Month-By-Month™

WHAT TO DO EACH MONTH TO HAVE A BEAUTIFUL GARDEN ALL YEAR

GARDENING
IN THE MID-ATLANTIC

Library of Congress Cataloging-in-Publication Data

Viette, André.
  Month-by-month, what to do each month to have a beautiful garden all year gardening in the Mid-Atlantic : Delaware, Maryland, Virginia, Washington, D.C. : by Mid-Atlantic experts, just for Mid-Atlantic gardeners! / Andre and Mark Viette with Jacqueline Heriteau. – Rev. ed.
       p. cm.
  Rev. ed. of: Month-by-month gardening in the Mid-Atlantic / André & Mark Viette with Jacqueline Hériteau. 2004.
  Includes bibliographical references and index.
  ISBN 978-1-59186-344-1 (alk. paper)
  1. Gardening–Middle Atlantic States. I. Viette, Mark. II. Hériteau, Jacqueline. III. Viette, André. Month-by-month gardening in the Mid-Atlantic. IV. Title.

  SB453.2.M527V54 2007
  635.0974–dc22

                                   2007040753

Published by Cool Springs Press
101 Forrest Crossing Boulevard, Suite 100
Franklin, Tennessee, 37064

First printing 2007

Printed in China
10 9 8 7 6 5 4 3 2 1

Managing Editor: Billie Brownell
Designer: James Duncan, James Duncan Creative
Horticulture Editor: Troy Marden
Illustrator: Bill Kersey, Kersey Graphics
Production Artist: S.E. Anderson

On the cover: Iris, photographed by André Viette

PHOTOGRAPHY AND ILLUSTRATION CREDITS

All illustrations by Bill Kersey, Kersey Graphics.
Neil Soderstrom: pages 26; 30; 40; 64; 76; 80; 84; 92; 130; 133; 137; 155; 156; 159; 162; 172; 188; 194; 199; 207; 220; 233; 234; 252
Thomas Eltzroth: pages 8 (top of page); 17 (top of page); 38; 45 (top of page); 71 (top of page); 87; 88; 90; 94; 96; 97 (top and bottom of page); 129; 147 (top of page); 165; 175 (top of page); 178; 184; 240; 242; 247; 255 (top and bottom of page); 272
Jerry Pavia: pages 45 (bottom of page); 63; 117 (bottom of page); 145; 147 (bottom of page); 166; 169; 181; 201 (top of page); 224; 258; 269; 275

Liz Ball & Rick Ray: pages 66; 71 (bottom of page); 175 (bottom of page); 201 (bottom of page); 214; 219; 249; 271
Andre Viette: Cover; pages 8 (bottom of page); 117 (top of page); 141; 196; 227 (top and bottom of page)
Pam Harper: pages 186; 254
Cathy Barash: page 251
Paula Biles: page 265
Charles Mann: page 36
Paul Moore: page 138
Netherlands Flower Bulb Association: page 53
David Winger: page 17 (bottom of page)

Month-By-Month™

WHAT TO DO EACH MONTH TO HAVE A BEAUTIFUL GARDEN ALL YEAR

GARDENING IN THE MID-ATLANTIC

ANDRÉ & MARK VIETTE

WITH JACQUELINE HÉRITEAU

COOL
SPRINGS
PRESS

Franklin, Tennessee
www.coolspringspress.net

DEDICATION

I dedicate this book to my mother and father, Jessie and Martin Viette, who instilled in me strong family values, a good work ethic, and a deep love of plants.

ACKNOWLEDGEMENTS

I want to thank the many people who have touched my life and made me a better person. Especially my wife, Claire, who has been by my side throughout my career and has given me such wonderful children—Mark, Scott, Holly, and Heather. And my son Mark, who works with me daily in the nursery, shares teaching duties with me at Blue Ridge Community College, and has been such an important part of the "In The Garden" radio programs. It has been a wonderful partnership. And my father, a great plantsman, who passed on to me his keen knowledge of plants and their culture.

I also wish to thank the many fine professors at Cornell University who helped mold my scientific mind. Rachel Carson changed my approach to the way we use our planet when I met her when I was just 24 years old. And I wish to recognize all my fellow members, past and present, of the New York Hortus Club, members who through the years have represented the finest in horticulture from New York City, New York, Connecticut, and New Jersey.

And finally, my very good friend and fellow author, Jacqueline Hériteau. Jacqui is a knowledgeable gardener and author of many distinguished books in the field of gardening. She is fabulous to work with and has the organization and work ethic to get things done.

André Viette
Fishersville, Virginia, February 20, 2004

CONTENTS

MEET THE AUTHORS

ANDRÉ VIETTE

Radio host of the weekly three-hour live nationwide call-in radio program "In the Garden," aired every Saturday from 8 to 11 am, a distinguished horticulturist, author, and lecturer, André owns the Viette Farm and Nursery in Fishersville, Virginia, (website: inthegardenradio.com) and is the former owner of the famous Martin Viette Nursery in Long Island, New York. A graduate of the Floriculture School of Cornell University, New York, instructor in horticulture at the Blue Ridge Community College, noted breeder of daylilies, and Past President of the Perennial Plant Association of America, André was honored in 2001 with the PPA Award of Merit for his contribution to the perennial plant industry. He holds the Garden Club of America 1999 Medal of Honor for his outstanding contribution to horticulture, and numerous other awards including Conservation Farmer of the Year. He has served on the Advisory Council of the National Arboretum, the Board of the American Horticultural Society, and is presently on the Board of the Lewis Ginter Botanical Garden and the Edith J. Carrier Arboretum.

MARK VIETTE

Nurseryman, lecturer, and contributor to horticultural journals, horticultural instructor at the Blue Ridge Community College, Mark Viette is alternate host as well as president and general manager of Viette Communications, which produces and distributes the national weekly radio call show, "In The Garden With André Viette." Mark is also director of marketing and sales for the André Viette Farm and Nursery. He holds a B.S. degree in horticulture from Virginia Tech and has completed several plant-finding trips to Europe and South America in search of exotic perennials to introduce to American home gardens.

JACQUELINE HÉRITEAU

Jacqueline (Jacqui) is the author of many noteworthy garden books, including *The National Arboretum Book of Outstanding Garden Plants* and the *Virginia Gardener's Guide*. With André, she co-authored *The American Horticultural Society Flower Finder* and the *Mid-Atlantic Gardener's Guide*. She is a Fellow of the Garden Writers Association of America and her contribution to gardening literature won her the 1990 Communicator of the Year Award from the American Nursery & Landscape Association. Jacqui also is the author of the *New England Gardener's Guide*, (Cool Springs Press, 2003) co-authored with her daughter Holly Hunter Stonehill.

INTRODUCTION

THE BENEFITS OF A MONTH-BY-MONTH GARDENING SCHEDULE

If you had all the time in the world, and were willing to use it to remember and record every move you and nature made in the garden all year long, it would look a lot like this book. The chapters that follow cover the major categories of landscape plants, starting with annuals and ending with water gardening—everybody's new love.

This is our collective garden log, a way to hang out over the back fence with you to answer your questions as they come up during the year. It's the next best thing to having your own decades-old garden log.

The month-by-month design is easy to work with, because our advice is always presented with the same "do this now" headings: Planning, Planting, Care, Pruning (or Grooming), Watering, Fertilizing, and Problems. The sidebar boxes are set apart to give you information that's different from the basic how-to and do-this-now type of information. We hope you'll find this book as enjoyable to read as it was for us to write.

CLIMATE

To help gardeners choose plants that will do well in our gardens, the USDA developed the Plant Hardiness Zone Map published in 1990 (although it is currently being updated). It assigns numbered zones to regions according to their average lowest winter temperature. The zone data on plant tags and in mail-order catalogs and garden literature indicate the regions in which you can expect the plant to survive winter.

Microclimates and Planting Dates. While the USDA zone map is a guide to what is likely to succeed in your yard, it isn't the last word about what or when you can plant. Spring and fall are the best planting seasons, and summer is okay for container-grown plants. But your community has a variety of spots that become warmer or cooler, sooner or later, than the prevailing climate.

Cold air sinks, so valleys and low spots are cooler than high ground. High hills and hillocks are colder than the zone indicates. Slopes facing north are colder than those facing south. Cities are 5 to 10 degrees warmer than the 'burbs and the country. Inland locations have greater fluctuations with early fall and late spring than the buffered maritime climates, and they have harder freezes.

Bodies of water modify temperatures. The seashore is warmer in winter than 10 to 20 miles inland. In spring the seashore is colder by 10 degrees or more since the ocean holds on to winter cold. In summer the shore is cooler because the ocean takes time to warm up. These same changes of zone occur around coastal bays, rivers, lakes, and even large ponds.

INTRODUCTION

ABOUT PLANT NAMES

Botanical plant names—which are in Latin, the language of science when the first herbals were written—tell you a lot about a plant.

A plant tag that reads *Picea abies forma pendula* is saying, this is a weeping Norway spruce. The Latin name breaks down like this: *Picea*, spruce, the genus, or overall group; *abies*, a species or category of spruce that came from Norway; *pendula* says this variety is pendulous, or weeping. Names between single quotes, such as *Spiraea japonica* 'Anthony Waterer' (pink spirea) indicate the plant is a named, or cultivated, variety, commonly called a "cultivar."

Don't get too hung up on cultivar names; new names turn up every season. 'Gold Flame' is the cultivar name for a pink spirea whose foliage is a fiery gold in spring and turns red, copper, and orange in the fall. If your local gardening center doesn't have it, ask for a golden-leaved pink spiraea, and your garden supplier should be able to tell you some choices.

In addition, every garden is home to microclimates—spots warmer or cooler than the prevailing temperatures. A south-facing wall can warm a corner. Shade cools it. White and reflective surfaces increase light and heat. A windbreak, a vine-covered pergola, a large tree, or a high hedge moderates summer heat and winter chill.

You can take advantage of these microclimates to try some plants that, by the book, aren't right for your climate. However, when it comes to flowering trees and big shrubs, stay with those recommended for your zone. Late frosts can devastate the flower buds on a camellia that isn't hardy in your zone even though the foliage and the plant make it. All these factors affect plant selection.

You can outwit the climate by choosing varieties that peak "early," "mid-season," or "late." Where the growing season is short, plant early varieties. When you want late season bloom, select late varieties. To enjoy a long season, plant all three varieties.

Another way to outwit a short growing season is to start seeds indoors early—in late winter for spring crops and in late summer for fall crops. Or, you can start seeds early outdoors in a cold frame or a hot bed (see November pages of Herbs & Vegetables) or in the open garden under "hot caps," cloches, tenting, and other solar collectors.

Two weeks after the date of the last annual frost, it generally is safe to transplant seedlings to the open garden. The outside temperature should have reached at least 55 degrees Fahrenheit during the day. The soil will still be cool. Transplanting too early leaves seedlings sulking. Tell your garden log when the first and last frosts occurred in your yard—that will be a better guide than any generalization experts offer.

Specific information on when to plant appears throughout the individual plant chapters.

LIGHT

Unless noted as a plant that flowers in shade, plants require six hours of direct sun to bloom well. Shade for plants means bright, not deep shade; examples are filtered light under a tall tree and all-day dappled shade under a tree with open branching.

If you are in warm Zones 7 and 8, you'll find that early morning sun is more beneficial than hot late afternoon sun for shade plants. In the Tidewater and the warmest spots in Zone 7, Washington, D.C., for example, shade-tolerant varieties benefit from protection at noon. The shade provided by lathing, a tall hedge, or a vine arbor will keep a shade plant safe. The plants can stand more noon sun when they are growing

in humusy moist soil and when you maintain a 3-inch layer of mulch over the roots in summer.

SOIL PREPARATION AND IMPROVEMENT

The best garden is one you can maintain without more effort than you have time to give. It begins with well prepared, good garden soil and sound garden practices.

The ideal garden soil has good drainage, lots of water-holding humus, and is loose enough so you can dig in it with your fingers. We evaluate garden soil in terms of its structure or composition, its pH, and its fertility.

Humus, the spongy remains of decomposed leaves, peat moss, and other organics, holds moisture and nutrients. It is the great modifier of rocky, sandy, and clay soils, but it's not a permanent fix. As plants grow, they deplete the organic content of the soil, and it loses its capacity to hold moisture and nutrients.

Soil pH. A plant's access to nutrients also depends on the soil's "potential of hydrogen," its relative acidity or alkalinity or pH. Soil of pH 7.0 is neutral; pH 4 is very, very acid; pH 8 is very alkaline. Most garden plants do best in soil whose pH is in a range between 5.5 and 6.5. Most herbaceous flowers and vegetables do well when the pH is between 6.0 and 7.0. For shrubs and trees, the recommended pH ranges far and wide.

Soil-testing kits for analyzing the pH of your soil are available at garden centers and from mail-order suppliers, as is everything you need to adjust the pH. To raise the pH of soils whose pH is too low, mix in 5 to 10 pounds of limestone per 100 square feet of garden bed. To lower pH that is too high, apply elemental fertilizer sulfur (water-soluble garden sulfur) at the rate of 5 to 10 pounds per 100 square feet. Other acidifiers are aluminum sulfate and iron sulfate; they act faster but do not last as long in the soil.

Fertilizing. Plants empty their larder of nutrients every season. To help plants to be all they can be, you must fertilize at planting time and at least once yearly in subsequent years.

The fertilizers we recommend are organic and release their nutrients slowly during the season, so we get solid stocky plants with loads of gorgeous foliage and flowers.

A sound annual soil maintenance program for an established garden includes these steps:

• Check and adjust the soil pH in late winter.

• Fertilize and add Rich Earth™ humate in late winter—late February, early March—before growth begins, and fertilize again in late summer or early fall.

• Water slowly and deeply as needed.

• Replenish the mulch cover after spring fertilization and before summer heat.

STARTING A RAISED BED

A raised bed, either a low berm or one surrounded by stones, bricks, or other material, is the best start a plant can have and an excellent solution to a site with poor drainage. You can start a

---

LIGHT NEEDS OF PLANTS

Full sun means at least six hours of direct, full sun. Part sun calls for four to six hours of direct sun, or dappled light all day. Shade can be two to three hours of direct sun a day, or bright dappled shade all day, such as the shade from a tall tree, for example.

Flowers, herbs, and vegetables need six hours of direct sun unless they are described as shade plants. In Zones 8 and 7, protection at noon—a trellis, the dappled shade of tall trees—may be needed. Plants growing in humusy moist soil and mulched 2 to 3 inches deep can stand more heat and sun. In Zone 6 with its cooler temperatures, plants growing in full sun may be able to stand the cold better.

INTRODUCTION

raised bed in the spring, summer, or early fall. It takes three to four weeks from start to planting. When you start a raised bed governs when you can plant. We favor late summer or early fall.

1. Use a garden hose to outline the bed. Island beds are the easiest to work since you can get at the middle from either side. Long, slow, gentle curves are easy to maintain and pleasant to look at.

2. Thoroughly water the turf covering the area to get the roots activated.

3. Spray the entire area with RoundUp® Weed and Grass Killer, following the instructions on the label. It takes about two weeks to completely die. As an alternative, you can remove the turf—the top layer of growth and its roots.

4. Cover the area with enough of the garden soil you can find that is most free of weeds to raise the soil level about 12 to 16 inches aboveground.

5. The next step is to determine the pH of the soil and amend it as needed to reach a pH between 6.0 and 7.0, following the procedures described in the Soil pH section previously.

6. Cover the bed with 3 to 4 inches of humus, enough so that one quarter of the content of the soil is organic matter. The humus can be decomposed bark, compost, partially decomposed leaves or seaweed, sphagnum peat moss, black peat humus, decomposed animal manures, or other decomposed organic material.

7. Next, for each 10-foot by 10-foot area, (100 square feet) add the following—available at most garden centers.

A new garden in full sun:
   Plant-tone 5-3-3—5 to 10 pounds
   Rock phosphate—5 to 10 pounds
   Greensand—5 to 10 pounds
   Clay soils only—gypsum 5 to 10 pounds
   Osmocote® 8-month—2 pounds

A new garden in shade:
   Holly-tone 4-6-4—4 to 7 pounds

   Superphosphate—3 to 5 pounds
   Greensand—5 to 10 pounds
   Clay soils only—gypsum 5 to 10 pounds
   Osmocote® 8-month—2 pounds

A new bed for bulbs in full sun:
   Bulb-tone—5 to 10 pounds
   Rock phosphate—5 to 10 pounds
   Greensand—5 to 10 pounds
   Clay soils only—gypsum 5 to 10 pounds
   Osmocote® 8-month—2 pounds

A new bed for roses:
   Rose-tone or Plant-tone—5 to 10 pounds
   Rock phosphate—5 to 10 pounds
   Greensand—5 to 10 pounds
   Clay soils only—gypsum 5 to 10 pounds
   Osmocote® 8-month—2 pounds

8. Next, with a rear-tine rototiller, which you can rent from a garden center, mix all this deeply and thoroughly. The bed should now be so soft you can dig in it with your bare hands.

9. When you are ready to plant, rake the bed smooth and discard rocks, lumps, and bumps.

10. Finally, pack and tamp the edge of the bed into a long, gradual slope and cover it with mulch to keep the soil from eroding. Or, frame the bed with low retaining walls of stone or painted cement blocks, 2-by-2 red cedar or pressure treated wood, or railroad ties.

Before planting in a new flower bed that has not been raised, mix into the existing soil the same proportion of supplements (except for the garden soil), and follow the same procedures as for a raised bed. If the area you are planting measures only 10 square feet, combine one-tenth of the amount of each supplement given for a raised bed of 100 square feet. If you have leftovers, they keep.

UNDERSTANDING FERTILIZERS
Whatever your climate, for unchecked growth and satisfying bloom, your plants need a continuous supply of nutrients. When to fertilize depends on the type of fertilizer you are using.

INTRODUCTION

Timing. Generally speaking, the time for the first application is before growth begins in spring, and the last application is as growth slows toward the end of the growing season.

The end of the growing season in Zones 6 and 7 falls some time between early September and early October. In Zone 8, Richmond and the Tidewater areas of Virginia, the time for the last fertilization is between the end of September and mid-October.

If you are using organic blends, such as Holly-tone or Plant-tone, then you will need to fertilize the first time a few weeks before growth is due to begin in spring, and then again toward the end of the growing season. Some plants, roses for example, need more.

If you are using only water-soluble chemical fertilizers, such as 5-10-10, which are immediately available to the plants, then you will need to fertilize every four to six weeks from beginning to end of the growing season.

If you are using time- or controlled-release chemical fertilizers, such as Osmocote® or Sierra®, then you will need to fertilize just before the plants start to grow and then repeat according to the formulation inscribed on the fertilizer container.

Fertilizer contents. To be all they can be, plants need the three primary plant nutrients—nitrogen for foliar growth, phosphorus for healthy roots and flower development, and potassium to maintain vigor—as well as a number of secondary and trace elements.

Fertilizers are made in formulations for plants that do best in either a low pH or a normal pH. Where soils are acid and the pH recommended for the plants is between 6.0 and 7.0, we recommend balancing the acidity by using a non-acid slow-release fertilizer blend such as Plant-tone. In soils whose pH is above 7.0, or up in the alkaline range, we suggest balancing the alkalinity by using Holly-tone or other fertilizer formulated for acid-loving plants.

Organic fertilizers. The organic fertilizer blends many horticulturists now favor may take up to four weeks before bacterial activity starts to make the nutrients available to the plants. Nutrients are then continually released over a three- to four-month period or longer. Water-soluble organic fertilizers that are immediately available to the plant can be found in both starter solutions and in products for foliar feeding for a quick pick-up if plants show signs of nutrient deficiencies. Garden centers carry soluble organics such as fish emulsion, liquid seaweed, the compost teas that are becoming popular, and manure teas made by steeping dehydrated manure.

Natural organic fertilizers have a positive effect on soil microorganisms and beneficial earthworms. In their presence, soil structure and aeration are improved. The organics break down gradually, depending on the amount of moisture in the soil, on the temperature, and on the microbial activity. Nutrients become available over an extended period of time, which decreases fertilizer run-off.

There are many organic fertilizer blends on the market, and each has its own rate of application. Fairly typical are the granular products Holly-tone and Plant-tone. They are sprinkled over the soil surface four to six weeks before growth is due to begin in spring, and then again toward the end of the growing season. They're easy to apply; just use your fingers to scratch handfuls of it about a quarter inch deep into the soil surface.

For Holly-tone 4-6-4, in a new bed apply ten pounds per 100 square feet; for an established bed, apply five pounds per 100 square feet. For Plant-tone 5-3-3, for a new bed apply ten pounds per 100 square feet; for an established bed apply five pounds per 100 square feet.

Supplemental organic fertilization. In addition to the two annual applications of organic fertilizers, we recommend four supplemental feedings.

Rich Earth™ humate is a mined product, a 100 percent natural rich humate soil which sup-

WATER CONSERVATION TIPS

- Water early in the morning, not when the sun is blazing because then you lose water to evaporation. Watering during the day reduces water loss by the plant due to transpiration, and that can be a good thing when the weather is very hot and plants are wilting.
- Mulch your gardens.
- Shut the hose off when moving between gardens.
- Turn the hose off at the faucet when you finish watering.
- Water deeply; when the water has penetrated to a depth of 6 to 8 inches, that's enough.
- Install rain barrels under drain pipes, and cover them with mosquito netting.

plies humic, ulmic, and fulvic acids containing over seventy trace minerals. It aerates the soil, improves water retention, conditions the soil, and enhances root development. Apply at the rate of 1 pound per 100 square feet of garden area.

Rock phosphate is a pure mined phosphate rock containing 32 percent total phosphate, which has been washed free of clay impurities. Phosphates help a good root system to develop and promote luxuriant flowering. Apply at the rate of 10 pounds per 100 square feet when planting.

Greensand, also known as glauconite, is a mined mineral-rich, ancient sea deposit that is an all-natural source of potash. Thirty-two or more micro-ingredients are contained in greensand. It helps to loosen heavy clay soil. It also binds sandy soil for a better structure. It increases the water-holding capacity of soils and is considered an excellent soil conditioner. It promotes plant vigor, disease resistance, and good color in fruit. Apply 5 to 10 pounds per 100 square feet of garden area.

Gypsum is a hydrated calcium sulfate that replaces sodium in alkaline soils with calcium and improves the drainage, aeration, and structure of heavier soils. It is an effective ammonia-conserving agent when applied to manured soils and other rapidly decomposing organic matter. It does not affect the soil pH. Apply at the rate of 5 to 10 pounds per 100 square feet in moderately clay soil; 10 pounds per 100 square feet in heavy clay soil.

Chemical Fertilizers. Granular chemical fertilizers, known as "complete fertilizers," are made up of the three essential plant nutrients—nitrogen (N), phosphorus (P), and potassium (K) in balanced proportions. Numerals on the bags, like 5-10-5, 10-10-10, and their variations, refer to the proportions of each essential element present in that mix. If you use only this type of fertilizer, make the year's first application just before the plants begin to grow in spring, and continue every four to six weeks until the growing season ends in your area.

If you use water-soluble fertilizers, they must be applied every two weeks, beginning two weeks before growth starts in spring and ending two weeks before the growing season is over. You would also add it to the water used as a starter solution at planting time, and for foliar feeding for plants showing signs of nutrient deficiency.

Slow-, Controlled-, or Time-Release Chemical Fertilizers. The complete chemical fertilizers have been packaged by scientists so they act like tiny time pills, releasing their nutrients over a specified period. The pellets are formulated to deliver nutrients at a slow, steady rate.

Examples are Osmocote® and Sierra® controlled-release fertilizers, which come in three to four month, eight to nine month, and twelve to fourteen month formulations. A similar product is Scott's controlled-release fertilizer tablets, which can last up to two years.

WATERING

From late winter on, there's usually enough rain to keep gardens growing through June. Summer

storms drench our gardens in July, but the unrelenting summer heat in Zones 7 and 8 often causes perennials and annuals to wilt at midday and some to stop growing. Late July and August is drought season here, and you will probably need to water two or three times a month before the fall rains arrive in September. One of the most important preparations for winter is a deep and thorough watering before the soil freezes; if the sky doesn't provide the rain, you must.

Overhead watering is fine as long as you water deeply. There's less waste if you water before the sun reaches the garden in the early morning or late afternoon or evening. In hot dry periods, daytime watering lowers leaf temperatures and reduces stress and plant water loss to transpiration. Evening watering is okay since dew naturally wets foliage every clear night anyway.

When watering, arrange to provide slow, gentle, deep watering. The ideal is to put down $1^1/2$ inches of water at each session. To measure, set an empty 1-pound coffee tin where it will catch the water, and record in your garden log the time it takes your sprinkler to deliver $1^1/2$ inches.

Electrically timed mechanical watering systems tend to ignore the weather and water too often and shallowly; however, they can do a good job if they are set up with the correct low-gallon nozzles and are timed to run long enough to water gently and deeply every week or ten days.

MULCHING

Keep a 2- to 3-inch layer of mulch on beds and around plants starting 2 to 3 inches from the central stem and covering an area that is wider than the plant's diameter.

Top off the mulch cover after the late winter/early spring fertilization. Check and replenish the mulch before the high heat of summer to keep the roots cool in summer. Maintain your mulch in fall to delay the freezing of the ground and to keep moisture available for roots that will continue to grow until the earth grows cold.

The need for additional winter mulch depends on the severity of your climate, and on the exposure of the beds. In the Mid-Atlantic, winter mulch can save plants that are borderline hardy from temperatures that are especially severe.

Apply winter mulch only after the ground has frozen hard, and remove it when you first spot signs of active growth in the plants. As a winter mulch we recommend airy organics like straw, pine needles, and pine boughs. Tent the plants so thinly you can still see some of the plant and the soil through the mulch. For coastal dwellers, marsh hay and salt hay from the shore are excellent winter mulches as they are weed-free, and they can be saved, covered, in a pile from year to year.

WEEDING AND GROOMING

Weeds start up in spring and come into their own in midsummer, along with drought and high heat. Before renewing or applying a summer mulch, rake the weeds up. If you get the little green heads before they're an inch high you won't have to hoe them when they are 8 inches high. If they get ahead of you, don't pull big weeds from bone-dry soil in a drought. Water the garden first, and then gently free the weeds and their roots. If you let weeds flourish and go to seed, they'll haunt you for years.

Grooming. To be at their best, plants need grooming, and that's true of water garden plants as well those grown in soil. In early spring, clear the gardens of last year's dead foliage, and prune to promote health and growth and to shape plants for beauty's sake. In summer, deadhead and shear spent blooms to encourage flowering this year and next.

Looking back on years of gardening, the moments that stand out in memory are the quiet times spent grooming the garden. Clipping box-

INTRODUCTION

woods in the cool early morning, birds calling; strolling the flower beds at sunset checking for spent blooms that need deadheading; weeding in summer; raking leaves on smoky autumn days, Canada geese calling overhead. These homely garden chores lift us out of our everyday lives and into the life of the garden and a promise of beauty that nourishes the soul.

KEEPING YOUR GARDEN HEALTHY

There are products available that help control the pests and diseases that plague us all—you'll find descriptions of the problems and Andre's recommended solutions in the Appendix. But the first defense against plant problems is to follow healthy garden practices. There's a huge bonus . . . lower maintenance. Here are some approaches that prevent difficulties—

• Introduce plant diversity into your garden and your neighborhood.

• Give cultivars of native plants a place in your design.

• Buy only healthy plants that are pest and disease resistant.

• Limit your choices to plants that thrive in your climate and your soil; these best withstand insect attacks and diseases to which the species may be susceptible, and they survive the normal droughts.

• Rotate crops of annual flowers, vegetables, and herbs.

• Clear out and destroy infested and diseased plants.

• Keep the garden free of weeds that are carriers of insects and diseases.

• When you can, buy from the nearest reliable full-service garden center or nursery, and ask for field grown or container stock that has proven successful in your area.

• Avoid plants identified as invasive.

Give Back to the Earth. Nourish the earth—and the earth will nourish your garden. Compost amends the soil; it can be used as a mulch, or it can be spread over the soil to a depth of 2 or 3 inches and dug or rototilled in. A handful of compost scratched into the soil around plants during the growing season is beneficial.

Some counties in the Mid-Atlantic give away wood chip mulches, and others are marketing composted waste. Northern Virginia's LeafGRO is effective and modestly priced.

You can, of course, make your own. Instructions appear in the October pages of Trees, the month we have lots of dry brown leaves, an important ingredient in compost.

Healthy leaves, weeds, grass clippings, vegetable garden debris, and vegetable or fruit peels are all excellent for composting. Don't compost fruit in bear country because it attracts them. Don't compost fish or meat, which attracts neighborhood pets. Don't compost garden debris that is diseased or harbors insects.

WELCOME TO GARDENING IN THE MID-ATLANTIC

What André Viette, Mark Viette, and I have written here is an overview of the rhythm of the year in a Mid-Atlantic garden. A truly beautiful garden is a very *healthy* garden. The gardening practices we recommend in the following chapters emphasize health over remedy. Our approach is easy on the environment. Happily, what is good for the environment is very good for the garden and for you, and not just in a grand save-the-planet design. Good garden practices equal healthy gardens, and that means lower maintenance, plus dollar savings, which equals happy gardeners.

Welcome to the wonderful world of gardening in Delaware, Maryland, Virginia, and the District of Columbia!

—Jacqueline Hériteau

USDA COLD HARDINESS ZONES

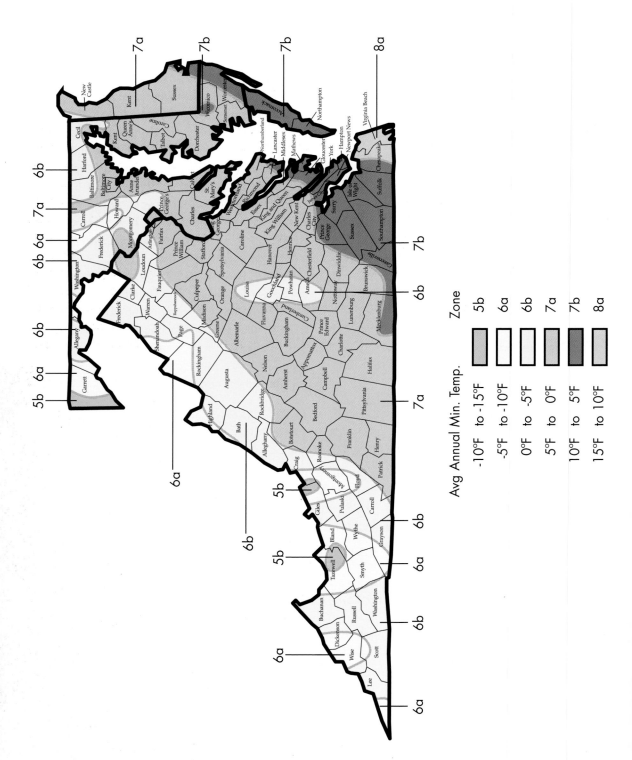

Avg Annual Min. Temp.   **Zone**

-10°F to -15°F	5b
-5°F to -10°F	6a
0°F to -5°F	6b
5°F to 0°F	7a
10°F to 5°F	7b
15°F to 10°F	8a

ANNUALS & BIENNIALS

Annuals, biennials, tender perennials, and tropicals are a delight to grow and dear to every gardener's heart. In our yards, all the plants in this group are one-year plants, but they are not all "true" annuals. Expect to replant them every year, but don't expect them to behave exactly alike.

True annuals. The botanist's "true" annual develops from seed, grows up and blooms, sets seed, and dies in one year. Zinnias, sunflowers, and marigolds are "true" annuals. Some true annuals appear to be perennial because they reseed themselves and come back year after year. Love-in-a-mist (*Nigella*), larkspur, and four o'clocks are among those that self-sow. The self-sown "volunteers" come into bloom at about the same time as seeds you sow in the garden.

Biennials bloom the second year after planting, not the first year, and they don't come back unless they are self-sowers. To have blooms every year, you must sow seeds or plant new plants every year. There are a few exceptions to the rule—like the forget-me-not species *Myosotis sylvatica*, which blooms from seed in just six weeks. Some biennials belong to genera that include annual and perennial species;

DID YOU KNOW?

Outstanding Self-Sowers
- Annual phlox, *Phlox drummondii*
- Annual rose mallow, *Lavatera trimestris*
- Bachelor's-button, cornflower, *Centaurea cyanus*
- Corn poppy, field poppy, *Papaver rhoeas*
- Cosmos, *Cosmos bipinnatus*
- Dahlberg daisy, *Dyssodia tenuiloba*
- Flossflower, *Ageratum houstonianum*
- Flowering tobacco, *Nicotiana* species and cultivars
- Larkspur, *Consolida ambigua* (syn. *Delphinium ajacis*)
- Love-in-a-mist, fennel flower, *Nigella damascena*
- Rose moss, sun plant, *Portulaca grandiflora*
- Spider flower, *Cleome hassleriana*
- Spurred snapdragon, toadflax, *Linaria maroccana* 'Fairy Bouquet'

Outstanding for Fall Color
- Annual aster, China aster, *Callistephus chinensis*
- Burning bush, red summer cypress, *Bassia scoparia* forma *trichophylla* 'Childsii'
- Coleus, painted nettle, *Coleus blumei*, *C. pumilus*
- Cosmos, *Cosmos bipinnatus*
- Dahlia, *Dahlia* x *hybrida* Unwin hybrids
- Flowering kale and cabbage, *Brassica oleracea* Acephala group
- Impatiens, busy Lizzy, *Impatiens walleriana*

- Lysimachia, *Lysimachia congestifolia* 'Eco Dark Stain'
- Mealycup sage, *Salvia farinacea*
- Ornamental pepper, *Capsicum annuum* var. *annuum*
- Pot marigold, *Calendula officinalis*
- Spider flower, *Cleome hassleriana*
- Sweet alyssum, *Lobularia maritima*
- Yellow sage, *Lantana camara*
- Wax begonia, *Begonia* Semperflorens-Cultorum

Outstanding for Cutting
- Annual Clary sage, *Salvia viridis* (syn. *horminum*)
- Annual phlox, *Phlox drummondii*
- Blue lace flower, *Trachymene coerulea*
- China aster, annual aster, *Callistephus chinensis*
- Cockscomb, *Celosia cristata*
- Cosmos 'Sonata White', *Cosmos bipinnatus*
- Globe amaranth, *Gomphrena globosa*
- Heliotrope, *Heliotropum arborescens*
- Marigold, *Tagetes* species
- Mealycup sage, *Salvia farinacea*
- Mexican sunflower, *Tithonia rotundifolia*
- Orange cosmos, *Cosmos sulphureus*
- Snapdragon, *Antirrhinum majus*
- Statice, *Limonium sinuatum*
- Sunflower, *Helianthus annuus*
- Zinnia, *Zinnia elegans*

for example, there's a perennial forget-me-not, *Myosotis scorpioides* (*M. palustris*). To know what to expect you must read the seed packet.

Short-lived perennials act like biennials and disappear after the second year. Examples are fragrant sweet William and furry-leaved silver sage, which raises a superb flower spike in late spring. These all must be replanted every year.

Cold-tender perennials, like geraniums, coleus, pentas, impatiens, lantana, and sweet potato vine, can't survive our winters, so they're treated like annuals. But, being perennial, they *can* live on for years. Several are worth potting up and bringing indoors for the winter. (See September, Care.)

Tropicals and **semitropicals**, like the gorgeous glory bush, *Tibouchina urvilleana*, and lovely bougainvillea are perennial in very warm climates. You can buy these as container-grown plants already blooming in late spring. They're great container plants and fillers for empty spots. They winter well in a greenhouse—but are so-so as houseplants. (Canna, dahlias, and other popular bulb flowers grown as annuals are mentioned in Chapter 2, Bulbs, Corms, Rhizomes, and Tubers.)

USES OF ANNUALS

Colorful Fillers. Summer-flowering annuals are the plants to use when you need to fill gaps in perennial beds after the spring flowers go by—zinnias and marigolds are prime examples. Seedlings of taller annuals help mask the oh-so-slow ripening of spring-flowering bulbs—sweet William, pinks, rocket larkspur, and garden balsam. Almost all annuals can be used to fill the wide-open spaces in new beds of perennials and shrubs. Annuals are a kitchen garden's best friend because they make it a popular destination.

Hedges and screening. Some annuals grow big enough to use as a temporary hedge—giant marigolds ('Climax'), and burning bush, (*Bassia scoparia* forma *trichophylla*), for example. Annual vines (see Vines, Ground Covers, & Ornamental Grasses) will envelop porches, poles, tree stumps, and garden eyesores for you in a matter of weeks.

Annuals as bedding plants. Bedding plants are flowers used in sequence to carpet large areas—for example, an early spring display of pansies, replaced as soon as they have peaked by upright bedding petunias. The lavish summer-long bloom of marigolds makes them excellent bedding plants.

Edging plants. Low-growing sweet alyssum, wax begonias, and ageratum are among many first-rate edging plants. They're often used to create ribbons of color spelling out municipal and business names and logos.

Baskets and planters. The cascading annuals are ideal for baskets and planters; they have a small root system that allows you to jam a whole lot in to a modest space. Cascade petunias are the stars. Close seconds are tiny, bright-as-sunshine creeping zinnias, *Sanvitalia procumbens*, a true annual, and the tender perennials *Scaevola aemula*, *Sutura cordata* 'Snowflake', and sweet potato vine. Spills of ivy and balcony geraniums, helichrysum, and variegated vinca (which often perennializes here) lend grace to flowery compositions.

Cutting flowers. Cut-and-come-again annuals are among the best cutting flowers. To have masses of blooms for bouquets, plant zinnias, snapdragons, and China asters. Give them a bed of their own in an out-of-the-way place. Or plant them in the kitchen garden—they'll make it beautiful!

Children's gardens. Annuals are a child's best garden friend. Quick popper-uppers like zinnias and sunflowers satisfy a youngster's need for early results. Seeing buried seeds grow, watching butterflies and bees seeking nectar, and sharing flowers and a garden's endless surprises gives children proud stories to tell.

STARTING ANNUALS AND BIENNIALS FROM SEED

For bedding displays and effective garden design, you will need enough seeds or seedlings of annuals to plant them in groups of five, seven, ten, or more; the smaller the plant, the more seeds you will need. Seedlings of the most popular annuals are readily available. Growing

DID YOU KNOW?

Outstanding for Drying
- Bells of Ireland, *Moluccella laevis*
- Everlasting, *Helipterum* species
- Foxtail, Italian millet, *Setaria italica*
- Globe amaranth, *Gomphrena globosa*
- Honesty, silver dollar, *Lunaria annua*
- Kiss-me-over-the-garden-gate, *Polygonum orientale*
- Love-in-a-mist, *Nigella damascena*
- Our lady's bedstraw, *Galium verum*
- Paper moon, *Scabiosa stellata* 'Drumstick'
- Pearly everlasting, *Anaphalis margaritacea*
- Salvia 'Blue Bedder', *Salvia farinacea*
- Sea lavender, *Limonium bonduelli*, *L. suworowii* (syn. *Psylliostachys suworowii*)
- Strawflowers, *Helichrysum bracteatum*
- Tall crested cockscomb, *Celosia argentea* var. *cristata*
- White sage, silver sage, *Salvia argentea*
- Zinnia, *Zinnia*

Outstanding for Edging
- Bedding begonia, wax begonia, *Begonia* Semperflorens-Cultorum hybrids
- Bluewings, *Torenia fournieri*
- Edging lobelia, *Lobelia erinus*
- Flossflower, *Ageratum houstonianum*
- French marigold, *Tagetes patula* varieties
- Impatiens, busy Lizzy, *Impatiens walleriana*
- Nasturtium, *Tropaeolum majus*
- Pansy, ladies-delight, *Viola* x *wittrockiana*
- Petunia, *Petunia* x *hybrida*
- Rocket candytuft, *Iberis amara*
- Rose moss, sun plant, *Portulaca grandiflora*
- Signet marigold, *Tagetes tenuifolia* (syn. *signata*) varieties
- Snapdragon, dwarf, *Antirrhinum* hybrids
- Sweet alyssum, *Lobularia maritima*
- Zinnia, Peter Pan series, dwarf varieties, *Zinnia* species

your own plants from seeds is a savings and allows you a much more interesting plant selection. You can save on seed costs, and avoid lots of leftover seeds, by sharing seed packets with friends.

You'll find annuals and biennials are easy to grow outdoors from seed. They also may be started indoors ahead of the outdoor planting season, as described in January, Planting.

When to sow seeds depends on how long the seeds take to germinate—some need twice as much time as others—and how "cold hardy" the seedlings are; that is, how much cold they can withstand. Seed packets label the seeds "hardy," "half-hardy," or "tender," and most packets suggest when and where to sow the seeds in the garden, and whether and when they can be started indoors to get a head start on the growing season.

Hardy. The seedlings of hardy annuals and biennials can take some frost. These do well sown in early spring, even before the last frost. Seed packets indicate that some can even be sown in fall after freezing temperatures have come.

Half-hardy. These seedlings are harmed by frost, but they tolerate cool, wet weather and cold soil. Most of the popular annuals are half-hardy (sometimes called semi-hardy). You would sow these seeds outdoors a couple of weeks after the last frost.

Tender. The seeds of tender annuals grow fastest and do best when they are sown outdoors after the air and the soil have warmed.

Sowing the seeds. The planting depth for seeds is usually given on the seed packet. The rule of thumb is to sow seeds at a depth about three times the seed's diameter, not its length.

CHAPTER ONE

Always sow seeds in moist soil, and always water them well after planting. If you can plant shortly after a rain and before the next one is expected, you won't have to water before and after.

Larger seeds are sown in "hills," groups of four to six, or three to five, equidistant from each other. Flowers for edging paths or the fronts of flower beds are usually sown in "drills," dribbled at spaced intervals along a shallow furrow. An easy way to make the furrow is to drag the edge of a rake or a hoe handle along the planting line.

FERTILIZING

In the Introduction to this book, we give detailed information about improving soil with organic matter and slow-release fertilizers. Make the effort to improve your soil, and it will carry your annuals through one growing season with little additional fertilization. If the annuals seem to slow after a first flush of bloom, they may benefit from a modest additional fertilization with a water-soluble organic fertilizer, such as seaweed or fish emulsion.

For established annual beds, we recommend that every year in late winter or early spring you recheck the pH, amend it if needed, and dig in organic fertilizers that release their nutrients over eight to nine months.

JANUARY
ANNUALS & BIENNIALS

PLANNING

Use pages torn from the many garden catalogs to create your own album of annuals. It is a real help in planning your garden. Put a sticky note by each plant reminding yourself where you think it would fit in your garden and why you pulled the page. Organize the plants according to their season of bloom. When considering flowers prone to powdery mildew, like **zinnias, verbena,** and **annual phlox,** choose disease-resistant varieties.

An album made up of catalog pages showing garden equipment and accessories you like is another useful reference and helps locate better pricing for expensive items.

Seed packets tell you whether the seeds can be started early indoors, and when. The introduction to this chapter explains how the "hardy," "half-hardy," and "tender" tags on packets relate to the seed's planting time. Seed packets tell you that speedy germinators, like **zinnias,** can be started indoors just four to six weeks before planting time but are often sown outdoors here. Slower annuals, like **petunias,** can be started indoors as many as fifteen weeks before the weather

will be warm enough to put them outdoors. For Zone 8, that would be about now. Get together the things you will need for the project.

Garden log. Make a record of the catalogs that provide the most useful information. Note the dates you placed your catalog order. Record the dates you started seeds indoors, and their progress.

PLANTING

Starting seeds indoors. This is a two-part project. First you sow the seeds and encourage them to germinate; then you transplant the seedlings and grow them into sturdy plants ready for their date with the garden.

Equipment. Commercial seed starting kits include strips of planting pockets, water-tight flats to hold them, and plastic covers to keep the soil moist while the seeds germinate.

You can improvise. For planting pockets and flats, use baking tins or porous cardboard egg cartons set on cookie tins. For a cover, tent the containers with clear plastic, the type used to insulate windows. Seeds that transplant with difficulty (the packet will tell you) you had best grow in individual peat pots. Use a sterile seed starting mix

for plants that will be moved outdoors in four to eight weeks. Use a commercial potting mix for plants that will be indoors eight to ten weeks. Soak clay and peat pots thoroughly before filling them.

Sowing the seeds. Moisten the planting medium in its bag so that it's moist but not so wet you can squeeze water out of it, and then scoop it into the containers. Seed packets tell you whether the seeds need to germinate in dark or with light. Sprinkle seeds whose packets say they need light to germinate over the growing medium, but don't cover them. Sow seeds that germinate in the dark in planting holes made with a pencil or a pointed stick—1/4 inch deep for medium-size seeds and 1 inch deep for large seeds.

To plant a flat, make shallow furrows in the potting medium, drop in the seeds, and cover them with the soil. Mix very fine seeds equally with sand, sprinkle them from a salt shaker, and cover them with a dusting of the starter mix.

Label each planting pocket, or row, to identify the seeds. Popsicle sticks sized to fit under the cover are a fine substitute for commercial row markers. Write the names on the labels with a waterproof marker.

Germination. Cover the flats for the week or two needed for germination. Moderate (ambient) light is enough at this stage. The annuals labeled "hardy" do not need bottom heat to germinate, and do best in a cool room or basement. Others germinate most rapidly with bottom heat, and in air temperatures of 65 to 70 degrees Fahrenheit. Heat mats are offered by catalogs and available at garden centers. A heating pad on Low will do the job; protect it from moisture with plastic film.

Check your flats daily. When most of the seeds have germinated, remove the covers, and move the flats to good light on a sill or in a light garden.

Water flats of seedlings from the bottom, or just mist the seedlings. Air the room often. Cool nights are beneficial. Seedlings that will be growing indoors for six weeks need good light to thrive.

An installation of two 4-foot fluorescent lights burning fourteen to sixteen hours a day is especially helpful if you plan to start a lot of your own seedlings indoors.

CARE

Change the water in which cuttings taken last fall are rooting and add two or three pieces of

EASY TO START INDOORS

- **Ageratum,** 8 to 10 weeks
- **Cosmos,** 4 to 6 weeks
- **Celosia,** 5 to 6 weeks
- **China aster,** 6 to 10 weeks
- **Cleome,** 6 to 10 weeks
- **Flowering tobacco,** 9 to 11 weeks
- **Mallow,** *Lavatera trimestris* 6 to 8 weeks
- **Marigolds, dwarf,** 8 to 10 weeks
- **Marigolds, tall,** 5 to 6 weeks
- **Petunia,** 11 to 15 weeks
- **Portulaca,** 10 to 12 weeks
- **Salvia,** 8 to 10 weeks
- **Snapdragon, dwarf,** 12 to 14 weeks
- **Snapdragon, tall,** 6 to 10 weeks
- **Verbena,** 8 to 10 weeks
- **Zinnias, dwarf,** 6 to 8 weeks
- **Zinnias, tall,** 4 to 6 weeks

charcoal, the kind that keeps the water in fish tanks clear.

GROOMING

Pinch back leggy cuttings and plants.

WATERING

Maintain moisture in pots of annuals and tropicals wintering indoors.

FERTILIZING

We gain almost a whole hour of extra daylight this month, so plants are starting to grow again.

Add a half-strength dose of houseplant fertilizer to the water for cuttings, plants, and tropicals stored indoors for winter that are showing new growth.

PROBLEMS

Damping off is a threat to seedlings. It's a fungal disease that attacks the seedlings at the base of their stems. It rots the stems so the plants fall over.

A sterile growing medium and good drainage help avoid the condition. The fungicide Thiram (Arasan) is a good preventative against damping off.

FEBRUARY

ANNUALS & BIENNIALS

PLANNING

As you finalize your catalog orders and buying plans, make sure there is a suitable place and space in your plan for each plant chosen. Heights and widths appear on the catalog pages in your album and on seed packets. Tall plants go to the back, mid-height in the middle, and shorties up front. The width measurement tells you how many of each type will fill the space.

Ordering seeds. Check your buying plans against your inventory of seeds that were left over or saved from last year and the cuttings and potted plants brought indoors last fall. List what you have, will order by mail, will buy at a garden center, and what you will have to go looking for. Seeds of the fragrant **petunias**, 'Celebrity White', 'Ultra White', and 'Apollo', for example, may take time to locate.

That done, you are ready to write up mail-orders and prepare shopping lists for later purchases at garden centers. Many mail-order houses now offer seedlings as well as seeds.

Garden log. Note design ideas picked up at flower shows and from visits to other gardens. Record the progress of the seeds started indoors.

PLANTING

Indoors. Zones 6 and 7: Start seeds for **ageratum, alyssum, China asters, geraniums, nicotiana, pansies, petunias, annual phlox, snapdragons,** and **stock.** (See Planting, January.) Zone 8 weather may encourage starting the hardiest of these outdoors late this month.

Sowing annuals outdoors. Most annuals sown outdoors come into bloom soonest when the seeds are sown where they are to flower. Seeds germinate most satisfactorily in moist, fluffy soil. If you can plant shortly after a rain and before the next one is expected, you won't have to water. If not, water well both before and after sowing the seeds.

The planting depth for seeds is usually given on the seed packet. The rule of thumb is to sow seeds at a depth about three times the seed's diameter, not its length.

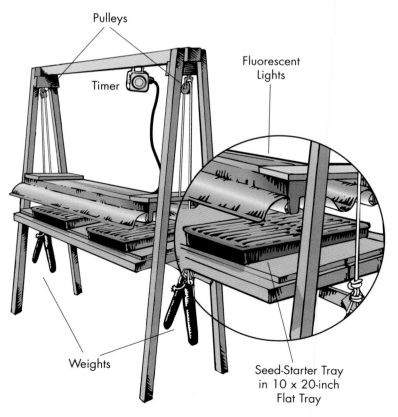

Pulleys

Timer

Fluorescent Lights

Weights

Seed-Starter Tray in 10 x 20-inch Flat Tray

The easy way to sow fine seeds evenly is to "broadcast" them, that is, sprinkle them over the bed. When the seedlings are up, thin them to the distance suggested by seed packets, or so that they are at least 3 to 5 inches apart.

Larger seeds are sown in "hills," groups of four to six, or three to five, equidistant from each other. Flowers for edging paths or the front of a flower bed are usually sown in "drills," dribbled at spaced intervals along a shallow furrow. An easy way to make the furrow is to drag the edge of a rake or a hoe handle along the planting line.

CARE

When the seedlings started earlier indoors become crowded, transplant each to an individual 3- to 4-inch pot filled with a good potting mix.

Seedlings that will be growing indoors for six weeks need good light to thrive. At this stage, an installation of grow lights burned fourteen to sixteen hours a day is especially helpful. If you plan to start a lot of your own seedlings indoors, it would be worth your while to invest in a light table.

Begin repotting plants brought indoors last fall, and pot up the strongest cuttings. (See March, New Plants from Stem Cuttings.) Continue to fertilize them.

If you planted a cover crop in your garden in the fall, (see October, Planting) turn it under now.

GROOMING

Pull out, and discard **ornamental cabbages** and **kale.** Deadhead the **pansies.**

WATERING

Water pots of transplanted seedlings as the soil becomes dry to the touch.

FERTILIZING

Do not fertilize transplanted seedlings until the appearance of two or three new leaves tells you the root system is growing again.

Every two weeks fertilize all the seedlings that will remain indoors another six weeks or more with a houseplant fertilizer at half strength.

PROBLEMS

Seedlings suffering from poor drainage, lack of air, and crowding are vulnerable to the fungus called "damping off," which rots stems near the soil surface. Discard affected plants, reduce watering, and increase light and fresh air. If the problem persists, mist the seedlings with a fungicide, such as Thiram (Arasan.)

MARCH

ANNUALS & BIENNIALS

 **PLANNING**

Take advantage of sales this month of fertilizers and other soil additives. But be cautious—these may be leftovers. If the price is a steal, make sure the bag is whole.

Go out to your garden, and reserve the space meant for the plants you've ordered. Take along a set of row markers on which you have written the names of the plants you will be setting out.

• In gardens of perennials and shrubs: outline each bay meant for annuals with a stick, and plant a row marker indicating the flower that goes there.

• In cutting and kitchen gardens: plant a row marker at the end of each row, indicating the vegetable or annual flower that goes there.

• In a garden for annuals: outline the bays, and press a row marker into the ground to designate which plant belongs where.

Garden log. Record the date of the last frost and when you planted what in your garden. Record the dates of any really good early plant sales. Chronicle the progress of seeds started indoors and your impression of the growing mediums used because you may want to try a

different brand next time. Record the arrival of seedlings ordered from catalogs and their condition on arrival.

 **PLANTING**

Prep your garden beds as soon as winter moisture has left the soil. A new bed needs the careful soil preparation described in the Introduction. An established bed for annuals also needs attention every year, as do areas reserved for annuals in gardens of perennials and shrubs.

The first step is to clean up the remains of last year's annuals. Take this debris to the trash. Don't compost it because there's a good chance organisms you don't want to encourage have developed over the winter.

Shortly before the last frost, gardeners can begin sowing seeds and planting seedlings of hardy annuals in garden beds, hanging baskets, window boxes, and large containers set in a sheltered spot. The fragrant **sweet pea** variety 'Sugar 'n Spice' is recommended for baskets.

Shortly after the last frost, you can sow seeds and plant seedlings of semi-hardy annuals. You can plant fragrant **sweet peas** outdoors now; these climbers need support—strings, brambles, obelisks. Soak or nick the

You can root stem cuttings by dipping the cut end into rooting powder, and then inserting the cutting into a gritty potting mix.

seeds before planting to aid germination.

In Zone 8 the last frost should occur sometime toward the end of March. In March the soil usually is still wet and cold, so it's not likely you'll need to water before or after sowing the seeds. Sow seeds of fast-growing annuals among the spring-flowering bulbs; as they grow up they'll mask the bulbs' yellowing foliage.

For detailed how-to instructions on sowing seeds and planting seedlings, turn to Planting, April.

Repot **geraniums, lantana,** and **mandevilla** saved from last year. Plant **pansies.**

CARE

Look over the cuttings and plants you brought indoors last year, and discard poor performers.

GROOMING

Pinch out the growing tips of seedlings that are becoming leggy.

Deadhead the **pansies** planted last fall to encourage blooming.

WATERING

Continue to water any indoor seedlings.

FERTILIZING

Every other time you water annuals wintering indoors, include fertilizer at half strength.

To assure the lavish production annuals are capable of, before planting each year André checks the pH of the garden soil and adjusts it to between 6.0 and 7.0. You can learn how to do this in the Introduction to the book. Then André works into the top 6 to 8 inches of the soil a gener-ous helping of nutrients (except when planting **nasturtiums**). An organic fertilizer will carry the plants through the whole growing season.

When working the soil, disturb as little as possible the area where self-sowers like **cleome** and **nigella** grew last year and where you had planted seeds of hardy biennials. Even if there's no sign of growth, the seeds are there and will germinate and develop soonest if undisturbed.

NEW PLANTS FROM STEM CUTTINGS

Cuttings and potted-up plants brought indoors last fall can provide you with new plants for your garden. Here's how you can multiply your holdings:

Geraniums. Cut off the top 4 inches of a sturdy, healthy stem just below a leaf node. Remove the leaves from the bottom 2 inches. Let the cuttings dry for a few hours or overnight. Then put them in a solution that is a gallon of water to which you have added 1/2 to 1 teaspoon of bleach, and set them in a sunny window. When they have grown a full set of roots—usually a matter of three or four weeks—transplant your cuttings to 3- to 4-inch pots filled with a gritty potting mix or non-clumping kitty litter. Or, root the cuttings in a rooting mixture. Grow your cuttings in a south-facing window.

You can also get cuttings to root by dipping the ends lightly in a rooting hormone and standing them in damp vermiculite or sand tented with plastic film. When the cuttings have developed enough roots to resist a slight tug, they're ready to transplant.

Coleus and wax begonias. Cut off the top 6 inches of a leafy stem just below a leaf node. Remove the leaves from the bottom 3 inches, then place the cutting in water containing a few drops of bleach, and set it in a semi-sunny window to root. When it has grown roots, transplant it into an all-purpose potting mix. Grow it in an east- or west-facing sunny window.

PROBLEMS

Spider mites can be a problem with indoor seedlings. See the section on Pests, Diseases, and Controls in the Appendix.

APRIL

ANNUALS & BIENNIALS

 PLANNING

Take the list of the annuals you are planning to purchase as seedlings to the garden centers and compare prices, sizes, and quality,

Garden log. Record the annuals that are coming into bloom as a prompt for plant combinations to try next year.

Record each and every planting date, and record how seeds and seedlings planted outdoors are doing.

 PLANTING

When you plant your baskets and container gardens, be sure to include annuals with a graceful drooping habit, like **variegated vinca, sweet potato vine,** and **cascade petunias.** Don't overplant! Leave space for second and third plantings of **petunia** seedlings. **Petunias** tend to play out in August, even when deadheaded regularly; adding **petunias** at three week intervals will keep the containers in full flower until early fall. The 'Surfinia' and 'Wave' **petunias** have more staying power than others.

Before filling moss-lined baskets with soil, patch or replace the moss so the earth won't dribble out. You'll find bags of moss at garden centers and florists. Fill your pots, windowboxes, and planters with commercial bagged potting mix that includes slow-release fertilizers and moisturizing polymers that will save you time watering.

Prepare containers too big to empty for planting by mixing slow-release fertilizer and 2 inches of compost into the top 6 inches of the soil.

In Zone 7 the last frost comes toward the end of this month. Zone 7 gardeners can sow seeds and plant seedlings of hardy annuals a little before that date, and of semi-hardy annuals a little after it.

When night temperatures are steady at 55 degrees Fahrenheit, you can put out seeds and seedlings of tender annuals and perennials

If the **icicle pansies** planted last fall look meager, give them a few weeks to grow out, and then fill the bed with fresh **pansy** seedlings, or with **primroses.**

To hide the yellowing leaves of your spring-flowering bulbs, plant big container-grown hardy biennials; **sweet William** and tall **snapdragons** are excellent possibilities.

Quick and easy transplanting instructions:

1. To prepare seedlings started indoors for life in the garden, harden them off for five or six days in a sheltered spot out of the wind and direct sun. The soil they are growing in will dry more quickly outdoors, so check it often and water as needed. Seedlings fresh from a greenhouse also benefit from a few days in a sheltered spot before being planted in the open garden.

2. When you bring home more flats of seedlings than you have time to plant (we always do), water them well, and place them out of direct sun until you are ready to transplant. Check the soil moisture daily, especially flats whose soil is hidden by foliage. A six-pack's tiny planting pockets can dry out in just hours on a hot, windy day, and you won't know it until the leaves collapse. That halt in growth isn't a good thing!

3. When you head for the garden to transplant your seedlings, take along a pail of water to which you have added starter solution or a dose of manure tea or liquid seaweed. If you followed the March suggestions to prepare beds for planting, you will not need additional fertilizer now.

4. Make planting holes with the end of your trowel for as many seedlings as you will be putting in the area. Remove an equal number of seedlings from their containers; use shears

to cut apart those that have grown together.

5. Before setting a seedling in its hole, gently unwind roots circling the rootball, and cut off those matted at the bottom. Set the seedlings upright in their planting holes, starting with the hole farthest from you. Add a half cupful of water from the pail to each planting hole.

6. When the water has drained, fill the holes with soil, and firm the soil around each seedling. The seedlings should be set in tightly enough so they resist a gentle tug. Pinch out the central stem and branch tips of the seedlings to encourage branching and more surfaces where flowers can develop.

7. Water the area with a sprinkler for half an hour or so. Apply a 2-inch layer of mulch all around, starting 3 inches from the crown.

OUTSTANDING ANNUALS FOR BASKETS

- **Bacopa,** *Sutera cordata* 'Snowflake'
- **Basket begonia,** *Begonia* x *tuberhybrida* Pendula Group
- **Black-eyed Susan vine,** *Thunbergia alata*
- **Cascade petunia,** *Petunia* x *hybrida*
- **Cigar flower,** *Cuphea ignea*
- **Creeping zinnia,** *Sanvitalia procumbens*
- **Edging lobelia,** *Lobelia erinus*
- **Fanflower,** *Scaevola aemula*
- **Impatiens, busy Lizzy,** *Impatiens walleriana*
- **Ivy-leaf** and **Balcon geraniums,** *Pelargonium peltatum*
- **Lady's-eardrops,** *Fuchsia* x *hybrida*
- **Nasturtium,** *Tropaeolum majus*
- **Painted nettle,** *Coleus blumei*
- **Rose moss,** *Portulaca grandiflora*
- **Sapphire flower,** *Browallia speciosa*
- **Trailing coleus** 'Trailing Rose', *Coleus rehnelthianus*
- **Verbena,** *Verbena* x *hybrida*
- **Water hyssop,** *Bacopa caroliniana*
- **Yellow sage,** *Lantana camara*

CARE

Transplant seedlings outgrowing their containers to larger pots.

GROOMING

Deadhead **pansies**, **primroses**, and other early spring annuals.

Pinch out the growing tips of plants that have become leggy.

WATERING

Seeds and seedlings in the garden need rain often enough during the next two or three weeks to maintain soil moisture. If spring turns dry, or if you see signs of wilting, water your seedlings deeply. Specific directions of deep watering are given in the general Introduction to the book.

FERTILIZING

Continue to fertilize seedlings of the tender perennials and annuals that will remain indoors until the air temperature reaches 55 degrees Fahrenheit at night.

PROBLEMS

Spider mites can be a problem for indoor seedlings. For controls check the section on Pests, Diseases, and Controls in the Appendix.

MAY

ANNUALS & BIENNIALS

PLANNING

On rainy days, cruise the garden centers searching for seedlings to fill gaps left by spring-flowering bulbs and other seedlings for late summer bloom.

Look for places in the garden where you could tuck in a few annuals that are fragrant at night and for flowers that will reflect moonlight—white, pale yellow, or pink. Seedlings of white **annual stock** are very fragrant late in the day.

Garden log. As spring gardens peak, visit public and private gardens looking for inspiration. Record the names of annuals and plant combinations you wish were blooming in your own garden right now.

Note when night temperatures reach a steady 55 degrees Fahrenheit. Also note what you planted when, and what is blooming.

Evaluate your spring garden and your responses to it.

PLANTING

In Zone 6 and where the last frost may come in mid-May, wait to plant seeds and seedlings of hardy annuals until a little before that date, and semi-hardy annuals a little after it.

When night temperatures reach 55 degrees Fahrenheit and above, sow seeds of tender annuals outdoors and set out seedlings of tender perennials grown indoors. The tropicals are safe outdoors now, too.

Where spring bulbs have gone by, make successive sowings of **zinnias** and **annual phlox.**

Sow late-blooming annuals and biennials for next year's display—either indoors, outdoors in a cold frame (see November, Herbs & Vegetables), or in an out-of-the-way place in the garden.

When the **pansies** and **primroses** fade, replace them with **edging lobelia** and follow with long-season low edgers like **wax begonias, dwarf snapdragons, dwarf marigolds,** and **dwarf zinnias.** Little **sweet alyssum** is a full-sun edger that will perfume evenings in late summer.

CARE

Thin self-sown and other seedlings to 2 to 3 inches apart.

If plants in hanging baskets and containers become crowded, remove the least vigorous seedlings.

GROOMING

Deadhead **pansies** and **primroses,** and shear **lobelia** to prolong the flowering cycle.

Monitor and pinch out the tips of branching annuals that develop one or more strong central stems. Continue to pinch

Thin seedlings to 2 to 3 inches apart.

them back until the stems are 6 inches long. Tall **snapdragons, salvia, stock, petunias,** and other cascading plants are among those that benefit from persistent pinching.

Weeding. Weeds aren't always ugly, but they always take up water and soil nutrients. They appear plentifully now, and by midsummer the big roots are hard to pull. A permanent mulch, close planting, and planting through a porous black plastic film keep them down.

Get rid of weeds early. Less than an inch high, you can rake them up. When they're 6 inches high, you'll need a hoe to cut them down. After that—well, the worst thing for a newly established garden is to have weeds flower and set seed there or nearby. They'll haunt you for years to come.

Don't pull big weeds from bone-dry soil—they're more tenacious than they are in moist soil, and the upheaval of the soil can reduce moisture. Water the garden first, then tug the weeds out gently but firmly to get the roots. Shake the soil back into the garden, and compost the weeds.

OUTSTANDING FOR FRAGRANCE

- **Evening stock,** *Matthiola tricuspidata, M. bicornis* 'Starlight Sensation'
- **Four-o'clock,** *Mirabilis jalapa*
- **Heliotrope,** *Heliotropium arborescens*
- **Large white petunia,** *Petunia axillaris, P.* F$_2$ hybrids
- **Mignonette,** *Reseda odorata*
- **Nicotiana hybrids,** *Nicotiana x sanderae*
- **Sweet alyssum,** *Lobularia maritima* 'Sweet White'
- **Sweet pea,** *Lathyrus odoratus* 'Cupani', 'Old Spice', 'Old-Fashioned Scented Mixed'
- **Wallflower,** *Cheiranthus cheirii*
- **Wild sweet William,** *Phlox drummondii*
- **Woodland tobacco,** *Nicotiana sylvestris*

WATERING

Unless the garden is moist from recent rain, before every planting gently and slowly water long enough to provide 1 to 1^1/$_2$ inches. Use an empty coffee tin to measure. After planting, water the area for half an hour more.

Maintain the moisture in newly planted seeds and seedlings. Unchecked growth is essential to the development of root systems strong enough to bloom and withstand summer heat. If you do not have a good soaking rain every week to ten days, water planted beds gently and slowly long enough to provide 1 or 2 inches.

This month begin biweekly checks of the moisture in plant containers; check the moisture level in small pots and hanging baskets every day or two.

FERTILIZING

Begin a regular fertilizing program for hanging baskets and container plants. They'll benefit from biweekly applications of a soluble fertilizer or manure tea at half strength.

PROBLEMS

Be on guard against aphids, spider mites, whiteflies, and, in rainy weather, snails and slugs. For controls, see the section on Pests, Diseases, and Controls in the Appendix.

JUNE
ANNUALS & BIENNIALS

PLANNING

Visit public gardens, and check out the plants used to replace spring bulbs.

Garden log. Record the dates of especially worthwhile plant sales held as spring ends.

Continue to record and date the development of this year's plantings.

It is far enough into the season now to evaluate the performance of transplants of rooted cuttings and plants saved from last year—**geraniums, coleus, impatiens, wax begonias,** and others—and decide whether this is something you want to do again in the fall. Was saving the **mandevilla** and **bougainvillea** worth the effort? Did saving plants save money?

PLANTING

Remove the last of the spring flowers, and replace them with seeds or seedlings of annuals that will bloom until frosts—blue and white **salvia, China asters, cosmos,** and 'Silver Cup' **mallow** (*Lavatera trimestris*) whose showy pink blooms light up the late garden. Sow seeds for a final succession planting of **zinnias** for cutting.

Make space in baskets and containers for fresh **petunia** seedlings. They'll keep color there after earlier plantings play out.

Use seedlings to fill gaps in flower beds as spring-flowering bulbs die away.

Volunteers of self-sown **snapdragons, French marigolds, cosmos,** and other annuals pop up every year, and they make good fillers. **Petunias** often volunteer, but they're so slow to bloom they're only worth transplanting where months of growing weather lie ahead.

CARE

To keep roots cool and weeds down, mulch flower beds 2 inches deep starting 3 inches from the crown of each flower. André uses fine grade hammermill bark and also recommends pine and hardwood bark, West Coast fir bark, cedar bark, and cypress. Coconut hulls are pretty, but they aren't best where mold is a problem. Compost and leaf mold (decomposed leaves) are beneficial mulches, but weeds and roots grow into them, and they decompose quickly in heat.

Staking. The tallest flowers benefit from staking—tall **snapdragons** and **zinnias,** 'Climax' **marigolds,** and **woodland tobacco.** Set the stakes within 2 to 3 inches of the stems. Choose stakes as tall as the plants are likely to grow. Tie the main stems loosely to the stakes with soft green wool, raffia, or cotton string.

GROOMING

Continue weed patrol. Root out prolific self-sowers like **love-in-a-mist** just as you would weeds.

Continue to pinch out the tips of the **petunias** and other cascading plants and branching annuals.

Snip off at ground level the stems of plants crowding others, as **nasturtiums** often will, and cut back the outer stems of perennials that are crowding annuals planted among them.

WATERING

Check the moisture in plant containers, hanging baskets, and windowboxes daily or every other day. On hot, windy days even large containers may need more frequent watering. Terracotta containers dry out especially quickly.

Maintain moisture in new plantings of seeds and seedlings. Annuals have shallow roots, and to grow they need sustained moisture. Water wilting plants at noon or in late afternoon.

DEADHEADING AND HARVESTING

Removing fading blooms stops plants from developing seeds and stimulates the production of flowers. It's called "deadheading." If your garden is small, you can enjoy pinching out dying blossoms. A big garden is something else: starting in June, André goes through his six acres of gardens with hand-held shears and deadheads spent flowers. It takes him about an hour to do the whole garden.

"Pinching out" is the quick and easy way to deadhead flowers on slender stems. Place your thumbnail and forefinger behind the bracts—the small scale-like leaves behind the petals—and squeeze the flower head off. To deadhead stems too thick to pinch out, use small pointed pruning shears made especially for this purpose.

Shearing may help plants attacked by mildew; take them down to the ground. Diseased foliage goes into the garbage—not into the compost pile. The new foliage may grow in clean.

Harvesting most annuals has the same effect as deadheading. Cut the stems of **zinnias** and **cosmos** just above a pair of leaves, which is where the next set of flowering stems will develop.

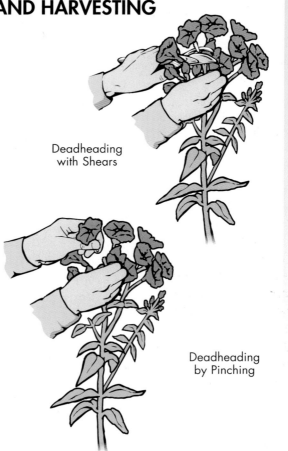

Deadheading
with Shears

Deadheading
by Pinching

FERTILIZING

Add enough compost or potting soil to plant containers to maintain the level where it was when you first planted them. Continue to fertilize with a half dose of houseplant fertilizer or weak manure tea every two weeks.

Annuals that have been blooming benefit from a sidedressing of compost, or a foliar feeding of liquid fish emulsion, liquid seaweed, manure, or compost tea.

PROBLEMS

Avoid overwatering in hot muggy weather because it encourages mildew. If powdery mildew appears, as it often does on ordinary varieties of **zinnias** and **annual phlox,** remove severely infected plants, thinning the bed to allow air all around. Check the plantings often, and take spent flowers, fallen petals, and leaves to the trash. Don't compost them. Spray the plant with André's remedy: a combination of 1 tablespoon of baking soda, and 1 tablespoon of ultra-fine horticultural oil in a gallon of water.

JULY

ANNUALS & BIENNIALS

PLANNING

Before your vacation, arrange to have the container plantings watered. Ease the chore by grouping them in a semi-shaded spot and providing each with a saucer. Investigate automatic watering systems.

Garden log. Note when dry spells begin and how long they last.

Weary of deadheading? Try annuals that self-clean next year—for example, **narrowleaf zinnias, wax begonias, impatiens, ageratum, pentas, New Guinea impatiens,** and **spider flower.**

PLANTING

Starting now until early August, seeds of hardy fall-flowering annuals can be started—**pansies, sweet alyssum, calendula** (try 'Pink Surprise'), and **ornamental cabbage** and **kale.** Biennials to start now include **foxgloves, money plant,** and **sweet William.**

In the warm Mid-Atlantic, **cleome, cosmos, sunflowers, zinnias,** and **marigolds** sown now may have time to bloom.

CARE

Remove crowded plants and poor performers from baskets and window boxes. If there is space and time, replant with fresh seedlings.

Monitor staked annuals, and tie the main stems and branches higher up.

GROOMING

Continue to deadhead. Pull out unwanted self-sowers. Snip off leggy **petunia** stems with only a few buds at the tips. Pinch off spiky **coleus** flowers, and cut back ungainly stems. Shear small-flowered plants such as **annual coreopsis** and **dwarf cosmos** to encourage a new round of flowers.

WATERING

Ageratum and other annuals that brown out in high heat will revive in the cool moist weather of early fall. For now, water but don't fertilize.

Water your compost pile when you water the garden, and turn it weekly.

Flower beds and new plants thrive with two to three hours of gentle rain every ten days to two weeks. At this point in summer André usually waters twice a month with hose-fed brass impulse sprinklers that deliver two gallons a minute. He runs them for twelve hours in each spot.

Overhead watering should not cause problems as long as you water deeply and the foliage dries between sessions. Watering early in the morning saves water loss to evaporation. Daytime watering lowers leaf temperatures and reduces stress, but evening watering is all right if you can't do it earlier.

Where mildew is a problem, water with soaker hoses to avoid wetting the foliage.

FERTILIZING

Plants that are blooming vigorously may benefit from a sidedressing of a handful of compost. Or, with a hose-end sprayer, apply diluted solutions of fish emulsion, liquid seaweed, manure, or compost tea to the foliage.

Continue to fertilize container plants every two weeks with a half-strength dose of liquid fertilizer.

Top the soil in containers with a layer of compost.

HARVESTING AND DRYING FLOWERS

As flowers used in potpourris and dried bouquets come into bloom, harvest the best specimens. Summer's dry heat speeds the process.

When harvesting for **potpourris**, pick the flower heads in a dry, hot moment of the day. Spread the petals over paper towels on screens. Set the screens to dry in a warm, airy, dry place.

For dried bouquets, harvest large, moist flowers like **zinnias** when the blooms are fully open. Single varieties are better for drying than doubles. Harvest dryish flowers like the **everlastings** and **salvia** just before the buds open. Cut fresh, healthy stems 12 to 14 inches long, and strip away all the lower leaves to prepare them for drying.

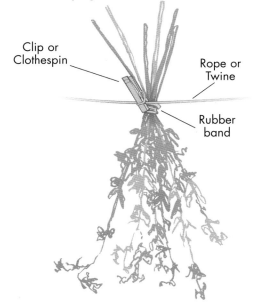

Clip or Clothespin

Rope or Twine

Rubber band

• **Air drying.** Tie the stems together in small, loose bunches, then enclose the heads in paper bags as they shed. Label the bags. Hang the bunches upside down for two to ten days, or until very dry, in a warm, airy, dark place. Direct sunlight fades the colors.

• **Silica gel.** Use this light, grainy gel to dry delicate, moist flowers like **cosmos.** Spread 2 or 3 inches of gel in a large box. Wire the flower stems, lay them on the gel, and cover them with more silica gel. In twenty-four hours check a flower; if it is dry, remove the others from the gel, and leave them on top of it for another day. Then store them layered in tissue in airtight, labeled boxes to which you have added a few tablespoons of silica gel. If gel clings to the petals, pour a little clean sand over them to remove the gel.

With use, the gel's blue crystals turn pink. To restore it for later use, spread the gel over cookie sheets covered with paper towels and heat in a conventional oven on low, thirty minutes for a 1-pound can. The gel turns light blue when it is ready to use again. The gel gets hot, so cool it in the oven five to ten minutes, and then store it in air-tight containers.

• **Oven-drying.** Dryish flowers dry well in a conventional oven on a low setting. A microwave oven at half-power can dry flowers in minutes. Dry a test flower for each batch to learn the length of time the others will need. Support the flower with a paper towel before drying it. The outside petals dry sooner than those inside.

To avoid over-drying in either oven type, check progress often through the oven window.

PROBLEMS

In hot, airless corners, aphids, spider mites, and whiteflies are a threat. Spraying with a Neem-based product helps.

If you see powdery mildew, remove the infected plants, and thin the bed to provide more air. Remove spent flowers, fallen petals, and leaves, and take them to the trash.

For other controls, see the section on Pests, Diseases, and Controls in the Appendix.

ANNUALS & BIENNIALS

PLANNING

Begin preparing places to plant the fall seedlings started earlier.

Garden log. Note how the annuals, in public, private, and your own gardens, are reacting to August drought. Those that are doing well are the ones you want to try next year.

PLANTING

Early this month you can start seeds of **pansies, calendula, flowering cabbage, kale,** and other fall annuals. Toward the end of the month, you'll find their seedlings at garden centers.

If you can find fresh **petunia** seedlings, add a final round to window boxes and hanging baskets.

In our warmest regions there's still time to sow **snapdragons, calendula,** and **stock.**

CARE

Do not let weeds mature!! They are drifting into your garden right now looking for a start.

Check the mulch. It decomposes rapidly in high heat and humidity.

At mid-month check staked annuals. If needed, install taller stakes.

GROOMING

Continue to deadhead and harvest flowers. The late summer annuals provide some of the year's loveliest bouquets. Our favorite bouquets include airy **cosmos** with spikes of **blue salvia,** mid-size **dahlias,** and stems of **basil** and **mint** for their sweet spicy aroma.

Attics and garages are hot and dry in August, perfect for air-drying **statice, blue salvia,** and others recommended in our July list.

Cut all older **petunia** stems back by two-thirds, and fertilize the plants.

Window boxes and railing planters showcase annuals beautifully.

WATERING

You will probably have to water this month. If you can, water in the early morning. Water slowly and well, as described in July. Where mildew is a threat, water the soil rather than the plants. In extreme heat, shower the garden at noon to lower the temperature and provide the plants with immediate relief.

Containers will have filled up with roots by now—so they need more frequent watering than earlier when plenty of moist soil surrounded the roots.

Water your compost pile when you water the garden. Turn it often.

FERTILIZING

The mulch you applied is decomposing and providing fresh organic elements, and the organic fertilizers added to the soil last spring are still making nutrients available.

But the self-sowing annuals that will give you next year's crop can use a little help. Rake a compost or a slow-release fertilizer into the soil under the parent plants. The seeds will do best if they fall into a 1- or 2-inch layer of humusy soil. When the seedheads begin to swell and

HARVESTING AND DRYING SEEDS

Harvesting seeds can give you great pleasure. To be sure you get the plant you expect from the seeds collected, harvest only seeds of *species*. Seeds of hybrids do not reliably repeat the qualities that are special; some or all may revert to the original species.

Harvesting. Harvest seeds that are ripe but not so ripe the seedheads drop or spew seeds to the ground. Ripe seeds are usually dark. When the vegetative envelopes swelling at the base of spent flowers begin to yellow and dry up, you can begin to harvest. Place the open end of a paper bag under a seedhead, and snip it into the bag.

Drying seeds. Spread seedheads and seeds on screens (try second-hand shops) lined with newspaper, and set them to dry in a warm, dry room until the seed envelopes are crackling dry, about five days. Separate the seeds from the chaff by rubbing the seedheads between your palms over a bowl. Gently blow away the chaff. Spread the seeds out to dry for another ten days.

Pour the seeds into glass jars, and cap them tightly. Check in a few days; if moisture has appeared inside the glass, air dry the seeds another few days. Store them in jars or small freezer bags. Label and date each one. Put a small mesh bag filled with flour into each container to absorb moisture. André stores seeds in the fridge.

dry, gather a few and scatter the seeds over the soil. Or, wait until the seedheads are dry and seeds are loose inside, and then shake the flower heads vigorously over the soil.

PROBLEMS

Aphid and spider mites love warm weather. Plants infested by spider mites have a faded, stippled look. Blow them away with a strong spray from the hose; rogue out badly infested plants.

If the damage is considerable, consider a non-toxic spray.

If mildew is a problem, spray with André's remedy: 1 tablespoon baking soda and 1 tablespoon of ultra-fine horticultural oil mixed well in a gallon of water. When mildew persists, clear the bed, rake out the remains of the plants, and dispose of them in the trash—do not compost.

For other controls, see the section on Pests, Diseases, and Controls in Appendix.

SEPTEMBER

ANNUALS & BIENNIALS

PLANNING

Right now, as you begin to plant the bulbs that will be the first to flower next spring, start to look for seeds of annuals you'd like to see coming up when the bulbs fade.

Garden log. Visit public and neighboring gardens, and keep notes on attractive combinations of fall bedding plants.

Note when the annuals in each of your gardens finished, when you removed them, which fall flowers you are replacing them with, and how they are performing.

Note where you have sown biennials and hardy annuals so you will know to leave the soil undisturbed when preparing the garden beds next spring.

PLANTING

Where frosts are early, begin to clear away played-out annuals. *Petunia integrifolia* and "Supertunias" in the Wave series withstand some frost so let them bloom on, along with the hardy **snapdragons** and **geraniums.**

Replace the soil in window boxes and containers you plan to replant for fall. The growing medium needn't include water-holding polymers. It does need

Imagine a colorful bed of flowering cabbages and kale ready for fall and winter; start seeds now. See page 41 for more on flowering cabbages and kale.

a four-month supply of slow-release fertilizer. Replant with seedlings of hardy annuals, such as **pansies, violas, flowering cabbage** and **kale,** and **calendula.** For its cascading foliage, plant **variegated myrtle,** which may winter over.

CARE

During dry spells, maintain soil moisture where you are encouraging self-sowers—**cleome, sweet alyssum, love-in-a-mist.**

Keep the compost pile moist, and turn it often.

When nighttime temperatures plunge towards 55 degrees Fahrenheit, move tender perennials and tropicals indoors.

Tropicals like **mandevilla** and **bougainvillea** thrive in a greenhouse and indoors in a sunny place. They may survive in a semi-dormant state in a frost-free garage, garden shed, or basement if you keep the soil damp. Move them when the garden soil is almost dry.

Several tender perennials make happy houseplants. **Impatiens** (African violet potting mix; semi-sun), **pentas,** and **browallia** do well indoors.

By September **coleus** plants are usually too big to bring in. We keep **coleus** by growing bouquets of cuttings in water. Here's how: Cut a dozen or more stems 12 to 14 inches long from your most beautiful **coleus** plants. Make the cut just below a node.

Strip the leaves from the bottom 6 inches, and arrange the stems in clean water containing six drops of a liquid fertilizer. Place the cuttings in a cool room in good light. Change the water every month, and add a few drops of liquid fertilizer. Pinch out flower spikes as they appear.

Geraniums can come indoors, too. Choose well-branched plants, hose them down gently, and repot them in clean clay pots filled with slightly gritty potting soil. Indoors, **geraniums** do best in a cool room in full sun.

Another way to keep **geraniums** is by rooting cuttings. Cut 4-inch stems just below a node. Dip the cut ends lightly in rooting hormone, and stand them in damp vermiculite or sand. Tent them with plastic film, and keep the film in place until the stems have developed enough roots to resist a slight tug. Then transplant the rooted cuttings to individual pots.

Wax begonias and **impatiens** make excellent houseplants and bloom all winter. Dig up healthy plants, rinse them, and pot the roots in a potting mix. Grow them in a sunny window.

GROOMING

Thin the late blooming annuals planted earlier.

MAKING A GERANIUM TREE STANDARD

A **geranium** (or a **lantana** or **rosemary** for that matter) with a strong central stem is easy to train as a tree standard. Repot it in gritty potting soil. Tie the central stem firmly to a straight, sturdy stake. Bring the plant indoors to a sunny window in a cool room. Turn it at least once a month so all sides get equal sun.

• In January or February when new growth begins, remove all the branches and leaves except those growing at the top of the central stem. Pinch out the tips of those branches to begin to shape the top into a globe.

• In May repot the plant, and move it outdoors for the summer.

• In coming years continue to prune, shape, repot, and stake the plant. Winter it indoors, and summer it outdoors.

• When the central stem reaches 4 feet, allow the plant to bush out at the top. Continue to pinch the branch tips to encourage it to bush out in the shape of a globe.

Harvest **impatiens** stems with half-opened buds for fillers for bouquets. A branch of one of the giant **marigolds** makes a bouquet all by itself.

Continue to deadhead and harvest late summer bloomers. Deadhead the **pansies.**

Attics and garages are still hot and dry, perfect for air drying **statice** and **blue salvia,** as described in our July tip.

At this season, weeds are sowing seeds everywhere. Rake up weeds and their seedlings!

WATERING

If a dry spell occurs, thoroughly water annuals sown recently.

FERTILIZING

Apply a light foliar feeding to **snapdragons** and other annuals that bloom until frosts.

PROBLEMS

Protect plantings you plan to bring indoors for the winter against whiteflies and spider mites by applying an insecticide. Occasional showers, fresh air, and applications of insecticidal soap should keep problems away.

For other controls, see the section on Pests, Diseases, and Controls in the Appendix.

OCTOBER

ANNUALS & BIENNIALS

PLANNING

As annual beds empty, their shapes emerge. This is an especially good time to make changes in the shapes and sizes of existing beds. Use a garden hose to outline potential changes and live with them a few days before you start to dig.

Planning a new bed for annuals? Start one now when you have time to grow a winter cover crop to improve the soil.

Early fall is ideal for dividing and moving most perennials. If you'd like to make more space for annuals next year in beds combining perennials and annuals, make the moves now.

Garden log. Record the date of the first light frost, the one that blackened the tips of the **impatiens** leaves. And record the date of the first hard frost.

Note the bedding plants used to replace faded summer annuals in public gardens.

Note the planting of a cover crop and its progress.

PLANTING

Once you've had freezing weather, scratch up the soil, add fertilizer, and sow seeds of spring-blooming hardy annuals and perennials that germinate in cool temperatures—**foxglove, money plant, stock, larkspur, calendula,** and **sweet alyssum.** (Note: **sweet alyssum** often self-sows.) Mark the beds so you'll remember not to disturb the seedlings next spring.

Cover crop. A cover crop is a planting of a fast-growing grass or legume that is sown in an empty bed or row to keep weeds out and which is turned under after it grows. Called "green manure," it provides the soil with organic matter that enhances soil structure, adds nutrients, increases microbial activity, and helps to break up compacted areas. According to *Wyman's Gardening Encyclopedia*, three successive sowings of cover crops have been known to turn barren soil into rich, productive loam.

If you are expanding a bed, you can use a flexible garden hose to outline the potential changes. Once you make your decision, use garden lime to retain the outline so you will know where to dig.

ABOUT FLOWERING CABBAGES AND KALES

The leaves of these fabulous **cabbages** and **kales** are streaked, splotched, and edged red, purple, and cream. As the temperature drops, the colors grow more vibrant. They're the garden's last chance at beautiful fall color, a perfect replacement for fading **garden mums**. If you didn't sow seed last spring or early summer, you can buy good-sized plants at most garden centers.

Ornamental cabbage is a real cabbage that looks like a huge rose edged with red, pink, or cream. One of the most beautiful is 'Color Up Hybrid', which is almost 12 inches in diameter, brilliantly splotched and streaked over 80 percent of the head.

Flowering kale, Peacock hybrid, is spectacular. Just 12 inches tall, it has feathery leaves that are extravagantly serrated or notched and make a remarkable display in red or white.

Like kitchen cabbages, the ornamentals are cool-season plants. They stay beautiful all fall and through mild winters into spring when they send up seedheads. Keep the flower heads pinched out, and the plants stay in shape longer.

The **flowering cabbages** and **kales** thrive in deeply-dug, well-drained, fertile soil that holds moisture.

(See photograph on page 38.)

In the Mid-Atlantic, cover crops sown for spring are **clover, alfalfa,** and **lespedeza;** for summer, **millet, sorghum,** and **supan; winter rye** and **winter wheat** grow when temperatures are barely above freezing.

Planting a cover crop is simple enough. Till a quick-acting fertilizer into the soil, then broadcast the seeds over the bed. Make sure the soil stays moist until the seeds have sprouted. Rake, dig, or till in your cover crop before the plants go to seed, and at least ten days before planting the garden.

CARE

Pull up, and compost frost-blacked **marigolds, impatiens,** and the tender annuals still out in the garden and in containers.

Turn the compost pile.

GROOMING

Continue to deadhead the **pansies, calendula,** and any other flowers blooming in the garden.

WATERING

If the weather turns dry, water the seedlings planted in late summer and early fall, the **pansies,** the areas around the self-sowing annuals, and the cover crop if you planted one.

FERTILIZING

Apply a light foliar feeding to **snapdragons** and other annuals that bloom until frosts.

PROBLEMS

Keep an eye out for whiteflies and spider mites on the plants brought indoors for winter. If occasional showers and applications of insecticidal soap don't keep them away, apply an insecticide.

For other controls, see the section on Pests, Diseases, and Controls in the Appendix.

NOVEMBER

ANNUALS & BIENNIALS

 PLANNING

If you have planted spring-flowering bulbs, the areas they occupy will be fresh in your mind. This is a good time to go through old garden catalogs looking for annuals you might plant next spring to hide the ripening foliage of those bulbs after they bloom.

Borrow garden books and videos from the public library that can teach you more about using annuals in garden design. Graham Rice's books, *Discovering Annuals* and *The Sweet Pea Book*, are a joy. One of Britain's most respected garden authorities, Graham now lives in America. The individual entries are a pleasure to read, and will inspire ideas for next year's gardens. The photography is superb.

Garden log. Record frost dates, and bring your garden log up to date.

If you don't have a garden log, this might be a moment when you have time to start one.

Computer or paper diary? A computer log is easy to adjust, change, improve. If you are computer literate and have a digital camera and photographer's software, you could include images with plant entries.

Writing in a diary takes time, but you may be more open to inspiration and pleasant memories. Holding a written diary in your hand can be a richer experience than looking something up on the computer.

Whichever way you go, a maintained garden log provides answers to many questions you ask yourself every year. A record of the effect of the weather on your annuals can be really helpful. USDA and American Horticultural Society climate zone maps divide our country into areas according to extremes of cold and heat. But in every yard there are microclimates, areas that are more or less exposed or sheltered. That affects what happens to annuals as well as to perennials.

Entries that remind you how various plants performed are invaluable when ordering seeds for the new season. Thoughts about plant and color combinations are worth keeping. You think you will remember, but when you start studying the year's new garden catalogs, the past season has a way of blurring at the edges.

 PLANTING

In frost-free areas you can still transplant cold hardy annuals.

 CARE

This is a good time to empty, clean, and store hanging baskets, window boxes, and other containers.

Stack wire baskets, and hang them from a rafter in a garage or basement. Before putting plastic and terracotta containers away for the season, clean them in soapy water with a stiff brush or a scrub pad. Rinse them, then dip them in a solution of half a cup of bleach to 3 gallons of water. Rinse them again in clean water, and store them upside down. Find a storage place for terracotta pots out of the weather because they tend to crack when they are left outside.

Take the soil from hanging baskets, small and medium pots, planters, and window boxes, and spread it over your compost pile. If you do not use your window boxes for holiday displays, turn them upside down.

GROWING SCENT-LEAF GERANIUMS

The **scent-leaf geraniums** you see at florist shops and garden centers are aromatic tender perennials that make great room fresheners. Happy indoors in the winter and outdoors in the summer, they have only modest blooms. But brush against the foliage, and the room fills with potent scents of nutmeg, mint, rose, or lemon. They're so potent that they're used fresh to flavor sweets and dried in potpourris. The varieties with the strongest aroma have small white or pale pink blossoms.

Lemon geranium (*Pelargonium crispum*) is the species to grow for leaves to use in finger bowls. Small and crinkly, the leaves have a lemony scent. The flowers are two-toned pink. Recommended are 'Prince Rupert', 'Mable Grey', and 'Lemon Fancy'.

Rose geranium (*P. graveolens*) is the one to choose for gift giving. Grown commercially for its sweet-scented essential oils, it is the most popular of the scented geraniums. The foliage is green-gray, and the flowers are rose-lavender with a dark purple blotch in the middle of the upper petal.

Apple geranium (*P. odoratissimum* 'Gray Lady Plymouth') is the plant to choose if you love variegated foliage. It has small, velvety, sweetly scented, ruffled leaves and bears white flowers.

Peppermint geranium, woolly geranium (*P. tomentosum*) is the plant to choose if you like the smell of peppermint. It has large, soft, fuzzy, grape-like leaves and bears tiny purple-veined white flowers.

 GROOMING

Remove dead annuals from the garden.

Deadhead plants you brought indoors for the winter.

 WATERING

If you hit a dry spell, water your plantings.

Maintain soil moisture in plants you brought indoors for the winter.

Water the compost pile, and turn it weekly.

 FERTILIZING

Do not fertilize the plants you brought indoors until they show signs of new growth in January.

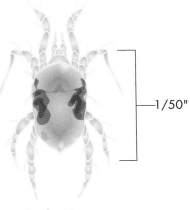

—1/50"

Spider Mite

PROBLEMS

Keep an eye out for whiteflies and spider mites on the plants brought indoors for winter. If occasional showers and applications of insecticidal soap don't keep them away, apply an insecticide.

For other controls, see the section on Pests, Diseases, and Controls in the Appendix.

DECEMBER

ANNUALS & BIENNIALS

 PLANNING

Go back to last year's garden log, and check your album of catalog pages of garden accessories. Order for the gardeners on your holiday list, and do family and friends a favor by telling them about tools and accessories you'd enjoy receiving.

Evaluate the progress of the tender perennials you brought indoors in the fall. Presented in a cache pot or a vase, some might make holiday gifts. If the plants lack light, invest in a light garden. Cuttings root well there, and in late winter and early spring a light garden promotes growth in seeds started indoors.

If you know now which seeds you intend to start indoors in February, use spare moments to make row markers for them.

Organize a seed-saver file. Organize your supply of seeds—those purchased that weren't used, and the seeds gathered in your garden. Nicely packaged, they make nifty stocking stuffers.

One of the most convenient ways we have found to file and store seeds is in a spiral binder with clear plastic sleeves. Place each variety of seed in its own small freezer bag. Mark the date on the bag, and store each bag inside its own sleeve in the binder. Slide a catalog image of the mature plant, and any comments you have, into each sleeve.

André stores seeds in small plastic bags in a refrigerator. Seeds are generally considered viable for three to five years after they have been gathered, though it may be that with each passing year fewer seeds will germinate.

Garden log. Record the progress of the cuttings of, or potted up, tender perennials you brought in earlier in the fall. Note especially whether there's enough light indoors for all you brought in—sunny sills, a picture window, or a Florida room—and whether you are enjoying them, or finding they take too much space and are too much work.

 PLANTING

Transplant well-rooted cuttings of the plants you brought in the fall.

 CARE

Indoors. Cuttings of **geraniums, coleus, impatiens,** and **wax begonias** growing in water should have masses of hair-like rootlets by now. Discard any that aren't rooting. If the water is growing murky, change it, and add a few small pieces of charcoal to keep it pure. André recommends adding $1/2$ teaspoon of bleach per gallon of water.

Outdoors. After cycles of freezing followed by thaws, check the **pansies, flowering cabbages,** and **kales** for signs of heaving—and heel them back in place.

 GROOMING

Indoors. Pinch out the tips of the **wax begonias** and **geraniums** you brought indoors as they get leggy.

Outdoors. Check the progress of spring-flowering seedlings growing in the open garden, and water them if December is dry.

 WATERING

Maintain the soil moisture in pots of tender perennials growing indoors.

 FERTILIZING

There is no fertilizing at this time.

 PROBLEMS

Continue to check for whiteflies and spider mites on the plants wintering indoors. Misting, fresh air, occasional showers, and applications of insecticidal soap should keep them healthy.

BULBS, CORMS, RHIZOMES, & TUBERS

Bulbs, corms, rhizomes, and tubers are a whole different category from annuals and perennials. Although each category has specific qualities, what they all have in common with each other is a bulbous type of structure. For the purpose of this chapter, we will refer to true bulbs, corms, rhizomes, and tubers as "bulbs." You can count on bulbs to bloom the first year planted, like annuals. And under the right circumstances, you can expect them to come back year after year, like perennials. What you need to be aware of when combining bulbs with annuals and perennials is that if you hope to have them perennialize you must allow the foliage to ripen at least six weeks after blooming before removing it. You also need to be aware that good drainage, one of the ben-efits from improving your soil as we recommend, is essential to bulbs.

There are bulbs that bloom in every season. In spring, daffodils and bluebells spread carpets of color in our woodlands. The perfume of the majes-tic lilies haunts summer gardens in late afternoon. Autumn crocus comes up when the leaves start to fall, and perfumed paper-white narcissus and hyacinths, golden daffodils, cheery amaryllis, and a host of others can be brought into bloom in your home all winter long.

Spring-flowering bulbs, the year's earliest show, are planted the preceding fall. They all tolerate our winter cold and summer heat with the possible exception of the alliums, which may not do well in the warmest reaches of Zone 8. Many come

CHAPTER TWO

DID YOU KNOW?

Which Is What?

• "True" bulbs are onion-like and have pointed tops and flattish bottoms that develop roots quite modest compared to the system of the same size perennial. Examples are daffodils, tulips, Dutch iris, and hyacinths. Stored within the bulb are the stem, the flower bud, and layers that are compressed leaves. Plant bulbs flat end down.

Some bulbs, like onions, are protected by a papery cover called a "tunic." Lilies and some other true bulbs have no protective cover; they are easily damaged and dry out quickly, so handle with care!

• Corms are roundish storage units that have flattish bottoms and a top that has one or more growing tips. This group includes crocus, gladiolus, crocosmia, and freesia. Plant these with the flattish part down.

• Rhizomes are fleshy lengths of thick, modified stem. They have lumpy tops and flattish bottoms from which the roots emerge. Examples are cannas and water lilies. Bearded irises, which grow from a knobbly rhizome, André groups with perennials. Lay rhizomes horizontally on the soil with the bottom down and the top even with the soil surface.

• Tubers are swollen rounded stems with "eyes," or growth buds, here and there. Think old potato. The eyes will grow roots or shoots, depending on their position in the soil. Examples are dahlias, caladiums, and lotus. Lay these horizontally under 2 or

3 inches of soil, or at whatever depth the supplier recommends.

Tulipology

Tulips have a romantic history. A Persian symbol of love and a major inspiration for artists, a potful of tulips in bloom makes a perfect holiday gift for lovers.

The tulip was brought to Europe in the mid-1500s from the court gardens of Suleiman the Magnificent in Constantinople. The species probably was *Tulipa gesneriana*, an ancestor of most modern hybrids. It had more in common with our little species tulips than with the spectacular modern hybrids. Species tulips are tulips as they evolved in nature, the original tulips from which all modern hybrids were developed. A few decades after their arrival in Europe, tulips were being grown in Holland.

The magic wrought on the Suleiman's bulbs by the Dutch growers so captivated people that speculation on the price of bulbs became a hazard to Europe's financial health. Laws had to be introduced to limit the prices. A single tulip was considered a suitable dowry for a bride, and in France a brewery was once exchanged for one tulip bulb. The market collapsed in 1637 ruining speculators, but 200 years later, one bulb of a rare type could still command a price of 650 pounds. Even today, a high price for a new variety is not all that unusual.

back year after year and multiply if protected from creatures that think of them as food.

Summer-flowering bulbs begin to grow after the nights turn warm—mid- and late June. Early and late varieties bring color to mixed borders and container gardens when they need it most, mid- and late summer.

The summer-flowering bulbs whose winter hardiness rating is north of Zone 6 may be planted in

mid-fall or mid-spring and need no special protection in winter. Those that are at the upper edge of their cold tolerance in Zone 6 are safer planted in mid-fall if they're provided with winter mulch. Examples are crocosmia and wood sorrel, *Oxalis adenophylla*.

Summer-flowering bulbs rated winter-hardy only as far north as Zone 8, canna, colocasia, and the perfumed tuberose, are best planted in mid-fall in

our region. In Zone 8 they may be safe wintering in the ground protected by a light winter mulch. In Zones 6 and 7, in autumn, lift, clean, and store the bulbs for winter indoors in a cool, dry place. Most need cool storage temperatures—between 35 to 50 degrees for bulbs such as canna, dahlias, and tigridia. Others can be stored at room temperatures—caladiums and colocasia for example.

Fall flowering bulbs are planted in summer for fall blooming. If you haven't grown these late bloomers, try a few this fall. Colchicum, fall crocus, and winter daffodil open showy blooms just aboveground in early fall, then in spring large glossy leaves rise and, after many weeks, disappear for the summer. The resurrection lily, *Lycoris squamigera*, produces exotic, fragrant, trumpet-shaped blooms from bulbs planted in August.

Bulbs for winter bloom indoors: In early fall, plan to pot up spring-flowering bulbs—we recommend tulips, daffodils, and perfumed hyacinths—which can be forced into early bloom in winter (see September). A few tropical bulb flowers can also be forced into bloom in winter, notably amaryllis (*Hippeastrum*) and perfumed paper-whites (see November).

PLANTING, MULCHING, DIVIDING

Light. Crocus, daffodils, bluebells (squill, scilla), and wood hyacinth bloom in partial shade, as do some of the smaller bulbs. But most big bulb flowers do their best in full sun, and need at least six hours of sun daily to flower a second year.

Soil. The garden and container soil in which bulbs do best is light and very well drained. Repeat, very well drained. Ideally, this is a raised bed on a slope. There are always exceptions to the rule; a few summer-bloomers tolerate moist spots—canna, Dutch iris, summer snowflake, crinum, rain lily, and spider lily.

The pH range most bulbs prefer is 6.0 to 7.0. There are exceptions to that rule, too. The most popular lilies prefer a somewhat acid soil (see About Lilies, February). For step-by-step instructions on creating a raised bed and adjusting soil pH, turn to the section on Soil Preparation and Improvement in the Introduction to this book.

When you are planting bulbs in an existing bed, the soil needs the same careful preparation as for a raised bed. Outline the area, then cover it with 3 to 4 inches of humus, enough so that one quarter of the content of the soil from the hole will be organic matter. Mix the humus into the soil as you dig it out of the hole, along with:

For every 100 square feet:
  Bulb-tone: 5 to 10 pounds
  Rock phosphate: 5 to 10 pounds
  Greensand: 5 to 10 pounds
  Clay soils only: gypsum 5 to10 pounds
  Osmocote® 8-month: 2 pounds

Planting. About bulb planters—they work well only if the soil has been well prepared. We recommend the Dutch method of planting bulbs, which is to use a spading fork to dig a generous hole or a bed, remove the soil and mix it thoroughly with the soil amendments above. Then, return 2 or 3 inches of improved soil to the hole, tamp it down, and plant the bulbs on top at the depth recommended.

Set true bulbs so the pointed tips are upright; set corms and tubers with the roots facing down. Set rhizomes horizontally in the soil with the roots down.

Winter mulch provides protection for bulbs whose cold hardiness is marginal in your area. For winter mulch, André recommends airy organics such as straw, pine needles, and pine boughs. For coastal dwellers, marsh hay or salt hay from the shore are excellent winter mulches.

Dividing bulbs is a way to multiply your holdings, and, in some species, it improves performance.

True bulbs growing well produce offsets that in three to four years may crowd the planting and cause the flowers to diminish. The best time to divide bulbs is after the foliage has withered.

Use a spading fork to dig and lift the bulbs, gently pull them apart or leave the clump intact, and replant. Bulblets (baby bulbs) need years to mature enough to bloom, so plant these in an out-of-the-way place.

You don't have to divide daffodils to keep them gorgeous . . . just fertilize them. Lilies, on the other hand, André recommends moving or dividing every four years.

You may divide rhizomes and tubers either before the growing cycle begins (easier since there is no foliage to contend with) or when it is over. Just cut the rhizome or tuber into sections that each contain at least one growth bud or eye. Tuberous roots, such as dahlias, do best when separated before growth begins.

Transplanting. Dutch growers tell us the best place for spring-flowering bulbs is in the ground. If lifted and stored, which once was recommended, they are susceptible to fungus and disease. But growers do recommend lifting and storing bulbs that can't survive winters in your garden.

Spring-flowering bulbs can be transplanted in spring, summer, or fall. You can move daffodils in bloom. Or wait until the flowers have faded, then cut off the flower heads, leaving the green leaves. Dig the plants with care so the roots are not damaged, and move the bulbs to the new location.

Summer-flowering bulbs that are hardy enough to be left in the ground in Zone 6 (-10 F winter lows) or Zone 7 (0 F winter lows) may be transplanted either in fall after the foliage has yellowed, or in spring just as growth begins.

Fall-flowering bulbs may be moved after the blooms fade. Those whose foliage comes up in spring, like the fall-blooming crocus, can be moved then.

Winter-flowering bulbs that have been forced into bloom indoors are weakened. Tulips and the smaller bulb flowers are best discarded. However, if you keep forced daffodils and hyacinths in a sunny window, water and fertilize them while the foliage ripens and dies down, then plant them in the garden in the fall, they probably will eventually bloom in their outdoor locations.

FERTILIZING

All bulbs need continuing fertilization if they are to thrive and multiply.

There are two schools of thought on fertilizing spring-flowering bulbs.

In their book *Daffodils*, daffodil gurus Brent and Becky Heath recommend applying a diluted organic fertilizer to spring-flowering bulb plantings from the time the tips show in spring until the bulbs bloom. They suggest fertilizing again in early fall with a slow-release product (5-10-12 or 5-12-20) such as Bulb Mate.

André recommends fertilizing spring-flowering bulbs as soon as they finish blooming with Bulb-tone at the rate of 4 to 6 pounds to 100 square feet, and again in early September.

André recommends fertilizing established summer-flowering bulbs in early spring before growth begins, and again in mid-fall.

PESTS

Squirrels, chipmunks, and voles truly believe you have set bulbs out just for their delight. All during the fall, squirrels are sure any bulb you plant is something they want—planters and hanging baskets not excepted. One year they tore up a heavy cardboard box of tulip bulbs I had stored on a second floor porch in D.C. Only daffodils are safe; they're toxic to wildlife.

The solution is to plant bulbs in VoleBloc or Soil Perfecta.

Deer love tulips and crocus too! Spraying is no guarantee they won't eat the flowers. What does keep them away for sure is a temporary chicken-wire enclosure (see the section on Pests, Diseases, and Controls in the Appendix) or bird netting.

JANUARY
BULBS, CORMS, RHIZOMES, & TUBERS

 PLANNING

A pleasant way to satisfy the hunger for spring flowers is to tear out garden catalog pages that show bulbs you especially like, and then to organize them into an album. Group together the spring-bloomers, summer-bloomers, fall-bloomers, and the bulbs that bloom in winter indoors. In February and in June use your album to help make decisions on which bulbs to order for the next season. When your choices have been made, place a sticky note by each plant chosen reminding you where to plant it.

Your annuals garden log (see January, Annuals) will suggest tall hardy annual flowers that, started early indoors, can be good follow-on plants for the bulb flowers.

 PLANTING

Plant **tulip** and **daffodil** bulbs that you didn't get into the ground last fall. The bulbs may produce plants that are stunted and small, but they have a chance of growing. One thing's for sure—if you don't get the bulbs in the ground now, they're toast. They won't last until next season.

 CARE

Early this month, check the dates and the timing chart on bulbs potted up for forcing last fall. Move those that have finished chilling into a warmer room, and begin to water and fertilize them as you do houseplants. In two weeks or so the shoots will grow tall and initiate flower buds. Place them in good light but out of direct sun. Feed a half dose of liquid fertilizer at every watering.

 GROOMING

When all the blooms are dead on **amaryllis** and other forced bulbs, cut the flower heads off, and move the plants to a bright sunny window to grow. But do not save the **paper-whites;** discard them.

 WATERING

Keep the soil just damp in pots of bulbs being forced, as well as in those that have finished blooming and that you hope to plant outdoors later.

Don't allow the soil of pots of tender or tropical bulbs wintering in a protected place to dry out completely; they are semi-dormant.

 FERTILIZING

At every second watering of bulbs after they've bloomed, add a half dose of liquid fertilizer for flowering houseplants, African violet fertilizer, for example, to the water.

 PROBLEMS

Aphids and fungus gnats can be a nuisance. Try rinsing aphids off with a kitchen sink spray or misting the plant with a horticultural soap.

Fungus gnats are tiny black gnats that hatch in potting mix and are a nuisance. Discourage them by allowing the soil to dry between waterings, and removing standing water from the plant saucers.

Discard forced bulbs you suspect of serious insect infestation, along with their soil.

FEBRUARY
BULBS, CORMS, RHIZOMES, & TUBERS

 PLANNING

Complete your order for summer-flowering bulbs. Mail-order suppliers won't ship until it's time to plant. Include some of the tropicals so popular now in Mid-Atlantic gardens. The big-leaved **cannas** and **ornamental bananas** are sensational accent plants in mixed borders and in containers. The tropicals make great container plants for the patio. *Tigridia* blooms last just a day, but a tubful is a riot of color. *Amarcrinum howardii*, a recent cross between the **amaryllis** and **crinum**, bears gorgeous pink flowers. **Lily-of-the-Nile** puts up exquisite blue, white, or pink trumpets and thrives for years indoors; a mature plant is magnificent in bloom. Combine **oxalis, caladium, coleus, variegated canna**, and **Oriental lilies** in complementary colors in a group of containers.

This year take the **dahlia** plunge! These six-footers rival **sunflowers**, real showstoppers at the back of a mixed border. Massed in the front of the bed, the smaller, bushier cactus-flowered varieties like pink 'Park Princess' are sensational.

 PLANTING

In Zone 8, late this month start new **tuberous begonias** and those saved from last year. Plant tubers 3 to 4 inches apart, hollow side facing up, round end down, in open trays of moist vermiculite or sphagnum peat moss or a combination of both. Keep the trays in indirect light at about 70 degrees Fahrenheit.

 CARE

There's still time to force **paper-whites** (see November), and many garden centers carry them this time of year.

Bring remaining spring-flowering bulbs potted up last fall for forcing into a bright, warm room, and water and fertilize as you do houseplants. When they bloom, move them to bright light but not direct sun, and keep the soil barely damp.

Daffodils, hyacinths, muscari, and other little bulbs may have a second life outdoors if they are allowed to mature on a sunny windowsill. Water and fertilize as you do houseplants. When the weather is warm enough, plant them outdoors in an out-of-the-way place. If the foliage dies down before you can plant outdoors, allow the soil in the pots to dry, and plant the bulbs when the weather warms.

Check stored **cannas** and **dahlias** for disease, and remove and discard tubers showing mold or rot.

 GROOMING

Deadhead **amaryllis** blooms, and grow the plants in a bright sunny window.

The **tulips** and **paper-whites** go to the compost pile. These bulbs cannot be forced again.

 WATERING

Maintain some moisture in pots of bulbs that are being, or have been, forced, and which you plan to replant later. Discard **tulips** that are finished, but continue to provide a sunny sill and to water and fertilize **daffodils** and **hyacinths** that look healthy.

Don't allow the soil in pots of tender or tropical bulbs wintering in a protected place to dry out completely; they are semi-dormant.

ABOUT LILIES

In late summer afternoons the perfume of the **Oriental lily** 'Casa Blanca' permeates the garden—an invitation to try these most majestic flowers.

The three major lily categories—**Asiatics, Trumpets, Orientals**—bloom in that order starting with the **Asiatics** in June/July and ending with the big **Orientals** in July/August. They have overlapping flowering periods since there are late **Asiatics** and early **Trumpets** and **Orientals**. Each bulb produces one big flowering stem.

Mail-order suppliers ship lily bulbs at planting time in spring or in early fall. The early-blooming **Asiatics** are best planted in fall. The late-blooming **Orientals** and **Trumpets** also are best planted in the fall, but may be planted in spring. Plant them as soon as possible. Container-grown lilies and lilies in bloom adapt to transplanting, but to plant a bare lily bulb that has sprouted a shoot over 2 inches long is bad news.

Give lilies a spot in full sun if your temperatures stay under 90 degrees Fahrenheit; in hotter areas, plant lilies in bright tall shade, or provide protection from direct noon and afternoon sun.

Lilies do best in slightly acid, fertile soil rich in trace elements. The **Asiatic lilies** require a pH between 5.8 and 6.8. The **Orientals** prefer pH 5.2 to 6.2, and do well with **azaleas**. The **Trumpets** are less particular. All lilies like cold feet, so mulch heavily, or underplant them with flowers such as **coreopsis** that do well in somewhat acid soil.

When the blossoms fade, pinch them off the flower stalk. When harvesting lilies, take no more than a third of the flower stalk, or it will be shorter next year. When flowering ends, cut the flower stalks to just above the leaves and allow the rest to yellow. Then cut the stalks to the ground—or leave them to mark the locations. In fall and again before growth begins in spring, fertilize the bed with Bulb-tone or Holly-tone at the rate of 4 pounds per 100 square feet. Mulch. Move or divide lilies every four years in the fall.

FERTILIZING

Monitor plantings of spring-flowering bulbs, and as soon as the tips show, water weekly with a diluted organic fertilizer and continue as they come into bloom.

At every second watering, add a half dose of liquid fertilizer for flowering houseplants to the soil for **amaryllis, daffodils,** and **hyancinths** still growing after blooming. Use bloom booster type fertilizers, like African violet food, which are high in phosphorus for promoting flower-bud initiation for next season.

PROBLEMS

Get rid of aphids by spraying them with a kitchen sink spray or misting the plant with a horticultural soap. Discourage the little black fungus gnats that hover over potting mix by allowing the soil to dry between watering and removing standing water from the plant saucers.

When forced bulbs finish blooming, discard any you suspect of insect infestation, along with their soil.

MARCH
BULBS, CORMS, RHIZOMES, & TUBERS

 PLANNING

Now that the early spring-flowering bulbs are showing their true colors, consider where you'd like to see more or different colors and plants next spring. Write your ideas on sticky notes, and place them in your bulb album (see Planning, January) as reminders when preparing your order this summer for October planting.

Plan to start tender and summer-flowering bulbs and tropicals indoors this month; organize pots and potting mixes.

 PLANTING

When danger of frost is over and the soil is free of winter cold and moisture, start planting hardy summer-flowering bulbs in the garden. For soil and planting recommendations, see Planting, in the introduction to this chapter.

True bulbs are planted flat end down. Don't leave scraps of their tunic covering around because squirrels will dig. **Lilies** and a few others have no protective cover so handle with care!

Corms are rounded; plant them with the flattish bottom down. Examples are **crocosmia, poppy anemones,** and **gladiolas.**

Rhizomes are fleshy lengths of thick, modified stem with lumpy tops—**bearded irises** for example. Plant these horizontally in the soil with the roots down.

Tubers are swollen rounded stems with growth buds, called "eyes," here and there. Think old potato. The eyes will grow roots or shoots, depending on their position in the soil. So plant them the way that seems right. **Caladiums** are an example.

Cold-tender and tropical bulbs must wait until the weather warms to go outdoors. **Dahlias** are an example. You can start them indoors now.

 CARE

When the **tuberous begonias** (see February, Planting) begin to grow, plant them in individual 6-inch pots filled with a mix of soil, compost, and peat. Move the containers to cooler temperatures, about 65 degrees Fahrenheit. When the shoots are 4 inches tall, transplant to 8- to 10-inch baskets or azalea pans filled with sterile soilless mix. Sprinkle enough damp sphagnum peat moss over the tubers to cover them.

Transplant forced **daffodils** and other forced bulbs that look healthy to an out-of-the-way place in the garden; do not remove the foliage. If the foliage has died, allow the soil in the pots to dry, and plant the bulbs when you can.

Easter lilies, *Lilium longiflorum,* can be transplanted to a sheltered sunny spot in the garden. Don't add wood ashes or lime; they need slightly acid soil.

 GROOMING

Discard forced bulbs you suspect of insect infestation, along with their soil.

Deadhead early **daffodils, tulips,** and other large bulb flowers that have finished blooming; allow the foliage to remain. The small bulb flowers are self-cleaning.

 WATERING

Indoors. Keep the soilless mix over **tuberous begonias** and other bulbs started indoors moist by sprinkling the surface.

Keep the soil moderately damp in pots of tender or tropical bulbs wintering in a protected place.

Outdoors. The early bulb flowers in the garden are growing full; sustained moisture is important at this time, so, if the sky doesn't do it, water slowly and deeply every ten days.

Water the bulbs whose foliage is being allowed to mature if the season is dry.

ABOUT DAHLIAS

In Zones 6 and 7, gardeners start **dahlias** indoors in March or April. In Zone 8, gardeners plant dahlias right in the garden in mid-spring and have them blooming still in early November.

1. Dahlias lifted and wintered indoors should still be attached to the main stem. Separate the tubers from the stems; include with each tuber a portion of the stem with a growth bud attached. Dahlia tubers you buy are ready to plant.

2. Line a pot that has drainage holes with landscaping cloth and 2 inches of gravel. Add 2 to 4 inches of damp soilless potting mix, or a mix of 2 parts peat moss, 1 part perlite, and 1 part vermiculite. Set the tubers on top, and cover them with 2 inches of the potting mix.

3. About four weeks later, when shoots appear, water the soil, and move the pot to a sunny spot. Keep the soil moderately damp.

4. As the shoots grow, add a few inches of soil until the soil is within 2 inches of the pot rim. When the dahlia stem is 12 inches tall, tie it to a stake.

5. Move the pots out to a protected spot when the air warms in May or June.

6. In Zones 6 and 7, dahlia tubers rot in the ground, even when mulched. So before frost

gets to them, lift and store them, unwashed, in dry sand or vermiculite at temperatures between 35 and 45 degrees. In Zone 8, dahlias can survive winters in the ground if they are heavily mulched.

FERTILIZING

When spring-flowering bulbs show their tips, water with a diluted organic fertilizer.

Early this month fertilize the hardy summer-flowering bulbs that are out in the garden. Scratch in Bulb-tone at the rate of 4 pounds per 100 square feet. For **lilies** use Holly-tone.

At every second watering, add a half dose of liquid bulb booster or African violet fertilizer for flowering houseplants to the soil for **amaryllis** and other forced bulbs you are growing after they've bloomed.

PROBLEMS

Deer love **tulips** and **crocus**! Spraying deer repellent is no

guarantee against them. What does keep them away is a temporary chicken-wire fence.

Get rid of aphids by spraying them with a kitchen sink sprayer or misting the plant with a horticultural soap. Discourage the little black fungus gnats that hover over potting mix by allowing the soil to dry between watering and by removing standing water from the plant saucers.

APRIL
BULBS, CORMS, RHIZOMES, & TUBERS

PLANNING

Do the plants around the spring-flowering bulbs screen the fading foliage? If not, consider investing in good-sized seedlings of annuals and in big container-grown perennials to mask the waiting period.

PLANTING

When all danger of frost is past, you can move the potted summer-flowering bulbs that wintered indoors out to the garden—**ornamental banana, canna, ginger lilies,** and **lily-of-the-Nile** (*Agapanthus africanus*), for example. Repot them, and begin weekly watering and fertilization.

Transplanting. You can move spring-flowering bulbs around in the garden after the plants go out of bloom. Do it while the foliage is still green; once the foliage dies the bulbs are hard to locate.

Prepare a new planting hole by loosening the soil and adding bulb fertilizer and compost. Then dig the clump, taking care not to damage the bulbs or roots, and plop it intact into the new planting hole. Allow the foliage to ripen naturally, just as you would have had you not moved the bulbs. After six or seven weeks the foliage will turn brown, and then you can cut it off at ground level.

The grass-like foliage of the small fall-flowering bulbs, **autumn crocus** for example, come up in spring; you can lift and transplant them in clumps anytime after the foliage comes up.

Dividing. After the foliage has died down but while you can still see it is the best time to divide clumps of spring-flowering bulbs. Use a spading fork to lift the clumps. Gently pull the bulbs apart. Replant clusters of two and three mature bulbs, and the biggest bulbs. Plant bulblets in an out-of-the-way spot because they must grow before they'll bloom.

You can dig and divide bulbs after the foliage is gone, but best get the job done before September when they will already be rooting. If you plan to move spring-flowering bulbs after the foliage has died, mark their positions now.

CARE

The **amaryllis** can be moved outdoors when the nighttime temperatures stay above 60 degrees Fahrenheit. Plant the pots up to their rims in full sun in well-drained soil. Water and fertilize them when you water other container plants.

You can remove **tulip** foliage when it has yellowed halfway down; if you hope to perennialize **tulips**, fertilize them now. **Darwin hybrids** and **species tulips** should be encouraged. **Tulips** that sent up foliage but failed to bloom this year we recommend you discard, or move to an out-of-the-way spot to mature.

GROOMING

Deadhead spring-flowering bulbs, leaving the stems intact. Allow the foliage to ripen six to seven weeks before you remove it.

WATERING

Maintain moisture in the container plants, the **tuberous begonia,** and the summer-flowering bulbs started indoors.

Keep the soil just damp in pots of bulbs that have finished blooming and that you hope to plant outdoors later.

Don't allow the soil of pots of tender or tropical bulbs wintering in a protected place to dry out completely; they are semi-dormant.

ABOUT DAFFODILS, NARCISSUS, AND JONQUILS

Narcissus is the botanical, or genus, name; the common name **daffodil** is often used instead. **Jonquils,** a type of *N. jonquilla,* are late bloomers that bear clusters of fragrant flowers on each stem. The immense variety of daffodils, their easy ways, and their imperviousness even to deer make them spring's favorite bulb.

Plant open woodlands with big, yellow daffodils in irregular drifts of twenty, fifty, or one-hundred bulbs, and they will carpet it with gold. A dusting of wood ashes in early September is enough to keep naturalized daffs blooming.

Plant early daffs, like 8-inch 'Jack Snipe', to edge flower beds and in rock gardens, containers, in the shelter of boulders, and along fences.

For bouquets, grow show-stoppers like 12-inch orange-cupped 'Jetfire', and 18-inch pink-cupped 'Chinese Coral'. Bouquets of **daffodils** are long-lasting; before combining just-cut **daffodils** with **tulips** or other flowers, place the **daffodil** stems in water overnight to detoxify.

For fragrance, in addition to **jonquils** plant **Polyanthus daffodils.** A favorite is 'Geranium' whose crisp white petals surround frilled orange cups. The perfumed paper-whites, so easy to force, belong to this group; they're not winter hardy here. Pot up **paper-whites,** a variety of **tazetta narcissus,** in late fall, and they will bloom and perfume your house in just a few weeks (see November).

Planting daffodils. Plant daffodils in the fall after the first hard frost. They thrive in full sun or partial shade in well-drained, slightly acid soil. Set large bulbs 8 inches deep, 3 to 6 inches apart; small bulbs 3 to 5 inches deep, 1 to 3 inches apart. Add a handful of 5-10-20 slow-release fertilizer as topdressing after planting. Deadhead the show daffs; naturalized daffs don't need it.

Perennializing daffodils. Most daffodils and jonquils perennialize. Allow the foliage to remain undisturbed until it has withered away. Binding the foliage while the leaves ripen cuts off light and oxygen the bulbs need to nourish the next year's flowers.

FERTILIZING

Every second time you water, include a half-strength dose of soluble fertilizer to the hardy bulbs growing in containers outdoors and to pots of **amaryllis**. Use African violet or bloom booster fertilizer for flowering plants.

You'll have bigger and more blooms next year if you fertilize spring flowering bulbs as soon as they finish blooming with Bulb-tone at the rate of 4 to 6 pounds for each 100 square feet, and repeat the dose in early September.

PROBLEMS

Daffodils, narcissus, and **jonquils** are safe from deer, but other flowering bulbs may not be. For controls, see Pests, Diseases, and Controls in the Appendix.

MAY

BULBS, CORMS, RHIZOMES, & TUBERS

PLANNING

Unhappy with bare spots where the spring-flowering bulbs have faded? Fill in the spots with **dahlias** ready to bloom, repeat sowings of perfumed **tuberose, rain lily** (*Zephyranthes*), **gladiola,** and other not very hardy summer-flowering bulbs. If you haven't already, try **canna** and **ornamental banana** this year; their big leaves are terrific fillers for empty spots at the back of the border. All of these need to be, or can be, lifted in fall and wintered indoors. That leaves the space free for the spring-flowering bulbs to pop up next year. If you set them in the garden in pots, moving them to a frost-free place for the winter is easy.

PLANTING

When the air warms, about when the **lilacs** bloom, you can plant the tender summer-flowering bulbs and tropicals started indoors or purchased at garden centers. Harden them off for a few days in a protected spot.

Set the plants 18 to 24 inches apart, according to mature size, in well-worked soil enriched with a slow-release, low-nitrogen fertilizer, 4-month formulation. Prepare sturdy stakes tall enough to support the upper third of the plants, like big **dahlias**, that will grow up to be between 18 inches and 4 feet. Insert the stakes deep into the soil 2 inches away from the plants that need staking. Firm the plants in their holes, and water them. When the stems are 12 inches tall, tie the main stems to stakes. Tie on other branches as the plant matures.

Mid-month, start planting sets of six or eight **gladiolus** for cutting, and repeat at three-week intervals until early August.

CARE

Move pots of **tuberous begonias, dahlias**, and other bulbs started indoors out now to a sheltered spot to harden off. In a week or ten days you can move them to their permanent summer location.

Move pots of **lily-of-the-Nile** and other tender bulbs and tropicals that wintered indoors in containers outdoors for a summer of R&R. Groom the plants. Repot those in small containers in fresh potting mix. Top-dress those too large to repot by adding 2 inches of compost to the container.

Stake the **lilies** growing in the garden, and mulch them to keep their feet cool; or underplant them with flowers that do well in somewhat acid soil, **coreopsis** or **lily-of-the-valley,** for example.

GROOMING

Clear away yellowing leaves of the **tuberous begonias,** and deadhead the male flowers. The showy blooms are male, and most are backed by a single female flower—it isn't necessary to deadhead the female flowers.

WATERING

Water potted **dahlias** often enough to maintain soil moisture, but avoid soaking them.

Keep the soil around the **tuberous begonias** evenly moist but not soaking.

Maintain the soil moisture of the **amaryllis** and the hardy bulbs growing in containers. As the season grows warmer, plants in small pots and hanging baskets may need watering every day.

FERTILIZING

At every second watering, include a half dose of fertilizer in the water for all your potted and basket plants.

ABOUT CALADIUMS

Start **caladium** tubers indoors about eight weeks before nights will be above 60 and day temperatures reach 70 degrees Fahrenheit.

1. Fill a flat with 2 to 3 inches of moist peat moss or sterile soilless potting mix.

2. Set the tubers about 8 inches apart with the knobbly side up and the little straggle of roots down.

3. Keep the growing medium damp. The tubers are slow to start but do well in a grow light stand or in a sunny glassed-in porch.

4. When they sprout, transplant them to containers filled with improved soil fertilized with Plant-tone. A container 8 to 10 inches in diameter can take four to five **caladiums**. Cover the tubers with 2 inches of fertile soil mixed with humus or peat moss.

5. When daytime temperatures reach 70 degrees Fahrenheit and nights stay above 60, move the **caladiums** outdoors in their pots, or transplant them to the garden. They do best in a semi-sunny or a lightly shaded location.

6. When temperatures drop below 70 degrees in the fall, harvest the tubers, allow them to dry, and store them at temperatures between 70 and 75 degrees.

Be warned: to a deer a caladium is prime time lettuce.

As the **tulips** finish blooming, spread bulb booster around those that you hope to perennialize.

You'll have bigger and more blooms next year if you fertilize spring-flowering bulbs as soon as they finish blooming with Bulb-tone at the rate of 4 to 6 pounds for each 100 square feet, and repeat in early September.

PROBLEMS

Japanese beetles can wreck the foliage of **canna, dahlias,** and some other bulb flowers. Pick them off by hand. To cut down on the populations, plan to spread milky spore disease over the area and the surrounding garden in early September. For other con-trols, turn to Pests, Diseases, and Controls in the Appendix.

Rake or hoe weeds away with a swing-head hoe. It's a push-pull oscillating hoe that cuts through weeds and cultivates the soil without disturbing the mulch.

To deter deer, spray with a new and different deterrent, or put up a barrier to keep the deer out. See Pests in the Appendix to the book.

JUNE
BULBS, CORMS, RHIZOMES, & TUBERS

PLANNING

Most of the mail-order catalogs arriving discount prices on early orders for fall- and spring-flowering bulbs. They offer a wide selection and ship at planting time. You'll also find the most popular, and newest, varieties at full service garden centers, but the selection may be limited.

Tear out catalog pages, and add them to your bulb album (see Planning, January); then make a planting plan that will keep bulbs blooming in your garden and indoors this fall, winter, and spring.

Fall-flowering bulbs. They are planted in summer or fall and bloom in September and October. Most are not much bigger than a crocus. Plan to plant them in drifts near paths to the house and in the front of shrub borders. **Resurrection lily,** *Amarcrinum,* and other full-size late bloomers we suggest planting in containers.

Spring-flowering bulbs. The small bulb flowers open in February and March, with *Iris reticulata,* **winter aconite, snowdrops,** and **hardy cyclamen** leading the way. It's a joy to watch their progress, so plant them in drifts by house entrances.

Intermediate-size bulb flowers provide the next wave of color—**squill, oxalis,** sapphire **scillas,** luminous **species tulips,** dainty white **leucojum**—on stems 6 to 24 inches tall. Use them to fill spaces in flowering borders between perennials and where you plan to plant annuals later.

Many of the large bulb flowers bloom toward the middle and end of spring, but there are early, mid-season, and late varieties of most, including the **daffodils** and **tulips.** Order a few dozen to scatter in groups in your flower borders. Plan to plant **tulips** for cutting in the kitchen garden. Naturalized **daffodils,** which are deer proof, light up shrub borders and woodlands. For their fragrance, plant groups of **hyacinths** near entrances.

PLANTING

You can plant the little fall bloomers as soon as you have them. The leaves of those already in your garden come up at this season, and then die down again in summer; before that happens, mark their positions to avoid digging them up when overplanting the area.

Continue planting sets of six or eight **gladiolus** for cutting, and repeat at three-week intervals until early August.

CARE

Move **tuberous begonias, dahlias, caladiums,** and other tender bulbs to their permanent place in the garden; they need some protection from noon and late afternoon sun.

Adjust the **dahlia** stakes as the plants grow.

GROOMING

Deadhead **tuberous begonias, irises,** and the other flowering bulbs. Remove **caladium** flowers as they appear; they aren't showy and detract from the foliage.

Cut the yellowed foliage of the spring-flowering bulbs off at the base. If there are some you wanted to move but didn't get to, mark the spot with plant marker or a golf tee so you'll know where to dig when you have time to move them.

WATERING

Check the soil moisture of small containers of summer-flowering bulbs, and the **tuberous begonias,** every two days. Don't overlook pots of **amaryllis** summering in the garden.

Where the hardy spring-flowering bulbs have bloomed, water only if you must; they are dormant now and most prefer to be rather dry. Underground automatic sprinkling systems spell death to most bulbs unless they're adjusted to water deeply, and only when moisture is needed—not every day, not every other day, not even every third day.

FERTILIZING

You'll have bigger and more blooms next year if you fertilize spring-flowering bulbs as soon as they finish blooming with Bulb-tone at the rate of 4 to 6 pounds for each 100 square feet, and repeat in early September.

Continue to fertilize **amaryllis** summering out in the open garden.

FALL-FLOWERING BULBS

A handful of fall-flowering bulbs bloom when everything else is going by except **pansies, mums,** and **flowering cabbage** and **kale.** Try some of our favorites:

- **Autumn daffodil,** *Sternbergia lutea*
  Planting time: late summer for fall bloom.
- **Colchicum,** *Colchicum* species
  Planting time: late summer or early fall for mid-late fall bloom.
- **Fall crocus,** *Crocus,* many fall-blooming species
  Planting time: summer for September or December bloom.
- **Hardy cyclamen,** *Cyclamen hederifolium*
  Planting time: July for late summer or early winter bloom.
- **Naked-lady lily,** *Amaryllis belladonna* (syn. *Brunsvigia rosea*)
  Planting time: early summer for early fall bloom.
- **Oxblood lily,** *Rhodophiala bifida*
  Planting time: early September for fall bloom.
- **Resurrection lily, hardy amaryllis,** *Lycoris squamigera*
  Planting time: August for fall bloom.

PROBLEMS

Hand-pick Japanese beetles and discard into a jar of soapy water. Try applications of Neem to discourage them.

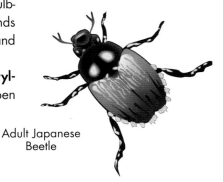

Adult Japanese Beetle

If spring has been wet, keep an eye out for fungal diseases. Pick and discard infected foliage. A fungicide may help control the problem. Try applications of Messenger, which is said to stimulate the plant's own defenses. For controls, turn to Pests, Diseases, and Controls in the Appendix.

To deter deer, spray with a new and different deterrent because they become used to what's been around for a while, or put up a barrier to keep the deer out.

JULY
BULBS, CORMS, RHIZOMES, & TUBERS

 PLANNING

Take advantage of the mail-order bulb suppliers' discounts for early orders. They start shipping as early as mid-August and can run out of popular varieties.

When purchasing bulbs, buy the largest ones you can find. They may cost a little more, but their performance more than makes up for the difference in price. Smaller sizes are good for naturalizing. Bargain mixes are a bargain only if they include first-rate varieties. Medium and small **hyacinth** bulbs are a good deal as the shorter flower stalks are less vulnerable to late storms.

Plan to try some of the beautiful little bulbs that bloom in September. The tender lavender hues of **colchicum** and **fall crocus** are very appealing in the midst of autumn's assertive reds, russets, and golds. Their leaves come up in spring and after many weeks disappear; the showy blooms rise when cool weather comes.

To make a showing with the little bulbs' flowers, order enough of each variety to plant drifts of twenty, fifty, or one hundred. For the mid-size bulbs to be effective you will need ten, twenty, or more of each. The big bulbs, the tall **Darwin tulips** for example, make a big splash planted in groups of as few as five or ten. Order **hyacinths** in groups of three or five of one color. Choose several **tulip** varieties for cutting with bouquets.

When ordering spring-flowering bulbs for forcing, select large size bulbs of varieties recommended for forcing. You'll need five **daffodil** or **tulip** bulbs for each 6-inch pot, and nine for a 12-inch pot. **Hyacinths** are planted three to a 5-inch pot. **Amaryllis** are planted one to a 6-inch pot, or three to a 12-inch pot.

 PLANTING

Plant the little bulbs that bloom in the fall in a sunny spot in the shelter of a stone wall or a big rock. Most will perennialize.

Dig planting holes and beds for the small bulbs 3 to 5 inches deep. But first cover the area with 3 to 4 inches of humus, enough so that one quarter of the soil will be organic matter. Then add to the soil from the hole the following organic amendments and fertilizers.

For every 100 square feet:
Bulb-tone: 5 to 10 pounds
Rock phosphate: 5 to 10 pounds
Greensand: 5 to 10 pounds
Clay soils only : gypsum 5 to
  10 pounds
Osmocote® 8-month: 2 pounds

To foil vole and squirrels, line the bottom of the hole or the bed with 2 inches of VoleBloc™ or Soil Perfector. Set the little bulbs 1 to 3 inches apart. Fill in all around them with VoleBloc or PermaTill so just the tips of the bulbs are showing. Cover with 1 inch of VoleBloc or PermaTill. Fill in with a mix that is 30 percent VoleBloc or PermaTill and improved soil.

Continue planting sets of six or eight **gladiolus** for cutting, and repeat at three-week intervals until early August.

 CARE

Tie tall **dahlias** and the **lilies** to the upper third of their stakes. Stake **gladiolus** as they gain height.

Mulch around summer-flowering bulbs to keep their roots cool and to maintain moisture now that the year's driest season is upon us.

 GROOMING

Harvest or deadhead **dahlias** and other flowering bulbs.

When harvesting **lilies**, do not take more than a third of the stem, or the stem will be smaller next year. After deadheading bulbs that have finished blooming, let the foliage ripen naturally. The stalks of the **lilies** and the foliage of the **Japanese irises** turn gold and bronze in late fall and can be quite beautiful.

Help flowers you harvest last longer by making an angled cut with clean shears, and at once plunging the stems into a big bucket of tepid water containing floral preservative.

WATERING

Check the soil moisture in hanging baskets and pots regularly, and water enough to keep the soil nicely damp.

Summer-flowering bulbs need sustained moisture to stay in top shape and resist the assorted pests and disease that strike about now. In July and August, regularly water deeply unless you have a soaking rain.

FERTILIZING

Add a half dose of soluble fertilizer to the water for bulbs growing in baskets and pots at every second watering.

SUMMER-FLOWERING BULBS

Summer-flowering bulbs are superb in big pots, planters, and barrels, and great fillers for empty spots in flower beds. Plan to lift those identified here as "tender" in fall, and store them indoors for winter.

- **Amarcrinum,** x *Amarcrinum howardii*, tender
- **Caladium,** *Caladium* spp., tender
- **Canna,** *Canna* x *generalis* cvs., tender
- **Crocosmia,** *Crocosmia* spp. and hybrids, hardy
- **Flowering onion,** *Allium giganteum*, hardy
- **Gladiola,** *Gladiolus byzantinus, G. hortulanus* semi-hardy standard, and minis
- **Lilies,** *Lilium* spp. and hybrids, hardy
- **Mexican shellflower,** *Tigridia*, tender
- **Ornamental banana,** *Musa velutina*, tender
- **Peacock orchid,** *Acidanthera bicolor*, tender
- **Peruvian daffodil,** *Hymenocallis narcissiflora* syn. *Ismene calathina*, tender
- **Poppy anemone,** *Anemone coronaria*, hardy
- **Rain lily,** *Zephyranthes* spp., tender
- **Summer hyacinth,** *Galtonia*, tender
- **Tuberose,** *Polianthes tuberosa*, tender
- **Wood sorrel, lady's sorrel,** *Oxalis* varieties, hardy

PROBLEMS

Keep weeds gone.

Pinch off and discard (do not compost) leaves or blossoms that show infestations or signs of disease. Spray infested plants with Neem.

If **dahlias** show signs of powdery mildew, thin the interior growth to improve air-flow. Spray with André's mix: 1 tablespoon baking soda and 1 tablespoon of ultra-fine horticultural oil mixed well in a gallon of water. For other controls, turn to Pests, Diseases, and Controls in the Appendix.

To deter deer, spray with a new and different noxious spray, or put up a barrier to keep the deer out.

AUGUST
BULBS, CORMS, RHIZOMES, & TUBERS

 PLANNING

Some mail-order houses ship bulbs for fall planting as early as mid-August. Bulbs you plan to force into bloom for winter indoors can be planted starting in September. You must wait until after a hard frost to start planting the hardy bulbs out in the garden. Store bulbs-in-waiting in a cool cellar, a crisper, or a cool garage. **Caution:** don't store bulbs with apples. Apples, along with bananas and some other fruits and vegetables, give off ethylene gas, which initiates flower buds in **bromeliads** but ruins the blooms in flowering bulbs.

Garden centers will soon be offering shrubs and trees at end-of-season sale prices, an invitation to consider starting a border of shrubs and bulbs. Spring-flowering bulbs do well under tall shrubs and deciduous trees, and even in the shade of evergreens tall enough to allow sun to reach the flowers. Don't top them with more than 2 or 3 inches of mulch; more will prevent the soil from draining and that will harm the bulbs.

 PLANTING

Late this month you can begin to transplant established spring-flowering bulbs marked in spring for moving. Use a pitchfork to lift them. Slowly slide the tines straight down into the soil just outside the marked position. If you feel resistance that could be a bulb, try the other side of the clump. When you have lifted a clump, ease it off the fork onto the ground. Pick through the bulbs, and replant the largest in soil fertilized with Bulb-tone in their new position. Plant the little bulblets in an out-of-the-way place to grow up.

 CARE

Crocosmia doesn't need deadheading. The flowers are followed by attractive seed capsules that look good with the sword-shaped foliage.

 GROOMING

Dahlias need deadheading and are good cut flowers, so don't skimp on bouquets. The crisp, almost translucent petals catch the light and in the paler shades are truly luminous. The dainty long-stemmed cactus types are beautiful massed as bedding plants, and make lovely bouquets. My favorite late summer bouquet combines **dahlias, basil** for the aroma, airy **cosmos,** plumes of **ornamental grasses,** and stems of **peegee hydrangeas.**

The best times to harvest **dahlias**—all flowers, really—is early morning or late evening. To give them a long vase life, re-cut the stems, and set them in 2 to 3 inches of water that is about 150 degrees Fahrenheit. Leave them there for a couple of hours, or overnight, then re-cut the stems for arranging.

When harvesting **lilies,** make the stalks you cut off less than a third of the overall height, or the plant will be smaller next year. When the blooms have faded, deadhead to where the leaves begin. The foliage of summer-flowering bulbs, like that of spring-flowering bulbs, must be allowed to ripen. Best to leave them to fall then cut the stalks to the ground—or leave them to mark the locations if you plan to divide them later in the season.

If **tall bearded iris** foliage is browning at the tips, cut the tips back to healthy tissue.

 WATERING

During droughts, **dahlias, lilies, crocosmia,** and the other summer-flowering bulbs need watering every week to ten days, as do the annuals and perennials. Watering overhead is okay.

FERTILIZING

If you have incorporated organic or slow-release fertilizers in your soil, your bulbs shouldn't need fertilizing now.

PROBLEMS

Weed faithfully. We use a swing-head hoe for weeding. It's a push-pull oscillating hoe that cuts through weeds and cultivates the soil without disturbing the mulch.

Mildew can be a problem. Pick off and destroy infected foliage; do not compost it. Spray infected plants with a sulfur-based fungicide recommended by your garden center, or spray with André's remedy: 1 tablespoon baking soda and 1 tablespoon of ultra-fine horticultural oil mixed well in a gallon of water.

Spider mites can be a problem now that the weather is hot and dry. Inspect plants not doing well, and if they are under attack, spray in the early morning with a miticide.

To deter deer, spray with a new and different deterrent.

ABOUT IRISES

The miniature **beardless irises** you see blooming in late winter and early spring are planted the fall before. Three and 4 inches tall, *Iris reticulata* is the first of the type to bloom. Charming in rock gardens and naturalized, plant these by the dozen, 2 to 3 inches apart, 2 to 3 inches deep in very well-drained soil. They do well in full or partial sun.

A second wave of **beardless irises** blooms toward mid-spring. These are the 20-inch tall **Dutch irises,** varieties of *I. hollandica*, and they also develop from bulbs planted the preceding fall. They need full sun, and are planted about 5 inches deep with 3 to 4 inches between bulbs.

In late spring and early summer the spectacular **bearded, Siberian,** and **Japanese irises** come into bloom. These are best planted and divided in spring or fall. The **tall bearded** (**German iris** hybrids) are divided in August and September.

The **bog irises** also bloom in late spring and early summer. The stately 5-foot **yellow flag,** *Iris pseudacorus,* bears bright yellow canna-like flowers. Rooted divisions are set out in early spring or fall in full or half sun in mucky, humusy soil that is moderately acid. Lovely varieties of the many-hued **Louisiana iris,** *I. hexagona,* bloom at about the same time and in the same type of soil. These **irises** can be divided anytime after they bloom.

Yellow Flag Iris

SEPTEMBER
BULBS, CORMS, RHIZOMES, & TUBERS

PLANNING

Working with the Planting Guide for Forcing Bulbs, plan a schedule for potting up and forcing bulbs for indoors this winter. You can start planting **hyacinths** for forcing indoors when outdoor nighttime temperatures fall into the 50s. Wait until closer to the holidays to pot up **amaryllis** bulbs and **paper-whites**.

PLANTING

Forcing bulbs for indoor bloom is a three-part project; pot up; chill twice (see Chilling); move to warmth to force blooming.

Tulip and **daffodil** bulbs take a standard pot, but the others are usually planted in bulb pans, which are half pots, or else in shallow bowls, boxes, or water-proofed baskets. Before planting, soak the pots and water the soil thoroughly. To avoid the diseases that can assail forced bulbs, pot them in a mixture of one-half sterile commercial potting medium and one-half good, gritty garden soil. As an added precaution, you can soak or dust the bulbs with a broad-spectrum fungicide.

Plant **hyacinths** about three to a 5-inch pot; plant **tulips** and standard **daffodils** five to a 6-inch pot, or nine to a 12-inch pot. Set **tulips** with the flat side facing out. Plant as many **muscari** and other small bulbs as there is space for. Set the bulbs just touching. Plant big bulbs so just the tip shows; cover small bulbs with potting mix.

Label the pots with the plant's name, the date, and when the bulb forcing guide indicates it will be time to initiate forcing.

Chilling. For the first chilling period, place the pots in the dark where temperatures are 40 to 60 degrees Fahrenheit—an unheated garage perhaps. After the first chilling period move the pots to colder temperatures—35 to 40 degrees Fahrenheit—a garden shed is likely to have the right temperature.

Water the waiting bulbs when the soil moisture feels dry.

Forcing. As the second chilling period ends and the bulbs are showing roots and shoots, move the pots for forcing to temperatures between 50 and 60 degrees Fahrenheit and into good, indirect light. They take about two weeks to come into bloom.

Toward the end of the month you can plant **Asiatic lilies** in the garden for next summer's bloom.

CARE

Store bulbs in a refrigerator crisper, away from fruit or vegetables, or in a cool garage or cellar until time to plant.

Between now and when the air turns icy in October, bring in pots of **amaryllis** from the garden. You can let the soil dry, or keep them growing. Either way, they need 55 degree temperatures for almost eight to ten weeks.

In Zone 8 when the **dahlia** tops die down, cover them with a winter mulch. In Zones 6 and 7,

In Zones 6 & 7, dahlia tubers must be lifted and stored in trays of vermiculate, sand, peat moss, or cedar chips in a cool location.

PLANTING GUIDE FOR FORCING BULBS

Planting Time Bulb	Container	Chilling Period 40/60 F	Chilling Period 35/40 F	Forcing Time
Sept./Oct.				
Hyacinth, French, Roman	Bowl/half pot	4–6 weeks	6–8 weeks	2 weeks at 65 F
Oct.				
Crocus, Daffodil, Narcissus	Half or three-quarters pot	6–8 weeks	4–8 weeks	2 weeks at 65 F
Grape hyacinth Muscari	Half pot	6–8 weeks	8 weeks	2 weeks at 65 F
Hyacinth, Dutch	Glass bowl, half or standard pot	6–8 weeks	6 weeks	2 weeks at 65 F
Tulips, large	Half, three-quarters, or standard pot	6–8 weeks	6–8 weeks	2 weeks at 65 F
Oct./Nov./Dec.				
Paper-whites	Bowl and pebbles	2–3 weeks	3–4 weeks, if shoots are up skip this	2 weeks at 65 F
Tazetta narcissus	Bowl and pebbles	2–3 weeks	3–4 weeks	2 weeks at 65 F

after the first killing frost, prepare to lift and store the tubers. Clear away the foliage, then gently lift the crowns and spread them out of direct sun to dry. Don't detach the tubers from the central stem. Don't wash them. Store them in trays of cedar chips, vermiculite, sand, or peat moss in a cool—35 to 45 degrees—area. Label each variety.

Store cold-tender and tropical bulbs at temperatures specified by the grower. For example, **caladiums** and **colocasia** need temperatures above 70 degrees; **tuberous begonias** and **crinum**, 35 to 41 degrees; **canna**, 41 to 50 degrees; **dahlia**, 35 to 45 degrees.

 GROOMING

Cut down **lily** stalks that are fully yellow; move or divide four-year old **lilies**.

Cut off the dying foliage of **irises** and other winter-hardy bulbs.

WATERING

Check the soil moisture in pots of bulbs being chilled weekly; water when the soil is dry to the touch.

Keep the soil damp in pots of tender perennials and tropicals wintering indoors; they are only semi-dormant.

 FERTILIZING

Spread Bulb-tone or wood ashes over established beds of spring-flowering bulbs at the rate of 4 to 6 pounds to 100 square feet.

 PROBLEMS

Spread milky spore disease where Japanese beetles have been evident.

OCTOBER
BULBS, CORMS, RHIZOMES, & TUBERS

PLANNING

As temperatures drop into the 50s, organize the planting of the spring-flowering bulbs. That's about six weeks before the ground freezes hard. If you plant them while the soil's still warm, bulbs risk developing fungus or disease. Bulbs planted too late risk having insufficient root development to survive the winter.

The **daffodils** go in first, after the first hard frost. The **tulips** and other large bulbs go next, after two hard frosts. The small bulbs—**muscari, crocus**—go in after the **tulips**.

While you are waiting, set the bulbs out in groups according to where you plan to place them in the garden. Their first year, spring-flowering bulbs will bloom even in shade. But to come back and to bloom, they need full sun, all-day light under deciduous trees, or bright shade under a limbed-up evergreen.

Plan to plant the little bulb flowers in groups of twenty, fifty, or one hundred of each variety; mid-size bulbs in groups of ten or twenty; big bulbs in sets of ten or fifteen; **hyacinths** in sets of three or five of each color.

For a lasting show, plant a three-tier bulb garden. Plant big bulbs on the lowest level, cover them with a few inches of soil,

You can plant crocus now to have spring flowers.

then plant medium bulbs, add a few inches more soil, and plant small bulbs on top.

PLANTING

Bulbs for forcing indoors. Continue potting up the bulbs the Planting Guide for Forcing Bulbs recommends starting this month (see the September sidebar and Planting).

Bulbs for the garden. When you are planting groups of bulbs, prepare planting beds rather than individual holes. (See Planting in the introduction to this chapter.) As a generalization, set large bulbs 4 to 6 inches apart and 8 to 10 inches deep; set bulbs under 2 inches in size

about 2 inches apart in planting beds 5 to 6 inches deep.

When planting large **daffodils,** dig the holes 3 to 6 inches apart, 8 inches deep; set small **daffs** 1 to 3 inches apart, 3 to 5 inches deep.

Plant very tall **tulips** 4 to 6 inches apart, 8 inches to 10 inches deep; set the **species tulips** 3 to 4 inches apart, 4 to 5 inches deep.

Plant **hyacinths** about 3 to 4 inches apart, about 8 inches deep.

Plant **wood hyacinth** about 2 to 4 inches apart, and 5 to 6 inches deep.

To create a naturalized drift. Dig an irregularly shaped planting bed, throw the bulbs out by the handful, and plant them where they fall.

To deter voles, moles, and squirrels, we urge you to plant all bulbs except **daffodils**, which are toxic to wildlife, with VoleBloc™ or PermaTill®.

At the end of the month plant **Oriental** and **trumpet lilies** in the garden for next summer's bloom.

CARE

You can move **autumn crocus** and other fall-flowering bulbs after they finish blooming. Lift the clump, and carry it to its new location.

Move or divide **lilies** that have been in place for four years or so.

Bring **tuberous begonias** inside when they begin to yellow. Let the soil dry to barely damp over five or six weeks, and then remove dead foliage. Store the tubers in a cool, dry place.

GROOMING

Cut the foliage of the **tall bearded** and **Dutch irises** to 2 inches.

WATERING

Monitor the moisture in pots of bulbs being forced for indoor bloom; if the soil is dry to the touch, water it. Keep track of the chilling periods.

Maintain a little moisture in pots of tender perennials and tropicals wintering indoors.

FERTILIZING

Clear dying foliage and dig up weeds from established beds of fall- and summer-flowering bulbs. Fertilize them with Bulb-tone 4-10-6 at the rate of 5 to 10 pounds per 100 square feet. For **lilies**, spread Holly-tone at the rate of 4 pounds per 100 square feet.

PROBLEMS

Clear the yard of anything that attracts deer—apples or pears, for example. Don't make pumpkins available, or ornamental bales of straw.

SEQUENCE OF BLOOM FOR SPRING-FLOWERING BULBS

To help you find ideal places in your garden for spring-flowering bulbs, we have arranged them here in the order in which they come into bloom:

LATE WINTER/EARLY SPRING
- **Early crocus,** *Crocus* spp. and cvs.
- **Daffodils,** *Narcissus* miniatures and early varieties
- **Snowdrops,** *Galanthus*
- **Winter aconite,** *Eranthis*
- **Squill,** *Scilla tubergeniana*
- **Dwarf beardless iris,** *Iris reticulata*
- **Glory-of-the-snow,** *Chionodoxa luciliae*
- **Grape hyacinth,** *Muscari* spp. and hybrids
- **Miniature cyclamen,** *Cyclamen coum*
- **Species tulips,** *Tulipa saxatilis, T. tarda, T. turkestanica*
- **Striped squill,** *Puschkinia scilloides*
- **Windflower,** *Anemone blanda*

MID- AND LATE SPRING
- **Daffodils,** *Narcissus* mid-season, late varieties
- **Hyacinth,** *Hyacinthus*
- **Late crocus,** *Crocus*
- **Lily-of-the-valley,** *Convallaria majalis*
- **Fritillaria,** *Fritillaria persica*
- **Silver bells,** *Ornithogalum nutans*
- **Spanish bluebell,** *Hyacinthoides hispanica*
- **Bluebell,** *Hyacinthoides non-scripta*
- **Summer snowflake,** *Leucojum aestivum* 'Gravetye Giant'
- **Starflower,** *Ipheion uniflorum* 'Wisley Blue'
- **Tulips,** *Tulipa* mid-season, late varieties
- **Wood sorrel,** *Oxalis adenophylla*

NOVEMBER
BULBS, CORMS, RHIZOMES, & TUBERS

PLANNING

Kits of **amaryllis** bulbs are sold this time of year, along with **paper-whites**. Both take only a few weeks to force, so they can be started shortly before the holidays if you wish to have them in bloom then.

PLANTING

Forcing freesias. These small funnel-shaped florists' flowers are so fragrant they are worth the patience and time it takes to force them into bloom indoors. The blossoms may be single or double, and the shades are subtle combinations of red, orange, yellow, and pink. Single flowered white **freesias** may be the most fragrant.

- To plant ten or twelve corms, provide an 8-inch standard pot.
- Fill the pot to within 2 inches of the rims with moist, sterile, somewhat gritty potting mix that is neutral or slightly acid—the cactus mix sold at garden centers will work.
- Arrange the corms on the soil with pointed ends up and 2 to 3 inches apart.
- Cover them with 1 inch of potting mix.
- Water thoroughly.

- Store the pots at about 55 degrees Fahrenheit for forty-five days—an unheated garage or a shed will do.
- When green shoots appear, move the pots to good light and temperatures of about 65 degrees Fahrenheit. Maintain the soil moisture, and fertilize the bulbs every two weeks with a soluble 20-20-20 fertilizer.
- Stake the stems as needed.

The flowers will appear in twelve to fourteen weeks and are long lasting.

CARE

Cover **crocosmia** and other bulbs at the edge of their hardiness in our region with a light winter mulch.

GROOMING

Cut down the remains of the **lilies, irises,** and other summer-flowering bulbs.

WATERING

Maintain the water level of bulbs being forced in pebbles or water.

Continue to monitor the moisture in pots of bulbs being forced. Do not allow them to dry out. Plants drink their food through rootlets, and if the rootlets dry out they will die. Until the bulbs grow new roots, the bulbs go hungry as well as thirsty. Growth will be severely checked and may not resume in time for forcing.

If rain fails, water new plantings of spring-flowering bulbs regularly to encourage rooting.

Maintain a little moisture in pots of tender perennials and tropicals wintering indoors; they are only semi-dormant.

FERTILIZING

If you haven't already, fertilize established beds of bulbs now. Spread Bulb-tone 4-10-6 at the rate of 5 to 10 pounds per 100 square feet. For **lilies**, spread Holly-tone at the rate of 4 pounds per 100 square feet.

PROBLEMS

Mulching areas planted in spring-flowering bulbs may discourage squirrels. But it encourages voles, so do not add mulch until the ground has frozen hard.

FORCING PAPER-WHITES, HYACINTHS, AND AMARYLLIS

Forcing paper-whites in soil. These sensationally fragrant varieties of **Tazetta narcissus** need seven to nine weeks to come into bloom. Choose bulbs not yet sprouted and plant them within four weeks. Keep **paper-whites** waiting to be planted in a dry warm room, about 60 degrees.

Plant the bulbs in bulb pans, six bulbs to a 6-inch pan, or twelve bulbs to a 10-inch pan. Set the bulbs up to their shoulders in gritty potting mix, and, to hold them in place, add enough gravel to cover the necks. Soak the soil in the pots, let the water drain, and set them to root in temperatures 45 to 60 degrees Fahrenheit. Water sparingly once a week until growth begins. See Planting, September, for further instructions.

Forcing paper-whites in pebbles. We find that sprouted **paper-whites** come into bloom quickly when forced in pebbles and water. Here are general instructions:

Choose a bowl that has no drainage hole and that is at about 4 or 5 inches deep. Fill it within 2 inches of the rim with marble chips, pea gravel, builder's sand, or PermaTill. Arrange the bulbs so they touch each other and are perfectly straight. Gently press the bottoms about an inch into the pebbles. Add water to just below the bottoms of the bulbs, and then add enough growing medium to cover the necks of the bulbs.

Store the containers in low light at cool temperatures, 45 to 60 degrees Fahrenheit, until they are well rooted and shoots are growing. Then move them to warmth and bright light; the warmer the room, the faster they grow—and go by.

Forcing hyacinths in water. Buy pre-chilled bulbs and "hyacinth glasses," glasses nipped in at the top so they suspend the bottom of the bulb just above the water. Fill the glass to just below the bottom of the bulb, and proceed as for forcing **paper-whites** in pebbles.

Forcing amaryllis. Use well-drained gritty soil and regular pots, not bulb pans. Plant these immense bulbs one to a 6-inch pot, or three to a 12-inch pot with the top third or half showing above the soil. Water the pots and the soil thoroughly, and set them in a warm room. Maintain soil moisture, and fertilize when you fertilize the houseplants. They should come into bloom in about five to six weeks at normal house temperatures. The flower stalk rises before the foliage, and the flower lasts up to two weeks.

DECEMBER
BULBS, CORMS, RHIZOMES, & TUBERS

 PLANNING

Catch up on entries for your garden log.

 PLANTING

Plant any remaining spring-flowering bulbs while the ground remains soft enough to dig in.

Amaryllis potted up at the beginning of this month still may come into bloom for the end of the year.

 CARE

Check **amaryllis** that dried down six to eight weeks ago for signs of growth. When a tongue of green appears, repot the bulbs in fresh fertile potting mix in the same pots, set them in bright indirect light in a warm room, and water and fertilize along with the houseplants. Wait to break off and repot offsets (baby bulbs) until the plants are in full growth in spring.

Monitor moisture in the soil of the bulbs being forced; water if the tops feel dry.

Mid-month, check the dates and the timing chart for bulbs being forced. Bring those that are showing roots and shoots into a warmer room and indirect light, and water and fertilize lightly when you water houseplants. When they are growing well, move them to good light, and out of direct sun. Keep the soil barely damp while they are blooming.

 GROOMING

When **amaryllis** finish blooming, cut the blossoms off, and continue to grow the plants in a bright sunny window.

 WATERING

As they come into bloom, water the soil of forced bulbs so it's slightly damp.

Keep the soil pots of tender perennials and tropicals wintering indoors damp.

 FERTILIZING

Include fertilizer when you water the **amaryllis.**

 PROBLEMS

When the growing medium is very wet, mold sometimes appears on pots of bulbs being forced. Move them to a place with good air circulation and allow the soil to dry down to barely damp.

Get rid of aphids by spraying them with a kitchen sink spray or misting the plant with a horticultural soap. Discourage the little black fungus gnats that hover over potting mix by allowing the soil to dry between waterings and removing standing water from the plant saucers.

CHAPTER THREE

HERBS & VEGETABLES

A kitchen garden should delight the senses with its color, aromas, and superb flavors. Vegetables, herbs, and fruit grown in your own garden and harvested at the peak of perfection have a wonderful aroma and a much finer flavor than store produce.

The first step in designing a kitchen garden that will become a favorite destination is to set it off handsomely. A picket fence has charm, and chicken wire will help keep out four-footed raiders. Make the entrance special with an antique gate, or a gated pergola supporting fragrant climbing roses. 'New Dawn' is perfect. Plan to train a grape vine over the fence, and an espaliered pear if there's space. Gussy it up a bit with ornate birdhouses, an antique sundial, and a water basin with a bubbler.

Make it exciting. Wake up your appetite. Grow lemon cucumbers, heirloom vegetables and fruits, exotic perfumed Galia melons from Israel, and pungent Oriental tat-soi greens. Pick baby heading lettuce and tiny squash, or plant a giant variety of pumpkin and aim for 600 pounds! Serve real haricots verts or true petits pois without concern for the price. Grow your own asparagus, rhubarb, strawberries, and artichokes.

Make it colorful. Plant bronze fennel, globe and purple basil as well as the sweet varieties, and variegated mint. Plant red, not green, romaine, Bibb and oakleaf lettuces; red scallions, not white;

yellow, purple, and orange sweet peppers along with red and green; scarlet, yellow, and purple runner beans; violet broccoli.

Make it interesting. Plant summer squashes with different shapes and colors—round 'Gourmet Globe', yellow 'Gold Rush', 'Butterstick', and pattypan 'Sunburst'. Add curly Russian kale for texture, arugula, radicchio, and mache for fall salads. Be tempted by little white and mauve eggplants, wildly colorful hot peppers, red new potatoes, yellow watermelons, golden beets.

Make it beautiful and fragrant. Plant rhubarb, and allow the magnificent flower heads to grow up. Edge the garden with aromatic perennial herbs—chives, variegated thymes, colorful sages, golden oregano, fragrant English lavender. The flowers as well as the foliage of the culinary herbs are edible. Center the beds on a little peach, plum, or apricot tree, and the air will be sweet when you arrive to plant the mid-spring crops.

Choose flowers whose colors and texture will enhance the beauty of the vegetables. Edge plain green vegetables such as spinach with brilliant 'Copper Sunset' mounding nasturtiums whose flowers and foliage are edible. Grow red-stemmed rhubarb chard with deep red 'Empress of India' nasturtiums. Back bush beans with pink or lavender 'Powder Puff' asters, and edge the row with blue ageratum or dwarf purple gomphrena and purple basil. Plant late tulips in the fall, and overseed the row in early spring with leaf lettuce and Johnny-jump-up violas. For fragrant summer bouquets plant aromatic basils with cosmos, snapdragons, and dahlias.

Intertwine snap beans with morning glories, and edge the row with blue salvia, white cosmos Sensation Strain 'Purity', and blue ageratum. Back the solid structures of the earth-hugging lettuces, beets, and cabbages with airy bronze fennel, tall snapdragons, caraway, or cosmos. These gardens can be prettier than flower gardens.

Caution: Don't combine edibles with poisonous plants—larkspur, foxgloves, and sweet peas are toxic.

START WITH A PLANTING PLAN

A plan is the first step in planning a kitchen garden. To put together herbs, vegetables, and flowers that will enhance each other, you need to partner varieties that mature at about the same time. The information you need is in garden literature and in mail-order herb, vegetable, and flower catalogues. There are early, mid-season, and late species and varieties.

PLANTING AND TRANSPLANTING VEGETABLES AND ANNUAL HERBS

Most vegetables (and some important culinary herbs) are annuals and must be replanted every year. Because we are all eager for early crops, many vegetables and herbs are started indoors.

Cool-season vegetables started indoors usually are ready to be moved out to the garden within four to six weeks. The young seedlings can be transplanted right from the flats the seeds were sown in.

Warm- and hot-season vegetables and herbs benefit from being grown for a few additional weeks in individual 2- to 4-inch peat pots before being moved out to the garden. In cold regions the bigger varieties of tomato may do best transplanted a couple of times to ever-larger containers. After transplanting vegetable and herb seedlings to larger pots, discontinue fertilizing until the appearance of two or three new leaves tells you the root system is growing again. At that stage, provide very good natural light, or grow the seedlings under continuous fluorescent light set about 3 inches above the seedlings. As the seedlings grow, raise the light to 4 to 6 inches overhead. Once the seedlings show strong growth, reduce the lights to fourteen to sixteen hours a day.

CHAPTER THREE

GROWING HERBS AND VEGETABLES

Here's an overview of the year in a kitchen garden:

1. In the fall or in early spring as soon as the cold and moisture have left the earth, turn the rows by hand or with a rototiller.
2. Check and adjust the soil pH and fertilize.
3. Plant cool-season vegetables starting in early spring.
4. Plant warm- and hot-season vegetables and herbs in May and June.
5. Harvest as crops mature. Replant the rows.
6. Clear the rows.

Soil. Most need well-worked, rich soil whose pH is between 6.0 and 7.0. See Soil and Fertilizing in this Introduction, and the April pages.

Light. Most herbs and vegetables do best in full sun. To provide as much sun as possible, arrange the planting rows in your kitchen garden to run east to west. At the north end set tall plants, like staked tomatoes, sunflowers, and corn (planted in blocks to assure pollination). At the south end, set low-growing things so they won't be shaded by the taller plants. Some cool-season vegetables whose enemy is heat—lettuce, peas, and spinach, for example—may last longer planted where the shade of taller plants cuts the heat of the late spring sun.

Spacing. Raised beds, or rows, about 36 inches wide are ideal as they can be worked from both sides comfortably. That gives you enough space to plant low-growing crops like lettuce and beets in the same row with flowers. When the seedlings are up, thin them out around the strongest flower seedlings. As the early vegetables are harvested, the flowers will fill in.

Big, rapid growers like eggplants, tomatoes, and summer squash need 24 to 36 inches around. To create a living mulch for these vegetables, plant spreading flowers like edging lobelia, *Lobelia eri-nus*, alyssum, nasturtiums, and multiflora petunias about 12 inches away. Where mildew is a problem avoid dense plantings, which cut down on air circulation.

SOIL AND FERTILIZING

To support the lavish productivity of an established kitchen garden, every year before planting season begins you need to check and adjust the soil pH as described in our Introduction.

In addition, a few weeks before planting, work into the top 6 to 8 inches of the soil a generous helping of nutrients (except for nasturtiums). Use an organic or an eight-month formulation of a controlled-release chemical fertilizer for vegetables and annuals. (See Understanding Fertilizers in the Introduction to this book.) That will carry the plants through the whole growing season. Scratch a full dose of fertilizer into the soil around the kitchen garden perennials—bramble fruits, asparagus, the berry patch, rhubarb, and the others—in early spring before growth begins.

The long-season hot-weather crops, along with tomatoes, benefit from a modest additional fertilization during the growing season. Prompts are given in the month-by-month pages that follow. André recommends using a water-soluble organic fertilizer, such as fish emulsion or liquid seaweed. In addition, before replanting a row that has already produced a crop, renew the fertilizer.

WATERING

Seeds need consistent moisture to germinate and grow. Before sowing seeds, unless the garden is moist from recent rain, water the soil slowly and thoroughly. Use a sprinkler or a hose that lays down 1 to 2 inches of water in five to twelve hours; set a coffee tin under the watering equipment to measure the time it takes to lay down that much water, and record it in your garden log. After the seeds are planted, water the area for half an hour or so.

JANUARY
HERBS & VEGETABLES

 PLANNING

Gather your favorite mail-order catalogs for herbs, vegetables, and annuals, and sketch a planting plan. Plan to maximize your garden's productivity by closely spacing the plants and by interplanting and succession cropping.

Interplanting or intercropping describes planting two or more compatible crops in the same row at the same time, like fast-growing **radishes** with **lettuce.** Or **sweet corn** with **pumpkins** at their feet. Or **tomatoes** with **basil** all around.

Succession cropping refers to keeping a row planted with a sequence of vegetables; when the first crop is harvested, you remove it and reseed the row immediately. For example, **radishes,** followed by **lettuce,** followed by **snap bush beans,** followed by late **carrots.**

If you plan to start cool-season plants, such as **peas, onions, shallots, leeks,** and **garlic,** in the garden in mid-February, late this month cover the area with black plastic to increase the warmth of the soil.

 PLANTING

Gather the equipment you will be using to start seeds indoors.

Zone 8 gardeners can sow seeds indoors now for the herbs that will need to grow pretty big before they can go outdoors to the garden, **lavender** for one. (See the Annuals chapter, January, Planting, Starting Seeds Indoors.) Some herbs are annuals, some perennial. **Parsley** is biennial. Our rule of thumb is this: for annual herbs, one plant per person in the household; for perennials, one plant or two. For **parsley,** six. Some hardy vegetables can be started indoors, too, such as **onion sets** (André strongly favors big yellow 'Candy') and **cabbage.**

The flowers of all the culinary herbs are edible and pretty as garnishes and in bouquets, so we plant more of those we use lots of, such as **lavender** and **basil.** The herbs thrive in containers.

 CARE

If you are overwintering cold-tender herbs, such as **rosemary,** in a cold frame (see November), monitor temperatures as the days grow longer and warmer, and ventilate to keep it moderately cool inside.

 GROOMING

Harvest and groom herbs such as **parsley** you brought indoors last fall.

Remove winter-damaged limbs from the fruit trees.

 WATERING

Maintain the soil moisture in herbs growing indoors.

 FERTILIZING

Add five drops of houseplant fertilizer to the water for herbs growing indoors.

 PROBLEMS

Damping off is a threat to seedlings. It's a fungal disease that attacks the seedlings at the base of their stems. It rots the stems so the plants fall over. A sterile growing medium and good drainage help avoid the condition. Applications of the fungicide Thiram (Arasan) help control the problem.

FAVORITE CULINARY HERBS

Arugula. Annual. Sow seeds indoors in late winter, outdoors in early spring; repeat in midsummer.

Basil. Annual here. Sow seeds in mid-spring, or set seedlings out when you plant **tomatoes.** For flavor, plant **sweet basil;** for pesto, and for freezing, 'Sweet Genovese'; for cooking and to make basil oil, **East Indian** or **holy basil;** for Oriental cuisine, and basil oil, plant **Thai basil;** for color and flowers, 'Purple Ruffles'; for containers, grow topiary-like tiny **bush basils.**

Chives. Perennial. Start seeds indoors in peat pots now to late February, or sow seeds in early spring where it is to grow. Set seedlings out in early April.

Dill. Annual. Sow seeds now in peat pots, or outdoors in early spring where the plants are to grow. Use the foliage fresh, or dry and store it. Allow flower heads to go seed, then dry seeds for cooking.

Cilantro/coriander. Annual. Sow seeds outdoors in early spring. In Zone 8, repeat in fall. The seed is the spice **coriander.**

Fennel. Annual. Sow seeds indoors four weeks before the last frost, or outdoors in mid-spring where it is to grow. For flavorful leaves, plant **sweet fennel,** *Foeniculum vulgare dulce;* the cultivar 'Rubrum' is the beautiful **bronze fennel.** The vegetable is **Florence fennel,** *F. v.* var. *azoricum.*

Lavender. Perennial. Sow seeds indoors now; transplant often. When the plant is 12 inches tall, transplant to the garden. For flavor, plant **English lavender;** harvest the stems before the buds break.

Mint. Invasive perennial. Grow **mint** in a large container. Plant root divisions in early spring, or in late summer where winters are mild. **Spearmint,** *Mentha spicata,* is the best all-round culinary **mint.**

Oregano. Perennial. See **Sweet marjoram.** For flavor, plant **common oregano,** *Origanum vulgare;* for edging the garden, plant **golden oregano.**

Parsley. Biennial. Start seeds indoors now. Set seedlings outdoors in March. In early September sow seeds near maturing parsley plants. Choose **curly parsley** for garnishing, chopping, and floral bouquets. Plant flat-leaf **Italian parsley** for salads and cooking.

Rosemary. Tender perennial. Sow seeds indoors now. Set seedlings out in mid-spring. In Zone 6, winter **rosemary** indoors. For cooking, choose *Rosmarinus officinalis;* as a garden ornamental, *R. o.* 'Lockwood de Forest'.

Sage. Sow seeds indoors in March. Plant seedlings outdoors in early spring. For flavoring, plant *Salvia officinalis.* For color, plant **tricolor sage.**

Sweet marjoram. Tender perennial. Sow seeds indoors in early spring or outdoors after the soil has warmed. A cousin to **oregano,** grow this one for use fresh.

Tarragon. Perennial. The best is **French tarragon,** *Artemisia dracunculus,* which is propagated from cuttings. For flavor, taste before you buy a plant.

Thyme. Perennial. Start seeds now. Transplant outdoors when the stem's 8 inches long. For flavor, plant **common thyme,** *Thymus vulgaris;* for display, 'Wedgewood English'; for containers, stepping stones, and in stone walls, **creeping thyme,** *T. serpyllum.* For edging, plant variegated 'Argenteus' and 'Aureus'.

HERBS & VEGETABLES

PLANNING

Prepare your garden tools for the season ahead. Treat all the wooden handles with applications of boiled linseed oil available where tools are sold. Oil your shears, trimmers, shovels, and spading forks. Service the rototiller, or take it to be serviced, and have the blade changed if necessary.

If you plan to set seedlings out in the garden early, consider whether they will need covering. Various types of cones including those called "hot caps" and "walls of water" are available.

Film tenting is also sold as protective covering and to keep insects and small pests away.

Ordering seeds and plants. Check your buying plans against your inventory of seeds left over or saved last year. List what you have, will order by mail, or plan to buy at a garden center. If prices are equal, buy perennials such as **asparagus** roots (three-year-old roots for quick results), **artichokes, rhubarb, strawberries, raspberries,** fruit trees, and **onion sets** from a garden center where you can see what you are getting.

Do a web search for items not found in your mail-order catalogs. We've had good luck with it. It's also worth your while

If a ball of earth packed between your hands sticks together when you press it, the soil is too wet to be worked.

checking catalog prices against prices at online garden sites.

When your plan is final, prepare catalog orders and mail them, and prepare shopping lists for purchases to be made at garden centers.

Check your supplies of small pots suitable for transplanting seedlings started indoors. Disinfect pots, flats, jars, and your potting table by washing them with a solution that is 1 part bleach to 9 parts water.

You may need more potting mix for indoor plantings, and for vegetables and herbs growing in hanging baskets and other containers. Look for bagged potting mixes that include water-holding gels, and for organic liquid fertilizers.

PLANTING

Indoors. All zones can sow seeds indoors for **cabbage, chives, fen-**

nel, sage, thyme, rosemary. (See Annuals, January, Planting.)

Outdoors. In Zone 8 the weather may encourage you to start a few of these herbs and vegetables outdoors late this month.

Elsewhere, when air temperatures are hitting 55 degrees Fahrenheit, you can begin to think of sowing cold-season crops out in the garden. **Peas** can be planted mid-February to mid-March, but cold soil may discourage quick growth. They tolerate some frost, and do well in air temperatures between 55 and 70 degrees Fahrenheit. **Potatoes** can go in St. Patrick's Day or later in April.

CARE

Indoors. When the seedlings started indoors become crowded, transplant each to an individual 3- to 4-inch pot filled with a good potting mix.

Seedlings that will be growing indoors for six weeks need good light to thrive. At this stage, an installation of grow lights burned fourteen to sixteen hours a day is especially helpful.

Repot herbs brought indoors last fall.

Outdoors. Early this month prune the **grape vines;** don't wait until later in the season as they will bleed, and that weakens the plants.

If you planted a cover crop in your garden in the fall (see Annuals, October, Planting), turn it under when soil is no longer cold and wet. The earth is ready to be worked when a ball of earth packed between your hands crumbles easily; if it sticks together, the soil is too wet.

GROOMING

Thin crowded seedlings. Groom potted herbs growing indoors.

WATERING

Water pots of transplanted seedlings as the soil becomes dry to the touch.

Maintain the moisture levels of indoor herbs.

FERTILIZING

Indoors. Every two weeks fertilize all the seedlings that will remain

---

POTTED KITCHEN GARDEN

Herbs and vertical vegetables make great container plants. Tidy herbs, like **parsley, globe basil,** and **thyme**, suit a window box and make pretty edgers for tall or short potted flowers. **Tomato** seedlings perform beautifully growing in pots, planters, and even garbage bags.

Shell beans and **eggplant** climb from a container as readily as from the soil. Small **summer squash, gourds,** or **cucumbers** can be trained to a teepee, three or four long poles tied together at the top like a Native American tent. **Melons** and even **pumpkins,** too, but the fruits will need the support of a sling made of a mesh bag or a section of pantyhose tied to the teepee when the fruits get big. Varieties with medium- to small-sized fruits carried high on the plant are more attractive for container growing than are the low-growing, heavy-fruited types.

Some of the perennial kitchen garden plants do well in big tubs and planters—**artichokes, rhubarb, strawberries, dwarf peach,** and columnar **apple** trees.

For window box, basket, and container plantings, we recommend a humusy commercial potting mix enriched with slow-release fertilizer. Mix a polymer such as Soil Moist into the soil, and you'll find maintaining moisture much easier. Where summers are cool, place containers in warm microclimates, in the reflected heat from a south wall, for example.

---

indoors another six weeks or more with a soluble houseplant fertilizer at half strength.

Outdoors. Zone 8: Check and amend the soil pH, and dig in organic or slow-release fertilizers. Fertilize established **asparagus** beds with a high nitrogen organic fertilizer. Fertilize other kitchen garden perennials, fruit trees, bramble fruits, and berry beds.

PROBLEMS

Crowded seedlings in soggy soil are vulnerable to the fungus called "damping off," which rots stems near the soil surface. Discard affected plants, reduce watering, and increase light and fresh air. If the problem persists, mist the seedlings with a fungicide such as Thiram (Asaran), or with 1 tablespoon of bleach to 1 quart of water, or 4 tablespoons of bleach to a gallon of water.

MARCH
HERBS & VEGETABLES

 PLANNING

The few perennial food plants are quite handsome. **Asparagus, red-stemmed rhubarb,** and **Jerusalem artichokes** or **sunchokes,** as the tuberous roots of tall, small-flowered **sunflowers** are often called, are decorative as well as delicious. Consider planting a few of these in front of, or alongside, the vegetable rows, and use sprawling **thyme** and **oregano,** two of the perennial herbs that are winter hardy, as edgers.

Alpine strawberries also make pretty edgers. But, if you love berries and cream, plant full-size **strawberries** in a bed of their own. Dwarf varieties of **apples** and **pears,** along with **peaches** and **nectarines,** are lovely in bloom and are used as center-pieces in ornate kitchen gardens; **dwarf apples** and **pears** make handsome, productive espaliers. **Grapes** can be trained to a fence, a pergola, and as an espalier.

The bramble fruits need a space of their own, off to one side.

You also can grow the perennial food plants in containers. Dwarf fruit trees can handle cold winters as long as the containers are 18 to 36 inches square or in diameter, and lined with a double row of large bubble wrap or styrofoam. In Zone 8, artichokes can stand a little shade in late afternoon.

 PLANTING

In Zone 8, you may be able to plant fruit trees, bramble fruits, **rhubarb, artichokes,** and **asparagus,** as the ground becomes workable.

Before transplanting vegetable and herb seedlings to the open garden, set them in a warm, sheltered spot outdoors to harden off for a few days.

When you are ready to plant:

1. Wet the seedlings thoroughly with tepid water containing fertilizer.

2. Open a generous hole in the bed.

3. Pour a little of the water into each planting hole.

4. Loosen roots that may be binding the rootball. Set each seedling upright and straight in its planting hole so the top of the rootball is just above the soil surface.

5. Fill the hole with soil, and press it down firmly around the stem.

6. Water well.

Seedlings growing together in a flat. Separate intertwined seedlings by slicing them apart with a sharp knife. Proceed as above.

Seedlings in planting pockets. Turn the flat upside down a little above the soil, and push one rootball at a time out of its pocket. Then transplant as described.

Seedlings in peat pots. Soak each peat pot thoroughly in a solution of 1 gallon of water to which you have added 1/2 teaspoon of liquid hand dish-washing detergent and liquid fertilizer. Then gently tear open the bottom third of the peat pot so the roots can tie into the earth. Set the pot and the plant upright in the planting hole, and proceed as above.

If you transplant to the open garden while frost threatens, plan to protect the seedlings with hot caps or something like Reemay®, a lightweight fabric used for the winter protection of ornamentals. You can save seedlings from an occasional night frost by covering them with newspaper, coffee cans, drycleaner's dry cleaning plastic or plastic film, old sheets, blankets, bedspreads, burlap. Don't allow the seedlings to dry out.

 CARE

In early spring remove the uppermost layer of straw on the **strawberry** plants. Leave the matted-down straw to make a clean bed for the berries to rest on.

Mulch the big perennial food plants—**asparagus, artichokes,** bramble fruits, and fruit trees. They benefit from annual mulching that will decompose and replenish the supply of humus in the soil.

GROOMING

Cut back **thyme, chives, sage, tarragon, oregano,** and other perennial herbs.

Prune the bramble fruits. Remove suckers (water sprouts) from the fruit trees.

WATERING

Maintain the moisture for seeds and transplants—those indoors, those in a cold frame, and those in the open garden.

Maintain the soil moisture in herbs such as **parsley** brought indoors last fall.

FERTILIZING

Indoors. Zones 7 and 6—Every two weeks fertilize all the seedlings that will remain indoors another six weeks or more with a soluble houseplant fertilizer at half strength.

WHEN TO PLANT WHAT

Cold Season Crops: These tolerate some frost, so you can plant them outdoors even before the last anticipated frost. They will grow well when air temperatures rise to between 55 to 70 degrees Fahrenheit. Early seeding doesn't always help because the soil is cold, and seedlings can rot as they germinate, just as a too-early planting of **potatoes** rots.

The perennial herbs, seedlings of **thyme, oregano, chives,** along with **parsley,** which is biennial, and the annual herbs **arugula, dill, onion sets,** and **garlic.**

Asparagus and **rhubarb,** along with **beets, broccoli, Brussels sprouts, cabbage, chicory, collards, kale, kohlrabi, leek, lettuce, peas, parsnip, radish, spinach, rutabagas, turnip greens,** and **turnips.**

These tolerate some cold but not frost: **artichoke, carrot, cauliflower, endive, lettuce, peas,** and **white potato.**

Warm season crops: These are readily damaged by frost. They do well at 65 to 80 degrees Fahrenheit, but sulk or rot in cold soil: **lavender, nasturtiums, summer savory, beans, cantaloupes, carrots, chard, corn** ('Kandy' 'Peaches & Cream', 'Silver Queen'), **cucumbers, muskmelon, sweet peppers, potatoes, pumpkin, squash, sweet corn,** and **tomatoes.**

Hot weather crops: These need air temperatures at least 65 degrees Fahrenheit. They do well in temperatures above 80 degrees Fahrenheit. They require a long growing season: **hot peppers, lima beans, shell beans, eggplant, okra, peanuts, sweet potato,** and **watermelon.**

Outdoors. Zones 7 and 6— Check and amend the soil pH, and dig in organic or slow-release fertilizers now.

Fertilize established **asparagus** beds with a high-nitrogen organic fertilizer. Fertilize the other perennials, the tree and bramble fruits, and **strawberries.**

PROBLEMS

Control rabbits and other pests with row covers or bird netting. A chicken-wire fence is one sure way to keep rabbits out. If there are woodchucks, leave the chicken-wire loose between posts; woodchucks can climb taut chicken-wire.

APRIL

HERBS & VEGETABLES

PLANNING

To make the most of your garden space, plan now to plant crops that will replace the cool-season vegetables.

Be prepared when temperatures reach 65 degrees Fahrenheit to set out seedlings, and sow seeds outdoors, for **nasturtiums, summer savory, beans, cantaloupes, chard, corn, cucumbers, muskmelon, potatoes, pumpkin, sweet corn, squash, rutabaga,** and **turnips.**

Order two- or three-year-old **asparagus** roots for planting this month. A plot 20 feet square, or a row 50 to 60 feet long, will produce all five or six people could want.

PLANTING

When the ground becomes workable, plant fruit trees, bramble fruits, **rhubarb, artichokes, asparagus,** and other perennial food plants.

When danger of frost is over, you can set out in the open garden seedlings of **artichokes, cabbage, cauliflower, chives, onion sets** (late April to early May), **fennel, sage, thyme,** and **rosemary.** In the open garden you can sow seeds for **carrots, endive, sunflowers,** and plant **white potatoes.** Plant **broccoli** ('Green Comet') and **lettuce** seedlings or seeds now through early May. In cool Zone 6, there still is time to plant **peas.**

And this is a good time to start **asparagus.** They'll be spring's first vegetable crop for the next twenty years. Plant two-, or better yet, three-year-old crowns; you can start harvesting the second or third year after planting. André's favorites are 'Martha Washington' and 'Jersey Knight'.

To prepare an asparagus bed, dig a deep, wide trench and mix in amendments such as composted cow manure, compost, and organic fertilizer.

Here's how to start growing asparagus:

1. Prepare deep, wide trenches 10 to 15 inches deep in rows 3 to 4 feet apart.

2. Loosen the soil in the trenches, and mix in rich composted cow manure, compost, and an organic fertilizer.

3. Set the crowns 18 inches apart in the rows, and cover them with 2 inches of soil.

4. Fill the trenches as the new shoots come up.

5. Do not harvest the first year, and harvest only a few stalks the second year. Fertilize the bed every year in spring before growth starts and when the stalks come in thin, which is also a signal to stop harvesting.

CARE

Keep weed seedlings raked up when very young, then as the good guys grow up, they'll shade out the weeds.

GROOMING

Keep an eye on the rows where you have sown vegetables, and when the seedlings start to come up thick and fast, thin the rows.

Close, dense planting shades out weeds; keep that in mind as you thin the rows.

DETERMINING THE pH FOR KITCHEN GARDEN SOIL

The soil elements most food plants need are readily available when the pH of the soil is between 6.0 and 7.0. The exceptions are **basil** (5.5 to 6.5), **blueberries** (4.5 to 5.5) **dill** (5.5 to 6.7), **eggplant, melon,** (5.5 to 6.5), **potatoes** (4.5 to 6.0), and **sorrel** (5.5 to 6.0).

Vegetable gardens produce multiple crops, and over time the soil tends to become acid, so testing annually is important. If your soil tests below pH 6.0, spread hydrated lime, and mix it into the soil. Try a small dose, and retest the pH a few weeks later. Applying ashes, preferably from the wood of deciduous trees, raises the soil pH and supplies water-soluble potassium as well, one of the essential nutrients.

If the soil of your vegetable garden tests above pH 6.8, apply water-soluble sulfur or iron sulfate. Ask an Agriculture Extension agent or an expert at your local garden center how. The treatment must be repeated after eight months or a year. Adding an acidic mulch such as composted sawdust, bark, leaves, pine needles, or cottonseed meal has a slow but lasting effect on pH.

The Agricultural Extension Service at your state university can provide sound advice about pH in, and the composition of, your soil. A reliable soil testing kit is sold by Cornell University; write for the Standard Kit pH 5.0 to 7.2, Cornell Nutrient Analysis Laboratories, 804 Radfield Hall, Cornell University, Ithaca, NY 14853.

WATERING

If rain fails, be sure to water seeds and seedlings deeply.

Water vegetables and fruits growing in containers every two to three days.

FERTILIZING

Weekly, include a half dose of a soluble organic fertilizer in the water for vegetables and fruits growing in containers.

PROBLEMS

Be tolerant of a small infestation of the insects that are food for the beneficials.

The buzz of a nearby bee can scare you, but they are essential to pollinate crops. Wasps are mostly parasitic and destroy countless whiteflies and aphids. Yellow jackets feed their young on many flies and caterpillars. Most lady beetles destroy aphids, mealybugs, and spider mites. There are beneficial beetles, flies that attack corn borer and cutworms, and midges that devour aphids. Other insects generally considered beneficial are dragonflies, lacewings, spiders, and beneficial mites.

To encourage these beneficials, avoid toxic sprays or dusts unless a crop is being truly harmed.

MAY

HERBS & VEGETABLES

PLANNING

Kitchen garden in a container. Growing herbs, vegetables, even dwarf fruit trees in containers solves problems of space, light, temperature. They'll thrive as long as the soil is fertile and the moisture sustained.

Low-growing culinary herbs such as **parsley** and **arugula,** and small and miniature vegetables like 'Tom Thumb', a tiny **heading lettuce,** do well in window boxes and big pots.

Rosemary thrives in a container. Train **rosemary** as a topiary ball or tree now, and you'll have sensational gifts to give in December.

Legumes and **squashes** can be trained to climb up into better light—**peas, beans,** including the beautiful **scarlet runner** and purple-stemmed **hyacinth bean, eggplant, summer squash, melons,** even **pumpkins** will grow up a teepee, a pyramid, or a trellis stuck into a big container.

Tomato varieties do well in containers. Small varieties of **cherry tomatoes** thrive in 8-inch pots and hanging baskets. The big heirloom and late keeper **tomatoes** need a 2- to 5-gallon container filled with good planting mix.

Many perennial food plants, such as dwarf and small fruit trees, **artichokes, rhubarb,** and the perennial herbs do well as container plants.

PLANTING

Sometime after the last frost, plant **tomato** seedlings. When temperatures reach 65 to 80 degrees Fahrenheit, other hot weather crops can go in, **hot** and **sweet peppers, lima beans, shell beans, eggplant, okra, peanuts, sweet potato,** and **watermelon.**

Sowing seeds. The classic way to sow vegetable seeds is in shallow furrows (drills) created by dragging the edge of a rake or hoe handle along the planting line. Then you dribble the seeds into the drills at spaced intervals.

Small, fine seeds, such as **lettuce,** are broadcast over damp, well-worked soil. Cover them with seed starting mix, and cover that with burlap to maintain the moisture during germination.

Seeds of vining plants like **cucumbers** and **winter squash** may be sown around a supporting teepee or bramble in groups of four to six, or three to five. Or, sow them at regular intervals front and back of trellising or chicken wire. If there's to be no support, sow the seeds in hills, that is in groups, with lots of room all around for the vines

to ramble away from the center.

When the seedlings are up, thin them to the distance suggested by seed packets, or so that they are at least 3 to 5 inches apart.

CARE

Pinch herbs to keep them shapely. Pinch out the growing tips of **snapdragons, basil, cosmos,** and other plants with central stalks, to keep them bushing out.

GROOMING

Harvest **lettuce** and other early crops as they mature.

Pluck weeds out while thinning vegetable seedlings.

WATERING

Seeds, and seedlings, need water right after planting, and enough the first three weeks to maintain soil moisture.

FERTILIZING

When **asparagus** spears come in thin, stop harvesting and apply a high nitrogen organic fertilizer such as dried blood or cottonseed meal.

ABOUT TOMATOES

Tomatoes are warm-season vegetables that flourish when nights reach 65 degrees Fahrenheit. In summer, the blossoms fall when days are above 90 and nights above 76 degrees Fahrenheit.

Determinate tomatoes are okay without staking, reach about 3 feet and ripen a big crop in a short time. They bear all at once, not continuously. If you want to get plants in and out to make place for other plants—choose determinate.

Indeterminate tomatoes need staking or caging, and they will keep producing continuously until stopped by cold. If you want a few plants that will bear over a long season, choose indeterminate varieties.

André and Mark plant a first crop May 1 to 15, of seedlings of 'Goliath', 'Park Whopper', 'Beefmaster', 'Mr. Stripey', Supersteak', 'Roma', and the antiques 'German Johnson', and 'Oxheart'. They plant a second crop July 4.

To grow your own seedlings, start the seeds for a first crop indoors in spring; or for a second crop outdoors in a cold frame, five to seven weeks before the outdoor planting date. Put them outdoors for the last ten days to harden them off.

If you are buying **tomato** seedlings, bypass those in small containers and already in bloom or fruiting, and choose vigorously growing healthy plants with the letters VFNA on the labels. That means they are resistant to the common insects and diseases that assail **tomatoes**.

Two weeks before planting time, dig an organic or timed-release 5-10-10 fertilizer into the soil along with hydrated lime to prevent blossom end rot. Mark adds a handful of gypsum for each plant to provide calcium without changing the soil pH. Set transplants so the first leaves are just above soil level; lay leggy plants in the ground horizontally with most of the stem buried and the head upright.

Mark places **tomatoes** 4 feet apart, with 4 to 6 feet between rows. Between plants he puts down a weed barrier, such as landscape fabric, and covers it with a layer of mulch.

When the plants start to set fruit, apply a soluble organic fertilizer.

When cool season crops are over, **peas** and **spinach** for example, pull them out and take them to the compost pile. Before replanting the rows, work an application of an organic or slow-release fertilizer into the soil.

PROBLEMS

Asparagus beetle may be deterred by planting **tomatoes** nearby.

If aphids appear at the tips of **tomato** stems, hose them off, or pinch the tips out and put them in the garbage. Ladybugs should control them later in the season.

Cabbage worms attack crops about now, the forebears of small white moths you see flitting around. Spray the foliage with Dipel, malathion, pyrethrin, Rotenone, or a Sevin insecticide.

Cutworms are the culprits when tender seedlings turn up topless. One solution is to create a collar to prevent the critters from climbing up to eat. When the crops are over, rototill the row, or by hand, turn and fluff the soil. That brings the eggs to the surface where they die.

JUNE
HERBS & VEGETABLES

PLANNING

You can save space in your garden, keep it healthier, and make harvesting easy by planning to stake tall flowers, and by growing vining vegetables with their heads in the air. Lead the first stems of **cucumbers, eggplant, peas, shell beans,** and small **summer squash** to a support. Surround **tomatoes** with a sturdy support system that will make the fruits easy to pick.

A fence, especially a chicken-wire fence, is a great support for **peas** and **beans.** If you don't have a fence, install a chicken-wire support 5 feet high by 30 feet long. That's 150 square feet of climbing room for **peas** and **beans**. An east- or west-facing wall is a fine place to espalier **pears** and **apples.**

A teepee is also a suitable support for **peas** and **beans,** and it's easily made. Just gather the tops of three to five tall, sturdy bamboo supports, and tie them together. You can make a cage for **tomatoes** by twining wire around a set of four tall sturdy wooden stakes. The stylized wooden teepees sold by garden centers last for several years, as do the many and various metal frames and cages.

When installing a support, set it close to the plants; if necessary, use green wool, raffia, or cotton string to lead stems and branches to the stake.

PLANTING

As the weather heats up, the cool-season crops come to an end. Early **turnips** are over. **Peas** are over. **Lettuces** and **spinach** begin to "bolt"—that is, they grow tall, produce seedheads, and taste bitter. So pull them all up and compost them.

Replant the rows with seeds or seedlings of any of these not planted earlier, such as **basil, nasturtiums, summer savory, cucumbers, green bush beans, cantaloupes, chard, corn, muskmelon, okra, sweet peppers, potatoes, pumpkins, squash,** and **tomatoes.** Replace the **spinach** with **New Zealand spinach,** a warm weather substitute.

CARE

When the early **strawberries** and **raspberries** start to ripen, protect your crop from the birds by covering the bed with nylon mesh, screening, cheesecloth, or a floating row cover.

Keep up the watering for any seeds or seedlings that you plant now.

Weed patrol is essential! Any that are allowed to mature and develop roots will be taking water and nutrients from the vegetables they are invading.

GROOMING

Continue to pull weeds, and thin vegetable seedlings.

WATERING

Keep an eye on plantings of **corn;** they need a good deep watering when the tassels at the top are beginning to show and when the silk is beginning to show in the ear.

Peppers need to be well watered now. Maintaining moisture evenly in the **tomatoes** helps prevent blossom end rot.

FERTILIZING

When the **tomato** plants start to set fruit, drench the foliage with a soluble organic fertilizer, such as fish emulsion. Water until it drips to the ground, wetting the soil beneath. The foliage absorbs nutrients quickly.

Repeat monthly until the fruits near mature size.

PROBLEMS

Watch out for corn borer and corn earworm. Corn earworm is also the tomato fruitworm, which winters in the soil as pupae. An environmentally friendly solution is in late fall to dig up and turn over the soil in infested areas.

THINNING SEEDLINGS

When you broadcast seeds, the seedlings come up too closely spaced for mature individual plants. You must thin the rows until each seedling has space enough all around to grow well. Seed packets indicate suitable spacing.

Thinnings of the root vegetables such as **turnips** and **beets,** and leafy vegetables, such as **lettuce** and **spinach,** are good raw in salads, and they add nutrients to stews, sauces, and soups. So think of thinning as early harvests of the row.

Here are some examples of our approach to thinning:

Carrots, like most root crops, don't transplant well. We broadcast the seeds over well-worked soil, and cover them a half inch deep. Germination takes several weeks. Then we thin the plants repeatedly until they stand about 3 inches apart and use the thinnings in salads, stews, and soups.

Kale thinnings are excellent greens. We scatter the seeds in a 4-inch band, then thin the seedlings several times until they are 8 to 12 inches apart.

We thin **beet** seedlings until the plants are 2 inches apart. But, you can leave some of the thinning until the extra plants are large enough to cook up as **beet greens,** which we like even better than fresh **spinach.**

Genetically engineered **corn** is resistant, but at this time there is a lot of controversy over genetically engineered plants.

Planting **corn** early helps, as does planting varieties that have resistance to the pest. You can also protect the rows with floating row covers. At the feeding stage they are discouraged by products that contain Sevin insecticide.

Asparagus beetles strip the foliage from the stems, and that prevents the plants from storing food for next season's production. Row covers may keep them away. Or, spray with a beetle control designed specifically for food plants, such as Rotenone and Neem products.

Protect **tomatoes** from tomato hornworm with Sevin when the fruit is getting to be $1/2$ inch in diameter.

JULY
HERBS & VEGETABLES

PLANNING

To enjoy the best of your kitchen garden, plan to harvest each species as it reaches peak flavor. Some vegetables maturing now must be kept picked to maintain productivity—something to consider when planning your vacation.

Individual seed packets offer guidance on harvest time. Here's an overview:

Herbs. The flavor of the perennial herbs is consistent all season. But **arugula** is a cool-season herb that is sweetest harvested very young. Take no more than a third of a **parsley** plant at one time. If it's hot, take only tip sprigs from your herbs however full they are. In extremely hot weather the plants shut down just as they do when cold becomes extreme. To strip them is to weaken the plant.

Leafy vegetables. Long-standing summer **lettuces** and **New Zealand spinach** may need watering but not harvesting while you are on vacation. **Chard** and **kale** have the best flavor in late summer and early fall, and you can pick side leaves until frost destroys the plants.

Root crops. There are early and late varieties. Spring **beets** are best harvested when 2 to 3 inches around; winter keeper varieties can stay in the ground until twice that size, or more. Spring planted **carrots** are best harvested at 2 inches around, when the orange shoulder shows through the soil. Winter **carrots** can stay in their rows until frost threatens; the longer they stay, the better the flavor. **Parsnips** taste best harvested in spring after a winter in the garden.

Legumes, peas, and **beans.** These must be picked when young, or the seeds in the pods will mature and the plants will slow or stop producing.

Squash zucchini. It tastes best harvested at about 5 inches and must be kept picked continuously to keep the plants producing. Other **summer squashes** taste best when picked young as well. The **winter squashes,** such as **butternut** and **Hubbard,** develop a fuller flavor when they are allowed to stay on the vine well into fall.

PLANTING

You can sow seeds now for the next round of cool-weather crops. Plant late-season varieties of **Brussels sprouts, cabbage, cauliflower, broccoli, chard,** and **kale.** Plant leftover seeds of cool-season **lettuces, arugula,** and **mache.**

Start seeds indoors or in a cold frame now for quick-bearing **cherry tomatoes.** Transplanted to a container that can be moved to a sheltered spot later, they will furnish your own fresh **tomatoes** well after the regular growing season. **Sungold tomatoes** are superb in stews and sauces and delicious fresh.

CARE

When the bramble fruits, especially **raspberries** and **cherries,** start to ripen, cover them with nylon mesh, cheesecloth, or a floating row cover to keep birds and deer (!) from harvesting your crop; the deer eat leaves and all.

GROOMING

For flavor, harvest **green beans, zucchini,** and **summer squashes** as they reach 5 to 6 inches long.

Harvest fruit trees consistently to avoid attracting deer.

Clear the plants of maturing vegetables to keep them producing.

In cool areas, when most of the tops of the **onions** break over naturally, the crop is ready to harvest. In warm areas, you can begin harvesting when about a third of the tops break over.

HOLLY'S BASIL OIL

5 packed cups fresh basil leaves, preferably Thai or Holy basil
1 quart mild olive oil

Strip off the leaves, and discard the stems. Pack the leaves into a measuring cup. Heat the oil until you can just bear to dip your finger in it. Bruise the leaves between your palms, and drop them into the oil. Remove the oil from the heat; cover the pot. Let the oil return to room temperature, then reheat it as before. Turn the heat off, cover the pot, and let the leaves steep 24 hours. Reheat the oil as before, let it cool to room temperature, then strain out the leaves. Bottle the basil oil, cap it, and store the oil in the refrigerator.

Basil (*Ocimum basilicum*)

WATERING

The water from a hose hit by July sun is as hot as hot tap water. No good for plants. So, run the hose until the water is tepid before you turn it on the garden. A vegetable garden needs at least 1 inch of water per week in summer.

Check the moisture in plant containers every three or four days; check small pots and hanging baskets every day or two.

Water your compost pile when you water the garden, and turn it weekly.

FERTILIZING

When the **tomato** plants start to set fruit, drench the foliage and the soil with a soluble organic fertilizer, and repeat monthly until the fruits near mature size.

PROBLEMS

Don't pull big weeds from bone-dry soil—the upheaval can cost soil moisture. Water first, then tug gently but firmly to get all of the roots. Shake the soil into the garden, and compost the remains.

Japanese beetles emerge this month. Spraying now with a Neem product may help. Plan to treat the garden and the lawn around with milky disease spores in late summer. It begins to be effective next year.

With summer's high heat and muggy air, fruits and vegetables become more susceptible to invasions of pests and diseases just as plants are crowding their rows. Thin the plants to let in more air. Plan to adopt a more open planting plan next year.

Since many fungal diseases thrive in a wet garden, water only in the early morning so the rising sun will dry the foliage. Spray **tomatoes** and **cucumbers** with copper fungicide.

AUGUST
HERBS & VEGETABLES

PLANNING

The best-tended kitchen gardens will show seasonal wear and tear. Wilted leaves, cracked or discolored skin, and yellowed stems are often caused by natural stresses of the growing season. Plan to keep your eye on these developments. If symptoms worsen and you can't identify or solve them, ask your full service garden center for help, or call an USDA Extension agent and apply the remedies recommended.

If you identify a symptom as a disease, before applying remedies to the plant, remove badly infected material and get it out of the garden. Put it into the garbage. Wash your hands well after handling diseased plants.

Be sure not to replant a crop that showed infection in the same

Cauliflower is a favorite fall crop.

spot in the garden, and don't plant any of its relatives there. (See November, Crop Rotation Equals Better Health.)

Here's another area of gardening where maintaining a garden log is essential. A record of when certain conditions occur, the names of the plants that exhibited the symptoms, and the methods that reduced the problem are your ally next year.

PLANTING

Garlic cloves planted now will produce a lush harvest of fat cloves next spring.

Plant seedlings of the last of the cool-season crops for fall harvests now—**cabbage, cauliflower,** and **broccoli**—along with **lettuce,** fall **radishes,** and **spinach.**

CARE

Weed seeds are maturing now. Water the garden, then tug on the weeds gently but firmly to get all of the roots up. Shake the soil clinging to the roots back into the garden. If you can't pull them without disturbing a nearby vegetable, cut the weeds back to the crown and put the seedheads in the trash.

GROOMING

Keep maturing **beans** and **summer squashes** picked to keep the plants producing.

As the weather freshens at summer's end, harvest all the herbs you wish to freeze or dry for winter use. You can strip **basil** and other annual herbs, but take

no more than a third of the **thyme** and other perennial herbs.

WATERING

Check the moisture in plant containers every four days; check small pots and hanging baskets every day or two.

A vegetable garden needs at least 1 inch of water per week in summer.

FERTILIZING

Water your compost pile when you water the garden, and turn it weekly.

For as long as the **tomato** plants are setting fruit, every four weeks drench the foliage and the soil with a soluble organic fertilizer and continue until the fruits near mature size.

PROBLEMS

If mildew turns up on plant foliage, spray with André's all-natural remedy: 1 tablespoon baking soda and 1 tablespoon of ultra-fine horticultural oil mixed well in a gallon of water.

If the stems of your **cucumbers** and **summer** and **winter squash** are rotting and the leaves yellowing, the culprit is the squash vine borer. The moth lays her eggs at

---

TOO-MANY-TOMATOES BRUNCH

Brunch for two. Cut one large **tomato** into slices half an inch thick, and spread each side lightly with crushed fresh **garlic.** In a heavy skillet over moderately high heat, melt a teaspoon of butter in a teaspoon of olive oil. Stir in a minced sprig tip of **basil**, then remove and discard it. Add the tomato slices, and sauté one side until slightly browned. Turn the slices, and break four eggs into the spaces around the tomato slices. Add salt and pepper, if you wish. Cover the pan, reduce the heat, and cook until the egg whites are set and glazed over. Serve at once with hot, crisp French bread and butter.

HARVESTING HERBS

Herbs are most flavorful harvested in the early morning before the sun dissipates the essential oils that give them flavor. Rinse herbs only if they're muddy. You won't have to rinse the foliage if you surround your herbs with mulch. We find herb foliage stays fresh for a week or so when we seal it in a vegetable bag lined with damp paper towel, and store it in the crisper.

To encourage an herb to bush out and be more productive, early on pinch out of the tip of the main stems. Remove herb flowers as they develop—they're edible and make charming garnishes.

When the plants have filled out, you can harvest the tender tip sprigs of the youngest branches at will without harming the plant. Never strip a plant of more than a third of its foliage, or it will have trouble maintaining itself. In summer's high heat—especially in very warm summer—herbs go into semi-dormancy. During this time, you should pick herbs sparingly, as the plants are unable to replace the missing foliage and will look awful and be slow to recover.

---

the base of the plant in early summer, and the worms eat the stalk and spread a virus that causes the stems to rot. Beneficial nematodes and *Bacillius thuringiensis* are controls.

To prevent this next year, dispose of the diseased plants now. Turn the soil, and fluff it to kill

larvae. Next year, plant resistant varieties. Plant through a square of foil, and cover the row with floating row covers to keep the moths away. When the plants get too big to keep the row cover on, mist the leaves regularly with garlic spray.

SEPTEMBER
HERBS & VEGETABLES

 PLANNING

Plan to double your pleasure in your kitchen garden by planning to store and preserve your harvests. Here are fast, easy ways to store vegetables:

Pick all the tomatoes you can; ripe, red ones, green ones, and those still white. You can still ripen the green and white ones.

Tomatoes. Pick all the ripe **tomatoes,** those turning color, and those whitening when frost threatens. Ripen reddish fruits on a sunny sill; wrap whitening fruits in newspaper, and store in a cool place. They will ripen over the next six weeks.

Freeze the fully ripe **tomatoes;** they're better for cooking than canned **tomatoes.** Select ripe, unblemished fruits, pop them dry into a freezer bag, and store them in the freezer. Before adding frozen **tomatoes** to a soup, a stew, or a sauce, run tepid water over the skins to make peeling easy.

Legumes and corn. Pick **snap beans** and **corn,** clean the crop, drop it into boiling water, wait two minutes, then remove and drain that portion you want to save, and freeze it. Parboil fresh **pole beans,** and freeze them; or, let the pods dry, shell the beans, dry them on screens, and store in paper bags. Or, let the vines dry, then shell the beans and store them.

Summer squash. Pick and rinse young **squash,** slice them up, drop into boiling water, wait two minutes, remove, then drain and freeze them. Cook frozen **squash** the same way you cook frozen **squash** from the market.

Strawberries, raspberries, blueberries. Pick clean, ripe fruit, remove the stems, toss the berries with granulated sugar, spoon them into freezer bags, and freeze.

 PLANTING

Clear out crops that have peaked, turn the rows, and replant them with seedlings of cool-season crops that mature in a short time—**lettuce, arugula, mache, chard,** and **kale.**

If your climate has less than two months growing weather ahead, plant in a cold frame, or plan to cover the rows when temperatures drop below 55 degrees at night.

Sow **parsley** seeds or seedlings; this year's crop will fade next spring.

 CARE

When temperatures fall below 65 degrees Fahrenheit, remove all the **tomato** blossoms to keep nutrients flowing to the ripening fruits.

Provide fall and winter protection for late crops. Cover the plants at night with row covers or old sheets, and they will ripen fruit for many days.

To stop Japanese beetles next year, spread milky spore disease on the soil and lawn around **raspberries** and **basil.**

Turn the compost pile weekly.

DRYING CULINARY HERBS

Ideally, we would all renew our supply of herbs at the end of every season. Drying herbs is a pleasant project. Harvest the herbs in the late afternoon on a hot, dry day.

Air drying:

1. Pick fresh, healthy branch tips 12 to 14 inches long. Strip the coarse lower leaves and discard. Gather the stems in loose bunches, and hang them upside down in an airy, dry, preferably dark place. When the stems are crackling dry, strip the leaves off, and discard the stems. Rub the leaves between your palms to break them up and to remove them from the tiny twigs they may be clinging to.

2. Pour the leaves into glass jars and cap tightly. After a few days, check to see whether moisture has appeared inside the glass. If yes, oven dry the herbs for two hours at 150 degrees Fahrenheit.

3. Store the herbs in small jars, and write the date and the name on the label.

Oven drying:

Spread the leaves out over paper towels, and heat them on low until crackling dry. How long depends on the herb and your oven.

Microwave drying:

Dryish herbs, like **thyme,** dry well in a microwave oven at half power. Experiment with timing when you can afford to ruin a batch or two. Drying moist herbs such as **basil** in a microwave keeps the color and the flavor. Prop several leaves on a crumpled paper towel, and microwave one or one-and-one-half minutes on High. A whole branch in our oven dries in three to four minutes.

 GROOMING

Keep maturing vegetables picked to keep the plants producing.

 WATERING

Plants growing in containers will need watering this month every ten days if you are without rain.

 FERTILIZING

As long as container plants are producing, continue to fertilize at half strength at every watering.

 PROBLEMS

If mildew continues to be a problem, clear the bed, rake out the remains of the plants, and dispose of it in the trash; do not compost. If the mildew is mild, spray with André's remedy: 1 tablespoon baking soda and 1 tablespoon of ultra-fine horticultural oil mixed well in a gallon of water.

OCTOBER
HERBS & VEGETABLES

PLANNING

Root vegetables and winter squash. They are ready to harvest this month; plan to keep them for winter eating.

Kale. Pick side leaves, rinse, bag them, and store them in the crisper. They will keep for a week or two.

Root crops. The flavor of **rutabagas** and **turnips** is improved by a light frost at maturity; **parsnips** are sweeter when they have wintered in the ground. **Beets** and **carrots** must be harvested before the ground freezes.

For short-term storage, harvest and clean the vegetables with their greens on; seal them in vegetable bags and store them in the crisper, and they will stay firm for at least a few weeks.

For long-term storage, remove the greens and layer the roots in damp sand in a spot where temperatures are between 33 to 40 degrees Fahrenheit. You also can store **beets, carrots, parsnips, rutabagas,** and **turnips** in a pit in the ground; line the bottom with clean sand, then layer in vegetables and sand, ending with a layer of sand. Cover the pit with bales of straw.

Winter squash and pumpkins. Keep maturing **winter squash** off the ground on hay or chicken wire to prevent the bottoms from rotting. Before frosts, harvest any

with a 3-inch stem. Wipe the skins clean with a damp cloth, and store indoors in a cool dry place; most varieties keep for two or three months; the big blue **Hubbard squashes** keep up to six months.

PLANTING

Early this month is ideal for moving or dividing most of the kitchen garden perennials, and the bramble fruits. It also is a good time to plant bramble fruits and fruit trees.

Before frosts hit, buy a few young plants of **basil, summer savory, bay leaf, rosemary,** and **chives.** They'll do well for a time on a sunny sill and will live for the winter in a cool Florida room.

October is a good month to prepare a planting bed for strawberries.

CARE

In empty rows, plant a cover crop such as **winter rye** to improve the fertility, texture, and water-holding capacity of the soil.

Compost all the healthy vegetative material. (See Trees, October, Composting.) Now, when you have fresh organic debris from the kitchen garden, and a yard full of fallen leaves, is the perfect time to refurbish or to start the compost pile.

GROOMING

Empty and clear the rows of vegetables that are finished, and turn the soil by hand or with a rototiller.

WATERING

If the season turns dry, water your seedlings, the cover crop if you planted one, and the kitchen garden perennials, especially any newly planted.

FERTILIZING

Scratch a little organic fertilizer in around the kitchen garden perennials. Turn the compost pile weekly.

ABOUT STRAWBERRIES

In cool regions, **strawberry** plants are set out in early spring as soon as the soil can be worked; in warm regions, they can be set out spring or fall.

They need a bed of their own. Soon after planting they send out runners that root new plantlets that can be used to start a new row, or to renew the original bed. The beds should be renewed every six years.

One-crop varieties bear early- or mid-season; everbearer varieties bear in late summer. A new type of everbearer described as "day neutral" produces its largest crop mid-season through fall. Plant two dozen of each for an all-season harvest.

A few weeks before planting, top a row 4 inches wide with 2 inches of compost or dried manure, and dig it in. Set the crowns at the level at which they were growing. The first season remove all the blossoms that form in spring; allow the everbearers to bloom and to set fruit from July on. Keep day neutrals clear of blossoms until mid-season and let them produce from mid-season through fall.

About six weeks after planting, **strawberry** plants send out runners. Remove all runners until the bed has been producing for three years. The fourth year allow them to root, and transplant them the following spring to start a new bed. The new bed will be in full production the following spring, and you can dig up the original bed.

When temperatures head towards 20 degrees Fahrenheit, cover the bed with a 6-inch straw mulch. After the ground has frozen hard, pile on a foot more of straw.

PROBLEMS

Discard remaining insect or disease infected garden debris in the garbage. Do not compost it. Where infestations have been severe, turn the soil; air destroys many of the organisms there.

Basil growing indoors may be attacked by whiteflies. Shower the plants, and especially the undersides of the leaves, every two days for ten days. If the problem persists, spray four times every seven days with Pyrethrum or Neem. If the problem still persists, discard the plants before they infect other houseplants.

NOVEMBER
HERBS & VEGETABLES

 PLANNING

If your soil is sandy, or lacking in humusy material, this is a good time to incorporate aged horse manure. There are many stables in our area, so locating a source shouldn't be difficult. Or dig in seaweed. Fall storms at sea usually leave drifts on the shore.

 PLANTING

About the only thing you can plant at this point are **Egyptian onions.**

 CARE

When temperatures head for 20 degrees Fahrenheit, cover **strawberries** with a 6-inch straw mulch.

 GROOMING

Clear the rows of everything but **parsnips,** which are improved by wintering in the garden. Turn the soil by hand or with a rototiller.

 WATERING

Maintain the soil moisture in herbs growing indoors.

CROP ROTATION EQUALS BETTER HEALTH

You can avoid encouraging pests and diseases by rotating your crops annually. The rotation rule applies not only to individual species, but also to members of that species plant family.

These six plant families benefit from crop rotation:

- *Cabbage group.* Broccoli, Brussels sprouts, cabbage, cauliflower, Chinese cabbage, collards, kale, kohlrabi, radishes, turnips
- *Carrot and parsley group.* Carrots, celery, coriander, dill, fennel, parsley, parsnips
- *Cucumber group.* Cucumbers, gourds, melons, squash, pumpkins, watermelons
- *Legumes.* Beans, peas
- *Onion group.* Chives, onions, garlic
- *Tomato group.* Eggplant, peppers, potatoes, tomatoes

Parsnip (*Pastinaca sativa*)

 FERTILIZING

Fertilize the fruit trees and bramble fruits.

 PROBLEMS

Basil indoors may be attacked by whiteflies. Shower the undersides of the leaves every two days for ten days. If the problem persists, spray four times every seven days with Pyrethrum or Neem.

CREATE A COLD FRAME OR A HOT BED

Cold frames and hot beds give plants a head start on the seasons. A handy person can make either.

A cold frame is a bottomless box sunk into the earth and roofed over with glass or plastic. In its warmth, seeds and seedlings germinate and grow weeks before they can be started in the garden. Garden centers offer cold frames ready to assemble, and lightweight portable styles enable you to move them around to protect late and winter crops. Some are equipped with solar-powered frame openers triggered by high temperatures.

The ideal position for a cold frame is facing south on a slope that sets the cover at a 45 degree angle to the sun. That allows water and snow to slide off. The day's heat keeps the inside warm at night. When the air inside reaches 90 degrees Fahrenheit, prop the top up to vent the box, or the heat will damage the plants.

Making a cold frame:

1. Use concrete blocks, bricks, or rot-resistant boards to make a frame 5 to 6 feet long by 3 feet wide by 3 feet high.

2. Make a cover for the cold frame from a pair of old storm windows. Or, staple heavy-duty plastic film to a wooden frame that fits onto the cold frame. Hinge the cover to the frame to make airing it easy.

3. Place an outdoor thermometer inside the cold frame where you can see the temperature without opening the cover.

4. In the cold frame, place flats, boxes, or pots filled with improved soil to plant in. Each season provide new improved soil.

A hot bed is much like a cold frame, but it has some insulation and is equipped with an underground heating cable regulated by a thermostat. The heat allows you to plant earlier than in a cold frame. When the heat is off, the hot bed serves as a cold frame. In horse and buggy days, hot beds were deeper, and bottom heat was provided by the decomposition of moist layers of straw, fresh horse manure, and leaves.

CEMBER

& VEGETABLES

PLANNING

Check last year's garden log for ideas for the coming season, and check your album of catalog pages of garden accessories. Early this month order the things you wish to give the gardeners on your holiday list. Do family and friends a favor by telling them about the seeds, tools, and accessories you'd enjoy receiving.

Organize a seed-saver file. Each season, we usually use up at least one packet each of **beans, peas, lettuces,** and the root vegetables. But we always have leftover seeds for **basil** and other herbs, **tomatoes** and **melons,** and others we plant several varieties of. Packets of seeds of space-consuming plants like

Arugula

cabbages, Brussels sprouts, and **kale** also take a few seasons to be used up.

We organize these leftovers in a spiral binder equipped with clear plastic sleeves. We mark the year on each packet, and place all the varieties of each species in the same sleeve. When we have one, we include a catalog image of the plant, and any comments we have.

Seeds generally are considered viable for at least five years. The older the seed, the fewer will germinate. You can check out how well older seeds will do by scattering a half dozen on damp paper towel and covering them with another sheet of damp paper towel. With indoor warmth they should sprout and tell you what percentage of the seed you can expect to see germinate if you plant them.

To avoid having a lot of leftover seeds, organize a seed-sharing project among your gardening friends.

PLANTING

Zone 8 may be warm enough to sow **arugula** and **mache.**

CARE

As temperatures near 20 degrees Fahrenheit, cover the **strawberry**

bed with a 6-inch straw mulch. When the ground has frozen hard, add a little more, but not so much you can't see some green through the straw.

GROOMING

Groom **parsley** and other herbs growing indoors.

WATERING

Maintain the soil moisture in herbs growing indoors.

FERTILIZING

Nothing to fertilize this month.

PROBLEMS

Continue the whitefly alert for the **basil** plants growing indoors. Showering the plants, and especially the undersides of the leaves, may lick the problem. If the problem persists, spray four times every seven days with Pyrethrum or Neem. If the problem continues to persist, discard the plants before they infect other houseplants.

LAWNS

A lawn is a highly visible part of your house. It can be a joy or a curse, depending on how you treat it.

There are four types of lawns: The lawn lover's lawn looks like the sod lawns you see in spring flower shows. Flawless. Fiercely defended nine months of the year against growth, weeds, wilts, pests, diseases, and droughts, it gives meaning and purpose to its caregiver's life.

The **nature lover's lawn** is a flowering meadow with a brush cut. Carpeted in spring with golden dandelions, blue violets, purple jewelweed, bright crabgrass, and jointgrass, ajuga, ivy, and other ground covers, here wildlife abounds—voles run, moles mound, birds enjoy a rich supply of grubs that will metamorphose into multi-hued Japanese and other beetles. In summer the wild flowers will self-sow then brown out leaving bare patches that save on mowing and watering.

The **environmentalist's lawn** is a work in progress—turfgrass is being replaced with ground covers, and there are motels for birds that will eat the grubs that feed the moles that fight the voles that dig the lawn that no longer surrounds the house that Jack built.

The **good gardener's lawn** is a hybrid of 1, 2, and 3. It's a beautiful lawn maintained by fertilizing adequately, mowing knowledgeably, and watering wisely.

FERTILIZING AND FERTILIZERS

A well-maintained lawn creates oxygen, removes pollutants from the air, traps dust and dirt, stops erosion, makes a fine playground, and enhances your home and the whole neighborhood. Like teenagers, turf grasses grow fast and need unchecked access to food, drink, and air to do well. The type of fertilizer you use decrees how often you need to fertilize.

Organic fertilizers. Organics release their nutrients slowly; two applications a year are enough. A Cornell University study found that using organic fertilizers may suppress some diseases, including brown patch, snow mold, dollar spot, and red thread. With organic fertilizers, herbicides, pesticides, and fungicides are usually applied separately.

Chemical fertilizers. Quick-release, balanced chemical fertilizers green the lawn overnight and are soon depleted, so you need to apply them four or five times a year. "Fertilizer-plus" products that include pre-emergent or post-emergent herbicides can be used to control crabgrass and broadleaf weeds. Insect and disease controls are usually applied separately.

Herbicides, pesticides, and fungicides are applied only when needed. Granular products applied with a drop-spreader are safest for the garden.

SOIL PREPARATION AND IMPROVEMENT

Soil pH. The condition of your soil impacts the lawn's access to the nutrients you spend real money and scarce time providing. If the pH of the soil is between pH 6.0 and 7.0 it should do well. The ideal pH for turfgrass is 6.5. Heavily cropped soils—like lawn soils—eventually become acid and have a lower pH reading. However, do not automatically apply lime to raise the pH. Some of our soils are naturally alkaline, and for these, the pH may need to be lowered, not raised. Check the pH of your soil annually, but adjust it only when adjustment is needed.

Sandy soil whose pH has been corrected is good for two years, clay soil for three. A pH check can be made any month. We recommend February before the first fertilization. (See February.)

Aeration (Coring). Running feet, foot traffic, heavy mowing equipment, bikes, cars, and loaded wheelbarrows all pack (compact) the top 2 or 3 inches of the soil into a dense layer. Compacted soil has no space for water or air, nor does it have growing room for roots. The solution is to aerate the soil by cutting out core plugs of sod so that water, air, and fertilizer can get down to where they are needed.

If the lawn is well used and beginning to bald or show a thatch buildup, aerate. If all is well, every two or three years, aerate to keep it that way. You can do it by hand, and you also can rent power equipment to aerate and dethatch. (See April and May.)

Thatch and dethatching. Grass clippings landing on the lawn are decomposed by the microorganisms there, and that adds nutrients to the soil. That layer of clippings is called thatch, and it's a good thing as long as the clippings are less than 1/4 inch deep. However, if the lawn gets too much fast-acting high-nitrogen fertilizer and water, it may grow quickly and the clippings may fall so thick and so fast the microorganisms can't keep up; that's when a layer of thatch a couple of inches deep accumulates, which is harmful. A lawn that feels spongy when you walk on it probably has thatch building to unhealthy levels. You can fix it by aerating and dethatching. You can also prevent thatch buildup. (See May.)

WATERING

Grass is programmed to thrive on a good soaking every week to ten days. Soak it more often, as nature does when we have a wet spring, and it will grow, use up the nutrients in the soil, and need mowing almost twice as fast. Water the lawn frequently and shallowly—every one to three days—and the roots will grow near the surface of the soil, which warms and dries out when the weather does, a bad place for roots to be. Excess water speeds up the rate of growth, which depletes the fertilizer and increases the need for water. That makes the grass vulnerable to drought, and more susceptible to the myriad pests and diseases lawns are heir to.

The watering program described in the July pages is easy on your time, effort, pocketbook, and lawn. Only your patience will suffer.

REPAIR AND RESTORATION

The rule of thumb is that if seventy percent of a lawn needs fixing, then you need a new lawn. If thirty percent or less is in trouble, it can be patched or restored.

Unhappily, it's a fact that on packed dirt only dandelions, crabgrass, and their associates grow readily. For lawn patching or restoration to succeed, you must mix humus and fertilizers into the soil before you seed or sod the area.

Repair. You can repair a small area with sod, new or stripped from somewhere else in the lawn, or by seeding the area. Lawn patching products include mulch and nutrients and are easy to apply.

Restoration. This involves sowing seed into an existing lawn after vigorously cultivating the ground with rented power equipment. (See August.)

Starting a new lawn. To seed or to sod, that is the question. It is not nobler to seed, just less costly. Sodding is faster, but the soil needs the same deep preparation and patient watering until it is established. Sod won't keep weeds out forever, and sod varieties are limited.

Seeding saves money. The bigger the lawn, the greater the savings. To seed 1000 square feet costs about $10, not including the humus, fertilizer, and other soil amendments the soil will need to get a good start. If you seed, you can choose from among the varieties of grasses in our turfgrass table.

Sod if you enjoy making magic. It's the way to have an instant lawn. The cost for a 1000 square foot area is about $200, if you do the work yourself. Your choice of grasses will be limited.

Timing for a new lawn. Cool-season grasses peak in spring, go semi-dormant in midsummer, and peak again in fall.

They're best started around Labor Day. Early spring is second best. Most seeds germinate when daytime temperatures are 68 to 95 degrees Fahrenheit.

Zoysia, a warm-season grass preferred by some in Zone 8, peaks in warm weather and is best planted in midsummer. (See September and November.)

MOWING

In our area mowing may begin as early as late March, goes weekly in May, slows with August heat and drought, slows for real in October, and ends in November. The rule of thumb is to mow every five to seven days during the peak season, and as needed at other times.

Good mowing equipment and knowledgeable mowing practices improve the beauty and the health of your lawn. In the long run that saves you time, effort, annoyance, and the cost of repairing what has gone wrong. Keep the mower blades sharpened, cut the grass high, and don't let the mowing get away from you. Don't overfertilize. Water wisely. Mow at the

CHAPTER FOUR

right height for the grass and the season. (See May, Mowing.)

The table of grasses for the Mid-Atlantic includes the mowing heights of each grass recommended.

About mowers. Buy the best equipment you can afford and the right size. That will make it easier and help you to keep up without feeling burdened. There are many sizes and types of mowers, but only two ways of cutting—reel or rotary. The reel mower does a better job but is slower. The rotary mower does a fine job and is faster. The most important thing to know about a mower is that it must be sharpened throughout the mowing season. Dull blades tear and damage the grass blades, and that shows up in the appearance of the lawn and the health of the grass plants. (See December.)

LEAVES AND YOUR LAWN

If there's just a scattering of leaves on your lawn, they'll dry and crumble into bits that the microorganisms in the soil will reduce to nutrients. The residue will blow away with winter winds and weather. But matted accumulations of leaves rob the grass of the sunlight it needs as growth continues through fall. The grass grows as long as the soil is warm, and it will remain warm in our region at least through November, and in Zone 8, even later.

Crunch the leaves under the lawn mower, rake and bag them, or grind them and distribute the bits over the garden with a blower-vacuum. (See October.)

COOL-SEASON AND WARM-SEASON GRASSES

For the Mid-Atlantic states in Zones 5, 6, and 7, André recommends cool season grasses. Even in Zone 8, tall fescues give you a greener lawn many more months than zoysia. Zoysia is a great grass for summer, drought tolerant, and

good looking, but it goes dormant and turns golden below 63 degrees Fahrenheit. To keep it green, some dye it green for winter, which makes it look like plastic turf, or it is overseeded with annual rye, and that's a chore.

Beware of too-good-to-be-true sales of grass seed.

CONTROLLING WEEDS, PESTS, AND DISEASES

Weeds, pests, and diseases attack lawns made vulnerable by lack of fertilizer and poor garden practices. There are ways to control them.

Cultural practices. Feed, mow, and water your lawn properly.

Biological methods. Apply agents such as beneficial nematodes, bacteria, and other organisms. A biological control becoming more available is endophytes—fungi bred to live within grasses and stop insect pests.

Chemical controls. Pre-emergent and post-emergent herbicides, and pesticides and fungicides—some natural, some manmade—are used to control weeds, pests, and diseases. Those now on the market are considered environmentally sound. Once again, we caution you to apply these only if really needed.

For an overview of how and when to do what, turn to the March pages.

WEEDS

All post-emergent liquid weed killers work best when the dose called for on the label is combined with 1 teaspoon of liquid dish detergent to each gallon of water.

Annual bluegrass. Prevent by applications of pre-emergent controls such as Betasan and Banlan made in early August and repeated one month later. There is no good post-emergent treatment.

Broadleaf weed seeds. These weeds, including dandelions, can be controlled by applications of

a pre-emergent broadleaf weed killer when the forsythia petals drop. Repeat in September and October.

Broadleaf weed plants. If a variety of weeds leaf out in May and June, apply a post-emergent broad-spectrum herbicide.

Chickweed, bindweed, ground ivy, violets, sorrel, and clover plants. Kill these weeds by applications in April and May of a post-emergent control such as 2,4-D+TurflonD; Dicamba 2,4-D+BanvelD; or Gordon's Trimec Broadleaf Herbicide. Repeat in September and October.

Crabgrass seeds. When the forsythia petals drop in late March or April, control by applying pre-emergent weed killers such as Betasan, Tupersan, Balan, Dacthal, Team, or Sidriron.

Dandelion, plantain, and other broadleaf weed plants. Control them by individual applications in April and May of 2,4-D and 2,4-D combinations.

Ground ivy. Control by applying a post-emergent control such as Gordon's Trimec Broadleaf Herbicide or 2,4-D+TurflonD anytime it appears.

Nutgrass. Apply a pre-emergent control such as Manage or Pennant when the forsythia petals drop in late March or April, and repeat one month later. When nutgrass first becomes visible in spring, and again ten days later, apply a post-emergent control such as Basagran, DSMA, MSMA, or Bentazon.

Wild onion (garlic). Apply a post-emergent control such as 2,4-D+ Dicamba (Banvel D) or 2,4-D+TurflonD in early spring when the onions first emerge, and repeat two weeks later.

PESTS

From November through March pests and diseases are on vacation. They're with you April through October.

Grubs. To control the larvae that become rose chafer or Asiatic beetle, in May and June, and again in August and September, apply biological controls such as beneficial nematodes; for the grubs of Japanese beetles, use milky spore disease. Or apply chemical controls such as Merit or Marathon.

Ants. Use Permethrin.

Chinch bugs. Apply Sevin, Permethrin, or Baygon in April and May, and again in August and September.

Cutworms. Use beneficial nematodes, Sevin, or Safer soap in spring.

Japanese beetles. Apply Neem, rotenone, or Sevin.

Sod webworms. In late June and again in late August and early September, apply Bt, Sevin, Permethrin, or Baygon.

DISEASES

To control a variety of diseases at one time, apply a broad-spectrum fungicide, or better yet a broad-spectrum systemic fungicide. Some André recommends are Daconil, Mancozeb, Chipco, Clearys 3336, and Bayleton.

Make the applications when the disease appears and twice a month in May, June, July, and August.

Fusarium blight (now called necrotic ring spot), copper spot, and dollar spot. They show up as a circle of dead grass with some green tufts in the middle. The disease will likely run its course. The controls are fungicidal copper or sulfur, Bayleton, or Cleary 3336.

Helminthosporum leaf spot and melting out. These diseases cause brown and black spots on the leaves, and the grass dies in irregular patches. Treat with a fungicide labeled for use on turf and melting out diseases, such as Fore or Heritage, every two weeks from the first appearance of the problem until it is gone.

Powdery mildew. It looks as though the leaves have been powdered. Powdery mildew turns up in shady spots, so try to get more light to the

CHAPTER FOUR

GRASSES

GRASS: Fine Fescues: chewings, creeping red, hard fescue
SHADE TOLERANCE: Excellent
PROBLEMS: Does not recover quickly from damage. Tends to lie flat and cause uneven mowing.
START AS: Seed in spring or fall.
SOW: 3 to 4 pounds per 1,000 square feet
MOWING HEIGHT: 2 to 2 ¾ inches

GRASS: Tall Fescue
SHADE TOLERANCE: Good
PROBLEMS: Older versions (Kentucky 31) tend to clump. Vulnerable to pythium, brown patch diseases, cutworms, sod webworms, billbugs.
START AS: Seed spring or fall; sod spring, early summer, or fall
SOW: Seed 6 to 10 pounds per 1,000 square feet
MOWING HEIGHT: 2¼ to 3 ½ inches

GRASS: Kentucky Bluegrass
SHADE TOLERANCE: Full sun best, also light shade
PROBLEMS: Heavy feeder, needs lots of water. Vulnerable to powdery mildew, fungal diseases, chinch bugs, cutworms, grubs, sod webworms

SOW: Start As: Seed 1 to 2 pounds per 1,000 square feet
MOWING HEIGHT: 2 to 2 ¾ inches

GRASS: Perennial Ryegrass
SHADE TOLERANCE: Some varieties tolerate some shade
PROBLEMS: Suffers in extreme heat—may get pythium. Vulnerable to brown patch, red thread, rust, snow mold, dollar spot.
START AS: Seed or sod in spring, early summer, or fall
SOW: Seed 4 to 5 pounds per 1,000 square feet
MOWING HEIGHT: 2 to 2 ½ inches

GRASS: Zoysia
SHADE TOLERANCE: Good
PROBLEMS: Is brown 6 to 8 months of the year in Zones 5 to 7. Chronic heavy thatch buildup.
START AS: Plugs or sod in spring
SOW: Plugs or sod
MOWING HEIGHT: 2 inches

area. Or control with applications of fungicidal copper or sulfur, or a systemic fungicide such as Bayleton or Banner Maxx applied twice a month from June through September.

Red thread and pink patch. Patches of grass turn light tan to pink, and pink threads bind the blades. From the time it appears, treat the lawn with a contact fungicide twice, seven to ten days apart.

Rust-infected leaves. These leaves are spotted yellow, orange, or brown. Rust is common in new lawns with a high percentage of ryegrass. It generally fades as other grass varieties

take over from the rye. Control with applications twice a month of sulfur, mancozeb, or manzate, or a systemic fungicide such as Bayleton and Banner Maxx, from the time it appears—usually May through September.

Snow mold. This is most prevalent in the cooler zones of our region and causes small to large gray or white matted patches of grass. Rake the lawn in early spring, and avoid overuse of nitrogen fertilizers.

JANUARY

LAWNS

 PLANNING

If your lawn mower was serviced when mowing ended last year, great! If not, see December for suggestions.

 PLANTING

Zone 7 can sow cool-season grasses even this early. Seed sown on frozen ground or a thin layer of snow will survive until moisture and warmth encourage germination.

 CARE

Walking on frozen grass damages it.

Shovel walk and driveways before applying snowmelt salts. Otherwise you risk damaging the lawn.

 MOWING

None needed.

 WATERING

If the lawn reaches under overhanging eaves and the season has been dry, that area may need water.

FERTILIZING AND FERTILIZERS

Save money by leaving grass clippings on the lawn. Reduced to their elemental forms by microorganisms in the soil, clippings can lower the amount of fertilizer needed by as much as thirty percent. Clippings from a 1,000 square foot lawn contribute 1/2 to 2 pounds of nitrogen depending on how much the lawn was fertilized.

Insect and disease controls are applied separately. (See March for timing.) Avoid fertilizing cool-season grasses (**zoysia** is okay) when temperatures are over 90 degrees.

When to fertilize:

Organic fertilizers. Organic fertilizers are applied twice a year. They can be applied in any season without danger of burning. Organics do not include herbicides, pesticides, or fungicides; these are applied separately and only when needed. The first fertilization is best made as grass starts into growth in early spring. For Zones 6 and 7 that's usually late February to April; for Zone 8 organic fertilizers can be applied as early as January. The second fertilization is best applied in September to October. The third fertilization is optional, and can be made December or January.

Chemical fertilizers. Chemical fertilizers are applied four to five times a year. Formulations are available that include pre-emergent or post-emergent controls for crabgrass and broadleaf weeds. For a new lawn, choose a fertilizer with an NPK of 1-1-1, or 1-2-2. For an established lawn, choose a fertilizer whose NPK ratio is 3-1-2 or 4-1-2. The first fertilization is best made as grass starts into growth in early spring. For Zones 6 and 7 that's usually February to March; for warm Zone 8 a chemical fertilizer may be applied as early as January. The second fertilization is April to June; the third is made June to August; the fourth is August or September. The fifth fertilization is optional and can be made October or November.

 FERTILIZING

An extra fertilization this month will benefit a lawn that hasn't been growing well. A light coat of granular fertilizer can be applied over a few inches of snow.

 PROBLEMS

In Zone 6, snow mold is possible. Just rake the patches clear, and avoid overuse of nitrogen fertilizers in the future.

FEBRUARY

LAWNS

PLANNING

If your lawn mower needs servicing, take it to the dealer now because this is the dealer's quiet season. Keeping the blades sharp is essential to giving the lawn a good cut, one that will be good for the lawn and good for the viewer.

PLANTING

You can overseed thin areas in late winter or early spring. It's okay to sow seed on a few inches of snow. For suggestions on how to repair damage—where a tree limb has fallen or a delivery truck has gouged the turf—and how to overseed a lawn, see August.

CARE

Check the pH of your lawn soil, and adjust it if needed.

If your lawn has developed low spots, top-dress it with improved soil now, and overseed it. (See September.)

MOWING

Mowing is not likely to be needed unless the weather has been warm in Zone 8.

SOIL pH AND LIME

To keep your soil in top condition for growing grass, check and adjust the pH annually.

The ideal pH for turfgrass is pH 6.5. Some gardeners lime their lawns every year, but you shouldn't lime by rote. Some soils in our region are naturally alkaline, and there the pH needs to be lowered, not raised.

The pH can be adjusted anytime the lawn isn't in full growth, but checking in February gives you time to correct the pH before the grass-growing season begins. A sandy soil whose pH has been corrected is good for two years; a clay soil is good for three years. But we recommend you check the pH every year. Kits for analyzing pH are sold at garden centers and by mail-order suppliers, as are products used for adjusting the soil pH.

- To raise the pH by 1 pH point, apply Dolomitic limestone:
  Sandy soil—50 pounds per 1000 square feet
  Clay soil—100 pounds per 1000 square feet

- To lower the pH by 1 pH point, apply elemental sulfur (water-soluble garden sulfur).
  Sandy soil—50 pounds per 1000 square feet
  Clay soil—100 pounds per 1000 square feet

Other acidifiers are aluminum sulfate and iron sulfate; they act faster but do not last as long in the soil as elemental sulfur.

WATERING

Water areas that have just been seeded or sodded.

FERTILIZING

The first application of an organic fertilizer can be made between now and April.

The first application of a chemical fertilizer can be made this month or next.

PROBLEMS

If wild onion (garlic) was a problem last spring, plan to apply a post-emergent control such as 2,4-D+Dicamba (Banvel D) or 2,4-D+TurflonD at first appearance.

MARCH

LAWNS

PLANNING

If you haven't already, get the lawn mower and trimmer into good condition, and sharpen the blades. Check supplies for your mower and trimmer.

PLANTING

Overseed areas where the grass is skimpy.

CARE

Check and adjust the soil pH. Aerate if you haven't in the last two years. Correct thatch build-up. Use a grass rake to fluff the soil, and discard debris.

MOWING

Begin to mow when the grass tops the height our turfgrass table recommends. (See page 102.)

WATERING

Water lawn areas that snow or rain can't reach.

FERTILIZING

The first application of an organic fertilizer can be made this month or next.

The first application of a chemical fertilizer should be made by the end of this month. (See January.)

PROBLEMS

If you've had crabgrass, when the **forsythia** petals fall, apply a pre-emergent broadleaf weed killer. If dandelions and other broadleaf weeds turn up as well, use a control that deals with both. If wild onion (garlic) pops up, apply a post-emergent control such as 2,4-D+Dicamba (Banvel D) or 2,4-D+ TurflonD, and repeat two weeks later. For other controls, turn back to the Pests and Diseases section in the introduction to this chapter.

HERBICIDES, PESTICIDES, AND FUNGICIDES

Herbicides. The best defense against weeds is a thriving lawn cut high. If a few weeds do appear, pull them by hand before they set seed. If lots of weeds appear, apply a post-emergent broad-spectrum herbicide. If crabgrass is a problem, apply a pre-emergent crabgrass killer. If broad-leaved weeds such as violets and dandelions are also a problem, use a broad-spectrum pre-emergent herbicide that kills weeds as well as crabgrass. Crabgrass germinates in late March or April, about the time **forsythia** petals fall and dandelions fluff out their seedheads. If the lawn is infested with a particular weed, apply a product specific to that weed as and when the label directs.

Pesticides. All lawns are home to insects, most of them beneficial. Biological and chemical controls are available if insects are numerous, but don't overdo; pesticides also kill beneficial insects. To get rid of harmful insects, you can use a combination of a chemical fertilizer plus a pesticide. If you are using an organic fertilizer, apply a broad-spectrum pesticide (insecticide) June to August. To control a specific insect infestation—Japanese beetles, for example—apply a control specific to the insect when and how the label directs.

Fungicides. Fungi cause lawn diseases. Most feed on dead vegetation, recycling it as soil nutrients. A few bad-guy fungi feed on live plants. Symptoms and controls are described in this chapter's introduction.

The best defense is a healthy lawn—fertilize adequately, mow correctly, water wisely, and keep your soil in good condition by adjusting the pH as needed by aerating (coring, plugging) every two or three years and by avoiding thatch buildup. Treat problems immediately.

APRIL

LAWNS

PLANNING

Evaluate the weed and pest populations in your lawn, and work out a plan to keep them under control. Get together last year's herbicides and pesticides. Figure out what you'll need, and acquire it now while garden centers are fully stocked.

PLANTING

Repair areas in the lawn that have been damaged by falling branches, snow-blowing equipment, and so on. (See August.)

CARE

If you haven't checked the soil pH, do it now.

Before mowing begins, rake away debris and fluff up the grass.

MOWING

Mowing begins in earnest this month. Keep the blades sharpened; a clean cut is a healthy cut. Set your mower at the height recommended in our turfgrass table for your type of grass. If you don't know what type you are growing, set the mower at 2$^1/_2$ inches.

WATERING

Water enough to keep the surface of newly sodded or seeded areas moist.

FERTILIZING

The first application of an organic fertilizer should have been made by the end of this month.

If your first application of a chemical fertilizer was made at the end of February, the second can be made between now and June.

PROBLEMS

If crabgrass or nutgrass have been problems, when the **forsythia** petals drop, apply a pre-emergent control; if they do leaf out, apply a post-emergent control. This month and next, watch for chickweed, bindweed, ground ivy, violets, sorrel, clover plants, dandelions, plantain, and other broadleaf weed plants. If there are only a few, pull them by hand. If there are many, kill them before they go to seed. If you spot chinch bugs, apply controls this month and next, and again in August and September.

Controls for each of these problems are suggested in the chapter introduction.

ABOUT AERATION (CORING)

To solve compaction, avoid thatch buildup, and condition the soil, aerate every two or three years. Aerating equipment punches 2- to 3-inch-deep holes in the soil, and lets fertilizer, air, and water penetrate. Aerators that are "corers" have hollow tines, and these are more effective than aerators with solid tines.

To aerate 1,000 square feet or less you can use a manual aerator. It looks like a spading fork, but the tines are hollow tubes. For a larger area, you need a drum-mounted aerator, or to hire a firm that is equipped to do the job.

The best time to aerate is when the grass isn't actively growing, early spring or fall. The day before, lightly water the grass so the tines will enter the soil easily. Before using the aerator, make a light application of fertilizer. Be thorough, and make two passes at right angles to each other with the aerator. Spread grass seed over the aerated area at the rate recommended on the bag. Water slowly and gently.

MAY

LAWNS

PLANNING

If you want to reduce the amount of water you use on the lawn, consider replacing outlying areas with a drought-tolerant ground cover.

PLANTING

You can seed or oversow areas of the lawn this month. (See August.)

CARE

May is a fine time to aerate and dethatch.

In Zone 8, if you suspect grubs, check late this month. Cut out and remove a square foot of turf 8 inches deep. If you find three or four grub larvae in the top 6 inches, apply a grub control. Check again in mid-August or early September.

MOWING

Mow often enough so you never have to cut off more than a third of the grass to maintain the height recommended. Keep the mower blades sharpened.

THATCH AND DETHATCHING

Grass clippings left on the lawn are returned to an elemental state by microorganisms in the soil and recycled as nutrients. A 1/4-inch layer of clippings is good; more is not. Clippings build when overdoses of pesticides kill the soil microorganisms, and when soluble high-nitrogen (N2) fertilizers and excessive watering push grass growth. Your lawn could need dethatching if it feels spongy to walk on.

- Look before you leap. Cut out a pie-shaped plug of turf that includes dirt with the roots. If the spongy layer between the grass and the soil measures more than 1/2 inch, dethatch.
- The best time to dethatch a cool-season grass is in early fall; dethatch **zoysia** in early spring.
- A convex rake with short knife-like blades in place of tines can be used to dethatch a small lawn. For a big dethatching job, a gas-powered vertical mower and power rake attachment is needed. If the thatch is thick, make two passes at right angles to each other.

WATERING

Water newly sodded or seeded areas.

FERTILIZING

Organic fertilizer. If the first application hasn't been made yet, do it now.

Chemical fertilizer. If your first application was in February, repeat now. If you made it in March, wait until May or June to repeat. If weeds are a problem, use a fertilizer that includes a post-emergent herbicide.

PROBLEMS

If dandelions, plantain, chickweed, bindweed, ground ivy, violets, sorrel, clover plants, or other broadleaf weeds appear, apply post-emergent controls before they go to seed.

Apply controls this month for the larvae that become chinch bugs, rose chafer, Japanese, Asiatic, and other beetles.

Rust may appear in new lawns with a high percentage of **ryegrass**. If rust shows up, spray immediately.

JUNE
LAWNS

PLANNING

The lawn's period of major growth is over till the weather cools in September; time to assess your mowing equipment and perhaps take advantage of sales to upgrade.

PLANTING

Sod installed now will do well as long as it is watered daily until it begins to root and grow again.

CARE

In Zones 6 and 7, if you suspect grubs in an area, check early this month. Cut out and remove a square foot of turf 8 inches deep. If you find three or four grub larvae in the top 6 inches, apply a grub control. Check again in mid-August or early September.

MOWING

Check the mowing height of equipment, and make sure it is at the height recommended for your type of turfgrass (see page 102).

Keep the blades on your mower sharpened.

Vary your mowing pattern to lessen the impact on the grass.

MOWING: THE SIX COMMANDMENTS

Good mowing practices help to keep the lawn beautiful and healthy.

1. Mow when the lawn is dry.
2. Keep the mower blades sharpened throughout the cutting season.
3. Cut the grass high. For the ideal height for your grass, refer back to the turfgrass table. Grass mowed higher than 2 inches develop extensive roots, reducing the need for water and nutrients. A Virginia study showed:
   - Cut grass 1 inch high: 43.1 weeds per 100 square feet (a plot 10 by 10 feet).
   - Cut grass 2 inches high: 2.5 weeds per 100 square feet.
   - Cut grass 3 inches high: .2 weeds per 100 square foot.
4. Mow often enough so you never have to cut off more than a third of the grass to maintain the height recommended in the turfgrass table. If your mower is set at $2^1/2$ inches, mow when the grass is $3^1/2$ inches high.
5. Use a mulching mower to make it easy for soil organisms to recycle clippings.
6. Vary your cutting pattern; that's easier on the grass.

WATERING

Keep the soil for newly planted seed or sod moist by watering every day or two.

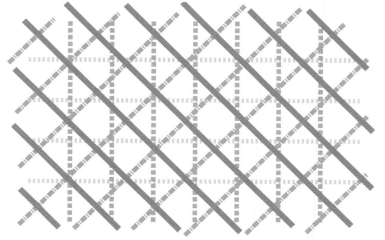

FERTILIZING

Organic fertilizer. If the first application hasn't been made yet, do it now. Organics can be applied anytime, but grass grows rapidly in spring and needs to have the nutrients replenished.

Chemical fertilizer. If you have not made the second application, make it now. If your second fertilization was in April, you can make the third application between now and August.

If weeds are a problem, use a fertilizer that includes a post-emergent herbicide. If insects are a problem, look for fertilizer-plus products that include a broad-spectrum pesticide.

 PROBLEMS

If you see broadleaf weeds in the lawn, apply a post-emergent broad-spectrum herbicide.

If you've had problems with rose chafer, Japanese beetle, Asiatic beetle, or other white grubs, apply controls now.

Watch out for sod webworms; initiate controls immediately.

Powdery mildew can appear about now. It occurs most often in shaded areas of the lawn. Initiate controls now, and continue throughout the summer.

Sod Webworm

HOW TO AVOID THATCH BUILDUP

- Remove less than 1 inch of grass blade when you mow. Use a mulching mower to double-cut the clippings, which makes it easier for the microorganisms in the soil to break them down.
- Avoid excessive dosing with pesticides that kill the soil microorganisms.
- Avoid soluble high-nitrogen (N2) fertilizers and excessive watering.
- Aerate every two or three years. Aeration helps avoid a big thatch buildup although it isn't enough alone to solve one.
- Beneficial insects speed the breakdown of thatch, so be conservative in your use of pesticides.

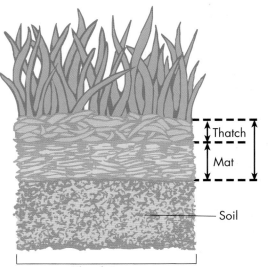

Thatch

Mat

Soil

Thatch Layer

JULY
LAWNS

PLANNING

As summer reveals the pests and diseases that love your lawn best, plan fall and spring strategies for reducing their numbers.

PLANTING

You can repair a lawn with sod now, but wait until late September for any serious seeding project.

CARE

The little moths hovering over the grass are laying the eggs of sod webworms—soon to become larvae. If you applied a control in June, the moths are a prompt that you must repeat in late August and in September.

MOWING

When you will be away for more than a week, arrange to have the lawn mowed. The growth rate of cool-season grasses is slowing, but if on your return you have to cut more than a week's worth of growth, the lawn will suffer.

Keep the mower blades sharpened.

WATERING

The lawn needs a good soaking every week, especially in very hot weather.

FERTILIZING

Chemical fertilizer. If you haven't applied your third fertilization yet, do it this month or next.

PROBLEMS

Look out for fusarium blight (now called necrotic ring spot), copper spot, and dollar spot; helminthosporum leaf spot and melting out diseases; powdery mildew; red thread and pink patch; and rust-infected leaves. As soon as you have identified a disease, apply the controls recommended in the chapter introduction. Repeat twice this month and next.

HOW TO WATER YOUR LAWN

Lawns need water every week. When you water, imitate a slow soaking rain. Then it will go deep, and the roots will grow down away from the heat and drought at the surface.

• When you water, lay down 1¹/₂ inches slowly and gently.

• Purchase a sprinkler that delivers the water slowly, avoiding wasteful runoff. Or, put down ³/₄ of an inch of water, wait an hour, and then repeat.

• Between 5 am and 10 am is the most efficient time to water. But water anytime your lawn retains footprints or grass blades curl inward. Where soil is thin—over rock outcroppings, for example—the grass dries out first and turns a bluish color, signaling that the lawn needs water.

• Watering systems deliver water at highly individual rates. To time how long it takes for your system to deliver 1¹/₂ inches of water, do this: With a waterproof marker, draw horizontal lines 1¹/₂ inches up from the bottom of the interior of five empty 1-pound coffee tins. Arrange the tins in a straight line out from the sprinkler to just inside its farthest reach. Turn it on, mark the time, and run the sprinkler half an hour. Check the water levels in the cans. Check at 15-minute intervals until the water reaches the 1¹/₂ inch marker lines. Compare the amounts of water in the cans. If some have less than others, overlap the areas the sprinkler reaches. Average the amounts and the time. Record the timing in your garden log. You think you'll remember but likely you won't.

AUGUST

LAWNS

PLANNING

When a high tide threatens a coastal lawn, flood it until the soil is so saturated it can't absorb much of the salt water.

PLANTING

August is considered a good month for repairing and over-seeding problem spots.

CARE

Grub damage becomes obvious during dry periods; apply grub controls.

MOWING

Mowing high is especially important during the hot dry months.

WATERING

Grass that is consistently and deeply watered has deep roots and will be just fine in spite of the heat and drought.

REPAIR AND RESTORATION: PATCHING

1. Level the sod and soil in the damaged area.
2. Cut away jagged pieces of sod.
3. Top with 3 to 4 inches of humus or topsoil. For each 10-by-10-foot area, add: Espoma Organic Lawn Food 5-3-5—5 to 10 pounds; Rock phosphate—5 to 10 pounds; Greensand—5 to 10 pounds; for clay soils—gypsum 5 to 10 pounds.
4. Mix this into the soil. For seeding or using a patching product, tamp it level with the lawn. For sod, tamp it down 1/2 to 3/4 inch below grade.
5. Sow seed, spread the patching product, or install sod, using, if possible, turfgrass matching the existing grass.
6. Fertilize the entire lawn lightly.
7. If you have seeded, cover it with straw so that only thirty to fifty percent of the soil is visible.
8. Water slowly and often to keep the soil moist until the seeds have (nearly) all germinated. When the grass is an inch high, reduce watering to every four or five days. After the first mowing, water deeply every seven days unless it rains.
9. Mow when the grass is 1/3-inch taller than its optimum height. For seeded lawn, avoid the riding mower until the soil is firm underfoot. For sodded lawn, use the riding mower after two or three weeks.

FERTILIZING

Chemical fertilizer. If you haven't applied your third fertilization yet, do it now.

PROBLEMS

Repeat controls for chinch bugs, rose chafer, and Japanese or Asiatic beetles. Apply pre-emergent controls for annual bluegrass. Treat again for sod webworms.

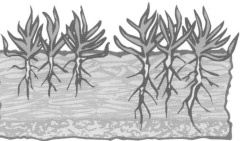

Compare the relationship between deep watering (illustration on the right) and the growth of roots.

September

LAWNS

PLANNING

Mid-fall is the best time to aerate because the grass isn't actively growing.

PLANTING

Labor Day is the beginning of the best season for repair, renovation, and starting a new lawn.

CARE

The best time to dethatch a cool-season grass is in early fall; dethatch **zoysia** in early spring.

MOWING

Keep the mower blades sharpened.

WATERING

Water if you have more than seven or eight days without rain, especially newly seeded or sodded areas.

REPAIR AND RESTORATION: RENOVATION

If thirty percent or less of the lawn is poor, patch. If seventy percent needs fixing, renovate. Mow the lawn as low as possible, then renovate by:

Option 1

If the soil isn't compacted, rent a slit seeder, which drops seed onto the soil after slicing it. Use half the seeds to plant in one direction, and then go over the area again in the other direction dropping the remaining seeds.

Option 2

• Cultivate compacted soil with a power rake to slice through thatch and into the soil so the seeds can touch the earth.

• Use a hollow tine core aerator to bring soil to the surface.

• Go over it again with the power rake to smooth out the cores and prepare for seeding.

• Distribute seed evenly with a mechanical spreader, preferably drop style. Make two passes at right angles to each other.

After the lawn has been seeded, follow steps 6 through 9, for Patching Your Lawn (see August).

FERTILIZING

Organic fertilizer. The second fertilization can be made this month or next.

Chemical fertilizer. If you have not yet made the fourth application, do it now.

PROBLEMS

For annual bluegrass, make the second application of a pre-emergent weed killer now, and repeat in October. For chickweed, bindweed, ground ivy, violets, sorrel, clover, and other broadleaf weeds, apply a post-emergent weed killer now.

Controls for sod webworm, rose chafer, and Asiatic or Japanese beetles must be applied in September. Repeat the spring treatments for chinch bugs this month and next.

Start or continue treatments for powdery mildew rust, fusarium blight, helminthosporum disease, red thread, and dollar spot.

STARTING A NEW LAWN: SEED OR SOD

September is the best month to sow seed for cool-season grasses; early spring is second. The best time to start **zoysia,** a warm-season grass, is in midsummer.

Seed

1. Spray the area with RoundUp to kill existing weed seeds. Wait seven to ten days, and then repeat.

2. Wait seven to ten more days, check the pH, adjust it if needed, and add the amendments and fertilizers described in the section on Repair and Renovation in August.

3. Rototill all this into the soil.

4. Sow the seed evenly using a mechanical spreader, preferably drop style. Make two passes, at right angles to each other using half the seed allotted on each pass.

5. Rake the seed into the top few inches of the soil.

6. Rent a lawn roller, and roll the seeded area.

7. Apply a straw mulch, thin enough so only thirty to fifty percent of the soil shows.

8. Water and mow. (See Repair and Restoration in August and September.)

9. Fertilize following the annual schedule given in this chapter.

Sod

1. Prepare the soil as for seeding; see steps 1, 2, 3.

2. Lay the sod in a staggered brick pattern so that the seam on one row of sod falls in the center of the previous row. Butt the edges firmly together, and, standing on a board laid over the previous row, tamp the seams firmly in place with the back of a rake.

3. Water enough to wet 4 to 6 inches of the underlying soil. For the next month, water deeply every four to five days unless you have rain.

4. Mow when the grass is a third taller than its optimum height. Use a hand mower (push mower) rather than a riding mower for the first season.

5. Fertilize following the annual schedule given in this chapter.

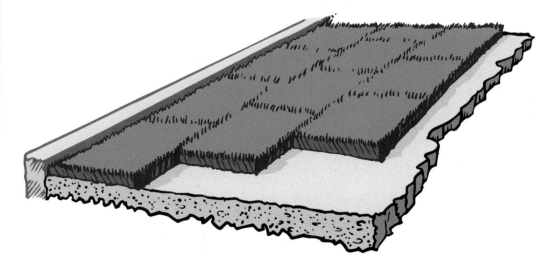

OCTOBER

LAWNS

 PLANNING

A healthy lawn is its own best defense against the weeds, pests, and diseases that cause deterioration. Use your experience with the lawn this year to plan a lawn care schedule that will build on current successes.

 PLANTING

The soil still has warmth, and the air is cooling, a happy time for cool-season grasses. You can still seed or sod, repair, overseed, or renovate early this month.

 CARE

The best time to dethatch a cool-season grass is in early fall; dethatch **zoysia** in early spring.

The best time to aerate is when the grass isn't growing, early spring or mid-fall. Now, while you are still expecting lots of fall rain, is a good time.

 MOWING

Grass growth is slowing. Mow only when the grass is a third taller than the cutting height we recommend for your type. Keep the mower blades sharpened.

LEAVES AND YOUR LAWN

Leaves are assets. Not one should leave your property. However, matted leaves rob the grass of the sunlight it needs as it continues to grow through fall. Grass grows when the soil is warm, and it will remain warm in our region at least through November, and in Zone 8, even later.

- As long as you can still see the grass blades through the fallen leaves, you can shred them with a mower, and leave them on the lawn to decompose into nutrients. To crumble, they must be mowed when dry.
- If or when the leaf layer is such that you can see just a little of the grass, mow, rake up the mess, spread it over annual beds and the kitchen garden, and dig it into the top 6 inches; that's next spring's supply of humus!
- When the leaf layer is about 4 inches deep, suck the leaves up in a blower-vacuum, and blow the residue over the surrounding lawn. Or, bag the ground leaves, and store them to use next spring as mulch.
- If the leaves get deeper than 4 inches, gather them into leaf bags, and put them on your compost pile. (See October, Trees.)

 WATERING

October should be wet, but if it isn't, water. For new lawns, follow the watering schedule recommended in September.

 FERTILIZING

Organic fertilizer. If you didn't make the second fertilization last month, do it now.

Chemical fertilizer. An optional fifth fertilization can be made this month to give the lawn a boost through winter.

PROBLEMS

To be effective, a September application of pre-emergent broadleaf weed killer to control annual bluegrass and/or broadleaf weeds must be repeated in October. That goes for controls for chickweed, bindweed, ground ivy, violets, sorrel, and clover plants.

Repeat the September treatment for chinch bugs this month.

For controls, turn back to the Pests and Diseases section in the introduction.

NOVEMBER

LAWNS

 PLANNING

If you are in snow country, lay in a supply of sand, non-clumping kitty litter, or environmentally friendly de-icing products that will enable you to have skid-proof paths and walks without harming the surrounding lawn.

 PLANTING

It's too late to seed or sod this year except in warm Zone 8; if the weather holds there, you can repair small areas.

 CARE

Seal herbicides, pesticides, and fungicides in their original containers. It is unwise to transfer them to unmarked containers, and in some states illegal. Store all three in a locked cupboard where they will be safe from the curiosity of children and pets.

Store granular formulations of all kinds, including fertilizers, in a cool, dry location to keep them in good condition for next year. Store liquid formulations away from direct sun and where temperatures do not go down to freezing. They may deteriorate.

 MOWING

The only thing left to mow should be small drifts of leaves; let the wind blow the chaff away. **Zoysia** lawns overseeded with **ryegrass** will need mowing all winter.

 WATERING

Water recently seeded or sodded areas if November is dry.

 FERTILIZING

Fertilizing is over for the year.

 PROBLEMS

Weeds, pests, and disease should be hibernating; you're on vacation now!

ABOUT TURFGRASSES

Turfgrasses are divided into two categories—cool-season grasses and warm-season grasses.

Cool-season grasses. Cool-season grasses are André's recommendation for our region. Even in warm Zone 8, **tall fescues** are better than **zoysia.** They peak in spring, go semi-dormant in summer, have a second peak season in mid- and late fall, and go semi-dormant for the winter. The best time to plant a cool-season grass is in early fall, around Labor Day. It thrives in fall's still-warm soil and cool moist weather. Early spring is the second best planting season. Seed will germinate as long as daytime temperatures are 68 to 95 degrees Fahrenheit.

Warm-season grasses. Warm-season grasses start up later in spring than the cool-season grasses, peak in summer, and go into winter dormancy sooner in fall than the cool-season grasses. A warm-season grass gets its best start planted in late summer. **Zoysia** is the warm-season grass used by some in Zone 8. It's a great grass for summer, drought tolerant, stands up to wear, and is good looking, but it goes dormant and turns golden below 63 degrees Fahrenheit. To keep it green, a green dye is used in winter, or it is overseeded with **annual rye** in late summer. Whether you use warm-season or cool-season grasses, read the label!! Beware of too-good-to-believe sales! Pay more but buy pure grass seed. Mixes including **annual rye grass** and chaff can lower not only the price but also the performance.

December

LAWNS

PLANNING

The giving time is near; draw up a lawn wish list.

PLANTING

Planting season is over. If you must repair a gash, use sod.

CARE

If you have a gas-powered lawn mower, run it until the tank is dry. Then, drain and replace the oil and clean the air filter. Next, oil the spark plugs and clean and store the engine. Finally, rinse the spreader and oil the wheels and put it away.

Shovel snow away before spreading de-icing products, and you will use less. Use snowmelt products safe for concrete and safe for grass and plants. Even better, use sand or non-clumping kitty litter.

MOWING

Zoysia lawns overseeded with **ryegrass** may need mowing all winter.

ABOUT LAWN MOWERS

A lawn that is more than a half-acre calls for a gas or electric powered mower. The blades have to be of good enough quality to hold an edge because dull blades harm the grass. Electric mowers are lighter and quiet, but suited only to smaller lawns; the farther you drag the cord, the lower the voltage, and the slower the mower. Battery powered electric mowers are heavier, but not limited by the length of the cord. Riding mowers make sense if the lawn is over an acre. If you have several acres to maintain, make it a tractor mower that can till, scoop snow, and pull large loads.

Reel mower. A reel mower cuts with a scissor-like action and does the best job when the blades are sharp, and set at the height right for the grass. Otherwise it tears and mashes the leaves and causes the tips to brown. This is a good choice for a lawn that is level and cut regularly. The cost and maintenance may be higher than a rotary mower.

Rotary mower. A flat circular blade rotating very quickly lops off the grass. The machine is easily maneuvered and does a fine job if the blades are sharpened regularly. If the blades aren't sharp, the lawn next day may look scorched or singed. Also, the whirling blades can be dangerous, so allow only adults wearing closed-toe shoes to operate it.

Mulching mower. A mower built for mulching has four blades rather than two, and recuts the grass as it moves, leaving behind very fine clippings that decompose and feed the lawn. It also grinds dry leaves finely in the fall. To work most efficiently, it must move slowly, and the turf must be dry.

WATERING

Hose season is over. Drain and store the hose before freezing weather.

FERTILIZING

Organic fertilizer. An optional third application can be made this month or next if you find your lawn can use extra help.

PROBLEMS

They're waiting for spring. Happy holidays!

PERENNIALS

To have a beautiful perennial garden, buy good stock, and put the right plant in the right place.

Some need light, some shade. A few do best in well-drained soil, but there are also bog lovers. Most perennials need slightly acid soil—some prefer slightly alkaline soil. Some take more cold than others. Information is widely available in mail-order catalogs and in books like our books on perennials and in our *Mid-Atlantic Gardener's Guide.*

The most beautiful perennial gardens include:

1. Flowers that bloom in each season—spring, summer, and early fall.

2. Foliage plants for color and for diversity.

3. A few small evergreens to anchor the composition and keep it green in winter.

4. Perennials with large distinctive leaves.

5. Tall, sculptural perennials, including ornamental grasses (see Chapter 9) and ferns that add structure to the composition.

6. Tropicals for accent.

To be everything you want it to be, choose perennials that:

1. Survive the extremes of winter and summer temperatures in your garden.

2. Will do well in the light your garden can give them.

3. Will peak when they will do the most for your garden design.

4. Will be resistant to pests and diseases.

COLD AND HEAT HARDINESS

A perennial's rating for cold and heat tolerance is the first consideration when you are making choices. Check it carefully; don't assume all varieties or cultivars of the same species have the same tolerance for cold and heat because tolerance differs.

Take peonies, for example. They are rated okay for Zones 3 to 8. They bloom early because they like it cool, and indeed must have a chilling period at below 40 degrees Fahrenheit in order to flower later. All varieties of peonies—early, mid-season, and late, and single and double forms—bloom fully in spring in our Zone 6 (and north). In Zone 7, the early and mid-season varieties bloom but fade quickly when the weather heats up. In Zone 8, only peony varieties advertised as early and mid-season are likely to have time to open fully before heat spoils them. Late peonies and the big semi-doubles and doubles often don't make it.

At the other extreme, heat tolerance is so meaningful for daylilies that they are grouped into categories for North and for South. There are many more rebloomers listed among daylilies and tall bearded irises for the South than for the North. Rebloomers usually flower a second time in late summer or fall, though some rebloom immediately after the initial flowering period, prolonging the display.

LIGHT

Most flowering perennials need full sun to flower completely unless they are described as plants for semi-shade or shade. In Zone 6, plants growing in full sun may be able to stand colder temperatures. In warm Zones 7 and 8, protection at noon—a trellis, the dappled shade of tall trees—may be needed.

Full sun means at least six hours of direct, full sun, especially the strong sun between 10 am and 4 pm.

Light or bright shade calls for four to six hours of direct—preferably morning—sun or bright dappled light all day.

Semi-shade can be two to three hours of direct—preferably morning—sun a day or bright dappled shade all day, such as the high shade of a tall tree.

A **southern exposure** provides the most light and in general is warmer, and that's good in Zone 6. A western exposure gets more afternoon sun than gardens facing east. That's not good in the warmer reaches of Zone 8 as the afternoon sun tends to be hotter. An eastern exposure gets the rising and noon sun, and that's best everywhere, especially in Zone 8. A northern exposure is cooler and doesn't dry out as quickly since it receives the least direct sunlight—not our first choice.

If you are in Zones 7 and 8, early morning sun is more beneficial than hot late afternoon sun for shade plants. In the Tidewater and the warmest spots in Zone 7, Washington, DC, for example, shade-tolerant varieties benefit from protection at noon. The shade provided by lathing, a tall hedge, or a vine arbor will keep a shade plant safe. The plants can stand more noon sun when they are growing in humusy moist soil, and when you maintain a 2- to 3-inch layer of mulch over the roots in summer.

CHAPTER FIVE

WHEN WILL IT BLOOM, COLOR, AND PEAK?

Most perennials come into bloom for the first time their second season and grow fuller each year thereafter until they reach a point where they need dividing (see the section on Dividing in this introduction).

A few perennials will bloom the first year from seed you sow directly in the garden, but most start to flower only the second year. To ensure a nice show of flowers the first season, buy a big container-grown root division or second-year seedling. Generally speaking, the larger the crown (and container and price) the fuller the floral display will be that year. If the perennial that you are interested in blooms in early or mid-spring—columbine, for example—you'll get more flowers the first spring if you set out a container-grown specimen in early fall than if you plant it in early spring.

Some catalogs ship perennials in spring "bare root," with planting instructions—astilbes, for instance. In our experience, these often flower fully only in the second season.

But when you need lots of a particular perennial—catmint for edging a big bed, for example—seeds are the way to go. But while annuals usually germinate within twenty days, most perennial seeds need more time. You can start seeds in flats indoors or in a cold frame. Perennials can also be started from seed sown in the garden, either in spring two weeks after the last frost date, or in summer up to two months before the first frost date. When fall sowing is recommended on a seed packet, it means those seeds will benefit from a chilling period. They can be sown in October and November and will germinate in the spring. The process, called "stratification," is described under Planting in the November pages of this chapter.

PLANTING

Soil for Perennials. The "good garden loam" perennials thrive in is more often created than inherited. Humus, the spongy remains of decomposed leaves, peat moss, and other organics, holds moisture and nutrients. Humus is the great modifier of both sandy and clay soils, but it's not a permanent fixture. As plants grow, they deplete the organic content of the soil, and it loses its capacity to hold moisture and nutrients.

The solution to assorted soil problems, including poor drainage, is to grow perennials in raised beds and in soil that has been improved and enriched with organic additives as recommended in the Introduction to this book. You will find information about adjusting soil pH, additives for soil, and creating raised beds under Soil Preparation and Improvement.

In addition to starting with the right soil, it is essential to follow a yearly and continuing fertilization and maintenance program for the soil.

Planting Procedures and Techniques. Whether you are planting in the soft soil of a new raised bed, or preparing a planting hole in an established perennial border, make the hole three times the diameter of the rootball, and twice as deep.

If you are preparing a planting hole in an established bed, test and amend the soil pH as described in the Introduction's information for preparing a raised bed, and then mix in 3 to 4 inches of humus, enough so that a quarter of the soil is organic matter. Mix in a slow-release organic fertilizer, half fill the hole with the amended soil, and tamp it down firmly.

When working with container-grown perennials, loosen the roots encircling the rootball. If you can't untangle them, make four shallow vertical slashes in the root mass and slice off the bottom half inch. Dip the rootball in a bucket containing starter solution. Half fill the hole with improved soil. Set the plant a little high in the hole. Fill the hole with improved soil, and tamp firmly. Water slowly and deeply, and then apply a 2- to 3-inch layer of mulch starting 3 inches from the crown.

The spacing for perennials depends on what size the mature plant will be. Front of the border plants under a foot tall need 12 to 18 inches all around. Intermediate sizes 1 to 1$^1/_2$ feet tall—which is most perennials—need 18 to 24 inches between plants. Larger plants need be set about 3 feet apart. Hostas and daylilies need 24 to 30 inches. Peonies need 3 to 4 feet. Cool climate gardeners find that close planting shades out weeds. Where warm, muggy summers encourage diseases, it's better to space each plant so it has plenty of air all around.

FERTILIZING AND FERTILIZERS

Fertilizing. To sustain growth and satisfying blooms, your perennials need a continuous supply of nutrients. The fertilization schedule for established beds begins in late winter or early spring. After that how often you fertilize depends on the type of fertilizer you are using.

But before that first annual fertilization, check the pH of the soil. Soil-testing kits are generally available in gardening stores as are the products you need to adjust the pH. To raise the pH of soils whose pH is too low, we mix in 5 to 10 pounds of limestone per 100 square feet of garden bed. To lower pH that is too high, we apply elemental fertilizer sulfur (water-soluble garden sulfur) at the rate of 5 to 10 pounds per 100 square feet. Other acidifiers are aluminum sulfate and iron sulfate; they act faster but do not last as long in the soil.

The growing season slows in Zones 6 and 7 early September to early October. In Zone 8, Richmond and the Tidewater areas of Virginia, the last fertilization can be between the end of September and mid-October.

Fertilizers. If you are using organic fertilizers such as Plant-tone, you will need to fertilize the first time about four to six weeks before growth is due to begin in spring, and then again toward the end of the growing season.

If you are using time- or controlled-release chemical fertilizers then you will need to fertilize just before the plants start to grow and to repeat according to the formulation inscribed on the fertilizer container. If you use a nine-month formula, that should carry you through the whole growing season.

If you are using only chemical fertilizers, such as 5-10-5, which are quickly available to the plants, then you will need to fertilize just before growth begins in spring, and repeat every six weeks from then until the end of the growing season.

PRUNING, SHEARING, AND DEADHEADING

You can improve the performance, and the health of some perennials, by selective pruning, shearing, and deadheading. Our suggestions on when to do it and which plants to do it to appear in the month-by-month pages that follow.

Pruning or shearing some perennials early in their growth cycles keeps the plants compact and encourages later and more, though usually smaller, blooms.

Removing fading and dead blooms—deadheading—from branching perennials stops the development of seeds, and stimulates the production of flowers. Starting in June, André goes through his six acres of gardens with hand-held

head shears and deadheads spent flowers. It takes him about an hour to do the whole garden. There usually is not a lot to deadhead at any one time.

Shearing is the way to deadhead plants with very small flowers—creeping phlox, miniature pinks, and baby's breath, for example.

WATERING AND MULCHING

Watering. Sustained soil moisture makes the nutrients in the soil available as well as water, and is essential to the growth and health of all the herbaceous perennials. Your zone and the condition of your soil will determine how often you need to water. Common sense—and the soil—will tell you that sandy soils need more frequent watering than clay soils. However, if you let clay soil bake dry, it will take forever to get it moist again. The soil in windy situations dries out more quickly.

André's rule of thumb for newly planted perennials is to put down 1 1/2 inches of water right after planting. Established flower beds need 1 1/2 inches of gentle rain every ten days to two weeks; if the sky fails, run your sprinkler or irrigation system long enough to lay down 1 1/2 inches of water. Set an empty 1-pound coffee tin under your sprinkler, and record how long it takes to accumulate 1 1/2 inches of water so you'll know for the future.

Winter moisture leaves the earth in March in Zones 6 and 7, earlier in the Tidewater. From late winter on there's usually enough rain to keep gardens growing through June. Summer storms drench our gardens in July, but the unrelenting summer heat in Zones 7 and 8 often causes perennials to wilt at midday, and some stop growing. Though that doesn't necessarily mean they are out of water, André recommends overhead watering anytime your perennials are

wilting. Late July and August is drought season in the Mid-Atlantic, and you will probably need to water two or three times before the fall rains arrive in September.

Even in the muggiest Mid-Atlantic regions, overhead watering is fine as long as you water deeply. However, there's less waste when you water before the sun reaches the garden in the early morning, and in late afternoon or early evening. Most commercial nursery owners, general gardeners, and farmers use overhead watering systems. During very hot, dry periods, watering during the day is a good idea because it lowers leaf temperatures and reduces transpiration and stress on the plants. Evening watering is fine, contrary to popular opinion; dew naturally wets foliage every clear night anyway.

André does not recommend electrically timed mechanical watering systems that ignore the weather and water too often and shallowly. However, they can do a good job if they are set up with the correct low-gallon nozzles, and timed to run long enough to water and gently and deeply every week or ten days.

One of the most important preparations for winter is a deep and thorough watering before the soil freezes; if the sky doesn't provide the rain, you will have to.

Mulching. André recommends keeping a 2- to 3-inch layer of mulch around perennials. A mulch deeper than 3 inches can bury the crown and kill some perennials. (See Mulching in the Introduction to this book.) Start the mulch a few inches from the crown, and spread it out over an area wider than the plant's diameter. That is enough to minimize the loss of soil moisture—saving water and the time applying it—and to moderate soil temperatures.

BASICS FOR A PERENNIAL BORDER

Here are fourteen easy-care summer-blooming perennials whose performance you can count on:

Front of the border

1. Catmint, *Nepeta* x *faassenii* 'Blue Wonder', for its mint-scented foliage and repeating blue blooms.

2. Cheddar pinks and other low-growing *Dianthus* species and hybrids, for their sweet, clove-scented mini carnations and grassy foliage.

3. Small and sprawling *Campanula* species and hybrids in blue-lavender or white.

Backed by

4. *Astilbe chinensis* 'Sprite', which is just 12 inches tall and has soft pink flower heads and ferny foliage.

5. Deep gold black-eyed Susan *Rudbeckia fulgida* var. *sullivanti* 'Goldsturm'.

6. Semi-evergreen *Sedum spectabile* 'Autumn Joy' for its succulent foliage and flower heads that change from early jade green to pink to rose to late rosy-rust.

Middle of the border

7. Silky flower heads of the many types and colors of phlox, but especially *Phlox paniculata* 'David' with its scented white flowers and mildew-resistant foliage.

8. Yarrow, *Achillea millifolium*, for its ferny, pungent odor, foliage, and lasting flower heads in lovely subtle shades.

9. Dwarf daylilies, especially *Hemerocallis* 'Stella de Oro' hybrids, for their multiple blooms and cascading foliage.

10. Shrub-like *Salvia* x *sylvestris* 'May Night' for its deep blue spikes; the rosy pink variation is 'Rose Wine'.

Back of the border

11. Tall mid-border spikes of the lovely pink hollyhock mallow, *Malva alcea* var. *fastigiata*, and white *M. moschata* 'Alba'.

12. Globe thistle *Echinops ritro* 'Taplow Blue', for its beautiful, deeply cut foliage and perfectly round, steel-blue spiky flower heads.

13. Tall, substantial daylilies, *Hemerocallis* hybrids, for their magnificent trumpet-shaped flowers and cascading foliage.

14. Six-foot *Rudbeckia* 'Autumn Sun' ('Herbstonne') for its showy, sunny yellow flower heads with swept back petals.

We replenish mulch after the late winter/early spring fertilization; again before the high heat of summer; and a third time in fall to slow the freezing of the ground, and to keep moisture around the roots that continue to grow until the ground grows cold.

The need for a winter mulch depends on the severity of your climate, the hardiness of the plants, and on the exposure of the beds. In Zone 6, the main purpose of winter mulch is to keep the perennials from heaving out of the ground as the ground freezes and thaws in winter and early spring. In Zones 7 and 8, a winter mulch can save perennials that are borderline hardy during especially severe winters. Apply a winter mulch only after the ground has frozen hard, and remove it when you first spot signs of active growth in the plants.

As a winter mulch, we recommend airy organics such as straw or pine boughs. Tent the plants so thinly you can still see some of the plant and the soil through the mulch. For coastal dwellers, marsh hay and salt hay from the shore are excellent winter mulches as they are weed free, and they can be saved, covered, in a pile from year to year.

CHAPTER FIVE

For year-round use we recommend organic mulches such as shredded bark and pine needles (which can be piled a little deeper) because they add humus and nutrients to the soil as they decompose.

WINTER CARE

When summer is over, we like to leave in place healthy seed-bearing perennials with woody upright structures, like black-eyed Susans. They're interesting in the winter, and they provide seeds for the birds. Some self-sow and will refurnish your bed.

In the late fall, clear away dead foliage; cut it off, rather than pull it off because that may damage the crown beneath. Look before you leap; be careful not to damage burgeoning stems.

To repeat a recommendation given above, it is most important that perennials facing winter receive a deep and thorough watering before the soil freezes.

DIVIDING PERENNIALS

You can help your perennials to stay healthy and productive by dividing and replanting them every few years. Division forces the crowns to grow new roots, and replanting provides an opportunity for you to refurbish the soil.

A plant signals when it's time to divide by producing fewer and smaller blooms, and by growing crowded and leggy. In our long growing season, many perennials benefit from division every four to five years.

You can divide in early spring before growth begins, but the best time of year for most perennials is toward the end of the growing season—late summer, and early fall. The soil is still warm enough then to keep existing roots growing while new roots are developing. Once the ground gets cold in late fall, planting divisions—especially of irises and daylilies—makes them susceptible to heaving.

For the method that is easiest on the gardener, try this: with a shovel, chop through the center of the crown and dig up one half. Amend and fertilize the soil around the section that is to remain where it is; it will grow on in lively fashion. Divide and replant the other section in improved soil. We recommend this method for peonies and other perennials slow to recover from being moved. This method allows for reproduction without interrupting the blooming cycle of the garden.

PESTS AND DISEASES

See Pests, Diseases, and Controls in the Appendix for complete information.

JANUARY
PERENNIALS

 PLANNING

If you haven't yet grown **daylilies,** make a New Year's resolution to explore their potential this year. One of André's favorites, **daylilies** bloom July through August in the gardens surrounding the Viette home in the Shenandoah Valley, and thousands more flower in the trial fields below the Viette nursery. Large-flowered **daylilies** typically open one to three blossoms per stem every day; the miniatures open three to seven blossoms per stem every day. **Daylilies** thrive in clay, loam, or sandy soils, and tolerate heat, wind, cold, and seashore conditions.

Here's how to grow **daylilies**:

• **Planting season:** The best planting time is spring. Soak tuberous roots for two to six hours before planting; plant container-grown **daylilies** anytime, but early spring is best.

• **Light: Daylilies** bloom most fully in full sun but do well in bright shade. In Zone 8, afternoon shade is beneficial.

• **Planting:** Prepare beds or planting holes in improved soil (see Soil Preparation and Improvement in the Introduction to the book). For fertilizer, use Plant-tone.

• **Bare root:** Fan the roots out in the planting hole, and set the crown so it is about 1 inch below the soil surface.

• **Container grown:** Set the crown so it is about an inch above the surface of the surrounding soil.

• **Spacing**: 24 inches apart for minis, 36 inches apart for large **daylilies**.

• **Watering:** Water gently and thoroughly after planting. The first season, water weekly unless it rains. Water established **daylilies** when needed.

• **Mulch:** Spread pine needles, pine bark, or hardwood bark 2 to 3 inches deep starting 3 inches from the crown.

• **Fertilizing:** Fertilize in early spring and in fall as recommended under Fertilizing and Fertilizers in the introduction to this chapter.

 PLANTING

Start seeds of fast-sprouting perennials indoors. It's a two-part project. First you sow the seeds and encourage them to germinate; then you transplant the seedlings and grow them into sturdy plants ready for their date with the garden. (See Starting Seeds Indoors under Annuals, January, Planting.) Seed packets tell you whether the seeds can be started early indoors, and when.

Outdoors. This month or in early February sow seeds outdoors of perennials that need to be stratified (chilled) in order to germinate. The November pages explain stratification.

 CARE

If you are without snow cover, make the rounds of your perennial beds to see if there are crowns that have been heaved. If yes, gently heel them in, and cover them with a winter mulch of evergreen boughs to keep the ground cold until winter ends. If there has been heaving, cover the crowns of **mums, veronica,** and other perennials whose basal foliage is showing.

Use only snowmelt products that don't harm plants, turf, or concrete.

 GROOMING

Prune back ornamental grasses that are looking weather-beaten. Use shears to cut the low-growing grasses and new plantings of the big grasses back to within a few inches of the crown. When a big grass begins to mature, simplify the annual haircut by roping the leaves together with sisal twine. Tie them all the way to the top so that they end up looking like a telephone pole. Then saw the top off a few inches above the crown. If you use a chain saw (as you must when a big grass reaches full size), take care not to catch the twine in the teeth!

WATERING

Indoors. Water often enough to sustain moisture in big containers of tropical (cold tender) perennials stored indoors for the winter.

Outdoors. Water the soil of containers of hardy perennials wintering outdoors if there's neither snow nor rain. Add just enough to keep the soil from drying out.

FERTILIZING

No fertilizing this month.

PROBLEMS

Damping off is a threat to seedlings started indoors, (described under Annuals, January, Problems).

SOIL AND WATER FOR CONTAINERS

André's recipe for soil for perennials to be grown in containers is:

2/8 good garden soil or bagged top soil
3/8 commercial soilless mix
2/8 compost
1/8 PermaTill or perlite

Add a modest application of Osmocote® slow-release fertilizer. To reduce watering chores, mix in a water-holding polymer, Soil Moist, for example. Line the bottom of the container with gravel or a piece of landscape fabric to keep the soil in.

Throughout July and August, check the soil moisture daily in small pots and baskets. On hot windy summer days, check the soil moisture in big containers every few days. When you water containers, pour it on until you see water dripping from the bottom.

You can minimize watering chores by planting in containers equipped with built-in water reservoirs or water rings that let the plant soak up the water from the bottom.

Frequent watering soon leaches the nutrients from the soil of small containers. To compensate, include a half dose of a water-soluble fertilizer every second time you water during the growing season.

NATURALIZE AND PERENNIALIZE

The two words are not synonymous. "Naturalize" applies to a garden plant that becomes a wildflower of the region. **Annual phlox** has naturalized on the Outer Banks of North Carolina and is considered a wildflower of the region. It is not, however, a native wildflower of the region. It has "naturalized."

Since there is no rule without exception, we confess the term "naturalize" is used by the industry about bulbs that "perennialize"—those that come back for four years or more. However, the term "perennialize" is correctly applied to plants that come back year after year but do not go wild.

It's a fungal disease that attacks the seedlings at the base of their stems. It rots the stems so the plants fall over. A sterile growing medium and good drainage help avoid the condition. The fungicide Thiram (Arasan) is a good preventative against damping off.

FEBRUARY

PERENNIALS

 PLANNING

While the cold keeps you housebound, look through your garden catalogs for summer-flowering bulbs, tender tropicals, aromatic herbs, dwarf evergreens, and flowering trees that can add to your pleasure in your gardens. Study your garden through the windows, and decide what to order now. It's time.

 PLANTING

Indoors. When seedlings started indoors become crowded, transplant each to an individual 3- to 4-inch pot filled with a sterile commercial potting mix. Give seedlings that will be growing indoors six weeks the best light available. An installation of grow lights burned fourteen to sixteen hours a day is helpful.

Outdoors. Early this month sow seeds outdoors of perennials that need to be stratified—chilled—in order to germinate. The November pages explain stratification.

The planting depth for seeds is usually given on the seed packet. The rule of thumb is to sow seeds at a depth about three times the seed's diameter, not its length.

The easy way to sow fine seeds evenly is to "broadcast" them, that is, sprinkle them over the bed. Cover them lightly with finely milled sphagnum moss or vermiculite. When the seedlings are up, thin them to the distance suggested by seed packets, or so that they are at least 3 to 5 inches apart.

Larger seeds are sown in "hills," groups of four to six, or three to five, equidistant from each other. Flowers for edging paths or the fronts of flower beds are usually sown in "drills," dribbled at spaced intervals along a shallow furrow. The easy way to make a furrow is to drag the edge of a rake or a hoe handle along the planting line.

 CARE

Early this month, replenish winter mulch of perennials that may have been heaved during freeze and thaw cycles. Protect perennials that retain green foliage during winter with evergreen boughs—for example, **garden mums, candytuft, Oriental poppies,** and **basket-of-gold.**

Start cleaning up the perennial beds; discard the debris, don't compost it, in case it harbors diseases and pests.

After the late winter fertilization described below, add enough fresh mulch to maintain a 2- to 3-inch layer. This organic blanket will stabilize soil temperature.

Check stored **dahlias,** and discard tubers showing mold or rot.

Use only snowmelt products that don't harm plants, turf, orconcrete.

Unless the winter is exceptionally warm, it is still too early to plant dormant bare-root perennials you may receive from eager beaver mail-order sources. Keep the plants in their packaging in a dark, cool, but frost-free place. You can plant in early March in Zone 8 and the Tidewater, mid-March in Richmond and Zone 7, and the end of March in Zone 6.

 GROOMING

Cut off battered **hellebore** foliage to make space for new growth and flowering. Be careful not to cut off new growth, which may already be showing.

Cut back the **ornamental grasses** before growth begins. When a big grass begins to mature, simplify the annual haircut by using sisal twine to rope the leaves together all the way to the top so that it ends up looking like a telephone pole. Then saw the top off a few inches above the crown. You can use a chain saw if you take care not to catch the twine in the teeth!

WATERING

Water transplanted seedlings started indoors when the soil is dry to the touch.

Maintain the soil moisture in containers of tropical perennials stored indoors. Water hardy perennials in containers wintering outdoors if you lack snow and rain.

FERTILIZING

Indoors. Do not fertilize transplanted seedlings until the appearance of two or three new leaves tells you the root system is growing again.

Every two weeks fertilize all the seedlings that will remain indoors another six weeks or more with a soluble houseplant fertilizer at half strength.

Outdoors. After your perennial beds have been cleaned up, prepare the soil for the season ahead:

• Check and adjust the soil pH.

• Apply Rich Earth humate.

LOVE LANGUAGE OF THE FLOWERS

For the Victorians, floral valentines spoke volumes because each flower has meaning in the "Language of the Flowers." The language was invented by Persian courtiers, and its influence is present whenever a lover sends roses to a sweetheart.

- **Anemone**—abandoned
- **Bachelor's Button**—single and blessed
- **Bluebell**—faithfulness
- **Blue salvia**—thinking of you
- **Carnation** white—love
- **Carnation** red—alas for my poor heart
- **Forget-me-not**—love that is true
- **Hyacinth** white—beauty
- **Jonquil**—desiring a return of affection
- **Lily-of-the-valley**—happiness returns
- **Pansy**—my thoughts are with you
- **Peach blossom**—I am captive
- **Pink single**—love that is pure
- **Rose**—love
- **Rose** yellow—jealousy
- **Tulip**—love

• If you are using organic fertilizers, apply them four to six weeks before growth begins.

• If you are using chemical fertilizers, apply them just before growth begins.

• If you are using time-release fertilizers, wait just before growth begins apply an eight-month formulation.

Container gardens of hardy perennials. Top dress the soil by scratching in an inch or two of humus and fresh potting soil that includes a nine-month formulation of a slow-release fertilizer.

PROBLEMS

Indoors. Seedlings started indoors that are crowded, or lack good drainage and air, may show symptoms of damping off, which rots stems near the soil surface. Discard affected plants, reduce watering, and increase light and fresh air. If the problem persists, mist the seedlings with a fungicide, such as Thiram (Arasan.)

Outdoors. When the **forsythias** come into bloom, apply a pre-emergent weed killer to the beds of perennials.

MARCH
PERENNIALS

PLANNING

Take advantage of sales this month of fertilizers and other soil additives. But be cautious—these may be leftovers. If the price is a steal, make sure the bag is unbroken. Moisture that gets into bags of cocoa hulls encourages mildew.

The first of the plants you've ordered will arrive soon; go to the garden and reserve the space meant for them. Take along a set of row markers on which you have written the names of the plants you will be setting out. Outline planting bays reserved for annuals, and plant row markers indicating the flowers you plant to put there.

Clean the birdhouses. Put out new ones. If mosquitoes are a problem, consider installing houses for purple martins and also for bats.

PLANTING

In Zone 8, gardeners can start **dahlia** tubers right in the garden anytime in mid-spring. They can survive winters in the ground if they are heavily mulched.

In Zones 6 and 7 we start **dahlias** indoors in March or April, set them out in the garden in May or June, and lift and store them indoors in September or October.

Dahlia tubers sold in spring are ready to plant. The tubers of **dahlias** lifted from the garden last fall and wintered indoors must be separated from the stem before planting. With each tuber be sure to include a portion of the stem that has an attached growth bud. For information on starting **dahlia** tubers indoors, see March in the chapter on bulbs.

Store dormant bare-root perennials received from too-eager mail-order suppliers in their packaging in a dark, cool, but frost-free place until time to plant; that is early in March for Zone 8 and the Tidewater, mid-March for Richmond and Zone 7, and the end of March for Zone 6 gardeners.

CARE

As new growth appears in your perennial borders, finish clearing away dead plant material and complete the fertilization of the beds. See Fertilizing in the February pages of this chapter.

GROOMING

Indoors. Pinch out the growing tips of seedlings that are becoming leggy.

Outdoors. Hellebores in a woodsy setting will multiply if you let them go to seed.

Cut back **Russian sage** leaving just 6 to 12 inches of woody stem. Pinch out the tips of the new growth when it emerges to encourage bushier growth.

WATERING

Indoors. Continue watering seedlings planted indoors in January. Water the soil in containers of tropical perennials wintering indoors. Add just enough to keep the soil from drying out.

Outdoors. If there's not much rain, water hardy perennials wintering in containers outdoors.

FERTILIZING

When to fertilize depends on the type of fertilizer you are using. The section on Understanding Fertilizers in the Introduction to the book explains how and when to use the various categories of fertilizer.

If you did not fertilize the garden last month, do it now. See Fertilizing in the February pages. Be sure to fertilize the soil of containers of tender and hardy perennials by scratching in an inch or two of humus and fresh potting soil that includes a

ABOUT ASTILBES

Astilbes are among the loveliest—and most useful—of all shade-loving perennials. In late spring and early summer the plants raise graceful plumes in mostly pastel shades. The deeply cut fernlike foliage is green or bronze, attractive both before and after flowering.

Astilbes are excellent fillers for the middle or back of the border and perfect for edging a woodland path, a stream, or a pond. You can achieve a lasting show by planting early, mid-season, and late bloomers. For instance: plant the white early-blooming favorite 'Deutschland', red 'Fanal', and pink 'Europa' with mid-season 'Ostrich Plume' ('Straussenfedder'), and late bloomers such as the **lilac** 'Superba' and little 'Pumila'.

'Pumila', a variety of *A. chinensis,* spreads by underground runners. The others spread by clump enlargement, and in time make large, dense mats. Catalogs ship bare-root **astilbe** crowns in early spring. Follow their planting instructions, and be patient. For a quick show, set out container-grown **astilbes** from early spring to late summer. **Astilbe** grows best in light shade in well-drained, rich, moist humusy soil. Summer drought and winter wetness are their worst enemies. Except for voles, which love them. For vole controls, see April in this chapter.

Astilbe

nine-month formulation of a slow-release fertilizer.

Most **ornamental grasses** need annual fertilization. The time for it is when signs of new growth appear. Apply a slow-release organic fertilizer such as Holly-tone Espoma Organic lawn food.

PROBLEMS

If your **peonies** were affected by botrytis last year—ugly blackened patches on the stems and foliage—spray emerging **peony** tips with Mancozeb or Manzate, fungicides.

Slugs and snails have not surfaced yet, but if winter has been warm and moist, they may be preparing an unwelcome appearance. Diatomaceous earth, a natural control, works in dry soil but isn't effective on moist soil. Instead, do them in with iron phosphate (Sluggo), slug and snail bait, and traps. You can make your own slug trap by pouring a little beer in shallow aluminum plates or empty tuna fish cans.

Deer sometimes graze the tender young leaves of **daylilies.** If you've run into this in the past, spray the foliage as it emerges with Deer-Off or some other evil-smelling liquid to keep them away while the plants grow up. If that has failed other years, lay chicken wire loosely over the tops. You can remove it when the tender leaves begin to grow up and get tough.

APRIL
PERENNIALS

PLANNING

Use your garden log to record dates your perennials bloomed to help plan your garden next year.

PLANTING

Indoors. Transplant seedlings started indoors that are outgrowing their containers to larger pots.

Outdoors. Plant as soon as possible your mail-order deliveries of bare-root and container perennials. Here's how:

1. Remove the wrapping, and clear away the moist packing materials. Soak the roots as directed by the supplier.

2. Dig a roomy planting hole large enough to accommodate

the roots spread out to their fullest extent.

3. Improve the soil from the hole with the amendments recommended in the introduction to the book under Soil Preparation and Improvement.

4. Build a firm cone of soil in the center of the hole. Make it high enough to place the crown of the plant a half inch or so higher than the level of the surrounding ground.

5. Center the roots over the cone, and spread them out into the hole.

6. Half fill the hole with improved soil, and tamp it down. Fill the rest of the way, and tamp that down.

7. Create a saucer-shaped depression around the crown.

8. Water the planting slowly, gently, and thoroughly.

9. Apply mulch 2 to 3 inches deep starting 2 to 3 inches or so from the crown of the plant.

CARE

You can divide four- to six-year old perennials that are losing productivity before spring growth begins. Fast-growing perennials, such as **asters,** *Eupatorium, Helianthus, Heliopsis,* and *Monarda,* are likely candidates. For how-to information, turn back to the

As soon as mail-order plants arrive, unpack them, remove the packaging, and soak the roots in water.

section titled Dividing in the introduction to this chapter.

In late April, lift and divide the roots of last year's **garden mums.** Discard the old centers, and plant the young roots in new places. You'll get a better show than you will if you leave them in same place for years on end.

When temperatures reach 60 degrees Fahrenheit, move containers of tropical perennials outdoors for the summer. Move containers of hardy perennials wintering in protected spots to their summer locations.

GROOMING

Indoors. Pinch out the tips of any leggy seedlings that are growing indoors.

Outdoors. Experiment with pinching back branching perennials by half an inch or so to encourage shorter, bushier growth, and more (though smaller) flowers. Perennials that benefit from this include **pink turtlehead,** *Veronica spicata,* and 'Autumn Joy' **sedum.**

Remove old, tired-looking stems from the **hellebores,** but allow the flowers to remain as the seeds will drop to the ground and germinate; in May, look for seedlings at the base of the plants, and transplant them to a humusy semi-shaded site.

WATERING

Outdoors. Seeds and seedlings in the garden, and perennials in containers, need rain often enough to maintain soil moisture. If spring runs dry, or if you see signs of wilting, water deeply.

FERTILIZING

If you are using only chemical fertilizers that are quickly available, such as 5-10-5, then you will need to fertilize garden and container plants every six weeks from beginning to end of the growing season.

PROBLEMS

Hoe and rake weeds away now, particularly around perennials towards the back of the border where they won't be as easy to spot when the garden fills out. Weed **lily-of-the-valley** beds when the flowers are in full bloom—that way you get to breathe in their exquisite perfume.

Watch out for aphids on the growing tips of **mums, coreopsis, sedum,** and **verbena.** Blow them off with a strong spray from the garden hose. Or remove the infested tips, and discard them.

ABOUT MOLES AND VOLES

You think "moles" when you see tunnels heaving the lawn, and blame them when perennials disappear and bulbs move around. But they are innocent. Moles eat bugs, grubs, and worms only. The culprits are voles, *Nicrotus* species. Often called pine or meadow mice, these small rodents are reddish-brown to gray, 2 to 4 inches long, and have short tails, blunt faces, and tiny eyes and ears. They live in extensive tunnel systems usually less than a foot deep with entrances an inch or two across.

Protecting the plant is easier than getting rid of voles. They dislike tunneling through coarse material. André keeps them away by planting with VoleBloc or PermaTill, which are bits of non-toxic, light, long-lasting aggregates like pea gravel with jagged edges. The stuff promotes rooting.

Established plantings: Dig a 4-inch wide, 12-inch deep moat around the drip line of perennials under attack, and fill it with VoleBloc, and mulch with VoleBloc.

New plantings: Prepare a planting hole 2 inches deeper than the rootball(s), and layer in 2 inches of VoleBloc. Set the rootball in place, and backfill with VoleBloc. Mulch with more VoleBloc.

If vole damage appears in winter:
- Bait the main area around the plants with a rodenticide.
- Pull the mulch apart, spray the crown lightly with a repellent, and put the mulch back in place.

The ants that crawl over **peony** buds are harmless; let them be.

When **hostas** break ground, watch out for slugs and snails (see Problems, March). If traces of leafminers appear on **columbine** foliage, remove and discard the leaves. If the condition persists, when the plants finish blooming, cut the foliage to the ground. It will regrow free of miners and be beautiful all summer. If leafminers are a continuing problem, replace your plants with *Aquilegia canadensis,* which is more resistant.

Blackened patches on **peonies** is Botrytis, a fungal disease. Immediately remove and destroy every affected part of the plant, and apply Mancozeb or Manzate, a fungicide. Make a note in your garden log for next March to spray **peony** tips when they first appear.

MAY
PERENNIALS

PLANNING

In our long growing season, many perennials benefit from division every four to five years. The signal it's time to divide is fewer and smaller blooms, a crown that is crowded, and stems that are leggy.

You can divide perennials that need help anytime before growth begins in the spring. But for most, the best time of year for dividing is toward the end of the growing season, late summer and early fall. Keep an eye on the productivity of the older perennials in your garden, and plan to divide those that need it this fall.

PLANTING

Try to get all your new perennials into the ground before the heat starts. For how-to information, turn to the section on Planting Procedures in the Introduction.

Replace perennials that aren't performing with big container-grown plants that will bloom this year.

Set tropicals growing in containers outdoors now, and transplant **dahlias** started indoors to the garden.

Move seedlings of perennials started indoors out to a sheltered corner to harden them off in preparation for planting them in the open garden.

As the spring-flowering bulbs in your perennial borders go out of bloom, replant the area with big seedlings of colorful annuals and aromatic herbs.

CARE

Prepare sturdy stakes tall enough to support the upper third of your taller tall plants, **delphiniums,** for example, and the big **dahlias,** that will grow to end up between 18 inches and 4 feet. Insert the stakes deep into the soil 2 inches away from the crowns. Firm the plants in their holes, and water them. When the stems are 12 inches tall, tie the main stems to stakes. Tie on other branches as the plant grows up.

GROOMING

Thin the seedlings of perennials sown out in the garden.

As the new growth of **cheddar pinks** and **creeping phlox** reaches a height of 4 to 6 inches, shear it back by an inch or so to encourage bushiness.

This doesn't work to **evergreen candytuft;** shear the plant immediately after blooming to encourage bushiness.

When the new shoots of **common phlox** are 8 to 10 inches high, remove all but four or five stems; this will result in bigger and better flowers, and, more important, will keep air circulating through the stems and help prevent powdery mildew.

WATERING

This month begin biweekly checks of the moisture in large plant containers; check the moisture level in small pots and hanging baskets every day or two.

Maintain the moisture in newly planted seeds and seedlings. Unchecked growth is essential to the development of root systems so they'll be strong enough to bloom and withstand summer heat. If you do not have a good soaking rain every week to ten days, water planted beds gently and slowly long enough to lay down 1 or 2 inches.

Water seedlings that show signs of wilting.

FERTILIZING

If you are using only chemical fertilizers, such as 5-10-5, which are quickly available to the plants, then you will need to fertilize garden and container plants every six weeks from beginning to end of the growing season.

PROBLEMS

Weeds are flourishing; scuffle and rake or hoe them away, every last one. Get those in the middle and back of the border before they disappear begin a screen of foliage.

Use the hose to blow away aphids, and to deter spider mites and whiteflies, which are especially fond of **coneflowers, daylilies, mums,** and **phlox.**

Early spraying with fungicidal formulations of copper will help to save susceptible perennials from blackspot, powdery mildew, rusts, and bacterial diseases such as bacterial leaf spots and wilt.

Scribbled tracings on **columbine** foliage is a sign of leafminer; when the flowers have finished blooming, cut the foliage to the ground. It will regrow healthy and make a lovely green filler all summer.

If the weather has been rainy, check your **hostas** and other shaded plantings for chewed leaf edges and shiny mucous trails—signs of slugs and snails. March describes controls.

A scuffle hoe is perfect for eliminating weeds, especially under established plantings.

JUNE
PERENNIALS

PLANNING

Plan to sow seeds of perennials if you need quantities of edgers and ground covers like **candytuft** and **catmint,** for example, and garden staples like **Shasta daisies, coneflowers,** and **coreopsis.** The seeds will be easiest to coddle sown in trays or flats kept indoors or in a cold frame. When the seedlings are 2 to 3 inches high, transplant them to an empty row in your kitchen garden, or to a sheltered spot in the flower beds. When the weather cools in September, transplant the seedlings to permanent homes in the garden.

PLANTING

Plant fillers, such as annuals, herbs, and tender summer-flowering bulbs, where the passing of spring-flowering bulbs leaves gaps in the flower beds. You can move bulbs whose foliage hasn't finished ripening to an out-of-the way spot if you need their space. Wait until the flowers have faded, and then cut off the flower heads but keep the leaves. Dig the root systems carefully to avoid damaging the roots, and move the whole clump to the desired location. Allow the foliage to ripen

naturally, just as it would have in its original spot.

CARE

Every few weeks adjust the ties on the tall flowers you have staked.

To keep roots cool and weeds down, renew the mulch on flower beds. André uses fine grade hammermill bark and also recommends pine and hardwood bark, West Coast fir bark, cedar bark, and cypress. Coconut hulls are pretty, but they aren't best where mold is a problem. Compost and leaf mold (decomposed leaves) are beneficial mulches, but weeds and roots grow into them, and they decompose quickly in heat.

GROOMING

Deadhead faded flowers at least twice a month. Removing dead blooms prevents a plant from developing seeds, and that stimulates the production of new flowers. Starting in June, André goes through his six acres of flower gardens with hand-held head shears and de-heads spent flowers; he is through in about an hour. There's not a lot to deadhead at any one time.

Shear to the ground plants showing the irregular serpentine tracings of leafminers. **Columbine** is very susceptible. The new foliage should grow in clean.

To keep the plants compact and improve flowering, around June 1 (and repeat July 1) prune back **garden mums** by a third, along with **asters, baby's-breath, bee balm,** 'Snow Bank' *Boltonia, Eupatorium, Helianthus, Heliopsis,* and **scabiosa.**

Shear back *Amsonia, Baptisia,* and *Artemisia* by half when they reach half their mature height. That will keep them from flopping later in the summer.

Deadhead **catmint** and other repeat bloomers to encourage a second round of flowers.

Trim back stems and shoots of perennials crowding their neighbors to maintain the definition between individual groups of perennials.

WATERING

Every day, check and adjust the soil moisture in small pots and baskets. On hot, windy summer days, check the soil moisture in big containers of perennials, and water as needed to keep the soil nicely damp.

If June has little rain, water the garden slowly and deeply every week to ten days. Apply

1¹/2 inches of water as measured in a 1-pound coffee tin or rain gauge.

Maintain moisture in new plantings. Water plants wilting at noon or in late afternoon.

FERTILIZING

Every two weeks add a half dose of fertilizer to the water for small containers. Add compost or potting soil to large containers of perennials whose soil level seems to be shrinking.

If you are using only chemical fertilizers, such as 5-10-5, which are quickly available to the plants, then you will need to fertilize garden plants every six weeks from beginning to end of the growing season.

PROBLEMS

Watch out for aphids and mites.

Handpick Japanese beetles—they're sluggish in the cool of early morning. Drop them into soapy water, and flush them down a drain. If they multiply, spray the plants with Neem, which will discourage feeding by adults. Try placing Japanese beetle traps far from the plantings you wish to protect, not among them. Insecticides containing Neem, rotenone, or Sevin insecticide are controls.

STAKING

Most tall perennials that are spaced properly and fertilized organically don't need staking. Weak growth is often the result of force-feeding with non-organic fertilizers. Wide spacing improves the plants' access to light and air, and that strengthens them. However, **delphiniums, lilies,** the tallest **dahlias,** and some other very big perennials usually do need staking.

When you set a new plant that needs staking—or when an established plant that will be very tall starts to grow—insert a stake as tall as the plant will be into the soil as close as you can get to the crown. Tie the main stem loosely to the stake with soft green wool raffia, cotton string, wool yarn, or strips of pantyhose. As the plant grows tie the main stem and branches higher up.

Stakes can be single, as shown in the illustration on the right, or a hoop stake, which encircles a plant within the stake.

Protect *Phlox, Monarda, Veronica,* and other plants that have shown signs of powdery mildew in the past with a mixture of 1 tablespoon baking soda, and 1 tablespoon of ultra-fine horticultural oil combined in a gallon of water.

JULY
PERENNIALS

PLANNING

Before your vacation, arrange to have the container plantings of perennials watered. Ease the chore by grouping the containers in a semi-shaded spot and providing each with a saucer. Investigate automatic watering systems.

PLANTING

In Zone 8, there is still time this month to start seeds of perennials outdoors. Though most perennials need two to three years to bloom from seed, some bloom in less than a year. Some that tend to come into bloom sooner are the large-flowered **tickseed** varieties *Coreopsis grandiflora* 'Goldfink' and 'Early Sunrise'; **purple coneflower, Shasta daisies, speedwell** (*Veronica spicata*), **oxeye daisy** (*Heliopsis helianthoides*), **violet sage** (*Salvia* x *superba*), and **yarrow.**

CARE

Tie tall **dahlias** and **lilies** to the upper third of their stakes.

Replenish the mulch in the perennial beds to keep their roots cool and to maintain moisture now that the year's driest season is upon us.

Take care to check and, when needed, water seeds started indoors or in a cold frame earlier. These baby plants need your attention in July and August.

GROOMING

Deadhead daily if you enjoy it, but anyway every two weeks, except for perennials whose seed pods you are planning to let develop.

Groom the garden, and trim back stems and shoots of perennials invading their neighbors.

To keep the plants compact and improve flowering, on July 1 prune back once again by a third the **asters, baby's-breath,** 'Snow Bank' *Boltonia,* **beebalm,** *Eupatorium,* **garden mums,** *Helianthus, Heliopsis,* and *Scabiosa.*

WATERING

Every day, check and adjust the soil moisture in small pots and baskets. On hot, windy summer days, check the soil moisture in big containers of perennials, and water as needed to keep the soil nicely damp.

If July has little rain, water the garden slowly and deeply every week to ten days. Apply $1^1/2$ inches of water measured in a 1-pound coffee tin or rain gauge.

FERTILIZING

If you are using only chemical fertilizers, such as 5-10-5, which are quickly available to the plants, then you will need to fertilize the garden every six weeks from beginning to end of the growing season.

Frequent watering quickly leaches the nutrients from the soil in small containers, so you must fertilize to compensate. Include a half dose of a water-soluble fertilizer every second time you water.

PROBLEMS

Continue to control infestations of Japanese beetles, aphids, mites, and whiteflies.

Keep an eye on **asters,** *Phlox, Monarda,* **dahlias,** and other flowers susceptible to powdery mildew. It often starts on the older, denser foliage at the base of the plant where there is less air. If you see a smoky film forming, thin the interior growth to improve air flow. Spray all the foliage of that plant and other susceptible and nearby plants with 1 tablespoon baking soda and 1 tablespoon of ultra-fine horticultural oil mixed well in a gallon of water. When the affected plants finish blooming, cut them back to the ground to promote clean healthy new growth. Destroy the prunings. Spray the clump and the surrounding soil with a fungicide for mildew.

PRUNING AND REBLOOMING

Deadheading—removing faded and dead blooms—encourages almost all flowering perennials to bloom on. To keep the plant shapely, cut off the stem of the spent bloom just above the next node on the stem. That's where the next flowering stem will arise.

Cutting back the stems of some perennials all the way down to the crown after the first flush of bloom is the way to encourage reblooming. Some that respond to this treatment are: **Catmint,** *Campanula carpatica, Centranthus, Echinops, Chrysanthemum* 'May Queen' and cultivars of the **Shasta daisies, daylilies** that are rebloomers, **delphiniums,** *Salvia nemerosa, Scabiosa, Stokesia, Tradescantia, Verbena, Veronica,* and **yarrow.**

Shearing tall fall-blooming perennials by half their height June 1 and again July 1, or no later than eight weeks before their scheduled bloom time, results in more attractive plants and better blooms. Some that benefit from this treatment are **asters, boltonia, chrysopsis, helianthus, heliopsis, mums, Russian sage,** *Salvia grandiflora,* and *Saponaria officinalis.*

Shearing spring bloomers soon after they finish blooming keeps them from getting leggy and promotes fuller bloom next season. Some that benefit from this treatment are **arabis, candytuft, creeping phlox,** and **sweet alyssum.**

Powdery mildew looks just like it sounds.

Control rust by avoiding overhead watering, and dispose of infected foliage and twigs, applying an anti-transpirant every other week, or spraying with a horticultural oil, Mancozeb, manzate, or sulfur of copper.

For other controls, turn to Pests, Diseases, and Controls in the Appendix.

AUGUST

PERENNIALS

 PLANNING

This month and next many garden centers keep cash coming in by staging sales that are very advantageous. They sell not only good-sized perennials at sale prices, but also many put hard goods on sale. So this is the moment to consider stocking up on flower holders, pots, and cachepots, as well as mulch, compost, wood chips for paths, tiles, and stones for hardscaping and so on.

Catch up on your garden log. Record the effect of staking taller plants and the result of cutting back **asters, boltonia,** and others that bloom in late summer and fall.

Evaluate the light reaching the flower beds. If some flowers are flopping forward, they may be short of light. Tree branches may have grown out and be casting shade on flower beds once in full sun. You can prune culprits now, the sooner the better. It takes full sun for most flowers to bloom up to their potential.

If you don't have the perfect planting site, then create one with a raised bed. See the directions in the Introduction.

 PLANTING

In spite of the heat and drought, container-grown perennials can be planted successfully this month as long as you water them every week or so, and hose them down gently if they show signs of wilting on especially hot days.

 CARE

Check and adjust the stakes supporting **boltonia,** the big **dahlias, lilies, Japanese anemones,** and other very tall flowers. Tie on straggling branches, and add stakes as needed to make sure the plants can handle the full weight of the plant in bloom.

 GROOMING

Dahlias need deadheading and are excellent vase flowers.

Continue to deadhead and shear spent blooms of **phlox, perennial salvia, scabiosa, purple coneflower,** and other summer-flowering perennials.

Remove dead, damaged, diseased, and insect-infested stems wherever they occur.

Shear **silvermound artemisia** to keep it from collapsing in hot weather.

 WATERING

Every day, check and adjust the soil moisture in small pots and baskets. On hot, windy summer

days, check the soil moisture in big containers of perennials, and water as needed to keep the soil nicely damp.

FERTILIZING

If you are using only chemical fertilizers, such as 5-10-5, which are quickly available to the plants, then you will need to fertilize garden and container plants every six weeks from beginning to end of the growing season.

Include a half dose of a water-soluble fertilizer every second time you water small containers.

PROBLEMS

High humidity and heat encourages powdery mildew. Avoid overhead watering. Cut down to the ground plants that have finished blooming, clear all fallen foliage, discard the mulch under the plants, and replace it with fresh mulch. Apply sulfur, ultrafine horticultural oil, copper fungicide, Immunox, or Bayleton to those afflicted plants that are not yet finished blooming. Make a note in your garden log next season to move the affected plants farther apart to increase air circulation. Or, if the infes-

ABOUT WATERING PERENNIAL BEDS

Climates and microclimates and the weather patterns from year to year affect the size, color, and health of perennials, their bloom time, their hardiness, and their seasonal performance. Understanding how heat and humidity affect your perennials helps you to water correctly.

• The hotter and drier the air, and the windier the weather, the more water your plants need. Don't water by rote; water when the soil feels dry.

• The sandier the soil, the more often your garden will need watering. You can offset sandy soil by incorporating plenty of humus in the soil before planting new plants.

• The windier the exposure, the sooner container plants and garden soil will dry out.

• The higher the heat, the drier the air will be, and the more likely you are to encounter spider mites infesting your plantings. Overhead watering humidifies the air and can help. Perennials growing in moist humusy soil and mulched 2 to 3 inches deep can stand considerably more heat, sun, and drought than plants without mulch.

• The wetter the season, the higher the humidity and the more likely the soil is to become waterlogged, especially in beds that don't drain well. Humidity encourages mildew, rust, and other negative conditions.

The first line of defense against disease in areas of high heat and humidity is to plant perennials advertised as disease resistant. Equally important is to provide your plants with very well-drained soil, a must for most perennials. Uncrowded, well-spaced plants have better drainage and good air circulation. The solution to finding the right spot where you want to put your perennials is to create a raised bed as described in the Introduction.

tation was very bad, in early spring replace the affected plants with mildew-resistant varieties.

Check for fungal leaf spot, and apply a fungicide if needed. If you see continuing signs of mites, hose the plant down regularly

and spray with insecticidal soaps or ultrafine horticultural oils.

SEPTEMBER

PERENNIALS

 PLANNING

This is an excellent month to plan—and start—new flower beds. Now to mid-October is ideal for planting.

The solution to assorted soil problems, including poor drainage, is to plant in raised beds whose soil that has been improved and enriched with organic additives. See Soil Preparation and Improvement and Starting a Raised Bed in the Introduction to the book.

 PLANTING

When rain and cool air arrive, transplant the seedlings started earlier to a nursery row, or to permanent places in the flower beds.

In Zone 6, September 1 to 15 you can divide and transplant perennials. In Zone 7, September 1 to mid-October is fine for dividing. In the warm Tidewater, the soil cools after Thanksgiving, so gardeners can divide as late as November 1. See Dividing Perennials in the introduction to this chapter.

 CARE

In Zones 6 and 7, after the first killing frost, prepare to lift and store **dahlia** tubers. Clear away the foliage, and then with a spading fork gently lift the crowns, and spread them out of direct sun to dry. Do not detach the tubers from the central stem. Store them in trays of cedar chips, vermiculite, sand, or peat moss in a cool dry area. Label each variety. Dig and store **canna, calla lilies,** and **glads** in a frost-free location.

In Zone 6, when temperatures head for 60 degrees Fahrenheit, move tropical perennials growing in containers to a frost-free shed or garage.

Clean up, and bring indoors to good light and a cool room potted perennials that winter indoors—**geraniums, impatiens, lantana,** and **mandevilla.** Keep the soil nicely damp throughout the winter.

Move big containers of hardy perennials to sheltered locations for the winter. You can also pack bags of leaves around them to keep the cold out.

 GROOMING

Continue to deadhead, and shear spent blooms.

 WATERING

September rains should keep the garden well watered, but check, and when needed, water small pots and baskets. There should be enough rain this month for the garden and containers of hardy perennials.

Include a half dose of a water-soluble fertilizer every second time you water small containers.

 FERTILIZING

If you are using organic blend fertilizers, such as Holly-tone or Plant-tone, then you will need to fertilize the last time a few weeks before the end of the growing season. The growing season slows in Zones 6 and 7 early September to early October. In Zone 8, Richmond and the Tidewater areas of Virginia, the last fertilization can be between the end of September and mid-October.

ABOUT ORIENTAL POPPIES

A spangle of these brilliant, beautiful blossoms lifts the spring/early summer garden from beautiful to extraordinary. Blossoms 5 to 10 inches across unfold crinkled silky petals in vibrant colors edged and splotched at the base in contrasting colors. The wiry stems bend to a whisper of wind, but withstand storms of amazing proportions. These gorgeous flowers last as cut flowers if you sear the bottom of the stem before putting it into water. The big fuzzy seedpods are great dried.

André specializes in **Oriental poppies**, and here are his recommendations for growing them:

1. Set out sturdy container-grown plants in early spring.

2. Plant in full sun, or bright shade. In Zone 8 they succeed under tall trees.

3. Soil with a pH 6.0 to 7.5 that is well-drained, deeply dug, light, somewhat sandy, and humusy is ideal.

4. Set the crown about $1^1/2$ inches below the soil level, and space the plants 2 to 3 feet apart.

5. Water gently and thoroughly after planting

6. Mulch 2 to 3 inches deep starting 3 inches from the crown.

7. Maintain moisture during the growing and flowering period, but don't water when the plants go dormant in the summer. Keep the bed on the dry side.

8. Remove the big, decorative seedheads, but allow the foliage to yellow and brown before removing it.

9. When the foliage begins to regrow in the fall, fertilize with Holly-tone, 4 pounds per 100 square feet. The fleshy taproot is difficult to transplant, but **Oriental poppies** rarely need dividing.

Oriental Poppy 'Turkemlouis'

If you are using only chemical fertilizers, such as 5-10-5, which are quickly available to the plants, then the last fertilization for garden and container plants will be six weeks before the end of the growing season.

If you are using time-release fertilizers in large containers and the garden, earlier applications should carry the plants through the end of the growing season.

 PROBLEMS

I'm a firm believer in radical weeding this month. Edge the flower beds to keep grass from creeping in. Then scratch up the soil around clumps of perennials, and get all the weeds out. That has the added virtue of opening up the soil so fall rains can give the plants a deep watering.

If **hostas** show signs of slug or snail damage, set out traps.

Remove, and discard every infected scrap of foliage and mulch from under plants that have been attacked by insects or diseases.

141

OCTOBER

PERENNIALS

PLANNING

Now that the foliage in the perennial beds is dying or has died down, you can evaluate the plant combinations. There's time ahead to make all things new for next year. Consider making places for colorful foliage plants and ornamental grasses. Some for up front, some for behind, but not directly behind, those up front, and some for farther back.

The silver-gray fuzz of **lamb's-ears** lightens the front of a border. Clumps of **dwarf bamboo,** *Pleioblastus fortunei,* add variety to the texture of middle rows. Variegated foliage appears light green, or gray green, at a distance. To change the texture at the back of the border, plant **verbascum,** a tall candelabra of a plant with felted, gray foliage. In shady areas, make room for colorful **hosta** varieties. The yellow-lime-green **hostas** are luminous, and some bluish **hostas** have wonderfully textured ribbed or quilted leaves.

Replace poor performers with sturdier lookalikes. **Delphiniums,** for example, that aren't doing all that well can be replaced with **hardy agapanthus** 'Bressingham Blue' or with dwarf **balloon-flower,** *Platycodon grandiflorus* var. *mariesii* and *Aconitum,* which

bear beautiful blue flowers that take more heat than the **delphiniums.** Seed sprinkled over a well-worked planting area might still have time to germinate this fall if the temperatures stay above freezing, and make enough growth to flower next year.

PLANTING

In Zone 7, you can divide and transplant perennials until mid-month.

In the warm Tidewater and Richmond areas of Virginia, the soil doesn't cool until after Thanksgiving, so gardeners can divide perennials up to November 1. See Dividing Perennials in the introduction to this chapter.

CARE

In Zone 8, move hardy perennials in containers to a sheltered corner for the winter.

In Zones 6 and 7, move tropical perennials that are still out in the open to a frost-free shed or garage.

Clear dead leaves from the flower beds, and compost them. They may be infested with pests and diseases.

Continue to root out weeds that appear in the flower beds. Dandelion seeds germinate well

in compost and must be rooted out, not just chopped off at the surface because they grow from root cuttings.

GROOMING

Cut **peonies** and **lantana** to the ground before the first frost.

WATERING

Outdoors. The most important preparation for winter is a deep and thorough watering of all new, established, in-ground, and container perennials before the soil freezes. If the sky doesn't do it, then you must compensate.

Indoors. Water the soil in big containers of tropical perennials stored indoors. Add enough to keep the soil from drying out.

FERTILIZING

In Zones 6 and 7, the growing season slows between early September and early October. In Zone 8, Richmond and the Tidewater areas of Virginia, the growing season slows between the end of September and mid-October.

If you are using fertilizers that are organic blends such as Holly-tone or Plant-tone, you should fertilize for the last time four to six weeks before the end of the growing season.

If you are using only chemical fertilizers, such as 5-10-5, which are quickly available to the plants, then the last fertilization should be just before the end of the growing season.

If you are using time-release fertilizers, a spring application of a nine-month formulation should carry the plants through the end of the growing season—no fertilizer need be added at this time.

PROBLEMS

Outdoors. Apply or change whatever deer deterrents you are using. The section on Pests, Diseases, and Controls in the Appendix explains why.

If vole runs appear around shrubs, bait the main runway with a rodenticide.

Indoors. Check **tropical perennials** moved indoors for whiteflies and spider mites. If you find problems, apply the controls recommended in the Pests section in the Appendix.

FOR WINTER INTEREST

In winter, ornamental grasses dance with the wind, woolly betonies stand tall above fallen leaves and evergreen edgers and ground covers rimmed with ice catch the sun and sparkle—if you have planted for winter interest. Here are a few of many perennials that stand out when storms of falling leaves give way to ice-blue skies and crisp winter air.

Blue false indigo, wild blue indigo, *Baptisia australis,* maintains its seed pods and leaves in winter.

Blue oat grass, *Helictotrichon sempervirens,* is a small grass whose gray-blue leaves last year-round.

Boltonia, *Boltonia asteroides* 'Snow Bank', has rich brown stalks and leaves in winter.

Carpet bugle, *Ajuga reptans* 'Burgundy Glow', maintains its variegated foliage—white, pink, rose, and green.

Chinese chives, garlic chives, oriental garlic, *Allium tuberosum,* keeps its white seedheads till spring.

Coreopsis, *Coreopsis verticillata* 'Moonbeam', retains its stems in winter, an interesting, dark feathery texture in the garden.

Edging candytuft, *Iberis sempervirens,* remains dark green most winters.

Hellebore, *Helleborus* species and cultivars, keeps its evergreen deeply divided foliage in winter.

Japanese anemone, *Anemone* x *hybrida,* and *A. hupehensis* var. *japonica.* The lean, branching stems are covered in winter with seedheads like cotton balls.

Lilyturf, *Liriope* cultivars, is evergreen until late winter.

Russian sage, *Perovskia atriplicifolia,* is like a huge white bird's nest all winter.

Sage, *Salvia officinalis,* the best-known culinary sage, retains its purple-gray foliage.

Siberian iris, *Iris sibirica,* has tall flowering stems that develop attractive seedpods. The grassy foliage turns rusty brown in fall.

Silver grass, *Miscanthus sinensis,* can soar to 6 or 8 feet, and in winter is all fine foliage and flower tassels, lovely with snow at its feet.

Spiraea, perennial spiraea, *Astilbe* species and varieties, keep their rich brown flower stalks in winter, and are particularly handsome in the snow.

Woolly betony, lamb's ears, *Stachys byzantina,* has big, semi-evergreen, gray leaves that remain in fall and winter.

Sedums 'Autumn Joy' and 'Vera Jameson', *Sedum spectabile,* retain their seedheads all winter. A new crown forms at the base preparing for next year.

November

PERENNIALS

PLANNING

This gray month, take the time to enlarge your horticultural knowledge. Here's the way horticulturists talk about flowers and explanations of what the words represent:

Anatomy of a Flower. Buds are enclosed in sepals; together they make up the calyx.

Petals develop next. Calyx and petals make up the corolla; and sometimes these come together and make a tube or cup, as with **daffodils.** Sepals and petals make up the perianth. Bracts are the leaves immediately behind the petals; they are small or scale-like leaves in most flowers, but very much larger than the flowers themselves in poinsettias.

Organs are inside the petals: The male organ is made up of stamens, and each stamen includes a filament (stalk); tipped with an anther; anthers form pollen.

Female organs are the seed-bearing carpels; when they fuse together in a blossom, the organ is called a pistil. Pistils may have three parts: an ovary in which seeds are formed, a slender style, which ends in a stigma. The stigma usually is either rough or sticky to hold the pollen that falls on it.

That's what fertilizes the seed.

PLANTING

Some seeds are programmed to withhold germination in the fall when they can be killed by winter frosts. They will germinate only after being exposed for a specific time period in the garden—typically four to eight weeks—to winter cold and moisture. Seed packets designate these seeds as needing "stratification" to germinate and tell you for how long. You can sow the seeds now in the garden, and they will germinate in the spring.

For more control of the stratification process, you can start them in containers. Here's how that works:

1. Sow the seeds in pots or trays, as described in Starting Seedlings Indoors in Annuals, January, Planting. Label and date the containers. Cover them with plastic film (plastic bags from the drycleaners for example) to keep the moisture from evaporating.

2. Keep the containers for the stratification period designated on the seed packet in an unheated garage, a shed, porch, or cold frame where they will be exposed to cold temperatures of less than 40 degrees Fahrenheit, but safe from snow, rain, and wind.

3. When the temperature climbs to between 45 and 60 degrees Fahrenheit, the seeds will begin to germinate—each species in its own time frame. Once the seedlings pop, remove the plastic, and begin the care program for seedlings described in Starting Seedlings Indoors.

Plan to have enough large containers for each seedling so you can grow them on until outdoors planting weather arrives in May or so.

CARE

In Zone 8, protect perennials that are borderline hardy with a winter mulch of pine boughs or straw on newly planted and evergreen perennials.

In the warm Tidewater and Richmond areas of Virginia, the soil doesn't cool until after Thanksgiving, so gardeners can divide as late as November 1. See Dividing in the introduction to this chapter.

GROOMING

If you would like your **garden mums** to perennialize, let the old stems stand as insulation for the new growth emerging at the base of the plants.

Let perennials attractive in winter remain. Even old flower stalks can be interesting. Seed-bearers feed the birds, and color their architectural branches rust, or rich brown or, in the rain, sooty black. *Sedum* 'Autumn Joy', **Siberian iris** in its rusty winter brown, the **coreopsis** bramble, and the dry leaves of *Allium tuberosum*, give the garden form while the earth rests.

WATERING

If the season is dry, water container and garden plants often enough to keep the soil from drying out. Before the first anticipated hard freeze, water thoroughly.

FERTILIZING

Fertilizer is not needed now because the growing season is over.

PROBLEMS

If you see signs of vole activity, bait the main runway with a rodenticide. See also the April pages of this chapter.

The beds are bare now, and dandelions and other weeds that have taken root are easy to spot and uproot.

BEST-OF-THE-BEST PERENNIALS

The Perennial Plant Association (PPA) is a professional trade association dedicated to improving the industry. André Viette has served as president. Each year the PPA chooses a Plant Of The Year rated according to multiseasonal interest and low maintenance. Here are recent choices. To keep up with Plant of the Year choices to come, check out **www.Perennialplant.org.**

- **Astilbe,** *Astilbe chinensis* 'Sprite' 1994
- **Coral bells,** *Heuchera* 'Palace Purple' 1991
- **Coneflower,** *Rudbeckia fulgida* var. *sullivantii* 'Goldsturm' 1999
- **Coreopsis,** *Coreopsis* 'Moonbeam' 1992
- **Creeping phlox,** *Phlox stolonifera* 1990
- **Feather reed grass,** *Calamagrostis acutiflora* 'Karl Foerster' 2001
- **Japanese painted fern,** *Athyrium nipponicum* 'Pictum' 2004
- **Penstemon,** *Penstemon* 'Husker Red' 1996
- **Perennial salvia,** *Salvia nemerosa* 'May Night' 1997
- **Phlox,** *Phlox* 'David' 2002
- **Purple coneflower,** *Echinacea* 'Magnus' 1998
- **Russian sage,** *Perovskia atriplicifolia* 1995
- **Scabiosa,** *Scabiosa columbaria* 'Butterfly Blue' 2000
- **Shasta daisy,** *Leucanthemum* 'Becky' 2003
- **Veronica,** *Veronica* 'Sunny Border Blue 1993

Japanese Painted Fern

December

PERENNIALS

PLANNING

Tools that make gardening easier become companions of sorts. You get attached. Good tools are expensive and make welcome gifts. Here's a handful—arranged in order of importance to us—that we use all the time when we work in the flower beds:

• A tool every seasoned gardener (and farmer) carries, but no one thinks of as a tool, is a little knife, a pocket knife, or a folding pruning knife, for digging up dandelions, cutting twine, impulse pruning—a thousand little jobs. It should be a size that is very comfortable in your palm, opens and closes easily, and is so well made it will last a lifetime.

• A pair of tiny shears for deadheading and harvesting flowers. Fiskars, manufacturers known for their line of pruning tools, make the little shears, and you can find the same type in shops with fabrics and sewing materials.

• For planting, the two most basic tools are a hand cultivator and a garden trowel. The fat-bellied type of trowel is the most versatile: the narrow variety incised with inches is mainly for planting bulbs. Painted trowels tend to peel. Cast aluminum is homely but light and durable; choose models whose handles are sheathed in plastic so they won't blacken your palms.

• The broad flat tines of a spading fork are the gardener's best friend when it comes to dividing perennials, loosening soil, and lifting perennials. (Jacqui is small, and finds tools designed for women easier to handle.)

• A shovel gets less use than a spading fork, but you'll need it to dig planting holes and move dirt and gravel.

• A hand rake (as opposed to a long-handled rake) for cleaning up flower beds.

• A swing-head scuffle hoe for weeding. It's a push-pull oscillating hoe with a double-edged blade that cuts through weeds on the forward and backward swing and cultivates the soil without disturbing the mulch.

PLANTING

Seeds that need stratification can be planted this month. See Planting, in the November pages.

CARE

Use only snowmelt products that don't harm plants, turf, or concrete.

GROOMING

Cut back perennials that have turned to mush due to frost, and discard them. Let plants with seeds of interest to birds remain—the **coneflowers** and *Heliopsis* for example.

WATERING

Maintain soil moisture in containers stored indoors, and also in containers of hardy perennials outdoors if there's neither snow nor rain. The roots need just enough moisture to keep the roots from drying out.

FERTILIZING

Fertilizer is not needed now because the growing season is over.

PROBLEMS

Before mulching your plants for the winter, remove fallen leaves and any remaining weeds.

ROSES

In full bloom a rose bush rewards you with the heart-stopping beauty of its flowers. The very best have a rich perfume that makes everything else go right out of your head.

True, like other great beauties, roses can be demanding, although some are more demanding than others. Pruning is a must; fertilizing, too. But when a rose's growing requirements are satisfied, it will perform in your garden beyond all expectations.

But the hardiness rating of a rose needs to be ascertained. In general you can expect the species roses, roses we haven't changed in any way, and many once-blooming old garden roses to be very cold hardy. These roses are growing on their own hardy roots. Of the repeat bloomers, rugosas are very hardy, and many David Austins, the Knock Out or Carefree series, and other bush roses are hardy, too. Miniatures and modern roses growing on their own roots are usually hardy.

Hybrid teas and other modern roses are "budded," a form of grafting, onto cold-hardy roots not their own; there are various reasons for this, such as improved vigor, cold hardiness, and disease resistance. If the top of a budded rose dies, the understock (or hardy root) will put forth its own

CHAPTER SIX

ABOUT ROSES

The rose is America's beloved favorite national flower. Since André and Mark first began teaching classes on roses at Blue Ridge Community College, Weyers Cave, Virginia, interest in roses has shifted. Gardeners still fall in love with, and exhibit, the unforgettable hybrid teas. But now landscaping roses that are easier to place and to manage, and miniature roses are very popular. The romantic old garden roses also have a strong following and the roses called "climbers' have many uses.

Climbers (pillar roses) and ramblers have long stiff canes that can be trained to grow up or sideways, and they occur in all rose categories. Climbing roses, and the floribundas, are the roses most often trained as "standard" or "tree" roses. Most bear large flowers singly or in clusters. Ramblers bear clusters of small flowers and bloom in spring and early summer. The initials CL after a rose's name stand for "climber." For example: CFL—climbing Floribunda; CHT—Climbing Hybrid Tea; and LCL—Large Flowered Climber.

---

canes, and these will not produce the desirable roses budded onto the roots. The label "own-root" on a rose is an indication that the rose was grown from a cutting and provides assurance that, if the top suffers in severe winters, the canes will grow back and eventually produce roses as before. Some very beautiful roses are budded, and we do plant them, but when winter hardiness is in doubt, we provide winter protection. You'll find suggestions in Winter Care for Roses, later in this introduction.

PLANTING

The humidity present spring and fall is kinder to new roses, but they'll succeed planted even in hot dry summer months if given adequate care. For a rose to bloom up to its potential, it must be placed where it has full sun, air all around it, well-drained top quality soil to grow in, and adequate fertilizer and water.

Roses are sold bare root, container-grown, and in plantable containers.

• Bare-root roses are available when it's time to plant them, in early spring before growth begins. Follow the suppliers' planting instructions exactly.

• Container-grown roses are available throughout the season, and you can plant them from late February/early March through to December 1.

• Roses in plantable containers are easy to plant, but they are available only in spring and early summer.

Light. The right place for a rose is one that receives at least six hours of direct sun, and eight is better in cold areas. In warm regions, they can handle more shade. Morning light is valuable because it dries the leaves, and helps prevent disease. Shade-tolerant roses, like the floribunda 'Gruss an Aachen', will bloom in partial light but may perform better in full. When talking roses, shade means bright, filtered shade.

If you lack full sun, choose shade-tolerant roses among hybrids of the musk rose, albas, rugosa roses, the lovely floribunda 'Iceberg', the Bourbon rose 'Zephirine Drouhin', and old garden roses 'Souvenir du Docteur Jamain' and 'Madame Plantier'.

Don't plant minis outdoors where the summer growth of taller plants will take away their sunshine.

Miniature roses growing indoors need all the light you can give them. If they are not getting enough light, try adding spot flood grow lights. And give them an occasional vacation under fluorescent lights in a light garden.

CHAPTER SIX

Soil. The ideal soil for roses has good drainage, lots of water-holding humus, and is loose enough for good root growth.

The pH of soil is a very important factor with roses. They prefer a slightly acid soil with a pH factor of 5.8 to 6.8. To raise the pH, mix in 5 to 10 pounds of limestone per 100 square feet of garden bed. If the pH is too high, lower it with an application of elemental fertilizer sulfur (water-soluble garden sulfur) at the rate of 5 to 10 pounds per 100 square feet. Aluminum sulfate or iron sulfate are acidifiers that act faster but do not last as long in the soil.

The planting hole for a bush rose needs to be at least 24 inches deep. If your soil is less than wonderful or if you have difficulty digging deeply enough, create a raised bed for roses. For instructions on preparing a new planting hole or bed for roses, turn to March.

Spacing. In addition to full sun, roses need air. Be sure to give your roses enough space all around for good air circulation. The rule of thumb is: compact roses need to be 2 to 4 feet apart. Climbing and heirloom roses need 5 to 10 feet between them. Miniature roses do well with just 18 to 24 inches all around.

FERTILIZING

Roses are heavy feeders, and the soil they grow in needs regular attention. The first chore of the year is to renew the soil—early spring, late February, or early March, is about right. Here's the drill:

1. Check, and adjust the soil pH.
2. Apply Rich Earth humate.
3. Fertilize:
   - If you are using an organic fertilizer, apply it four to six weeks before growth begins.
   - If you are using a chemical fertilizer, apply it just before growth begins.
   - If you are using a time-release fertilizer, just before growth begins apply an eight-month formulation.
4. Renew the mulch. This organic blanket will stabilize soil temperature and renew the humus content of the soil.
5. Every three to five years enrich the soil by applying rock phosphate, greensand, and gyp-

---

ARS AND AARS RATINGS

Two major influences on the U.S. world of roses are the nonprofit American Rose Society (ARS) and All-America Rose Selections (AARS). The ratings given roses are national ratings based on how roses perform nationwide. Some do better or worse regionally than the national rating. Local rose societies and growers will know.

The ARS is an association of rosarians who rate rose introductions on a scale of 1 (worst) to 10 (best). The ratings average individual ratings given by beginners as well as experienced rose growers. They are printed yearly in the "Handbook for Selecting Roses" available from the ARS. The highest rating given even the enduringly popular roses, 'New Dawn', 'Double Delight', 'Iceberg', 'The Fairy', and 'Bonica', reach no higher than 8.7.

The rose gardens near ARS headquarters in Shreveport, Louisiana, are open to the public during the growing season. Their website can help you locate local rose societies. You'll find their address in the Appendix.

The AARS is a nonprofit association of rose growers and rose producers that introduces and promotes roses judged exceptional in their trial programs. They are headquartered in Chicago. The roses judged go through a two-year field trial. The AARS seal of approval has influenced rosarians since 1938.

sum, the granular soil additives used in preparing a bed for roses (See March.) Measure it all into a pail, and spread the stuff over the planted area. Rain will do the rest.

PRUNING, DEADHEADING, AND HARVESTING

Roses bloom more fully when they are pruned and deadheaded.

Pruning. Roses must be pruned annually to remain shapely and stay healthy and productive. The best time is late in their dormant period before the buds begin to swell and new leaves appear—March and April. But late is better than not at all. The exception to the spring-pruning rule is one-time bloomers. They are pruned after they have finished blooming because they bear their flowers on the previous year's growth.

Prune to remove any cane thinner than a pencil and all damaged, weak, and nonproductive canes. That allows the plant's energy to go into flower production and larger, healthier canes. Hybrid teas and exhibition roses are pruned hard when the goal is to encourage a few large blooms. The cluster-flower roses and compact roses are pruned lightly to encourage growth and maintain their shape. For detailed information on when and how to prune the various categories of roses, turn to February.

Deadheading and harvesting. Removing spent blooms encourages the bushes to produce. Harvesting roses for bouquets is a form of deadheading—so indulge!! If you don't, blooms that were pollinated may begin to form seedpods (hips), which takes away energy needed for growth and flower production. Miniatures, small polyanthas, species, and carpet roses generally do not need deadheading.

Deadheading and pruning is over about October 1. Let the last roses on hybrid teas produce hips. That causes the plant to undergo chemical changes that slow growth, inhibit blooming, and generally prepare for dormancy by focusing on "hardening" the canes. The formation of hips tells the plant that it's done its job and can now rest.

WINTER CARE FOR ROSES

To help roses harden off and mature for winter, stop using high nitrogen chemical fertilizers about six weeks before the first frost. Instead, make the last fertilization a slow-release, organic product such as Espoma Rose-tone or Plant-tone. It will work slowly over winter without promoting top growth, which can be harmed by fall frosts.

When cold weather threatens, stop deadheading and allow the flowers to go to seed and form rose hips. The formation of hips encourages the

PRUNING CUTS FOR ROSES

Where you cut—whether pruning, deadheading, or harvesting flowers—shapes the bush's future. Roses tend to send a strong lateral (sideways) cane (branch-stem) out from the node just below a cut. You can keep the center of the bush open by making all cuts about 1/4 inch above an outward facing bud or leaf cluster. Use sharp bypass shears.

• Always cut at a diagonal, a 45-degree angle. Make the top of the cut the side the bud or leafset is on.

• When deadheading or harvesting roses, make the cut just above the first five- or seven-segment leaf below the flower or an outward facing bud. If this would cause too much of the cane to be removed, make the cut at a three-segment leaf instead.

• The first year, cut back to the first three- or five-segment leafset. In following years, cut far enough down to get to a five-segment or seven-segment leafset or bud that is facing outward. This will open up the plant.

ROSE COLLECTION FOR BEGINNERS

Climbers
- Fragrant blush-pink 'New Dawn' and 'White Dawn'.

Flowering Carpet Rose
- Low-growing, wide spreading white 'Jeeper's Creepers'.

Hedge Roses
- Sprawling bramble with clusters of small shell-pink flowers 'The Fairy' and vibrant pink 'Betty Prior'.

Hybrid Tea Rose
- Very fragrant red-and-cream blend 'Double Delight' and coral-red 'Fragrant Cloud'.

Miniature Rose
- Yellow 'Rise 'N Shine'.

Shrub Rose
- Care Free rose series and the Knock Out series, especially 'Rainbow'

plant to slow growth and blooming, and harden the canes in preparation for dormancy. When the bush is bare of leaves, to prevent disease and fungus from overwintering, remove every scrap of leaves and other debris on the ground. Spray the bush with dormant oil to kill insects and diseases on the bush and on the ground. Water the plant thoroughly before the ground freezes hard.

PESTS

Weeds. When weeds, including grass and dandelions, get going under roses they can be painful to remove. So rake weedlings out early. If you must hand weed, wear leather gauntlets. Keep earth covered with 2 to 3 inches of mulch to keep new weed seeds from sprouting.

Deer love roses. Sprays containing very bitter Bitrex may keep deer away if they're not starving. The only sure protection is to screen the roses with chicken wire. It isn't noticeable at a distance. For controls, turn to Pests, Diseases, and Controls in the Appendix.

Voles. Voles (short-tailed pine or meadow mice) are most active October to March. They can girdle roots and canes of roses under mulch. To control them:

- Bait the main area around the roses with a rodenticide.
- If you expect more winter weather, pull the mulch apart, spray the stem and the lower branches lightly with a repellent, and put it back in place. If winter is almost over, don't replace the mulch.
- To protect new and established plantings, see About Moles and Voles, in April, Perennials.

INSECTS AND DISEASES

The first line of defense is to plant pest- and disease-resistant roses, to give your roses lots of air all around, to fertilize, and to water well. When you encounter an infestation, treat it, and immediately remove every scrap of infected vegetation from the plant and the ground.

For additional information on rose problems, turn to Pests, Diseases, and Controls in the Appendix.

JANUARY
ROSES

 PLANNING

Take this respite from the garden to learn more about roses. Mail-order catalogs from the rose specialists named in the Appendix are great teachers. Make an album of catalog pages of roses you would like to try. Go out to the garden and scout likely places to plant them.

Roses that climb (CL) need 5 to 10 feet between plants. Train them to climb or ramble, and the canes will cover split rail fences, stone walls, pillars, posts, pergolas, or arches. A large-flowered **climber** trained to a trellis makes a beautiful backdrop for a rose garden. **Ramblers** and **miniature climbers** are excellent basket and container plants.

Large-flowered **bush roses** need 3 to 4 feet between plants. These roses are all about big, breathtakingly beautiful flowers, ideal for exhibition and for collectors. The group includes **modern hybrid tea (HT)** and **grandiflora (GR)** roses. The plants are large, upright, leggy, and need a bed of their own. In formal gardens **hybrid tea roses** are set off, parterre style, in geometric shaped beds edged with low hedges of clipped **boxwood** or **lavender cotton,** *Santolina chamaecyparissus.*

Cluster-flowered **bush roses** need 2 to 3 feet between plants. Mediumsize, these easily managed roses bear clusters of flowers all season. They're excellent in big perennial borders, and grouped in transitional spaces. Some can be pruned just with hedge shears. The **floribundas** (many-flowered) are planted in Europe along the roads and in parks. The **modern bush roses,** including the peachy-pink AARS 1987 winner 'Bonica' and other Meidilands, are hybrid ever-bloomers growing on their own roots. Smaller **polyanthas** like the rambling, fragrant seashell-pink 'The Fairy', make pretty, low, carefree hedges. The **English** and **David Austin roses** are graceful plants that bear very pretty flowers in the style of **old garden roses**, but with more modern disease resistance built in.

Compact and **patio roses** need 2 to 4 feet or more. Compact roses, 2 to 4 feet tall, somewhere between **miniatures** and **floribundas,** bloom freely all season. They are planted in perennial borders, for hedges, as ground covers, as edgers, and as fillers for rose beds. The Flower Carpet Group has a 5-foot spread.

Miniature roses need 18 to 24 inches between plants. The enchanting **minis** bloom all season, are winter hardy, disease-resistant, and are easy to grow indoors, too. The upright forms are 12 inches high and 6 to 18 inches across, and make pretty edgers. Those with trailing branches are lovely basket and container plants.

Heirloom, rugosa, and **species roses** need 5 to 6 feet or more between plants. **Heirloom roses** are **old garden roses,** a passport to time travel. Many are exceptionally fragrant. Most bloom once for about four weeks in early or mid-spring, on canes 3 to 6 feet long. The modern trouble-free **rugosa roses** are tall stiff bushes with spiny upright canes, perfect for tall hedges, as windbreaks, and as barriers to intruders. Deer don't trouble them, and they are excellent at the seashore.

Some rose species are excellent subjects for a naturalized garden. The magenta-pink **Virginia rose** (*Rosa virginiana*) is extremely cold hardy, and has brilliant autumn foliage.

 PLANTING

Lay out a new rose bed now, and you will be ready to start digging it when cold and moisture have left the earth next month.

CARE

Indoors. If **miniatures** growing indoors aren't blooming, add spot grow lights for the evening.

Outdoors. Check and adjust the winter mulch and other forms of protection for in-ground roses.

PRUNING

Deadhead **miniature roses** indoors; remove crossing and crowded stems to keep the center open.

WATERING

Indoors. Keep the soil moderately moist for **miniatures.** Shower them every two weeks. Every other time you water, moisten only the soil, not the leaves.

Maintain moderate soil moisture for tender roses wintering in containers indoors, and for containers of hardy roses sheltered in a cold garage or shed.

Outdoors. If winter has been dry, water the roses out in the garden.

GROWING MINIATURE ROSES INDOORS

Miniature roses that do well indoors are available from florists and garden markets. Some favorites are 'Rise 'n Shine', 'Little Jackie', 'Red Beauty', and 'Starina'. To grow a mini indoors:

• Repot it in a clay pot lined with pebbles or PermaTill, and filled with a potting mix that includes a water-holding polymer.

• Grow it on a south-facing windowsill, under grow lights, or in a window greenhouse.

• Keep the plant cool at night.

• Water the soil, not the leaves, when the surface feels dry to the touch.

• Fertilize at every watering with a half dose of a water-soluble fertilizer.

• Deadhead back to the first five-leaflet set.

• Prune out crowded and crossing stems to keep the center open.

• Remove infected foliage and stems at once.

• Shower every two weeks.

• In May move the plant outdoors to a semi-sunny spot for a summer vacation.

FERTILIZING

Fertilize **miniature roses** growing indoors at every watering with a half dose of a water-soluble plant food for flowering plants, such as African violet, or some other bloom booster.

PROBLEMS

Indoors. If spider mites attack **miniatures,** rinse the plants every two weeks. Air the room daily. Segregate infected plants. See also Problems in the introduction to this chapter.

Outdoors. If vole runs appear around the roses, treat the area with a rodenticide.

FEBRUARY

ROSES

PLANNING

When ordering new roses, make sure they withstand your winters. Be wary of roses that have no hardiness rating; growers don't always know how new roses will perform. It's also a good idea to be skeptical of winter ratings based on experience in Britain—plants perform differently there.

Species roses, and many once-blooming **old garden (heirloom) roses** are very cold-hardy. Of the repeat bloomers, **rugosas** are very hardy, and many **David Austins** and **modern bush roses** are okay. **Miniatures** and **modern bush roses** growing on their own roots are usually hardy. If the tops suffer, canes will grow back and bloom. This isn't applicable to roses that bloom just once. They flower in spring only on the last year's canes—no old canes, no flowers. Many yellow and lavender roses are especially tender.

Hybrid teas and other budded roses. Propagation identified as "own-root" and the rootstock as hardy in your area are fine. Their hardiness depends on natural resistance to cold. Killed to the ground, shoots from the rootstock will regenerate and bloom "true" to the parent variety.

Protecting roses against winter weather is an added safeguard against loss and a necessity for roses not growing on their own roots. In warm Zone 8, tender roses may winter over without protection.

PLANTING

In Zone 8 the soil may have warmed enough to plant.

CARE

When the annual fertilization is complete, add enough fresh mulch to maintain a 2- to 3-inch layer starting about 3 inches from the central stems.

PRUNING

Indoors. Continue to deadhead and groom the **minis.**

Outdoors. Look your roses over now, and evaluate the when and how of the pruning job ahead.

If you want to slow the growth and promote flowering in some roses, root prune them. The best time for it is early spring before growth begins. With a spade, sever the roots in a circle all around the bush to where the roots are about the size of your little finger. If you encounter roots you need a saw to cut, you are too close. If the roots are web fine, you are too far out.

WATERING

Indoors. Keep the soil—not the leaves—moderately moist for **miniatures.** Maintain soil moisture for containers of hardy roses sheltering in a garage or shed.

Outdoors. If winter has been dry, water the roses outside.

FERTILIZING

Late this month, or in early March, about four to six weeks before your roses start to grow:

• Check and adjust the soil pH.

• Fertilize with an organic fertilizer (see Fertilizing Roses in the introduction to this chapter).

• Apply Rich Earth humate.

PROBLEMS

Remove the mulch under roses troubled by blackspot last year. Allow the area to dry, then spread new mulch.

Smother overwintering insect eggs with an ultrafine (dormant) horticultural oil spray. There are temperature limits for effectiveness, so read the label.

If vole runs appear around the roses, bait the main runway with a rodenticide.

ABOUT PRUNING ROSES

Wear thick leather gloves, and use sharp, clean pruning shears for small canes, and a small pruning saw for large canes.

• Pruning begins: Zone 8: end of February; Zone 7: mid-March; Zone 6: mid-April.

Basics

• Place pruning cuts so the center of the bush remains open for maximum air circulation.

• Make cuts $1/4$ inch above an outward-facing bud or leafset. Cut at a 45-degree angle with the high side on the side the bud or leafset is on—the outward facing side.

• Squeeze a drop of white glue over the cut ends of larger canes to keep borers out.

• Scrub the woody surface of the bud union with a brass wire brush (sold by hardware stores) to clear dead tissue and stimulate growth.

Pruning Established Roses

• **All roses.** Before or as the buds swell, remove dead canes, any growth skinnier than a pencil, and canes crossing the center that are growing in the wrong direction and crowding others. Cut winter-damaged canes back to healthy green wood. Leave enough stem above the bud union for new growth to develop.

• **All roses.** Saw off old woody canes as close to the bud union as possible.

• **All budded roses.** Remove suckers growing from below the bud union of **hybrid teas, grandifloras,** and other budded roses—or they will take over.

• **Hybrid teas and grandifloras.** Cut **hybrid teas** back to six well-placed canes and **grandifloras** back to eight canes. Reduce the canes a third, to 14 to 18 inches long.

• **Floribundas and polyanthas.** Cut three-year old canes off at the bud union. Cut two-year old stems back by half. Cut back new canes by a third, or to just below where they bloomed last year.

• **Modern bush roses, 'Bonica' and the Meidiland family.** Trim branch tips back to shape the plant.

• **Cluster-flower bush roses, heirloom, and species roses.** Prune lightly to shape the plant.

• **Miniatures.** Remove all but the best four or five canes, and cut those back by a third.

• **Climbers.** For the first two years, prune to remove unproductive canes. After that, prune out the oldest canes leaving five or six healthy canes, and shorten their side shoots by two-thirds.

• **One-time bloomers.** Prune shortly **after** they have flowered.

• **Carpet roses.** Prune the canes back to 6 inches.

• **Rugosa roses.** Cut unproductive older canes back to the ground.

A pair of leather gauntlet gloves is a must to protect your hands when pruning roses.

MARCH

ROSES

PLANNING

When winter moisture and cold leaves the soil, you can start planting new roses.

PLANTING

Preparing a rose for planting:

- **Bare root.** Keep the rose in its package in a dark, cool place until planting time. The roots need to be soaked in tepid water before planting—usually six to twelve hours.

- **Container-grown.** Make shallow slits in the container sides, and peel the pieces away. If roots wrap the rootball, make four shallow vertical cuts in the sides of the rootball, and slice off the bottom 2 inches.

- **Roses in plantable containers.** Open the top, and maintain the soil moisture until you are ready to plant. Follow the package planting directions.

CARE

When the **forsythias** start to bloom, remove the winter mulch and other protective materials from the roses—but don't get ahead of the weather.

Don't just guess at the width of the planting hole—measure for the correct size.

NEW PLANTING HOLE

1. Outline a hole at least 20 inches wide. Dig a hole twice as deep as the rootball.

2. Test the pH of the soil. Bring to the site the products needed to adjust the pH, along with the fertilizers and amendments recommended for a new 100 square foot bed, (see the facing page, "New Bed for Roses." If the area you are planting measures only 10 square feet, combine one-tenth of the amount of each supplement given for a bed over 100 square feet.

3. As you dig, every 4 or 5 inches mix a portion of the fertilizer and amendments into the soil from the hole. The soil by the side of the hole is now "improved" and ready for the next step.

4. Pack in enough improved soil to place the graft (bud union—a thickened node at the base of the stem) at the right depth. The right depth depends on your plant-hardiness zone. In Zone 6, budded roses do best planted so the graft lies 1 to 2 inches below the soil surface. In Zone 7, the bud union can be at soil level. In Zone 8, the bud union may be slightly above the ground.

5. **Bare root rose.** Firm a cone in the center of the mound, drape the roots over it, and spread them out in the hole. **Container rose.** Settle the rootball on packed improved soil so the stem is straight. **Plantable container.** Make sure the container sits straight in the hole.

6. Backfill with improved soil. Pack it firmly over the roots, or around the rootball, or the plantable container. Shape the soil around the crown into a wide saucer (water basin), and create a rim around it that will keep rain or hose water from running off. Water the soil slowly, gently, and thoroughly with a sprinkler, a soaker hose, a bubbler, or by hand. You need to put down $1\frac{1}{2}$ inches of water. Or, slowly and gently pour on 10 to 15 gallons of water from a bucket. Mulch 2 to 3 inches deep starting 3 inches from the main stem.

Adjust the leads and supports for **climbers**.

Return container roses that sheltered in a garage or shed to the garden, fertilize, and prune them.

PRUNING

Indoors. Deadhead **miniature roses.**

Outdoors. Roses are best pruned before the buds swell (see February); keep an eye on their progress.

WATERING

Indoors. Maintain the soil moisture of **miniature roses.**

Outdoors. Keep the soil in containers of roses sheltering in a garage or shed moderately damp. Water hardy roses outdoors in containers and in the ground if you run into a dry spell.

FERTILIZING

Prepare established rose beds for fertilization:
- Check and adjust the soil pH.
- Apply Rich Earth humate.

NEW BED FOR ROSES

Any airy, sunny, well-drained site soil can be made into a fine bed for roses. Start three to four weeks early so soil amendments will settle in before you plant.

1. Choose a site with full sun—six hours, eight in cold areas. Farther south, roses can take more shade.

2. Lay out the bed. Check and adjust the pH. Thoroughly water the turf.

3. Spray with RoundUp® Weed and Grass Killer. The turf will be completely dead in about two weeks. Or, remove the turf (and compost it).

4. Cover the bed with 3 to 5 inches of organic material—any combination of decomposed bark, compost, partially decomposed leaves, sphagnum peat moss, black peat humus, or well-rotted animal manure.

5. For every 100 square feet of garden bed, spread on these long-lasting organic fertilizers and amendments:

> Rich Earth humate: 1 pound;
> Rose- or Plant-tone: 5 to 10 pounds;
> Rock phosphate: 5 to 10 pounds;
> Greensand: 5 to 10 pounds;
> Clay soils: gypsum 5 to 10 pounds;
> Osmocote® eight-month: 2 pounds

6. With a rear-tine rototiller, which you can rent from a garden center, mix all this as deeply as the rototiller will go. Rake the bed smooth, and discard rocks, lumps, and bumps.

- Every three to five years enrich the soil by applying phosphate, greensand, and gypsum.

Turn ahead to April, Fertilizing where the timing for various types of fertilizers is explained.

PROBLEMS

Remove old mulch under plants that had blackspot last year. Allow the area to dry, then spread new mulch.

Apply an ultrafine (dormant) horticultural oil spray to smother overwintering insect eggs. There are temperature limits for effectiveness, so read the label.

If vole runs appear around the roses, bait the main runway with a rodenticide.

APRIL
ROSES

PLANNING

Keeping a record of which bush did what and when will be helpful next year when you are preparing to amend the soil and prune your roses.

PLANTING

Brighten your porch, patio, or steps with roses planted in containers. The **miniatures** thrive in moss-lined baskets, planters, and clay or cement containers. **Compact** and **patio** cluster-flowering varieties and **tree roses** bloom nonstop in a container.

CARE

If you did not prepare the soil in established rose beds with an annual fertilization last month, do it now:

• Check and adjust the pH.

• Spread an application of Rich Earth humate.

• Every three to five years enrich the soil by applying phosphate, greensand, and gypsum.

PRUNING

Indoors. Continue to deadhead **miniature roses.**

Outdoors. If you have not yet pruned your roses, do so now. The rule is to prune before the buds break. But late is better than not at all. See February for recommended timing. The exception to the early spring pruning rule are one-time bloomers. Prune this type after blooming as they bear their flowers on the previous year's growth.

Prune first-year plants only lightly to allow them to concentrate on establishing a strong root system.

WATERING

Indoors. Keep the soil for **miniatures** moderately moist. Wet the soil, not the leaves.

Outdoors. Maintain soil moisture for **tender roses** sheltering in a garage or shed, and in **hardy roses** outdoors in containers and in the ground. Roses are growing now and must have $1^1/2$ inches of water every week—that's 2 to 3 five-gallon bucketfuls.

FERTILIZING

Before growth begins, fertilize the soil around in-ground and container roses. How far in advance depends on the type of fertilizer you are using. Mark the date in your garden log, and note on your calendar when the next application is due.

• **Organic fertilizers.** Early this month, or four to six weeks before growth begins, apply to every 100 square feet of bed:

Rose-tone or Plant-tone:
  5 to 10 pounds
Rock phosphate:
  5 to 10 pounds
Greensand:
  5 to 10 pounds
Clay soils only:
  gypsum 5 to 10 pounds
Osmocote® eight-month:
  2 pounds

The next application is due in early summer, about six weeks from now, and every six weeks until September 15.

• **Timed-release fertilizers.** Four to six weeks before growth begins, apply an eight-month formulation.

Supplement this with foliage feedings of water-soluble organic or fast-acting liquid fertilizers if the roses fail to bloom up to expectation or show a lack of vigor.

• **Chemical water-soluble complete fertilizer.** Make a first application just before growth begins. The next applications are due in six weeks, and every six weeks ending September 15.

PROBLEMS

Weeds are popping up. Rake them away.

Spray with an anti-desiccant spray or André's remedy for blackspot and mildew. If you have had serious infestations, start spraying with a rose fungicide.

A rose leaf with blackspot, one of the most common rose problems.

GROWING ROSES IN CONTAINERS

Smaller roses do well in containers. **Miniatures, rose trees,** smaller **Meidilands, floribundas,** and some **hybrid teas** are all candidates.

• **Light.** Provide at least six hours of sun each day. Turn the pot often to keep the bush growing evenly all around. A movable container makes it easy to take advantage of shifting light. Garden centers offer plant saucers and containers equipped with casters.

• **Container size.** For a **miniature rose,** a 6-inch pot that's 5 inches deep is sufficient. For **standard roses,** provide a tub that is at least 18 inches in diameter and 14 inches deep. Save watering time by planting in a container with a built-in water reservoir or water ring that lets the plant soak up the water from the bottom.

• **Preparation.** Soak porous containers—clay, wood— before adding soil, or they will take moisture from the soil you put into them. For winter protection, wrap the interior with a double row of large bubble wrap or Styrofoam™.

• **Planting.** Line the bottom with PermaTil®, then fill with this mix: $1/4$ good garden soil or bagged top soil, $1/4$ commercial soilless mix, $1/4$ compost, and $1/4$ sand, or $1/8$ perlite and $1/8$ PermaTill. Add a modest application of Osmocote® slow-release fertilizer and a water-holding polymer such as Soil Moist to help maintain moisture. Soak the growing medium before you plant.

• **Watering.** After planting, water well and maintain soil moisture thereafter.

• **Fertilizing.** Liquid feed every two weeks with a half strength dose of a good rose or container plant fertilizer.

• **Winter care.** Before freezing cold temperatures, store the container in a detached, unheated garage, shed, or cool basement. A rose needs to be cold enough to go dormant but must not freeze. Water lightly once a month.

Aphids cluster on rosebuds and cane tips. Spray them off every morning with a hose, or spray with Neem or insecticidal soap.

Deer are up, hungry, and enjoy tender new shoots and rose foliage. For controls see Pests, Diseases, and Controls in the Appendix to the book.

MAY

ROSES

PLANNING

Other gardener's roses, like some-one else's grass, always look better. That's usually because we see them from a distance.

But to get a notion of how stunning roses can be, visit some of the public rose gardens in our area because roses are in full bloom. Bring a notebook, and write down the names of those you must have—then look for them a garden centers. They're brimming with roses this time of year, all in top condition.

PLANTING

May is a fine month for planting new roses.

Fill gaps in the rose bed with leafy annuals such as **salvias, wave petunias,** or **sun coleus.**

CARE

Repot **miniature roses** growing indoors in fresh soil, and put them outdoors in bright light, but not in direct sunlight, to prepare them for summer outdoors.

PRUNING

Prune one-time bloomers when they finish blooming. See February for recommended timing.

To keep roses looking good and producing flowers, dead-head religiously—that is, remove spent blooms. Deadheading is especially important with large-flowered roses, the **hybrid teas,** and **grandifloras. Miniature roses** and the small **polyanthas** and **species roses** generally do not need deadheading.

To deadhead, make the cut a 45-degree diagonal just above the next five- or seven-segment leaf down the stem. The first year cut back to the first three- or five-segment leafset. In following years, cut far enough down to get to a five-segment or seven-segment leafset or bud that is facing outward. This will open up the plant.

WATERING

As the weather warms, begin daily checks of the moisture in the soil of roses growing in small pots and baskets. Water enough to keep the soil from drying out.

From late spring to mid-autumn, roses growing in big tubs may need watering every four to six days, or weekly. The larger the container, the less often it will need watering.

Make sure in-ground roses receive $1^1/2$ inches of water every week—that's two or three 5-gallon bucketfuls.

FERTILIZING

Liquid feed roses growing in containers every two weeks with a half strength dose of a good rose or container plant fertilizer.

For in-ground roses, six weeks after your first application of organic blend fertilizers or chemical water-soluble fertilizer, repeat the application. The usual timing is early summer, but it depends on when you make the first application.

Supplement this with foliage feedings of water-soluble organic or chemical liquid fertilizers if the roses fail to bloom up to expectation or show a lack of vigor.

PROBLEMS

Use a hoe to root out weeds creeping into the mulch under the roses.

If blackspot or powdery mildew appear, remove, and discard (do not compost!!) every leaf and spoiled blossom on the plant and petals on the ground. Prune out diseased canes. Apply a rose fungicide according to the label directions.

Aphids cluster on rosebuds and cane tips. Use a strong spray of water to blow them away in the early morning. If they persist, spray with Neem or insecticidal soap.

Enlarged view of an aphid nymph.

HARVESTING ROSES

- Harvest roses early, before the sun gets to them.
- Take to the garden a 5-gallon plastic bucket filled with lukewarm water containing floral preservative, clean sharp pruning shears, and thick gauntlets.
- Choose stems whose buds haven't fully opened.
- The first year make the cut just above the first three- or five-segment leafset. In following years cut far enough down to get to a five-segment or seven-segment leafset or bud that is facing outward.
- Immediately plunge the cut stem into the water bucket, remove the foliage that will be below the water line, and condition the roses in fresh water overnight in a cool place.
- Scour the bucket and vases with a dilute bleach solution ($^1/_2$ teaspoon of bleach per gallon of water) each time they are used.

Aphids clustering on a rose stem.

At the first spell of hot, dry weather watch out for spider mites. Three applications of Permethrin or Pyrethrum at five to seven day intervals will help you to control these pests. Be sure to spray the undersides of the leaves.

Roses that are wilting, yellowing, and seem stunted may be troubled by nematodes. The control is applications of ground crab shells.

Deer nibble the tender new wood and leaves on roses and eat the flowers and the buds; the Pests, Diseases, and Controls section in the Appendix has suggestions for controlling them.

JUNE
ROSES

 PLANNING

The roses that didn't sell this spring may be on sale now—or soon. Be tempted but be wise. Check out the rootball, and go for plants whose leaves are shiny, green, and plentiful—no yellowing, no stippling, and no little spider webs.

 PLANTING

If you haven't tried **miniature roses** yet, see what's on sale at the garden markets this month. The **minis** bloom freely and will almost surely come back better than ever next year. The little blossoms are somewhat reserved about sharing their scent, but it's there. 'Starina', 'Jennifer', 'Pacesetter', and 'Party Girl' are among scented **minis**, and some say 'Rise 'n Shine', which bears beautiful little yellow flowers shaped like a **hybrid tea**, is perfumed.

Many **miniatures** are hybrids of 'Minima', a selection of the **China rose** (*Rosa chinensis*). One of the wonderful characteristics the **China rose** imparted to modern roses is summer-long bloom. Pot yours up in September, and bring it indoors, and it will bloom all winter.

Ramblers and climbers must be tied to supports.

 CARE

Top up the mulch around the roses before heat gets intense.

Attach the new growth of the **climbers** and **ramblers** to their supports.

 PRUNING

Check budded roses, and remove new canes coming from the rootstock below the bud union.

Deadhead **hybrid teas, grandifloras,** and other show-time roses.

Prune one-time bloomers as soon as possible after they finish blooming. See February for likely timing.

 WATERING

New and established roses growing in good soil need 1 to $1^1/2$ inches of water each week, from the sky or your watering system. Or, slowly pour two or three 5-gallon bucketfuls of water around and in the water basin.

Miniature roses growing in small pots and baskets probably need water daily. Check the roses growing in big containers every couple of days, and water when the soil feels dry a few inches down. Water until the water runs out the bottom.

 FERTILIZING

Liquid feed roses growing in containers every two weeks with a

ROOTING CUTTINGS TO MULTIPLY YOUR ROSES

Propagating roses by softwood cuttings is a fascinating project, and a thrill when you succeed. Some easy to propagate from softwood and semi-softwood cuttings are **old roses, English roses,** and **miniatures.** Take cuttings from the ends of new canes that are green to semi-green and whose flowers have lost almost all their petals.

1. Set a 2-gallon baggie upright, and pack the bottom with 6 inches of sterile potting mix well-moistened with water containing 1 teaspoon of soluble rose food for every 4 quarts.

2. Shake about 2 inches of rooting hormone powder Number 3, or Root-tone, into a small glass.

3. Take the cutting in early morning. From the blossom end, count down four leafsets to a five-leafset, and cut the stem off about an inch below.

4. Working in the shade, cut the top off about a half-inch above the top leafset. Remove the leaves from the bottom 2 inches. Mist the foliage. Score the bottom inch or so of the stem vertically. Dip the wounded end in the rooting powder, and knock off the excess.

5. Bury the cut end upright in the middle of the potting mix deep enough to cover the wounds. Press the soil up around the stem.

6. Mist the cutting, blow the baggie full of air, and zip it closed.

7. Place the baggie in bright, indirect light.

8. Sometime between two and six weeks there should begin to be roots showing along the bottom of the baggie.

9. When top growth begins, acclimate the cutting to the air in the room. Each day for the next two weeks unzip the baggie a little more, and leave it open a little longer. Start with four hours the first day.

10. Fill a pot as big as the baggie to within 4 inches of the top with half potting soil and half peat. Set the baggie on top, and slit the bottom. Gently firm the soil up around the roots.

11. In about a week move the pot outside, and week by week expose it to increasingly stronger light. Maintain the soil moisture. In September, transplant the plant to the garden, and cover it with an open mulch of hay or evergreen boughs.

---

half strength dose of a good rose or container plant fertilizer.

The second application of organic blend fertilizer or chemical water-soluble fertilizer was due six weeks after the early spring application. Do it now if you haven't done it yet.

 ## PROBLEMS

Deer nibble roses, buds, and leaves; deterrent sprays may not keep them away. See the section on Pests, Diseases, and Controls in the Appendix.

Continue to root out weeds, and look out for aphids, spider mites, thrips, blackspot, and powdery mildew. If you have already sprayed without effect, switch to another control.

Japanese beetles get busy now. This rather handsome metallic green and coppery-maroon insect wrecks the flowers and chews the leaves and stems as well. In early morning knock them into soapy water, and destroy them.

If there are wild grape vines on your property, root them out; they are an attractive host plant for the Japanese beetle. Grub-proof the lawn and gardens now, and there should be fewer Japanese beetles next year. But that won't stop them from flying in. Beetle traps are effective only if they are placed far away from the roses. If Japanese beetles become a real problem, apply insecticides containing Neem, rotenone, or Sevin.

JULY
ROSES

PLANNING

This month and next, visit public gardens, and gardens noted for roses—and smell the roses. Note the names of those that are really fragrant, and plan to try them. For the perfumed roses to be truly fragrant, I find they need to grow in full sun—eight hours.

PLANTING

You can plant **container roses** now—at home and even at the shore. If Japanese beetles are ruining your roses, try one they don't pay much mind to, the **rugosa rose**. *Rosa rugosa* is a tall (5 feet or more) native of China, Russia, Japan, and Korea that does so well at the seaside it is used to create windbreaks in very exposed positions.

Yes, it's tall and thorny, but modern cultivars bear clove-scented single or double flowers that are quite lovely, and the rose hips are spectacular. Most bloom for quite a while in spring, and some repeat bloom.

The roses are very cold hardy, and resist not only the Japanese beetle, but also many other pests. The only pruning needed is the removal in early spring of older canes to encourage vigorous new growth.

One of the most beautiful is 'Frau Dagmar Hastrup', which bears light pink roses and is so dense it can be pruned repeatedly without much diminishing the production of flowers. The flowers of 'Therese Bugnet' are large, flat, slightly fragrant deep pink and repeat some. Almost thornless 'Linda Campbell' produces large clusters of crimson flowers with six to seven flushes of blooms.

When preparing containers for a seashore garden, use commercial potting soil rather than the sandy soil of the area. The humidity in the air reduces the need to water, but check the soil moisture often anyway.

CARE

Heat is here. Check and replenish the mulch under the roses.

PRUNING

Harvest and deadhead **hybrid teas** and **grandifloras.** The ever-blooming roses that bear clusters of small flowers generally do not need deadheading, but if they aren't producing as expected, groom and deadhead them, and apply a liquid fertilizer.

WATERING

This month and next check the soil moisture daily in small pots and baskets. They may need a good soaking almost every day. Roses growing in big containers in hot windy places may need watering every three to five days now. Water until you see water dripping from the bottom of the container.

Make sure in-ground roses receive $1^1/2$ inches of water every week—that's two to three 5-gallon bucketfuls.

Keep roses that suffered from powdery mildew well watered. Unlike blackspot, wet conditions actually inhibit the development of powdery mildew. It cannot reproduce in water. While it thrives in high humidity, it forms on dry leaves. Warm dry days and cool dry nights are ideal for powdery mildew. A weak or stressed plant is more susceptible to disease.

If blackspot is a problem on the same plant, water the roots and avoid wetting the foliage.

FERTILIZING

Liquid feed roses growing in containers every two weeks with a half strength dose of a good rose or container plant fertilizer.

The third application of organic blend fertilizer or chemical water-soluble fertilizer is due six weeks after the second application, in midsummer.

If roses fertilized with a timed-release chemical fertilizer are failing to bloom as expected, or look peaked, supplement it with foliar feedings of water-soluble organic or fast-acting liquid fertilizers.

Roses that have been in bloom all season and are slowing production or that aren't growing vigorously, may respond to foliage feedings of water-soluble organic or fast-acting liquid fertilizers.

PROBLEMS

Weed! Don't let them get going!

Mites attack roses stressed by hot weather and drought. Make them miserable with vigorous hosing of the leaves, and especially the undersides of the leaves, every day or two for a week. If there are signs of webs on twigs and leaf stems, apply Neem or an insecticidal soap.

If caterpillars become numerous, spray with a biological control such as *Bacillus thuringiensis*. Other controls are Sevin or malathion insecticide, pyrethrin, or rotenone.

ROSES WITH OUTSTANDING FRAGRANCE

There are fragrant roses in every category, many among the **hybrid teas,** the **English roses,** and **old garden roses.** Some very fragrant roses gardeners posted on the American Rose Society website are:

'Mr. Lincoln'

Hybrid Tea Roses
- 'Double Delight' (mentioned most often), red-white bicolor
- 'Fragrant Cloud', reddish- orange
- 'Mr. Lincoln', dark red
- 'Crimson Glory', red
- 'Chrysler Imperial', red
- 'Papa Meilland', dark red
- 'Perfume Delight', pink

English Roses
- 'Gertrude Jekyll', pink
- 'Othello', dark red

Old Garden Roses
- **Alba rose** 'Felicite Parmentier', soft pink edged cream
- **Damask rose** 'Mme. Hardy', white
- **Tea rose** 'Sombreuil', cream-white (climber)
- **Bourbon rose** 'Souvenir de la Malmaison' (climber)

If Japanese beetles persist, spray their bodies with a pyrethrum product. It's a contact sport.

The rose midge larvae causes deformed buds and dead branch tips. Prune off and destroy buds and tips that are infested. Spray with Neem every five days as directed.

Deer may be eating your roses and their foliage; see Pests, Diseases, and Controls in the Appendix of the book.

AUGUST

ROSES

PLANNING

During late afternoons in August, the scent of perfumed roses is heady because the fragrant oils have been volatilized by a whole day of hot sun. Once upon a time oils drawn from the scented florals were our only source of fragrance. The roses that scented the old potpourris are still available. It's fun on a lazy, fragrant summer evening to dream of planting a garden of roses for making potpourris. You would interplant the roses with **English lavender,** *Lavandula officinalis,* whose lasting scent when dried makes it a "must" in recipes for dry perfumes.

The scented **Bourbon roses** in general, and the very fragrant pink 'La Reine Victoria' in particular, would be good candidates. Many of the **cabbage roses,** *Rosa centifolia,* are sweetly fragrant, including the cultivar 'Fantin Latour'. The **damask roses** are fragrant, including the beautiful white 'Madame Hardy'. If you have room for only one rose for potpourri, choose the rose grown commercially for its scent, *Rosa gallica* 'Officinalis', the **apothecary rose.** This rose is unique in that the petals are more fragrant after drying.

PLANTING

If roses go on sale and you haven't the inclination to plant your purchases in August's high heat, buy them anyway, and grow them in their containers until September brings cooler and better weather for planting. **Miniature roses** are safe in their original container as long as you keep it watered. The larger roses will do better while waiting if they are repotted in a larger container.

Rosa gallica 'Officinalis'

CARE

If the foliage of the **hybrid teas** is wilting in temperatures over 90 degrees Fahrenheit, help them recover by misting the leaves with a mild solution of liquid sea-

weed. Apply it in early morning before the sun starts to climb.

PRUNING

Deadhead the **hybrid teas** and the **grandifloras**.

Remove suckers growing up from under the bud union of your **hybrid roses**, along with any diseased or damaged canes.

WATERING

This month and next check the soil moisture daily in small pots and baskets. They may need a good soaking almost every day. Roses growing in big containers in hot windy places may need watering every third or fifth day. Water until it is dripping from the bottom of the container.

Make sure inground roses receive $1^{1}/2$ inches of water every week—that's two to three five-gallon bucketfuls.

Keep roses attacked by powdery mildew well watered. Wet conditions actually inhibit the development of powdery mildew. If blackspot is a problem in the same plant, water roots, and avoid wetting the foliage.

FERTILIZING

Liquid feed roses growing in containers with a water-soluble fertilizer every two weeks.

The third application of organic blend fertilizer or chemical water-soluble fertilizer was due six weeks after the second application, in midsummer. If you haven't done it yet, do it now. If the roses look as though they need a quick pick-up, spray a liquid fertilizer on the foliage.

If roses fertilized with a timed-release chemical fertilizer are failing to bloom as expected or look peaked, supplement it with foliar feedings of water-soluble organic or fast-acting liquid fertilizers.

PROBLEMS

Roses weakened or stressed by hot dry weather are especially vulnerable to mites, aphids, and Japanese beetles.

Control rust by avoiding overhead watering, and dispose of infected foliage and twigs, applying an anti-transpirant every other week, or spraying with a horticultural oil.

ENGLISH ROSE POTPOURRI

The ancient recipe that follows is from my book *Potpourris and Other Fragrant Delights*, which was published here and in Europe some years ago. Gum styrax is from the resin of the tree *Styrax officinalis*, and it is the "benjamin" mentioned in the old stillroom potpourri recipes. Gum benzoin and oil of benzoin are substitutes and are offered by several online suppliers.

> 3 cups dried petals of a fragrant rose
> 2 cups dried lavender buds
> 1 cup lemon verbena leaves
> 1 tablespoon ground allspice
> 1 tablespoon fresh-ground cinnamon
> 1 tablespoon fresh-ground cloves
> $1/4$ ounce or more gum benzoin, gum styrax, or oil of styrax

Combine all the dry ingredients, then add in the gum benzoin, gum styrax, or oil of styrax, mixing as you go until the scent seems satisfyingly strong. Seal the container, and set it to cure in a dark, dry place, shaking the contents every day. Put the potpourri into a decorative container that has a close-fitting lid.

Uncap the container when you wish to scent a room, but keep it well covered at all other times.

Control powdery mildew by applying an anti-transpirant, and by maintaining good air circulation.

Control blackspot by removing fallen leaves, pruning out diseased twigs, and avoiding wetting the foliage.

Viral diseases may strike now. There's no remedy. Symptoms are a mottling or mosaic discoloration of the leaf or ring spots. In most cases removing the infected plant is the only control.

Continue weed patrol.

Deer may be eating your roses and their leaves; see Pests, Diseases, and Controls in the Appendix.

September

ROSES

 PLANNING

Time to begin thinking about winter protection for your roses. You will not need to do much to protect the **old garden roses, miniatures, rugosas, species roses,** and other roses growing on their own roots.

Budded roses are less certain to survive winter without help. The first line of defense for those roses is to plant the bud union at the proper depth as described in March. Check bud unions now of budded plants, and, if need be, dig and replant the roses this month. The November Care section has detailed instructions on winter care of budded roses.

 PLANTING

As the weather cools, repot the **miniature roses,** rinse and spray them with insecticidal soap, and bring them indoors to a sunny sill.

September is a fine month for planting as well as transplanting roses, so take advantage of end-of-season sales to complete your rose collection.

 CARE

To help roses harden off and mature for winter, stop the use of high nitrogen fertilizers about six weeks before the first frost.

If you did not check and adjust the pH of the soil in your rose beds in March or April, you can do it now. Roses prefer a slightly acid soil, pH 5.8 to 6.8. To raise the pH use 5 to 10 pounds of limestone per 100 square feet of garden bed. If the pH is too high, lower it with an application of elemental fertilizer sulfur, (water-soluble garden sulfur) at the rate of 5 to 10 pounds per 100 square feet. Aluminum sulfate or iron sulfate are acidifiers that act faster but do not last as long in the soil.

 PRUNING

Let the last blossoms on **hybrid teas** develop into rose hips. It causes the plant to undergo chemical changes that slow growth, inhibit blooming, and generally prepare for dormancy by hardening the canes. The formation of hips tells the plant that it's done its job and can now prepare to rest.

 WATERING

Indoors. Keep the soil for **miniatures** moderately moist. Moisten the soil, not the leaves. Shower them every two weeks.

Outdoors. Check soil moisture daily in roses growing outdoors in small containers. Water big containers every week or so unless you've had a soaking rain.

Make sure in-ground roses receive 1 1/2 inches of water every week—that's two to three 5-gallon bucketfuls. If you are using a watering system or a hose, measure the amount in a 1-pound coffee tin, or use a rain gauge, available from garden centers and catalog suppliers. The plants must be well watered before the ground begins to freeze.

 FERTILIZING

If you are using organic or water-soluble chemical fertilizers, the last application in Zones 6 and 7 should be made between early September and early October. In Zone 8, Richmond and the Tidewater areas of Virginia, make it between the end of September and mid-October. If you are using a timed-release fertilizer and applied an eight-month formulation in early spring, it will carry the roses all the way through October.

'The Fairy'

PROBLEMS

Continue to check your roses for signs of aphids and spider mites.

Powdery mildew remains a threat. Remove and destroy the leaves on the plants affected, and replace the mulch beneath with fresh mulch.

Rake away, and destroy mulch under roses that have had black-spot, mildew, and other problems. Let the soil air and dry, then apply fresh mulch.

Root out weeds and grasses that have crept into the mulch under big roses.

Deer may be eating someone else's apples instead of your roses, but don't count on it.

ABOUT HEDGE ROSES

A rose hedge is a pleasure and an effective barrier. The height you want to achieve indicates the variety to plant.

Low borders. Miniature roses make pretty borders for rose gardens, and they bloom all season. 'China Doll' tops out at about 18 inches, and covers itself with clusters of $1^1/2$-inch light pink, semi-double blooms.

Low hedges. The rose advertised as the "living fence" hedge is 'The Fairy', a **polyantha** under 30 inches that blooms all season. 'The Fairy' and other polyanthas grow into brambly hedges covered with clusters of roses under 2 inches.

Medium hedges. The vigorous **floribundas,** which are cluster-flowered bush roses that bloom all season, make fine hedges 4 to 5 feet tall. Our favorite is 'Betty Prior', whose vivid pink flowers and emerald green foliage stay beautiful all summer. The **Meidiland group** of roses develops into wide-spreading naturalized hedges that bloom all season with little care. 'Bonica', an upright 4- to 5-foot bush, bears 3-inch fully double shell pink flowers set off by rich deep green glossy leaves.

Tall hedges. The **rugosa roses** grow into tall, very thorny hedges that withstand strong winds and sea spray. The only pruning they need is the removal in early spring of older canes to encourage vigorous new growth. The flowers of the modern cultivars are quite beautiful, and many produce spectacular rose hips.

OCTOBER

ROSES

PLANNING

If your winter temperatures will fall to 10 degrees Fahrenheit or lower, be prepared to cover **floribundas, grandifloras, hybrid teas,** and other budded roses. (See the Care section of November.) Late fall before the ground freezes is about the right timing.

Be wary of covering roses before the temperature falls to 28 degrees Fahrenheit as that may keep the rose from hardening properly and will slow the onset of dormancy, leaving it vulnerable to frost. Cover the rose too late, however, and it may be damaged by the cold.

PLANTING

This month, apply potassium to the soil to help winterize your roses.

When tree leaves start to change color is an excellent moment to plant new roses, and to start digging and transplanting roses. In Zone 8, you can plant roses throughout October, November, and into early December. In Zone 7, you can still plant roses in October and November. In Zone 6, you can plant roses in October and into the very beginning of November.

CARE

Begin to prepare **climbers**, roses growing in containers, and **tree roses** for winter:

Climbing Roses. Climbers exposed to high winds will do better with protection in winter. Spray the canes with a rose fungicide or dormant oil, and use an anti-desiccant, such as Wilt-Pruf®, to help them withstand winter dryness. Clear fallen leaves and mulch from the soil beneath the climber, and apply new mulch about a foot deep.

Untie the canes from the trellis or fence. Wrap them with an insulation material (such as you use to keep pipes from freezing), and then retie them in place. If the stems are very flexible, you may find it easier to just lay them along the ground, and cover them with a foot of soil or mulch.

Container Roses. In Zone 6, as temperatures plunge toward 28 degrees, move roses growing in containers to an unheated garage or shed. First, remove the leaves, cut the canes back to 36 inches, tie them together to make the container easy to move, and clear the mulch away from the soil surface. Add new mulch, move the containers to their winter quarters, then water the container thoroughly.

Standard or Tree Roses. Prepare **tree roses** growing in containers for winter as recommended for **container roses**, above. Before temperatures reach 28 degrees Fahrenheit, move them to an unheated garage or shed.

A **tree rose** growing in the ground needs winter protection. Remove the leaves, clear away old mulch, and replace it with new mulch. Tie the canes together loosely. Enclose the plant in salt hay wrapped in burlap, translucent white plastic, or roofing paper, and tie the bundle

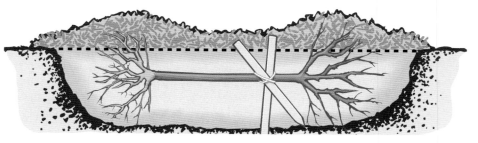

Tree roses growing in Zone 6 may need to be placed on their sides in a trench topped with soil and mulch to protect them from winter.

together with a cord to keep everything in place.

In Zone 6, a **tree rose** growing in an exposed location may need more help. Cut free one side of the roots, then tip the entire **tree rose** over into a trench. Cover it with a foot of soil topped by mulch.

PRUNING

As the weather cools, stop dead-heading, and allow the roses to form rose hips. That encourages the plant to slow growth and blooming, and harden the canes, all in preparation for dormancy.

WATERING

Indoors. Check pots of **miniatures** every day or two, and keep the soil moderately damp. Rinse them every two weeks to discourage spider mites.

Outdoors. One of the most important winter preparations for all roses is a final deep and thorough watering before the ground freezes.

Renew the mulch; that protects the ground from freezing, which keeps moisture available for roots.

ROSE HIP JAM

When you plan to make rose hip jam, avoid spraying the roses whose hips you want to use with anything bad for your health. The **rugosa roses** produce the biggest and most colorful rose hips, and generally are pest- and disease-resistant, so their hips are good candidates for jam making. Wait until after the first frost to pick the hips, and choose the biggest.

This recipe was given to me by my friend, the late Sally Erath.

Frances Chrystie's Rose Hip Jam

4 cups rose hips
1 cup water
Sugar (as needed, see below)

Place the rose hips, and the water in a large pot over medium heat. Cover, and simmer about 30 minutes, until the fruit is very tender. Force the pulp through a fine sieve.

Measure the pulp, then return it to the pot. For each cup of fruit pulp, stir in 1 cup of sugar. Simmer for 10 to 15 minutes, or more until the mixture is thick. Remove the pot from the heat, and skim off the foam. Pour the jam into jelly glasses cleaned and dried in your dishwasher. Fill the glasses to within $1/2$ inch of the rim, and seal with melted paraffin.

Store in the refrigerator.

FERTILIZING

Fertilizing is over for now.

PROBLEMS

When the roses have lost their leaves, prevent disease and fungus from overwintering by removing fallen leaves, old mulch, and weeds under the roses. Spray with dormant oil to kill bacteria on the bush and on the ground.

If vole runs appear around your roses, bait the main runway with a rodenticide.

If you've been troubled by rodents in winters past, wait until after a hard frost, then mound VoleBloc or PermaTill all around the main stem of each rose bush, and cover that with a winter mulch.

November

ROSES

PLANNING

Now that the leafy season is over and the garden bare, evaluate the setting you've given your roses, and consider which might do and look better moved to another spot.

PLANTING

You can still plant and transplant roses if the weather stays comfortable.

CARE

Winter protection for roses is meant to keep the canes from drying in bitter winds, to avoid cold damage to the canes and bud union, and damage to the crown when alternate thawing and freezing cycles cause the soil to heave it.

In the Tidewater region of Virginia, established roses require little winter protection other than a winter mulch.

In Zones 6 and 7 for their first winter, protect newly planted roses and the **miniatures,** even those rated winter hardy in your area. As the temperature heads toward 28 degrees Fahrenheit:

1. Cut the canes back to 36 inches, and tie them together with string. These canes will be trimmed back further in the spring to remove portions winterkilled.

2. Spray the canes with an anti-desiccant.

3. The "thaw/heave" cycles that can occur when warm spells hit can heave the crown from the ground. Mulch will prevent the ground from thawing. So:

- Cover the crown or the bed at least a foot deep with tree leaves. Do not use rose leaves as they may harbor disease. Oak leaves are best as they are more resistant to rot and seem to drain better.

- Or, cover the bed with straw.

- Or, spread a mound a foot deep of soil from another part of the garden over the base of the plant. Bark, fresh compost, or shredded leaves can be used instead of soil.

4. Along with any one of the mulches listed, in Zones 6 and 5 and in sites exposed to stiff wind, protect the canes:

- Wrap the whole plant in burlap or Reemay®.

- Or, encase the plant in a cage of wire and straw.

- Or, wrap the plant in straw covered with burlap and tied with rope.

You can protect roses from thaw/heave cycles by burying the crowns with up to a foot of soil.

- Use rose cones made of Styrofoam™ as protection. You need to trim and defoliate the rose first, then mound the crown with 12 inches of soil and mulch. Tie up the canes, place the protective cone over them, and set a weight on the cone to keep it from blowing away.

PRUNING

Cut back long canes of big roses that look as though they could be whipped around by wind. Save other pruning of long canes for late winter and early spring as branch tips generally have some winter die back, and you'll have to prune them then anyway.

WATERING

Indoors. Keep the soil for **miniatures** moderately moist. Shower them every two weeks, but the other times you water them, wet the soil, not the leaves.

Outdoors. A major danger to roses in winter is lack of water before the plant is completely dormant. One of the most important winter preparations is a deep and thorough watering before the ground freezes.

Maintain moderate soil moisture for hardy roses in containers, and for containers of hardy roses sheltering in a cold garage or shed.

FERTILIZING

To encourage blooming, fertilize **miniature roses** growing indoors under grow lights with a light application of African violet or another of the liquid bloom booster fertilizers.

PROBLEMS

Indoors. Spider mites are a threat to **miniature roses.** Pale, fine stippling on leaves is the giveaway. Spray affected plants in a kitchen sink every day or two for a couple of weeks. If that doesn't work, spray with insecticidal soap. Air the room every day.

Outdoors. To prevent disease spores from infecting new growth when it comes along in the spring, strip off the leaves, and pick up all fallen leaves under your roses. Remove the mulch below diseased plants, and replace it with fresh.

If vole runs appear around your roses, bait the main runway with a rodenticide.

DISEASE-RESISTANT SHRUB ROSES

Two groups of roses are making roses easier to grow than any of us ever imagined! They are varieties in the Knock Out series and the Care Free series. These everblooming shrub roses don't have much fragrance, but they are disease-resistant and hardy in Zones 4 - 9.

'Knock Out Cherry Red Blend' was the AARS winner for 2000. It has a light, tea-rose scent. A pink and then a double-flowered red followed.

'Knock Out Rainbow', a deep coral pink with a yellow center, was the AARS 2007 All America Rose Selection

'Carefree Delight', a single-flowered pink blend, was the AARS Selection for 1996. 'Beauty' is a semi-double coral pink; 'Wonder" is a creamy hot pink blend; and 'Sunshine' is a medium yellow.

December

ROSES

PLANNING

Update your garden log.

PLANTING

A raised bed for roses solves drainage problems and gives the roses a very good start. Get the project under way three to four weeks before you plan to plant. In our area, you can plant roses from late February to December 1.

See Starting a Raised Bed in the Introduction to the book for complete details.

CARE

If **miniature roses** growing indoors aren't flowering, increase the light by adding grow lights after dusk and putting them under fluorescents in a light garden.

PRUNING

Deadhead **miniature roses** indoors.

GIFTS FOR THE ROSE GARDENER

Grooming and pruning roses are essential to their health and beauty. Here's a set of tool rose growers love to give—and to receive:

1. For pruning and cleaning up—a set of bypass pruners; get the scissor type, not the anvil type, which crushes the stems.

2. For removal of large woody canes at the graft—a pruning saw small enough to access the graft area so the cut can be made flush with the main stem.

3. For cutting canes $1/2$ inch diameter or greater—lopping shears with 18-inch handles.

4. To scrub loose bark away from the bud union—a brass wire brush about 2 inches wide by 3 inches deep. Hardware stores sell them.

5. To seal pruning cuts on canes greater than $1/4$ inch diameter to prevent cane borers from entering—clear nail polish or white glue.

6. To save hands and arms from scratches—long leather gauntlets.

WATERING

Indoors. Keep the soil moderately moist for **miniatures** growing indoors.

Outdoors. Don't let the containers of hardy roses sheltering in a cold garage or shed dry out.

If December is short of snow or rain, water the roses overwintering in the open garden.

FERTILIZING

To encourage blooming, fertilize **miniature roses** that are growing indoors under grow lights with a light application of African violet or another bloom booster fertilizer.

PROBLEMS

Indoors. Dry air invites spider mites to adopt **miniature roses;** air the room every day. When you water **container roses**, water the soil, not the foliage.

Outdoors. If vole runs appear around the roses, bait the main runway with a rodenticide.

CHAPTER SEVEN

SHRUBS

Shrubs give the most pleasure for the least maintenance. What do established shrubs really need? Annual fertilization. Water during droughts. Mulch. Winter care. Regular maintenance of this type, and its timing, is easy to understand and provide.

More complex is the annual pruning that enhances a shrub's structure and its production of flowers and foliage. Pruning takes thought because when and how differs with each shrub group. As does the plant's "habit," the natural form a well-grown shrub will have when it matures if well pruned.

Guides to pruning the various categories of shrubs that appear on the pages for March and for May will help you to sort it out.

For the rest, you will find that shrubs that are pest- and disease-resistant, and are given a good start are worth many times over your investment in money and time.

Design. The growth "habit" of shrubs and hedge plants you choose to add or subtract have a tremendous impact on the traffic flow and the design of your garden. Like other structures—trees, fences, hedges, furniture, statuary—shrubs are the "bones" that anchor the garden design. Shrubs may be arched (forsythia), rounded (barberries), upright (*Kerria japonica* 'Pleniflora'), or columnar (dwarf Alberta spruce, *Picea glauca* 'Conica').

The most interesting shrub borders include a variety of tall and small flowering, foliage and

ABOUT HEDGES

To help you decide whether a hedge is for you, here's some advice from seasoned hedge keepers:

• Be sure you will have enough time available to keep your hedge trimmed. Hedges trimmed with hand pruners have a more natural look . . . and that takes time.

• Don't site a hedge on your property line using shrubs whose branches will reach into the neighbor's space. The neighbor can legally remove branches and roots invading his/her space.

• Choose species suited to the light and ground space available for the length of the hedge.

• Buy young shrubs, 3 feet or shorter. They are less expensive and adapt quickly.

• If the hedge will run through both tall shade and real shade, choose species that succeed in either light. Among candidates are most hollies, including American, Foster's, and Japanese holly, and longstalk holly, *Ilex pedunculosa*, Canadian hemlock, and 'Otto Lukyen' laurel, *Prunus laurocerasus*. In the shadiest area plant the shrubs closer together.

For more about hedges, see Planting in September.

---

berry plants, evergreen and deciduous types, and a variety of shapes and colors.

PLANTING

Bare-root shrubs. In early spring before growth begins, mail-order suppliers ship some shrubs bare root. Ascertain the size of a mail-order purchase before deciding it's a bargain. Follow the shipper's instructions for planting exactly.

Container-grown shrubs. In the Mid-Atlantic, you can plant container-grown shrubs from early spring—late February and March—through summer and fall until December 1. Buying locally allows you to select shrubs whose flower and foliage color, and structure, are exactly what you expect.

Balled-and-burlapped shrubs. You can plant B&B shrubs from early spring until December 1. Evergreens are best moved August, September, and into October. In summer, avoid buying B&B shrubs dug in spring that have been sitting for months in the open air with their bare rootball naked to the wind and sun. B&B shrubs dug in spring and "heeled in," that is protected by mounds of mulch or soil, stay in good condition. We recommend paying extra to have large B&B shrubs planted and guaranteed by the supplier.

Light and spacing. Many shrubs got their start in light shade under tall trees in a forest or at its edge. So most can do with less than a full day of sunlight. Azaleas, rhododendrons, and gardenias do very well in the filtered light of tall trees.

Space shrubs at distances that allow plenty of space for the lateral development of branches. To calculate the best spacing for two or more young shrubs, add together the widths given on the plant tags, and divide by two. To occupy the bed while young shrubs fill out, plant shade-tolerant hostas or ferns, and annuals such as impatiens, pentas, and caladiums. Avoid airless corners.

Soil. The information on Soil Preparation and Improvement and pH given in the Introduction to the book applies to shrubs.

Digging the hole. Make the planting hole three times as wide and twice as deep as the rootball. Loosen the sides of the hole, and blend the soil taken from the hole with the organic amendments described in Soil Preparation and Improvement in the Introduction. Half fill the bottom of the hole with improved soil, and tamp it down to make a firm base for the roots.

Set the shrub so the crown will be an inch above ground level. Half fill the hole with improved soil.

Tamp it down firmly. Finish filling the hole with improved soil, and tamp it down firmly. Shape the soil around the crown into a wide saucer.

Water the soil slowly, gently, and thoroughly with a sprinkler, a soaker hose, a bubbler, or by hand. You need to put down 1 1/2 inches of water (see Watering). Or, slowly pour on 10 to 15 gallons of water from a bucket.

Mulch newly planted shrubs 2 to 3 inches deep starting 3 inches from the main stem. Replenish the mulch as needed to keep it 2 to 3 inches deep.

Growing shrubs in containers. You can grow a shrub in a container outdoors indefinitely-a hardy shrub, that is-providing the container is large enough to insulate the roots from winter cold. (See April, Growing Shrubs in Containers.)

Transplanting shrubs. Spring and fall through November are the best seasons to move shrubs. Evergreen shrubs can be transplanted spring and fall through October. You will find information on moving large established shrubs under Planting, in the February pages. Move flowering shrubs well before, or after they have bloomed.

WATERING

Newly planted and transplanted shrubs need sustained moisture—for the first eight weeks, two or three 5-gallon bucketfuls of water around the roots weekly throughout spring unless you have sustained soaking rains. In summer, every week or ten days, unless you have a soaking rain, slowly and gently lay down 1 1/2 inches of water. In fall, even after cold sets in, shrub roots continue to develop so water often enough to prevent the soil from drying out. One of the most important winter preparations is a deep and thorough watering before the ground freezes.

PRUNING

You can reduce the amount of pruning your shrubs will need by selecting dwarf and slow-growing varieties. This is most important when choosing shrubs for hedges. But even dwarfs grow, albeit slowly, so even they may need some pruning to maintain their size. See the introduction to the Trees chapter for the proper ways to prune.

We prune shrubs at different seasons and with a variety of purposes:

To rejuvenate. Prune drastically in late winter while still dormant to rejuvenate leggy shrubs. Take away no more than a third or a quarter of the branches in one season. Make the cut about a foot from the ground. Repeat the process the next two years until the pruning project is complete.

To encourage flowering. Prune shrubs that flower on the current season's wood—butterfly bush and vitex for example—well before growth begins to encourage the production of many new flowering shoots. Prune shrubs that bloom on last year's wood, azaleas for example, when they finish blooming, because they soon start initiating flower buds for the next season.

To stimulate fullness. Prune shrubs when they are growing actively to encourage more, bushier growth. Fresh, young shoots that are cut back by half immediately begin to grow lateral shoots.

To encourage branching. To encourage more foliage in broadleaf evergreens that branch, azaleas and abelias, for example, prune succulent new shoots while they are growing actively back by half. Rhododendrons are different; cut just above a whorl.

To limit growth. Prune leafy plants after the season's growth to reduce the leaf surfaces, which limits the sugar synthesized and sent to the roots, and that limits next year's growth.

To top a plant. Top a shrub or a hedge after the season's growth has been completed to maintain the current height.

JANUARY
SHRUBS

PLANNING

In winter your garden reveals its "bones," the naked woody structures that anchor the landscape. Take the garden catalogs arriving now to a comfortable chair by a window, and consider what a few new shrubs, or a hedge, could do for your view. You can start planting new shrubs as early as March, but we recommend waiting to plant a new hedge until fall.

Flowering shrubs. For flowers early to late spring and four-season greenery, consider varieties of flowering broadleaved evergreens—**mountain laurels, rhododendrons, azaleas. Evergreen azalea** foliage adds shades of plum and maroon to the fall scene, and some are flecked with gold. **Kaempferi azaleas,** including 'Armstrong's Fall' and 'Indian Summer', rebloom in September, just as **nandina's** lipstick-red berries begin to shine.

Shrubs for fragrance. In their season of bloom, shrubs that bear fragrant flowers become garden destinations. **Winter daphne,** *Daphne odora* 'Aureo-marginata', scents the garden early on, followed by the perfumed **viburnums.** You can count on **mock oranges** for late spring perfume, and in November the tiny blooms of **sweet holly olive** (*Osmanthus*

Oregon grape

heterophyllus) fill the air around with a haunting fragrance.

Evergreen shrubs for perennial beds. If you have not included shrubby evergreens in your flower beds, plan to try a few this year. The lively green anchors the beds off season. We use the dark little **mugo pines** that way. A trio of small, clipped ball-shaped **boxwoods** among the perennials adds greenery and a smile. Small, columnar evergreens like **dwarf Alberta spruce,** *Picea glauca* 'Conica', are sensational in a large flowering border. **Alberta spruce** is attacked by spider mites, so make a note to keep it sprayed periodically with horticultural soaps.

Evergreen shrubs for hedges and edging. The **junipers** (*Juni-*

perus spp. and cultivars), the indestructible **yews** (*Taxus*), the handsome **Meserve hybrid hollies** (*Ilex* x *meserveae*) 'Blue Boy' and 'Blue Princess', and **dwarf variegated hollies** make handsome hedges, great edging for paths and driveways, and foundation plants.

Deciduous shrubs for seasonal change. Flowers and foliage that changes with the seasons is the domain of the leaf-losing shrubs. In early fall the **dwarf winged spindle tree,** *Euonymus alata* 'Compacta', is a blaze of pink-scarlet. *Spiraea* and the silver-backed leaves of **willowleaf cotoneaster** (*Cotoneaster salicifolius* 'Autumn Fire') turn purplish when the weather is cold. Yellow **Japanese barberry** (*Berberis thunbergii* 'Aurea') and golden **Scotch heather** (*Calluna vulgaris*) brighten dark corners. Cultivars of the exquisite **Japanese maple** (*Acer palmatum*) rival the crimson of the **swamp maple.** The beautiful cultivar 'Osakazuki' is yellow to light green in the summer and turns a stunning fluorescent red in fall.

Berried shrubs for winter interest. The bright berries of both evergreen and leaf-losing **hollies, barberries,** and other berried shrubs cheer winter's gray skies. **Oregon grape** (*Mahonia aquifolium*), *Nandina domestica,* and **sweet box**, *Sarcococca hookeriana* var. *humilis*, add dabs of shiny red to the seasonal mix. Bright blue/black or white berries follow the flowers in many species.

PLANTING

Give your out-of-bloom gift **azalea** a sunny spot on a sill since it, along with **mums** and **poinsettias,** is among plants that test high as air purifiers. When blooming is over, transplant the **azalea** to a larger pot filled with a mixture that is one-fourth garden soil and three-fourths peat moss. Keep the soil moist, and when new growth appears, at every watering apply an acid-type fertilizer at one quarter the recommended strength. Increase that over a four-month period until you are fertilizing at

the strength recommended on the container. Forced **azaleas** are not usually hardy here, but if you summer it outdoors and expose it to several cool, but not freezing, fall nights before bringing it in, it may bloom again.

CARE

Free evergreen branches from snow or ice. Use a broom to brush away snow or ice accumulations that might harm hedges.

Renew the anti-desiccant spray on **camellias** and other **broad-leaf evergreen shrubs** growing in exposed positions. If they are suffering, wrap them in Reemay.

PRUNING

Remove branches damaged by heavy snow and winter storms.

WATERING

Indoors. Water shrubs wintering inside as needed.

Outdoors. Without snow or rain, the soil may run dry around

shrubs growing next to foundations and under overhangs, and shrubs in containers that are under arbors and similar shelters. During the January thaw, give them a slow, thorough watering.

FERTILIZING

Tropical hibiscus, potted **gardenias,** and other tender shrubs brought indoors last fall are beginning to grow again; add a half strength dose of water-soluble fertilizer at every second watering.

PROBLEMS

Indoors. Monitor **tropical hibiscus** and shrubs growing indoors for signs of spider mite, whitefly, and other problems. See Pests, Diseases, and Controls in the Appendix for controls.

Outdoors. Repair or renew deer deterrents and sprays. Check and adjust burlap covers and chicken-wire cages protecting shrubs.

If vole runs appear around shrubs, bait the main runway with a rodenticide.

SHRUBS FOR FLOWER ARRANGEMENTS
- **Butterfly Bush**, *Buddleia* x *weyeriana* 'Honeycomb'
- **Bigleaf Hydrangea**, *Hydrangea macrophylla* 'Amethyst'
- **Drooping Leucothe**, *Leucothoe fontanesiana*
- **Highbush Cranberry**, *Viburnum trilobum* 'Compactum'
- **Lilac**, *Syringa vulgaris* 'Beauty of Moscow'

FEBRUARY

SHRUBS

PLANNING

When the buds on branches of shrubs that flower in early spring are swelling, harvest a few to force into bloom indoors.

Place your catalog orders for shrubs now.

PLANTING

In Zone 8, the soil may have warmed enough to do some transplanting. Small shrubs can be moved anytime before growth begins. Moving very large shrubs is a two-year project. Known as root pruning, the process also slows growth by depriving the plant of nutrient intake.

Year 1. Before growth begins, sever the roots in a circle all around the trunk of the shrub to stimulate root growth within the circle.

Year 2. This time next year, tie the branches together at the top. Dig a trench outside the root-pruned circle, lift the rootball onto a big piece of burlap, and tie the burlap up around the trunk. Very gently transport the plant to its new location. Prepare the soil, and plant the shrub as described in Planting in the introduction to this chapter, and then free the branches and prune out damaged twigs.

CARE

Clear snow, dead branches, and winter debris from the shrubbery, especially the **boxwoods.**

After the late winter fertilization (see Fertilizing), add enough fresh material to maintain a 2- to 3-inch layer of mulch starting about 3 inches from the central stems.

PRUNING

Thin **forsythias, quince,** and other spring-flowering shrubs well before they bloom, and use the branches for forcing into bloom indoors.

You can prune summer-flowering shrubs February, March, or April.

Prune out evergreen branches damaged by winter storms.

To rejuvenate the **hollies,** prune heavily in late winter to early spring. You can cut the plants down to about a foot from the ground.

WATERING

Indoors. Water shrubs growing indoors as needed.

Outdoors. The soil is usually still wet from winter rain and snow, so no watering should be needed this month, except for new transplants. Throughout spring, unless you have a soaking rain, pour two or three 5-gallon bucketfuls of water around the roots once a week.

FERTILIZING

Indoors. Fertilize **tropical hibiscus** and other tender shrubs brought indoors last fall at every second watering.

Outdoors. Check and adjust the soil pH in the beds of shrubs, especially any that aren't performing well, including **azaleas, rhododendrons,** and other acid-loving plants. To raise or lower the pH, see Soil Preparation and Improvement in the book's Introduction.

Fertilize the beds late this month or early next month. The section on Understanding Fertilizers in the Introduction to the book explains how and when to use the various types of fertilizer.

Halve the amount of fertilizer for mature hedges; do not over-stimulate when you no longer have a lot of room for growth.

PROBLEMS

Indoors. Watch shrubs growing indoors for signs of whitefly, spider mites, and other pests. If you find problems, look up controls in the Pests, Diseases, and Controls section in the Appendix.

Flowering cherry 'Kwanzan'

Outdoors. Check and adjust burlap covers and chicken-wire cages protecting shrubs from deer.

As the ground thaws, voles get lively; they can damage young shrub roots. If vole runs appear, bait the main runway with a rodenticide.

To keep rabbits, woodchucks, and other rodents away from shrubs, try chemical fungicide formulations such as Thiram (Arasan) and hot pepper wax.

Before buds on plants suspected of insect infestation break, spray them with horticultural oil. The oil smothers insects and their eggs.

FORCING FLOWERING BRANCHES

In late winter, branches of spring flowering shrubs (and trees) can be forced into bloom indoors. The time to harvest the branches is when the buds begin to swell. The warmer the zone, the earlier the forcing date.

Harvest branches 2 to 3 feet long and heavily studded with buds. Monitor the water levels in the containers—it may need topping twice a week.

Cold method. Press the cut ends into snow or icy cold water, and let them rest two days in a cool, dark place. Fill tall vases with cool water, recut the branch ends, and arrange the branches in the vases. Set them in the sun next to a window.

Warm method. Bring the cut branches indoors, and place them in tall containers in water at bath temperature—90 to 110 degrees Fahrenheit. Tent the containers and the branches with plastic, and set them in a dim, warm room. The warmth and humidity will encourage the scales covering the flower buds to expand, and activate dormant buds.

Here are a few of our favorites:

• *Chaenomeles,* **Japanese quince, flowering quince;** cut February to mid-March; force for two to five weeks; bloom period, four to seven days.

• *Cornus florida,* **dogwood;** cut mid-March; force for two to four weeks; bloom period, seven to ten days.

• **Forsythia;** cut February to mid-March; force for one to three weeks; bloom period, seven days.

• *Malus,* **apple, crabapple;** cut mid-March; force for two to three weeks; bloom period, seven days.

• *Prunus calleryana,* **flowering pear;** cut late January to mid-March; force for two to five weeks; bloom period, seven to fourteen days.

• *Prunus persica,* **flowering peach;** cut early February; force for four to five weeks; bloom period, seven days.

• *Prunus serrulata,* **Japanese flowering cherry;** cut late January to mid-March; force for two to four weeks; bloom period, seven to fourteen days.

• *Prunus triloba,* **flowering plum;** cut late January to February; force for three to four weeks; bloom period, ten days.

• *Salix* species, **pussy willow;** cut February; force for one to two weeks; bloom period, indefinitely if allowed to dry. (Remove the bud scales, and when they reach the fuzzy bud stage, remove the branches from the water.)

• *Syringa,* **lilac;** cut early March; bloom period, four to six weeks; bloom period, three to seven days.

MARCH

SHRUBS

PLANNING

March is a great month to plant the shrubs you'd like to add to the garden.

Begin to plan the pruning of shrub borders and hedges.

PLANTING

As soon as winter cold leaves the ground, you can start planting new shrubs. Use Tree-tone, Holly-tone, or Plant-tone as fertilizers.

Container-grown shrub. To free the shrub, tip the pot on its side, and roll it around. If it's too large for that, slit the sides of the container, and peel off the pieces. If roots wrap the rootball, make four shallow vertical cuts in the sides of the rootball, and slice off the bottom two inches.

Bare-root shrub. Keep the shrub in its packaging in a dark, cool place until you are ready to plant. Soak the roots in tepid water six to twelve hours before planting.

B&B shrub. Handle the rootball gently, and as little as possible. Avoid disturbing the burlap, twine, or wire basket as you put the rootball into the planting hole. After the rootball is in the hole, cut the twine around the trunk, and cut off or push the ends of the burlap into the hole. If the cover is plastic, cut away as much as possible, and poke holes in what remains.

Follow these steps for planting:

1. Dig a planting hole three times as wide and twice as deep as the rootball; after planting, the crown of the shrub should be about an inch above the soil line.

2. Mix into the soil from the hole the amendments recommended under Soil Preparation and Improvement in the Introduction to the book.

Half fill the bottom of the hole with the improved soil, and tamp it down. Make a firm mound in the center of the hole, and drape the plant roots over and around the mound.

CARE

Indoors. To keep a **gardenia** indoors in good condition, put the pot on a saucer of moist pebbles, grow it in a sunny window, and air and mist the plant daily. When you water, add a half dose of water-soluble fertilizer for acid-loving plants.

Outdoors. Remove covers from protected shrubs. March winds can blow hard enough to disturb the mulch applied last month after fertilizing the beds; top it off if necessary.

PRUNING

Shear hedges. The pruning guide for deciduous shrubs on this month's pages and the May guide for evergreens will help you to determine when to clip shrubs and hedges.

In mid-March, shear damaged (and browning or whitened) **boxwood** branches back to live growth. To regenerate a multi-stemmed deciduous shrub that is overgrown, before it begins to grow, take out a third or a quarter of the branches. Make the cut about a foot from the ground.

Remove the containers from shrubs prior to planting.

Deadhead and prune back flowering shrubs that bloom on the current season's wood now before the buds break. Cut **butterfly bush,** *Buddleia,* back to 6 to 12 inches from the ground to force new growth. To encourage flowering and maintain a shrubby height and form in **shrub althea (rose-of-Sharon)** and **crapemyrtle,** prune older branches back to a strong outward facing bud.

You can prune summer-flowering shrubs this month and in April.

WATERING

Indoors. Water shrubs wintering inside as needed.

Outdoors. Maintain the soil moisture in new and transplanted shrubs. Pour two or three 5-gallon bucketfuls of water around the roots once a week throughout spring.

FERTILIZING

Indoors. Continue to fertilize **tropical hibiscus, gardenias,** and other tender shrubs at every second watering.

Indoors and outdoors. Before growth begins, top-dress the soil of shrubs growing in containers indoors and outdoors. Tip the containers on their sides, and gently remove the top 2 inches

---

PRUNING GUIDE FOR DECIDUOUS SHRUBS

Dead or damaged wood. Prune anytime between late winter and early autumn.

Flowering shrubs that bloom on new wood. Prune in late winter or early spring, well before growth begins.

Flowering plants that bloom on old wood. Prune right after they bloom to avoid removing next year's flower buds that develop on new growth.

To encourage dense branching. Prune during active growth; cut back by half succulent stems beginning to grow lateral shoots.

To control height. Prune after new growth has fully developed. Cut into the old wood.

To slow or dwarf growth. Prune after the season's new growth is complete.

---

of soil. Replace it with a fertile potting mix that includes Hollytone. Renew the mulch.

Outdoors. Fertilize beds not fertilized last month. Avoid fertilizing flowering shrubs shortly before blooming. That stimulates growth at a time when you want the plants to direct their energy into flowering. If you've missed the right moment for fertilizing, wait to fertilize until after they have bloomed.

PROBLEMS

Indoors. Watch shrubs growing indoors for signs of whitefly, spider mites, and other problems. If you find problems, look up controls in the Pests, Diseases, and Controls section in the Appendix.

Outdoors. Before the buds begin to swell, apply a dormant horticultural oil spray to insect-infested shrubs. These dense oils smother the insects and their eggs.

In deer country, apply a new and different spray to vulnerable shrubs (**rhododendrons, arborvitae,** and other broadleaf evergreens), and replace old deterrents with new deterrents. (See Pests, Diseases, and Controls in the Appendix.) If deer are very audacious, surround small treasured shrubs with temporary chicken-wire screens; for larger plantings, try unobtrusive bird netting.

Voles are active in March. If you see vole runs, bait the main runway with a rodenticide.

APRIL

SHRUBS

PLANNING

Considering adding shrubs with colorful foliage and/or bark to brighten your shrubbery border. Some of our favorites are **golden privet,** *Ligustrum x vicaryi*, and **variegated gold-dust tree,** *Aucuba japonica* 'Variegata'. At a distance the foliage of **variegated bigleaf hydrangea,** *Hydrangea macrophylla* 'Variegata', and *Weigela florida* 'Variegata', and 'Wine & Roses' are a lovely soft jade.

PLANTING

You can transplant container-grown and B&B shrubs all the months ahead until about December 1. Evergreen shrubs may do best August through October. But right now the new stock at your garden center is likely to be in top condition. Before buying a container-grown shrub, tip it partly out of the pot, and make sure the rootball isn't heavily rootbound.

CARE

Indoors. Repot **azaleas, gardenias, citrus,** and other tender shrubs outgrowing their containers, and as soon as the weather

Hydrangea 'Bluebird' Lace-cap type

stays above 60 degrees at night, move them outdoors for summer R&R. Place them in bright indirect light.

Outdoors. Don't be alarmed if **crapemyrtles** and some other late shrubs don't come to life when you expect them to. Wait until June before deciding they didn't survive winter.

PRUNING

As flowers fade on shrubs that bloom on the previous year's wood, prune back branches that are compromising the natural form of the shrub, and older nonproductive wood.

Prune **azaleas** when they finish blooming to a shape suggesting

a layered cloud; don't just shear off the branch tips.

WATERING

For a shrub's first season, unless there's a soaking rain, throughout spring slowly and gently pour two or three 5-gallon bucketfuls of water around the roots once a week.

Water shrubs growing in containers as needed.

FERTILIZING

Outdoors. Mophead and **lacecap hydrangeas** bloom colors may be cream through rose to dark blue. The color depends not only on the variety, but also on the soil pH. Acidity makes aluminum in the soil more available, and that's what keeps the flowers blue. A pH of 5.0 to 5.5 results in a soft blue color. To maintain pink, the soil must be in the pH range of 6.0 to 6.5 or slightly higher. Test the soil now. If the pH needs adjusting, see Soil Preparation and Improvement in the Introduction to the book. The time to adjust the pH is before new growth begins to emerge.

If you are using chemical fertilizers, you should be fertilizing every six weeks or so. Check the section on Understanding Fertilizers in the Introduction to the book for timing.

At every second watering, add a half dose of a water-soluble fertilizer to the water for shrubs growing in containers.

PROBLEMS

Outdoors. Continue preventive measures to protect your garden from deer.

Aphids, whiteflies, and spider mites are gearing up to get you down. **Azaleas** growing in full sun are especially susceptible to spider mites and lacebugs. Three applications of Permethrin or *Pyrethrum* at three to four day intervals will help you to control these pests. Be sure to spray the undersides of the leaves.

GROWING SHRUBS IN CONTAINERS

You can grow almost any shrub successfully in a container as long as it has good drainage and is big enough to hold enough soil to protect the roots from winter cold. Casters on the bottom of the larger containers make moving easier.

Container. For a small shrub, a container 14 to 16 inches in height and diameter is enough. Start a young larger shrub, like **Japanese maple,** in an 18- to 20-inch tub, and plan to move it to a 30-inch tub.

Insulation can keep containers from cracking in winter's cold. Wrap the interior of containers that will remain outdoors for the winter with a double row of large bubble wrap or Styrofoam before filling them with soil. You can provide added winter protection by packing bags of leaves around the containers in fall.

Soil. The ideal container soil is a fertile semi-soilless mix. André's recipe is: 1 part good topsoil, 1 part horticultural perlite, and 2 parts coarse peat moss. For every 7 inches of planter height, add $1/3$ cup slow-release fertilizer, and 1 cup dehydrated cow manure. Adding a soil polymer, such as Soil Moist, can reduce watering by as much as 50 percent. Soak the growing medium before you plant. After planting, water until water runs out the bottom. Apply and maintain a 2- or 3-inch layer of mulch.

Watering. From late spring to mid-autumn, plan to water weekly or biweekly. The larger the container, the less often you will have to water it. Containers with built-in water reservoirs, or with water rings that let the plant soak up the water from the bottom, help to keep the soil moist.

Fertilizing. Once a month during the growing season, add a water-soluble fertilizer, seaweed or manure tea, to the water.

In late winter before growth begins, top-dress the soil. Tip the container on its side, and gently remove the top 2 inches of soil. Replace it with fresh fertile potting mix that includes Holly-tone slow release fertilizer, and renew the mulch.

Scale is a problem with hollies and camellias. Spray with summer weight horticultural oils or Neem.

Rake up weeds as they raise their little green heads to avoid dealing with mature ones later.

Late this month gypsy moths may appear. Spray with a biological control such as *Bacillus thuringiensis*. Other controls are Sevin or malathion insecticide, pyrethrin, or rotenone.

MAY
SHRUBS

PLANNING

Spring gardens are peaking in the Mid-Atlantic, a wonderful time to visit public and private gardens. Check out the **azalea** collection at the U.S. National Arboretum in Washington, and note the names of some you would like to see in your shrubbery border.

When the weather keeps you out of the garden, visit your full-service garden centers looking for must-haves and bargains.

Investigate the many **viburnums**. Some of these big handsome shrubs bear flowers that are spicily perfumed, and many have colorful foliage and fruits in fall. Some bloom with the **flowering cherries**, some as late as the end of June. The earlier types bear large rounded flower heads and are called **"snowball"** or **"semi-snowball"** varieties.

'Mohawk' and 'Cayuga' are two of several superb fragrant disease-resistant cultivars introduced by the late great plant hybridizer, Dr. Donald R. Egolf of the National Arboretum. **"Double-file viburnums"** bloom later, and they perch rows of pure white flowers all along the tops of their branches; Dr. Egolf's 'Shasta' is a superb example.

PLANTING

May is a fine month for planting new shrubs and transplanting shrubs that have finished blooming.

Fill gaps left by the passing of the spring-flowering bulbs by planting big seedlings of flowering annuals, along with young tropical shrubs and tender shrubs from last year that you wintered indoors.

CARE

Indoors. Move indoor shrubs that still are indoors outside to bright indirect light for their summer vacation.

Outdoors. To keep summer's downpours from eroding the soil around your shrubs, and to protect their roots from the coming heat, replenish the mulch. Make it 2 to 3 inches deep starting 3 inches from the main stem.

PRUNING

Prune shrubs that bloomed on last year's wood when the flowers are finished.

Deadhead **rhododendrons** very carefully; pinch out the dead blossoms, taking care not to damage the tiny emerging leaf buds right behind them.

As **azaleas** finish blooming, clip or prune 2 to 3 inches off the branch tips that have flowered.

To lower an **azalea** or a **rhododendron** that is getting too tall, take a third of the oldest branches back to 12 inches. Aim at creating a layered look.

Prune **forsythia** by taking older branches right back to the ground. If you leave a stump, new branches will develop there

Doublefile Viburnum

in a direction that crosses other branches.

Cut a few central stems of **nandina** bushes right to the ground.

Scorched lower branches of evergreen shrubs may be from salt damage that occurred when streets or sidewalks were de-iced; drench the soil to leach out the remaining salts, and cut out the damaged branches.

Dog urine also can turn a shrub lower branches yellow, especially **boxwoods.** Drench the soil, and fence the area, and spray the plants with dog and cat deterrent.

WATERING

If watering, or April rains, have eroded the soil on sloping shrub borders, shovel it back up the slope, and reestablish saucers around the plants to catch and hold the rain.

For a shrub's first season, unless there's a soaking rain, throughout spring slowly and gently pour two or three 5-gallon bucketfuls of water around the roots every week.

FERTILIZING

Twice a month add a water-soluble fertilizer, or dilute seaweed or manure tea, to the water for shrubs growing outdoors in con-

---

PRUNING GUIDE FOR EVERGREENS

Winter and snow damage to evergreens is best pruned before growth begins.

Dead or damaged wood on evergreen conifers can be removed at any time.

Flowering broadleaf evergreens that bloom on new wood, like **abelia,** should be pruned in late winter or early spring before growth begins.

Flowering broadleaf evergreens that bloom on old wood—**azaleas** and **rhododendrons** for example—should be pruned immediately after they bloom and before they initiate new growth to avoid cutting off buds being initiated for the following season.

To slow or dwarf a broadleaf evergreen, after its main spurt of growth, remove up to a third. You can cut the main stem (leader) back to the first side shoots, but don't take off more than has grown the last year or two.

To encourage dense branching in evergreens whose growth is initiated by candles (new, candlelike growth), cut the candles back by half when growth is complete. Prune the tips of **yews, junipers,** and **hemlocks** lightly anytime during the growing season.

To establish a shape, prune evergreen shrubs and hedges when they are three to five years old.

For holiday greens, prune lightly in December.

---

tainers, and to the annuals and tender and tropical shrubs summering in the shrubbery border.

How often the in-ground shrubs need fertilizing depends on the type of fertilizer you are using; for that information, turn to section on Understanding Fertilizers in the Introduction to the book.

PROBLEMS

Early this month gypsy moths may appear. Spray with a biological control such as *Bacillus thuringiensis.* Other controls are Sevin or malathion insecticide, pyrethrin, or rotenone.

Apply or change whatever deer deterrents you are using. See the section on Pests, Diseases, and Controls in the Appendix.

Mugo pines and other needled evergreen shrubs that show denuded branch may be under attack by pine sawfly larvae. Spray the affected plants with Bt (*Bacillus thuringiensis*).

Keep the beds weed free.

JUNE
SHRUBS

PLANNING

When the color of a shrub's blossoms matter, buy it from a local garden center when you can see the plant in bloom. Buying locally will also provide an opportunity to:

• Select the very best cultivars for your area.

• Check the undersides of the leaves, and the crotch of the branches for signs of insects.

• Check the condition of the rootball. It's okay if a few roots circle the rootball and there's a thin mat of roots at the bottom; much more than that will need removal, however, and the plant will need time to recover.

• Get good cultural advice.

PLANTING

Transplant **azaleas** that have finished blooming.

If shrubbery borders look bare, plant seedlings of **flowering maples,** *Abutilon,* and **tropical hibiscus.** In September you can pot them up, and winter them indoors as houseplants.

CARE

If wands of willowy **butterfly bush** get flattened by rain and

Be prepared to hand water newly planted shrubs, if needed.

wind, stake them. They can be pruned and shaped throughout the summer.

Make sure the mulch around hedges and shrubbery is a full 3 inches deep—no more—before heat arrives.

PRUNING

Finish deadheading late-blooming **rhododendrons** and **azaleas.** Deadhead **tropical hibiscus, flowering maples,** and other tender shrubs.

To let light and air into the interior of old clipped **boxwoods,** remove older inside branches.

After the first flush of new growth in **evergreen hedges,** trim the top and sides to keep the height down and the greenery full. Keep the top narrower than

the bottom so light can reach the lower branches, or they will lose their leaves.

Cut the succulent new shoots on **deciduous hedges** in half.

Prune elongated **boxwood** shoots after new growth is complete to keep them trim and beautiful.

WATERING

A newly planted shrub needs a good soaking every week to ten days in summer. If it doesn't rain, slowly and gently pour two or three 5-gallon bucketfuls of water around the roots.

Every few days check the soil moisture in shrubs growing in containers, and water as often as necessary to keep it nicely damp.

FERTILIZING

New growth is emerging in the **mophead** and **lacecap hydrangeas**—time to adjust the bloom color toward pink or blue by increasing or decreasing the soil acidity. A pH of 5.0 to 5.5 results in a soft blue color. For pink keep the soil pH 6.0 to 6.5 or slightly higher. To adjust the pH, see Soil Preparation and Improvement in the Introduction to the book.

How often the in-ground shrubs need fertilizing depends on the type of fertilizer you are using; for information, turn to the section on Understanding Fertilizers in the Introduction to the book.

At every second watering, add a half dose of a water-soluble fertilizer to the water for shrubs growing in containers.

PROBLEMS

Repair and/or renew deer deterrents and sprays.

Check **rhododendrons** and **azaleas** for lacebug damage. The leaf surfaces will be dull, speckled, pale, and the undersides will show specks of insect excrement. Spray the foliage at intervals with horticultural oil or insecticidal soap.

Whitefly and spider mite damage shows up as spotted and blanched leaves. Remove dead or severely infected twigs, and spray with Neem at intervals until the infestation is gone. See Pests, Diseases, and Controls in the Appendix.

Keep the beds clear of weeds. If they mature and go to seed, there will be an army to rout later on.

ROOTING CUTTINGS TO MULTIPLY YOUR SHRUBS

Azaleas, winterberry, magnolias, nandina, osmanthus, coniferous evergreens, and many other shrubs can be rooted from semi-hardwood cuttings taken June and July. New green growth that is just turning brown and hardening is what is meant by "semi-hardwood." Snap a twig, and if the bark clings to the branch, it's likely semi-hardwood.

Here's how it works:

1. Prepare a rooting box about the size of a seed flat and 5 to 6 inches deep. It must have drainage. Fill the box with 4 inches of a moist mix of equal parts peat and perlite or coarse sand. With a pencil, make twelve equidistant planting holes.

2. Cover the bottom of a saucer with rooting hormone powder Number 3, or Root-tone.

3. In early morning, cut a dozen semi-hardened branch ends 4 to 8 inches long at a point about 1 inch below a leaf cluster. Remove the leaves from the bottom 3 inches. Mist the foliage.

4. Working in shade, remove a strip of bark 1/2 to 1 inch long on the side of each cutting close to the cut end. Lightly coat the cut ends and the wounds in the rooting powder.

5. Insert the cut ends 2 to 3 inches in the rooting box, deep enough to cover the wounds. Press the soil up around the cuttings.

6. Water well, and enclose the box in clear plastic. Use hoops made of wire coat hangers to support the plastic, and punch a few tiny holes in the plastic for ventilation.

7. Place the box in a shaded, sheltered location. Check the soil moisture every five days; the cuttings mustn't dry out.

8. In about six weeks, test the cuttings to see if they are rooted. Very gently tug on a couple of the cuttings; when you meet real resistance, they are rooted.

9. Transplant the rooted cuttings to pots filled with equal parts potting soil and half peat.

10. Gradually expose the pots to increasingly strong light while keeping the soil moist. In September, transplant them to the garden, and protect them with a light mulch of hay or open evergreen boughs.

JULY

SHRUBS

PLANNING

Keep abreast of research on natural controls and improved shrub varieties. Find time for a trip to the U.S. National Arboretum in DC to learn more about the many improved and disease-resistant varieties of popular shrubs introduced in recent decades by scientists working there.

Many new mildew-free **crapemyrtles,** superior **viburnums** like **hardy hibiscus (shrub althea, rose-of-Sharon)** and the **doublefile** beauty called 'Shasta', were selected and introduced by the late great Dr. Donald R. Egolf. **Euonymus** specimens at the National Arboretum are now free of scale insects, a pest that can make growing these beautiful evergreen shrubs a never-ending battle. Scales on the insect's back literally protect them from insecticides, but USDA scientists found predator beetles in Korea that attack and control the pest at the Arboretum without the aid of insecticides.

PLANTING

When planting shrubs in containers at the seashore, use commercial potting soil rather than the sandy soil of the area. The humidity in the air reduces the need to water, but check the soil moisture often anyway.

You can continue to plant container-grown shrubs this month. B&B shrubs, too, but don't buy B&B shrubs whose rootballs have been sitting unmulched and baking at a garden center since they were dug in early spring.

CARE

After heavy summer storms, check, and if needed, replenish the mulch around shrubs.

To prevent plant damage from coastal storms, spray the upper and lower sides of the leaves with anti-desiccants.

PRUNING

Groom and prune back the spring-flowering shrubs and hedges.

Continue to deadhead **tropical hibiscus, flowering maples,** and other shrubs that bloom all summer.

Toward the middle of the month, you can take a half inch off leggy shoots of older **azalea** shoots; do not prune new growth—that's where next year's flowers will be.

WATERING

Shrubs growing in big containers are likely to need watering every four to seven days, the smaller containers more often. Containers with built-in water reservoirs, or with water rings that let the plant soak up the water from the bottom, minimize watering chores.

Late July is drought season, and you will probably need to water the garden two or three times before the fall rains arrive in September. If you go ten days without rain, water slowly, and deeply, especially newly planted shrubs. Shrubs slow their growth to adapt to high heat unless forced by shallow watering and inappropriate fertilizing to grow

WHEN IS A SHRUB A SHRUB?

A forester's definition of a shrub is a multi-trunked woody perennial plant reaching not more than 10 to 20 feet at maturity. Some woody plants can be trained either as trees or shrubs, **crapemyrtle**, for example, and **shrub althaea, lilacs, witchhazel, shadblow, smokebush**. Yes, even **lilacs**, though so often they are trained to a single stalk so they look like small trees.

when the weather isn't supporting growth.

Before going on vacation, group shrubs growing in containers in light shade, make sure each one has a generous saucer, and water them thoroughly.

FERTILIZING

At every second watering add a half dose of a water-soluble fertilizer, liquid seaweed, or a manure tea to the water for shrubs growing in containers.

How often the in-ground shrubs need fertilizing depends on the type of fertilizer you are using; for information, turn to the section on Understanding Fertilizers in the Introduction to the book. If you are using chemical fertilizers, you should be fertilizing every six weeks or so.

PROBLEMS

Continue preventive measures to protect your garden from deer.

When you see the first Japanese beetles, go after them. Japanese beetle traps are effective, provided they are placed far away from the plantings you are trying to protect, not among them. In the cool or early morning, knock the beetles off into a jar of sudsy water. Do not install pheromone traps that attract beetles from

---

SHRUBS AT THE SHORE

These plants tolerate salt spray and sandy situations at the shore and inland, too. Most require well-drained soil.

- **Adam's-needle,** *Yucca filamentosa.* Big, dramatic evergreen rosette of sword-like leaves that sends up 6-foot flower spikes.
- **Bayberry,** *Myrica pennsylvanica.* For Zone 6 and north. Beautiful big shrub with gray-green, semi-evergreen leaves that are aromatic when crushed.
- **Beach plum,** *Prunus maritime.* Round bush that bears clusters of white blooms followed by purplish fruit.
- **Fragrant elaeagnus,** *Elaeagnus pungens.* Tall evergreen shrub that bears fragrant white flowers in September and October.
- **Hydrangea,** *Hydrangea* species and varieties. Deciduous shrubs with huge flower heads in mid- and late summer.
- **Inkberry,** *Ilex glabra.* Black-berried, usually evergreen, shrub to 3 feet high. 'Leucocarpa' has white fruit.
- **Japanese rose, rugosa rose,** *Rosa rugosa.* Tall rugged bush that bears handsome roses and brilliant fruit.
- **Juniper, creeping juniper,** *Juniperus horizontalis;* **shore juniper,** *J. conferta.* Spreading gray-green evergreen foliage and blue berries.
- **Lavender cotton,** *Santolina* species and varieties. Gray-leaved, low, evergreen shrubs with aromatic leaves and inconspicuous flowers.
- **Scotch broom,** *Cytisus scoparius.* The arching stems bear pea-like flowers in spring or summer.
- **Tamarisk, salt cedar,** *Tamarix ramosissima.* For Zone 7 and north. Tall shrubs with delicate leaves and feathery clusters of flowers in late summer.
- **Vicary golden privet,** *Ligustrum* x *vicaryi.* Small-leaved evergreen for tall hedges.

---

everywhere. Spray serious infestations with *Pyrethrum*.

Whitefly, mealybugs, scale, spider mites, and aphids multiply in hot, airless spots and will spoil the leaves even if they don't do permanent damage. Spray infestations two or three times with some form of Neem, *Pyrethrum,*

or horticultural soaps—they won't harm the environment. You can also use horticultural oils. See the Appendix for more details on Pests, Diseases, and Controls.

Continue to weed shrub beds.

AUGUST
SHRUBS

PLANNING

If you are interested in adding a hedge to your yard, lay it out, and order the plants now, so you can start planting when the weather turns cool in early September.

Formal hedges are clipped and follow symmetrical lines—straight with squared corners, a circle, an oval, a triangle. Hedges facing each other left and right are common. Shearable evergreens like **boxwood** and **privet,** or naturally columnar evergreens like **dwarf Alberta spruce,** *Picea glauca* 'Conica' are used.

Informal hedges have loose habits and follow lines that curve and lead off at angles. Choose open, asymmetrical shrubs like **forsythia** and *Juniper chinensis* 'Hetzii'. Or plant a compatible mix, such as **mugo pines, potentillas,** and 'Crimson Pygmy' **barberry.**

Texture. For a close-up hedge, choose fine-textured *Pyracantha* and **Korean box.** For a distant hedge, choose coarse foliage, like the **Meserve hollies** and **holly olive.**

To slow growth and keep an informal hedge attractive, trim it at least once a year. Trim a clipped hedge at least twice a year. Hand shears are better than hedge shears for informal and natural styles.

PLANTING

Fall is considered by André as the best planting season in our area. You can plant this month, but if you wait until the leaves start to turn in October, the plants will benefit. Evergreen shrubs do well moved August through October.

CARE

If the harvest from your **highbush blueberries** is shrinking, blame birds or bears. You may be able to save remaining berries by covering the bushes with bird netting. Console yourself with the thought of the vibrant color **highbush blueberry** foliage brings to the garden later in the season.

PRUNING

Give hedges their final trimming for the year.

WATERING

You will probably need to water all the shrub beds two or three times before the fall rains arrive in September. The ideal is to put down 1 1/2 inches of water at each session. To find out how long your watering system takes to deliver that much water, mark 1 1/2 inches on the inside of an empty 1-pound coffee tin or other container, and set it where it will catch the water.

Overhead watering is fine as long as you water deeply. There's less waste if you water before the sun reaches the garden in the early morning or late afternoon or evening. In hot dry periods, daytime overhead watering lowers leaf temperatures and reduces stress. Evening watering is fine since dew naturally wets foliage every clear night anyway.

André doesn't recommend electrically timed mechanical watering systems that ignore the weather and water too often and shallowly. But he does believe they can do a good job if they are set up with the correct low-pressure nozzles, and timed to run long enough and to water and gently and deeply every week or ten days in periods of drought.

Continue to water shrubs in containers as needed.

FERTILIZING

If shrubs fertilized with a timed-release chemical fertilizer are failing to bloom as expected, or look peaked, supplement with foliar feedings of water-

SHRUBS FOR HEDGES

- **Barberry, Japanese barberry** 'Crimson Pigmy', *Berberis thunbergii*; **yellow Japanese barberry,** *B. t.* 'Aurea'; **evergreen barberry,** *B. linearifolia, B. verruculosa*
- **Boxwood, English box,** *Buxus sempervirens,* 'Suffruticosa', and 'Arborescens'; **dwarf littleleaf box,** *B. microphylla* 'Compacta' and 'Kingsville Dwarf'; **edging box,** *B. s.* 'Suffruticosa'; **Korean littleleaf box,** *B. microphylla* var. 'Koreana'
- **Common buckthorn,** *Rhamnus cathartica*
- **Canadian hemlock,** *Tsuga canadensis*
- **Cripp's golden Hinoki falsecypress,** *Chamaecyparis obtusa* 'Cripsii'
- **Dwarf Alberta spruce,** *Picea glauca* 'Conica'
- **Dwarf Chinese juniper,** *Juniperus chinensis* 'Mas,' 'Spartan'; **golden juniper, dwarf Colorado blue spruce,** *Picea pungens* 'Glauca' and 'Fat Albert'; *P. p.* 'Glauca Montgomery'
- **Dwarf winged spindle tree,** *Euonymus alata* 'Compactus'
- **Firethorn,** *Pyracantha coccinea*
- **Forsythia,** *Forsythia x intermedia* 'Spectabilis'
- **Fragrant/sweet olive,** *Osmanthus fragrans* 'Aurantiacus'; **holly olive, hardy sweet olive,** *O. heterophyllus*
- **Germander,** *Teucrium chamaedrys*
- **Glossy abelia,** *Abelia x grandiflora* cultivars
- **Holly,** including the **Meserve hybrids** 'Blue Boy' and 'Blue Princess'; **Foster hybrid hollies,** *Ilex attenuata* 'Fosteri #2'; **Japanese holly,** *Ilex crenata; I. c.* 'Convexa'; *I. c.* 'Helleri'; *I. c.* 'Microphylla'
- **Leyland cypress,** *Cupressocyparis leylandii* (classed as a tree but shearable)
- **Myrtle,** *Myrtus communis*
- **Nandina, heavenly bamboo,** *Nandina domestica* 'Umpqua Warrior'
- **Oleander, rose-bay,** *Nerium oleander* cultivars
- **Photinia, Fraser's photinia** or **red tip,** *Photinia x fraseri*
- **Potentilla, shrubby cinquefoil,** *Potentilla fruticosa*
- **Privet, Amur privet,** *Ligustrum amurense; L. x ibolium;* **California privet,** *Ligustrum ovalifolium;* **wax-leaf/Japanese privet,** *Ligustrum japonicum* (*Texanum*)
- **Pyramidal American arborvitae,** *Thuja occidentalis* 'Emerald' (Classed as a tree.)
- **Roses, polyantha/floribunda/rugosa,** *Rosa* species and varieties
- **Santolina, lavender cotton,** *Santolina* species and varieties
- **Sawara falsecypress,** *Chamaecyparis pisifera* 'Boulevard'; *C. p.* 'Filifera Aurea'
- **Wintercreeper euonymus,** *Euonymus fortunei* 'Gracilis'
- **Yew, English yew,** *Taxus baccata* 'Fastigiata'; **dwarf Japanese yew,** *T. cuspidata* 'Nana'; **upright Japanese yew,** *T. c.* 'Capitata'; **Hick's Japanese yew,** *T. x media* 'Hicksii'

soluble organic or fast-acting liquid fertilizers.

If you are using chemical fertilizers, fertilize every six weeks or so.

PROBLEMS

Change deer deterrents and sprays around in the garden.

If your berries are harvested before you can get to them, there may be a bear in the vicinity. If, in addition, bear sightings are reported, it's probably not a good idea to put out bird feeders this winter.

Clear the beds of all weeds; don't let them grow up and go to seed!

SEPTEMBER

SHRUBS

PLANNING

If you've been wanting to do something positive for the environment, plant a rain garden this fall to handle runoff from severe storms and to preserve water.

A rain garden is sited where the runoff from concrete surfaces goes, or where building gutters empty. It is designed to take flooding. The center is slightly lower than the soil level so water can pool there. The plants use up the runoff so it goes into the soil of the rain garden and doesn't all go into the water table, sewers, or streams. Runoff water often carries pesticides, herbicides, heavy metals, and other toxins.

Rain garden plants are bioremediators—their roots and foliage tie up toxins. Some excellent plants for a rain garden are **birches, ornamental grasses, coneflowers, rudbeckia, weigela, baptisia,** and **coreopsis.** Other plants include **river birch,** North Lights series **azaleas, red-osier dogwood, asters, astilbe, campanula, hostas, salvia, Siberian iris, Joe-Pye weed, red milkweed,** and **switchgrass.**

PLANTING

Late plant sales and perfect planting weather combine to make this a fine time to install a hedge.

Laying out the bed. Make the width of the bed equal to the height of the shrubs at maturity. For a 1- to 2-foot high hedge, make the bed 18 inches wide; for a hedge 3 feet tall, make it 3 feet wide; for a hedge 15 feet tall, make it 15 feet wide. Columnar plants need less space. For a double hedge, measure the width of the bed starting with the outside plant on either side.

Planting. Prepare a trench 12 to 18 inches deep, and improve the soil. Set low-growing shrubs 18 inches apart for a single row. For a double row set them zigzag 12 inches apart; to keep out intruders, weave chicken wire between the shrubs. Crowded shrubs can be moved later to replace failed plants. Finish the bed with 3 inches of mulch.

Fertilizing. Encourage growth the first two years by fertilizing in late winter, again after the main spurt of growth, and again in fall. As the hedge matures, fertilize at half strength when you feed other shrubs.

Prepare a bed for planting by digging a trench about 12 to 18 inches deep.

CARE

In Zones 7 and 6, pot up and move **tropical hibiscus, flowering maple** and other tender shrubs indoors when the thermometer hits 60 degrees Fahrenheit. Hose them down, and then spray them with insecticidal soap before the move.

Toward the end of the month in Zone 6, move hardy shrubs growing in containers to sheltered locations for the winter.

PRUNING

Deadhead fall-flowering shrubs.

WATERING

Indoors. Water shrubs wintering indoors as needed.

Outdoors. Even after cold sets in, the soil stays warm, and roots continue to develop, so water both established and new shrubs sufficiently to keep the soil from drying out.

Pour two or three 5-gallon bucketfuls of water around the roots of newly planted shrubs once a week throughout fall unless you have good, soaking rains.

PRESERVING LEAVES AND BERRIES

Branches of evergreen leaves. Broadleaf evergreen foliage—*Magnolia grandiflora*, **holly, euonymus**—are preserved by splitting and mashing the branch ends and immersing them in a solution that is 2/3 drugstore glycerin and 1/3 water, warmed to 80 degrees Fahrenheit. Leave them there until the color of the leaves changes—some darken, some lighten—then air-dry them.

Trailing stems. Ivy and other trailing stems can be preserved by laying them for 6 or more days in a solution of half glycerin and half water.

Berry branches. Stems of berries can be preserved by dipping them in a solution of half-and-half wood alcohol and clear shellac, and then hanging them upside down over newspapers to drip dry.

Baby's-breath. This airy plant air-dries quickly. It also can be preserved by leaving the stems overnight in a solution of 1 part glycerin to 2 parts water, and then hanging them upside down in loose bunches.

FERTILIZING

Indoors. Add a half strength dose of fertilizer to shrubs indoors at every fourth watering.

Outdoors. The last fertilization of in-ground shrubs is toward the end of the growing season. If you are using organic or water-soluble chemical fertilizers, the last application in Zones 6 and 7 should be made between early September and early October. In Zone 8, Richmond and the Tidewater areas of Virginia, make it between the end of September and mid-October. If you are using a timed-release fertilizer and applied an eight-month formulation in early spring, it will carry plants all the way through October.

PROBLEMS

Indoors. Check shrubs for whitefly and spider mites. Find controls in the Pests, Diseases, and Controls section in the Appendix.

Outdoors. Change whatever deer deterrents you are using. If there are bears in your area, don't stock a bird feeder.

Continue to search for and destroy weeds.

OCTOBER

SHRUBS

Burning Bush

winter. **Willowleaf cotoneaster** 'Autumn Fire' has purplish leaves and scarlet fruits. The **fothergillas** turn brilliant yellow and orange-red. **Chokeberry** 'Brilliantissima', a cultivar of *Aronia arbutifolia,* 'William Penn' **barberry,** the **American smoke tree, chittam-wood, sweetspire,** and some of the **sumacs** are others with exceptional autumn color.

The colorful stems of shrubby **red-** and **yellow-twig dogwood** brighten the scene in winter, especially when there's snow on the ground.

 PLANTING

When the leaves start to change color is a good time to dig and transplant shrubs. Excellent months for planting are October, November, and into early December. Evergreen shrubs may do better planted this month rather than next.

Plant open spaces in the shrubbery border with spring-flowering bulbs. For ideas, turn to the October pages of Chapter 2, Bulbs, Corms, Rhizomes, and Tubers.

 CARE

Zone 8, move hardy shrubs growing in containers to a sheltered corner for the winter.

 PLANNING

Visit nearby public gardens and learn more about the shrubs that blaze into color in the fall. Foliage in the **azalea** collection at the U.S. National Arboretum will be showing streaks of plum, maroon, and gold. While you are there, look for the **witchhazel** 'Diane', *Viburnum* 'Cayuga', and ask about other National Arboretum introductions whose fall foliage is exceptionally rich.

The reddest leaves at your garden center are likely to belong to the *Euonymus* called **burning bush,** or the **dwarf winged spindletree.** The most fluorescent yellow foliage will be on little **Japanese maples** 'Osakazuki' and 'Sangokaku', whose bark becomes brilliant coral-red in

Zones 6 and 7, move shrubs that are borderline hardy and still out in the open to a frost-free shed or garage.

PRUNING

From now until next spring the only pruning you should do is to remove diseased or dead wood.

WATERING

Indoors. Water indoor shrubs as needed.

Outdoors. Unless you have good soaking rains, pour two or three 5-gallon bucketfuls of water around the roots of newly planted shrubs once every week this fall.

The most important preparation for winter is a deep and thorough watering of all shrubs, new, established, in-ground and in containers, before the soil freezes; if the sky doesn't provide the rain, you will have to.

FERTILIZING

Indoors. Add a half dose of fertilizer to the water for shrubs growing indoors at every fourth watering.

Outdoors. In Zones 6 and 7, the time for the last application of fertilizer is between early September and early October.

ABOUT BOXWOODS

Deer are smart enough to avoid **boxwood**, which is toxic to animals. That's one more plus for this slow-growing, small-leaved evergreen shrub whose refined foliage and tolerance for shearing and reshaping have made it an outstanding subject for hedging, edging, and topiary treatment since the days of classical Greece.

In the Mid-Atlantic, some long-lived slow-growing **English box,** *Buxus sempervirens*, dates back to Colonial times. Unclipped, its natural shape is billowing and somewhat pyramidal, and it grows to 15 to 20 feet.

Six-foot 'Vardar Valley' tolerates cold and drought. Columnar 'Graham Blandy', and 5-foot gray-green-silver 'Elegantissima' are excellent accent plants. Five-foot 'Green Mountain' stands repeated shearing and holds its rich green color in winter. For warm dry climates the 3- to 6-foot **littleleaf boxwood** cultivar 'Morris Midget' is a popular choice.

A container-grown **boxwood** transplants easily in fall or spring. In well-drained humusy soil, pH around 6.0, it thrives in sun or light shade. **Boxwoods** don't tolerate salt or wet feet, but once established, they can stand some drought. Fertilizing every two or three years is enough for slow-growing **English box.**

In mid-March shear damaged, browning, or whitened **boxwood** branches back to live growth. Prune elongated shoots in late spring after new growth is complete to keep the plants trim, bushy, and beautiful.

Save the clippings of overgrown **boxwoods** until December, and use the branches to make holiday roping and topiary trees.

In Zone 8, Richmond and the Tidewater areas of Virginia, the last fertilization can be between the end of September and mid-October.

PROBLEMS

Indoors. Watch shrubs moved indoors for signs of whitefly and spider mites. If you find problems, look up controls in the Pests, Diseases, and Controls section in the Appendix.

Outdoors. Apply or change whatever deer deterrents you are using.

If vole runs appear around shrubs, bait the main runway with a rodenticide.

NOVEMBER

SHRUBS

 PLANNING

To enjoy the beauty that is unique to the garden in November, learn to appreciate the wonderful structures nature bares when the foliage falls. The twiggy forms of naked shrubs, **barberries** for example, are quite beautiful in winter. **Deciduous hollies** like the National Arboretum introduction 'Sparkleberry', *Pyracantha,* many of the **viburnums,** and other berried shrubs are colorful assets, and attract birds. **Oregon grape,** *Nandina,* and **sweet box** (*Sarcococca hookeriana* var. *humilis*) add scraps of color to the seasonal mix. In some species blue, black, or white berries follow the flowers, and add winter interest.

The tiny white blooms of evergreen *Osmanthus* spread a sweet subtle perfume in the cool November air, almost miraculous at this season. **Aucuba** and other needled evergreens, **crapemyrtle** bark, **oakleaf hydrangea's** towering stems, **southern magnolia** leaves, the **viburnums, Virginia sweetspire**—nature's fall parade rivals spring if you take the time to stop and to really see, feel, smell, breathe in the seasonal changes.

 PLANTING

In Zone 8, when the outdoor temperatures head for 60 degrees Fahrenheit, pot up **tropical hibiscus, flowering maples,** and other tender shrubs growing in the open garden to containers, spray them with insecticidal soap, and move them indoors.

November, into early December, it is still okay to plant deciduous shrubs that are either container grown or balled and burlapped. The air is cold, but the earth still has warmth.

 CARE

Winter protection for shrubs is applied to keep the foliage from drying in bitter winds, and to avoid damage to the crown especially of newly planted shrubs when alternate thawing and freezing cycles cause the soil to heave it. Apply an anti-desiccant spray to the foliage of **camellias** and other broad-leaved evergreen shrubs growing in exposed positions, or wrap them in Reemay or burlap.

 PRUNING

Even in Zone 8, it's too late to prune shrubs now; pruning will encourage new growth that won't have time to harden before winter.

 WATERING

Indoors. Water indoor shrubs as needed.

Outdoors. A major danger to newly planted shrubs in winter is lack of water before the plant is completely dormant. One of the most important preparations for winter is a deep and thorough watering of your shrubs before the ground freezes. If the sky doesn't do it, then you must.

Maintain moderate soil moisture for hardy shrubs and those that are less hardy and sheltering in a cold garage or shed.

FERTILIZING

Indoors. At every fourth watering, add a half dose of water-soluble fertilizer to the water for **tropical hibiscus, flowering maple,** and other shrubs moved indoors for the cold months.

Outdoors. Fertilizing is over for the shrub garden this year.

ABOUT SHRUBS THAT BEAR BERRIES

The shrubs that produce berries are colorful late-season and winter assets. To make sure you will have the show of berries you hope for, before buying a plant for its berries, ask your supplier about the pollinating needs of the species. For some species of berry-producing shrubs you will need to make sure a male pollinator is nearby in order to guarantee a showy crop of berries.

Most plants have male and female flower parts in the same flower, and they self-pollinate—don't need outside help to produce berries. Other species include both male and female flowers separately on the same plant. These don't require pollinators either; just a little shaking by the wind will do the trick.

But some important berry-producing shrubs are not unisex; they develop as either female or male plants. They're referred to as "dioecious" shrubs. Among popular shrubs that are dioecious are **aucuba, bayberries, fringe tree, hollies, skimmia,** and **yews.** The female of these species must have a suitable male pollinator within pollinating reach to produce a heavy crop of berries. Female plants generally produce the showiest fruit, and they also litter the most.

As a rule of thumb, you can provide one male shrub and expect it to cross-pollinate two to ten females or more, depending on species and location. In a neighborhood with many gardens, you may not need to provide a male pollinator. Your garden center or nursery supplier will be able to advise you.

PROBLEMS

Indoors. Watch shrubs moved indoors for signs of whitefly and spider mites. If you find problems, apply the controls recommended in the section on Pests, Diseases, and Controls in the Appendix.

Outdoors. In deer country, wrap **rhododendrons** and other susceptible **evergreens** in chicken wire cages. Change whatever deer deterrents you are using.

If vole runs appear around shrubs, bait the main runway with a rodenticide.

One form of winter protection can be to erect burlap screens around shrubs.

December

SHRUBS

PLANNING

Browse your catalogs for holiday giving—to yourself and others.

If you worry lots about pests and diseases, ask Santa for a Brunton MacroScope—a microscope that focuses from infinity down to 18 inches, and lets you see insects at a distance of 6 feet! (**www.closetoinfinity.com**)

Gifts that gardeners deeply appreciate and never have too many of are superior pruning tools. Inexpensive pruning tools don't cut well and don't last. Good pruning tools cost more, but with care they last a lifetime. A gardener with lots of shrubbery needs four basic pruning tools:

1. The tool that goes where the gardener goes is a pair of bypass pruning shears. Really good shears snap through twigs and small branches as effortlessly as a hot knife cuts butter.

2. Long-handled lopping shears are bypass shears long enough to reach the interior of large shrubs.

3. To cut through main stems and larger branches, you need a little pull saw. Half handle and half short blade with multifaceted teeth, it makes a deep cut as you pull back.

4. For anyone who owns a hedge, scissor-like handheld hedge shears are essential. If the hedge is a long one and meant to be trimmed, then electric or gas shears are almost essential.

A good pruning tool is a treasure, to be cleaned and wiped with an oily rag after each use. After pruning diseased plants, disinfect tools by dipping them in a solution of 1 part bleach to 9 parts water.

PLANTING

You can still plant deciduous shrubs the first days of this month. In Zone 8, some winters are mild enough to plant all winter long.

CARE

After storms, check and adjust the protective covering on shrubs.

With a broom, as soon as possible after a heavy snowfall, free evergreen shrubs that are weighed down. Use only snowmelt products that don't harm plants, turf, and concrete.

PRUNING

Prune overgrown **boxwoods** and evergreens lightly to obtain material for making roping, swags, topiary trees, and wreaths for the holidays.

WATERING

Indoors. Water shrubs indoors as needed.

Indoors/Outdoors. Maintain the soil moisture on shrubs growing indoors, and new shrubs outdoors as well if the season runs dry. Make sure the shrubs are watered thoroughly and deeply before the ground freezes.

FERTILIZING

Indoors. Don't fertilize shrubs indoors until new growth begins.

Outdoors. Fertilizing is over for the year.

PROBLEMS

Indoors. Watch shrubs growing indoors for signs of whitefly and spider mites. If you find problems, apply the controls recommended in the Pests, Diseases, and Controls section of the Appendix.

Outdoors. The scent-carrying oils in evil-smelling deer deterrents don't volatilize in cold air. If you see a lot of deer, wrap **rhododendrons** and other endangered shrubs in chicken-wire cages for the winter.

If vole runs appear around shrubs, bait the main runway with a rodenticide.

TREES

A well-grown tree is a gardener's pride and joy, a property's defining element, and an asset of great majesty and beauty in every season.

A tree is the largest plant in the garden, so its silhouette as it matures should be your first consideration when you are choosing a new tree. Each species has a recognizable volume and sculptural structure— spreading, pyramidal, oval, vase-shaped, round, columnar, clumping, or weeping. When adding— or deleting—trees, aim for a variety of silhouettes. Variety makes a landscape more interesting.

Evergreen and deciduous. You can count on evergreens to block unwanted views with a highly textured wall of green foliage winter, spring, summer, and fall. If you want a really solid green presence, consider a broadleaved evergreen— the hollies thrive here and come in many sizes and shapes. The majestic evergreen magnolias have beautiful leaves in addition to extraordinary flowers. Conifers that have flat scale-like leaves— American arborvitae and the fast-growing Leyland cypress, for example—also present a substantial silhouette. The needled evergreens—hemlock, pine, and spruce—have an airier presence.

A deciduous tree's great asset is that it does lose its foliage annually. You can count on deciduous trees to change your garden view beginning with spring's tender greens and throughout the year. Many deciduous trees are famous for flaming fall finales—'Autumn Glory' maple, for one. In winter

the bare branches and twigs of the deciduous trees frame the sky and the clouds scudding by, and their bark presents arresting textures—the silky gray kid of the American beech, for example, and the chalky white of river birch.

Flowering trees. All trees flower. In early spring the red maples wrap their twigs in tiny, garnet velvet leaf buds, and the willows drip golden catkins. But a real flowering tree in bloom is a sky-high pastel bouquet. There are lots of species to choose from. Your property, if big enough, can host a flowery parade from March when the ornamental cherries bloom until mid-fall when the last fragrant blossom falls from the little Franklin tree, *Franklinia alatamaha*. Double your pleasure by selecting flowering trees that bear colorful fruits. Or opt for fragrance, and plant a scented flowering apple, or Yoshino cherry *Prunus* x *yedoensis* 'Akebono,' or Chinese witch-hazel, *Hamamelis mollis*.

PLANTING

Location. Site large trees where they will reach full sun as they mature. Many small flowering trees are understory plants that developed in the partial shade of a forest, and they will thrive in partial light. If you are trying a tree that is at the edge of its cold hardiness zone in your yard, such as a dogwood or a redbud, place it in a spot that provides shelter from the north wind. Don't plant a tree, large or small, in an airless corner, or close to a wall or overhang.

Space trees at distances from each other that allow plenty of space for the lateral development of branches. Columnar trees can be set more closely than pyramidal trees. Large shade trees are best when set 75 feet apart. The absolute minimum for a street tree is 8 feet in every direction, and 12 feet is better.

Don't plant tall trees near electric or phone lines, and avoid proximity to pipes and septic systems.

Before placing a large tree in the vicinity of a garden, consider not only how the shade under the branches will affect the plants, but also how the shade the mature tree will cast at various times of the day and the year will affect the garden design. Don't plant so close to a sidewalk or patio that the big roots that develop near the trunk will heave the paving.

When to plant. In our area, you can plant trees from March through the end of November. When the leaves start to change color is the beginning of an excellent planting season—October, November, and even into early December in mild years. Choose early spring for planting balled-and-burlapped (B&B) trees considered difficult to transplant, Florida dogwoods and magnolias, for example.

It is okay to plant container-grown and B&B trees in summer, providing the rootballs haven't been baking on the tarmac at a garden center since early spring. B&B trees whose rootballs have been "heeled in," and protected by mounds of mulch or earth, stay in good condition even in summer.

Bare-root trees. In early spring before growth begins, mail-order suppliers ship young trees bare

ABOUT PRUNING CUTS

When you remove a large limb, follow the three-cut pruning method to avoid stripping bark from the trunk:

1. About a foot out from the trunk, cut from the bottom of the branch upward about a third of the way through the limb.

2. A couple of inches out, or beyond the first cut, cut from the top of the branch down. The branch will break away cleanly.

3. Find the collar or ring at the base of the limb where it springs from the trunk. Taking care not to damage the ring, remove the stub. From the collar, an attractive, healthy covering for the wounded area can develop.

Current wisdom says "no" to painting or tarring these cuts. That said, André prefers to paint large wounds caused by removing big branches with orange shellac; the alcohol in the shellac disinfects, and the cuts are sealed.

root. Before placing your order, ask about the size and age of the sapling so you know what you are getting. The tree will be shipped at the right planting season. Follow the shipper's instructions for planting exactly.

Container-grown and B&B trees. Container-grown and balled-and-burlapped trees can be planted from early spring, through summer and all fall up to December 1. Big trees are now being grown in 10-, 15-, and even 50-gallon containers. B&B trees dug in spring and protected in the months since by mounds of mulch or soil stay in good condition. B&B packaging is usually reserved for very large trees. Container and B&B trees are more costly than bare-root trees.

Save on costs by choosing young trees. Young trees knit into their new environments quickly; trees 7 to 8 feet tall soon overtake the growth of 15-foot trees set out at the same time.

Soil and pH. Within a year or two, a new tree will send roots out well beyond the amended soil of its planting hole, so your greatest successes will be with species growing in native soil whose pH matches their pH needs. However, amending the pH of the planting hole helps them get started and is useful for hard-to-transplant specimens like sweetbay magnolia, American hornbeam, and sour gum.

Digging the hole:

1. Make the planting hole for a tree three times as wide and twice as deep as the rootball.

2. Loosen the sides of the hole, and blend the soil taken from the hole with the organic amendments described in Soil Preparation and Improvement in the Introduction to the book.

3. Half fill the bottom of the hole with improved soil, and tamp it down very firmly to make a solid base. Instructions for planting bare-root trees may call for the creation of a cone in the center of the hole, over which the roots are to be spread.

4. Plant the tree in the hole so the trunk is 1 to 2 inches above the level of the surrounding earth.

The weight of a container or B&B tree on unsettled soil will cause it to sink some after planting.

5. Half fill the hole once more with improved soil. Tamp it down firmly. Finish filling the hole with improved soil, and tamp it down firmly. Shape the soil around the crown into a wide saucer.

6. Water the soil slowly, gently, and thoroughly with a sprinkler, a soaker hose, a bubbler, or by hand. You need to put down 1 1/2 inches of water. (See Watering.) Or, slowly pour on two or three 5-gallon bucketfuls of water.

7. Mulch newly planted trees 3 to 4 inches deep starting 3 inches from the trunk out to the edge of the saucer. Replenish the mulch as needed to keep it 3 to 4 inches deep.

STAKING

It isn't essential to stake a young tree unless the stem or trunk shows a tendency to lean or to grow at an odd angle. Remove the stake when the tree is growing straight and true.

WATERING

Newly planted and transplanted trees need sustained moisture. For the first eight weeks, pour two or three 5-gallon bucketfuls of water around the roots once a week. The first summer, water every week or ten days, unless you have a soaking rain. Slowly and gently lay down 1 1/2 inches of water. Set a 1-pound coffee can or other container under the sprinkler or the hose, and record how long it took to put 1 1/2 inches in the can—then you'll know.

When the weather isn't supporting growth, young trees adapt by slowing down unless forced to grow by shallow watering and inappropriate fertilizing. In fall, even after cold sets in, roots continue to develop, so water often enough to prevent the soil from drying out.

After the first year or two, most trees require watering only in times of severe drought.

JANUARY
TREES

PLANNING

Sit down with your mail-order catalogs by a window overlooking your garden, and dream about trees. January winds bring a big sky, and the possibility of a new vision for your landscape.

Adding a tree makes a big difference to the overall design. Balanced plantings create a sense of security and well-being. Pairs of same-size shrubs or trees lining a walk or a driveway express balance, and are perfect for a formal dwelling. You can add a dynamic to balanced plantings by duplicating a silhouette without duplicating the plants that create it. Combining the arresting silhouettes of the symmetrical evergreen **incense cedar** and the stylized **Serbian spruce** with the sprawl of wide-spreading pyramidal **maples** and clumping **birches** adds interest to the view.

PLANTING

A live Christmas tree (see December) can begin to deteriorate after ten days indoors in a heated house. As soon as possible move the tree outdoors. If you have not prepared a planting hole (see Planting, November and December), place the tree in a sheltered spot, and cover it with 14 to 18 inches of leaves kept in place by evergreen boughs. As soon as you can, dig a hole, plant the tree, and then mulch the area (see Planting in the introduction to this chapter).

Repotting larger indoor trees is difficult and necessary only every three or four years. Other years in late winter before new growth begins, remove the top 2 inches of soil, and replace it with 2 or 3 inches of compost or fertile potting soil.

CARE

Established trees. Use a broom to brush away accumulations of snow and ice on the lower branches of the evergreens.

New trees. Renew the anti-desiccant spray—a coating that keeps leaves from losing moisture—on evergreen trees, especially broadleaf evergreens in exposed positions. Check and adjust the burlap protecting new trees.

PRUNING

Outdoors. Prune away winter and snow damage before growth begins. Cut down old and injured trees. Cut the wood of deciduous trees into logs the size of your fireplace, and stack them to dry. Evergreen wood is soft and bad for your chimney, so make it into chips to top paths, or compost it.

Indoors. Remove dead flowers from **flowering maple** and **hibiscus,** as well as yellowing leaves and twigs crowding the crowns of indoors trees, and **ficus,** for example. Pinch out all but half a dozen or so of the tiny lemons developing on a **Improved Meyer lemon** tree.

Before planting, review a layout of your landscape to determine where a tree should be sited.

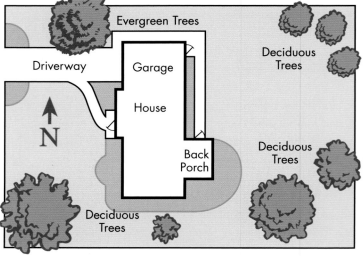

WATERING

Trees growing outdoors in containers under overhangs and other shelters don't benefit from snow fall and may need watering.

If you have planted a live Christmas tree, water it as you do other new trees.

Maintain the soil moisture of the indoor trees, for example, **citrus, ficus, tropical hibiscus, flowering maples,** and **palms.** Mist and air the room daily or often.

FERTILIZING

When you see new growth in indoor trees, begin adding a half-strength dose of fertilizer at every second watering.

PROBLEMS

If you see vole runs, bait the main runway with a rodenticide.

Deer go for the tips of reachable branches of **arborvitae, yews, cedars,** and other evergreens. Spraying may deter them, but wrapping them with burlap or chicken wire is a surer safeguard. Deer also nibble bark; check the wraps on newly planted trees.

Apply dormant horticultural oils to small trees before growth begins to smother insects that have wintered over.

PRUNING EVERGREEN TREES

• Pruning woody plants stimulates growth, so avoid heavy pruning in summer when the plant is preparing to go dormant.

• Dead or damaged wood on evergreen conifers can be removed at any time.

• Winter and snow damage is best pruned before evergreens are actively growing.

• To encourage dense branching in evergreens with candle-like new growth, cut the candles back by half. Prune the tips of **hemlock** branches lightly anytime during the growing season. Prune **yews** and **junipers** lightly or heavily anytime during growth.

• To establish a shape, prune evergreens (sparingly) when they are three to five years old.

• To slow or dwarf a broadleaf evergreen tree—**hollies,** for example—when growth ends, cut back no more than 20 percent of the new growth. You can reduce the main stem back to the first side shoots, but don't remove more than has grown the last year or two.

• To have holiday greens, save some pruning of new growth on **hemlocks, hollies, spruce,** or **cedars** until December.

WINTER CARE OF INDOOR TREES

For trees that live indoors in winter, a bright, airy, cool room is best. Daytime temperatures should be between 68 and 75 degrees Fahrenheit with a drop of 7 to 10 degrees at night, and humidity between 30 and 60 percent. Temperatures higher than 68 degrees take the humidity from the air.

Air the room daily for about ten minutes unless it's freezing outside, and mist the plants with water at room temperature. If the room is warm, run a humidifier, keep wet sponges around, and grow the plants on saucers filled with wet pebbles. Keep the soil evenly damp, not soaking wet. When there's new growth, include a half-strength dose of houseplant fertilizer at every second watering.

Supplement inadequate window light with spot grow lights. Check for insects often. For controls, see Pests, Diseases, and Controls in the Appendix. Every few weeks remove yellowing or damaged foliage, dead flowers, branches that cross, and those that are becoming ungainly. When repotting, use houseplant soils.

FEBRUARY

TREES

PLANNING

Place catalog orders for trees now. Buy only resistant cultivars of trees that we've noted as susceptible to problems.

PLANTING

Bare-root deciduous trees can be planted about a month before the last freeze; mail-order suppliers ship them dormant at your planting time. Here's a general view of how to plant them:

1. Soak the roots as instructed by the supplier.

2. Dig a planting hole twice as wide and deep as the roots.

3. Loosen the sides of the hole, and blend the soil from the hole with the organic amendments described in Soil Preparation and Improvement in the Introduction to the book.

4. Half fill the bottom of the hole with improved soil, and tamp it down **very firmly** to make a solid base. In the center of the hole build a cone. Gently separate the roots of the tree, and arrange them over the cone. Set the tree so the crown is 1 inch above the level of the surrounding earth.

5. Half fill the hole with improved soil, and tamp it down. Fill the rest of the hole with improved soil, and tamp it down firmly. Shape the soil around the crown into a wide saucer.

6. Slowly pour on ten to fifteen gallons of water.

7. Mulch newly planted trees 3 to 4 inches deep from 3 inches out from the trunk to the edge of the saucer.

CARE

Established trees. Remove snow weighing down evergreen limbs and damaged and dead branches.

New trees. After fertilizing (see Fertilizing), top off the mulch to keep it 3 to 4 inches deep starting about 3 inches from the trunk.

Check the stakes and ties of newly planted trees. If the ties are damaging the bark, loosen them a little. If the tree is growing straight and true, remove the stakes.

If cycles of thawing and freezing have heaved roots, press them back into place, and replenish the mulch to insulate the soil.

If you have planted a live Christmas tree, check and maintain the soil moisture.

PRUNING

Prune spring-flowering trees well before they bloom.

This month and next prune summer-flowering trees. Clear out underbrush, saplings, and weed trees crowding desirable trees in woodlands and groves. You can use a string trimmer to level small growth. Use bypass pruning shears—powerful shears with a scissor-like action—to take down saplings. Then remove diseased and dead trees and trees crowding others. Prune out big branches that could fall on driveways and paths in a storm. Remove from deciduous trees any limbs spoiling the symmetry of the structure.

Remove dead and damaged limbs from mature deciduous trees, and all that cross other limbs or crowd the center of the tree. If the soil beneath appears compacted, loosen it with a hoe—take care not to damage roots near the surface. Then fertilize and water generously.

Root-pruning of deciduous and evergreen trees to check growth and prompt flowering can be undertaken now before growth begins. Use a spade to sever the roots in a circle around the trunk. Go out to where the roots are about the size of your little finger. If your spade encounters

Bypass shears

roots you need a saw to cut, you are too close; if the roots are web-fine, you are too far out. Water well, and fertilize after root pruning.

WATERING

Outdoors. Check the soil under broadleaf evergreen trees; the foliage continues to lose water through transpiration during the winter, and if snow or rain has been scarce or if the soil under the mulch is dryish, water.

If there's no snow and no rain, water all your new outdoor plantings thoroughly.

Indoors. Water trees growing indoors, **citrus, ficus, tropical hibiscus,** and **palms.** Mist and air them daily or often.

OUTSTANDING FLOWERING TREES

- **Callery pear,** *Pyrus calleryana* 'Aristocrat', 'Chanticleer', 'White House'
- **Common smoke tree,** *Cotinus coggygria*
- **Crapemyrtle,** *Lagerstroemia indica* and hybrids
- **Chinese dogwood,** *Cornus florida* hybrids, *C. kousa, C. x rutgersensis* Stellar Series
- **Eastern redbud,** *Cercis canadensis*
- **Flowering cherry group,** *Prunus sargentii* species and hybrids
- **Flowering crabapple,** *Malus* hybrids
- **Franklin tree,** *Franklinia alatamaha*
- **Japanese snowbell,** *Styrax japonicus*
- **Japanese stewartia,** *Stewartia pseudocamellia*
- **Southern magnolia,** *Magnolia grandiflora* 'Little Gem', 'St. Mary's', 'Lennei', *M. stellata* 'Waterlily'
- **White fringe tree,** *Chionanthus virginicus*
- **Witchhazel,** *Hamamelis* x *intermedia* hybrids

FERTILIZING

Add a half-strength dose to the water for trees growing indoors every second time you water.

Fertilize newly planted trees the first two or three years. When the buds begin to break, scratch in an application of Holly-tone for acid-loving trees, and Plant-tone for the others. Established trees in lawns, shrub, and flower borders should be okay with the fertilizer applied to the surrounding lawn and beds.

PROBLEMS

Voles can damage the roots of young trees. Bait the main runway with a rodenticide to prevent their damage.

To keep rabbits, woodchucks, and other rodents away from new trees, try chemical repellents and fungicide formulations such as Thiram (Arasan) and hot pepper wax.

Deer are definitely up and hungry. Spray evergreen foliage that is munching-height with deer repellents. Check and adjust burlap covers and chicken-wire cages.

Before the buds open on trees suspected of insect infestation, spray them with horticultural oil. The oil smothers insects and their eggs.

MARCH

TREES

PLANNING

If you want to plant a street tree, get municipal permission and their recommendations for trees that tolerate urban conditions. If it's up to you, choose trees that stay under 20 to 30 feet, or narrow understory trees—examples are the **American hornbeam** and **columnar flowering pear** 'Capital'. The **London plane tree** 'Columbia', which was introduced by the National Arboretum, is a fine shade tree for wide streets. Water and fertilize the tree until it is well-established, and then water during droughts.

You can pave around a tree to within 2 feet of the trunk if the paving is set in sand and gravel.

PLANTING

It's spring planting—and transplanting—time when winter cold and wet leave the ground. Pack a ball of earth between your hands, and if it crumbles easily, it's ready to be worked.

Detailed instructions for planting appear in the chapter introduction. To prepare a tree for planting:

Container-grown tree. To free the rootball, tip the container on its side and roll it around. If it is too large for that, slit the sides of the container, and peel the pieces away. If roots wrap the rootball, make four shallow vertical cuts in the sides of the rootball, and slice off the bottom 2 inches.

Bare-root tree. Leave the tree in its packaging in a cool dark place until you are ready to plant. Soak the roots in tepid water as directed by the planting instructions, or six to twelve hours before planting.

CARE

New trees. Remove trunk covers from protected trees. If a tree that was staked is growing straight and not being heaved, remove the stakes. After fertilizing, renew the mulch.

Trees in containers. Before growth begins, top-dress the soil.

Remove the top 2 inches of soil, and replace it with soil enriched with Holly-tone or Plant-tone, as appropriate. Renew the mulch.

PRUNING

Outdoors. You can prune summer-flowering trees this month and in April. Harvest branches from flowering trees that can be forced into bloom indoors, **flowering cherry trees, crabapples,** and **dogwoods,** for example. (See Forcing Flowering Branches into Bloom Indoors in February, Shrubs.) If sap starts to flow, never mind. It will stop when the tree leafs out.

The ends of **hemlock** branches can be lightly pruned throughout the growing season. Prune **yews** and **junipers** anytime during the growth cycle.

Remove any branches heading into the center of the tree or crossing others.

Prune newly planted trees lightly the first few years to control the development of the scaffold (the limb structure). Remove branches heading into the center of the tree or crossing others.

Never take away more than 20 to 25 percent of a tree's growth; this is called "dehorning," and it causes "water sprout" growth. To learn how to prune your own trees, study the trunk and branch structures of well-grown trees in arboreta and public gardens.

Indoors. Continue to deadhead and groom indoor trees.

WATERING

Outdoors. For new and transplanted trees, including a live Christmas tree, pour two or three 5-gallon bucketsful of water around the roots weekly throughout spring unless you have a soaking rain.

Regular check the soil moisture of hardy trees growing outdoors in containers, and water enough to maintain soil moisture.

Indoors. Continue to maintain the soil moisture of indoor trees, such as **citrus, ficus, tropical hibiscus,** and **palms;** mist the trees, and air the room often.

FERTILIZING

Indoors. Add fertilizer at half-strength dose to the water every

---

PRUNING DECIDUOUS TREES

• **Winter damage.** Prune anytime.
• **Damaged branches.** Prune them before the leaves fall—they're easier to spot.
• **In fall.** Prune lightly in fall when the plant is preparing to go dormant.
• **Flowering trees that bloom on new wood.** Prune them before growth begins in late winter or early spring.
• **Flowering trees that bloom on old wood.** Prune immediately after they bloom to avoid cutting off branches where buds are being initiated for the following season.
• **To control height.** Prune after the season's new growth has fully developed.
• **To slow or dwarf growth.** Prune in summer when the plant has stopped growing.

---

second time you water. Mist often with water at room temperature.

Established trees. If, in its third or fourth season, or later, a tree isn't growing well, fertilize.

Stunted growth and leaves that are uncharacteristically red or dark green may signal a shortage of phosphate. Applying a fertilizer with a higher ratio of phosphate should improve matters. Weak stems and a susceptibility to disease might be caused by a shortage of potash; fertilizer with a higher ratio of phosphorus and potash would help.

PROBLEMS

If you see vole runs, bait the main runway with a rodenticide.

If you didn't spray with a dormant horticultural oil last month, do it now. These botanical oils sprayed on the egg and immature stages of insects smother them.

If you spot bagworm webs or tent caterpillars, in the cool of the evening, scoop the tents out with a stick and destroy them. The other way is to spray with a biological control such as *Bacillus thuringiensis*. Other controls are Sevin or malathion insecticide, pyrethrin, or rotenone.

To keep deer away from evergreens and newly planted trees, spray with a repellent they have not smelled recently. Circle small trees the deer are damaging with chicken wire; for larger trees, use unobtrusive bird netting.

APRIL

TREES

PLANNING

Need more colorful trees? Check out the yellow and yellow-green evergreens. **Cripps golden Hinoki cypress,** *Chamaecyperis obtusa* 'Crippsii', is fast-growing and has rich golden-yellow foliage. Some of the new **Japanese maple** cultivars are breathtaking when sun shines through the leaves. **Variegated hollies** and **beeches** are quite beautiful. Enter the names of trees that catch your fancy in your garden log, and plan to buy them at a local nursery late in the season when you can see the summer color and maybe buy at a bargain price.

PLANTING

You can transplant newly planted container-grown trees the first two years without trauma.

Small well-established trees can be moved successfully if you plan ahead.

Year 1. Before growth begins, sever the roots in a circle all around the trunk to stimulate root growth within the circle.

Year 2. The following year tie the branches together at the top. Dig a trench outside the root-pruned circle, lift the rootball onto a big piece of burlap, and tie the burlap around the rootball. Very gently drag the plant to its new location. Prepare the soil, and plant the tree as described in the introduction to this chapter. Free the branches, and prune out damaged twigs.

Protect your young trees from mower damage by surrounding the trunk with a 3-inch layer of mulch that starts 3 inches from the trunk.

CARE

Established and new trees. Mow with care around the trunks of trees young or old. If the mower consistently gets too close, keep it away by surrounding the trunk with a ring of mulch 3 inches deep. A 3-inch deep mulch starting 3 inches from the trunk keeps the roots cool and weeds down—and replenishes the organic material in the soil beneath.

Container tree. Root pruning every two or three years keeps a tree growing well, and dwarfs it without impairing its form. The best time for root pruning is late winter before growth. A small tub can be tipped onto its side, and the rootball slipped out. Disentangle roots binding the bottom of the rootball, and cut away roots growing straight down the outside of the rootball. Next, add a layer of fertile soil mix to the bottom of the tub, and center the rootball inside.

If the tub is too big for this operation, then slide a hand-pruning saw inside the container, and sever an inch of the roots growing around the outside of the rootball. Remove the top inch or two of the soil covering the rootball. Push soil mix down into the sides of the tub, and add 2 or 3 inches to the top of the rootball, and then renew the mulch 3 inches deep. Water the container thoroughly.

PRUNING

The ends of **hemlock** branches can be lightly pruned throughout the growing season. Prune **yews** and **junipers** lightly or heavily anytime during their growth season.

Remove "water sprout" growth from tree limbs, and suckers from around the base of the fruit and other trees and on tree trunks and branches.

WATERING

Water the soil in containers of trees growing indoors, and those you have moved outdoors. Always use water at room temperature.

Water hardy trees growing outdoors in containers when the soil feels dry. You will need to water less if you included water-holding polymers in the container soil.

For new and transplanted in-ground trees, including a Christmas tree, pour two or three 5-gallon bucketfuls of water around the roots once a week throughout spring unless there's a good rain.

FERTILIZING

Indoors. At every second watering, add a half-strength dose of fertilizer to trees growing indoors—**citrus, ficus, palms,** and others.

Outdoors. Frequent watering leaches nutrients from the soil in containers, so start monthly applications of a water-soluble organic fertilizer, seaweed or manure tea, for example.

In-ground trees growing in lawns and flower and shrub borders will get all the fertilizer they need when you fertilize the surrounding lawns and borders.

PROBLEMS

Continue protecting your trees from the deer.

Scale may turn up on your **hollies.** Spray with summer-weight horticultural oils or Neem.

Rake up weeds.

Late this month tent caterpillars emerge. Spray trees with signs of infestations with a biological control such as *Bacillus thuringiensis.* Other controls are Sevin or malathion insecticide, pyrethrin, or rotenone.

Pick off the cone shaped nests of bagworms and destroy them.

MAY

TREES

 PLANNING

To furnish your yard with song—and to keep insects down—look for places to plant a few trees that meet the needs of birds. They nest in the branches of evergreens like **Canadian hemlock**, *Tsuga canadensis*, and **white pine**, *Pinus strobus*. They eat the fruit of **American holly**, *Ilex opaca*, and **red cedar**, *Juniperus virginiana*. The tiny fruits of the flowering, or ornamental, fruit trees are staples for birds—beautiful cultivars like the **crabapple** *Malus* 'Narragansett', the **Florida** and *Cornus kousa* **dogwoods**, and **weeping cherries**. Many native trees bear fruits birds love—**chokecherry**, *Prunus pennsylvanica*, and **wild red cherry**, *P. virginiana*, and **American hornbeam**, *Carpinus caroliniana*, a lovely shade tree.

 PLANTING

This is a fine month to plant new trees.

Crapemyrtles are slow to start up, so if new plants seem to have died, wait until late next month before deciding you must replace them.

 CARE

Indoors. When nighttime temperatures stay steady at 60 degrees Fahrenheit and above, start moving your indoor trees—**citrus, ficus, tropical hibiscus,** and **palms**—outdoors for a summer vacation. Summered out in the bright light on a porch or under a tall tree, they'll survive less favorable winter conditions indoors.

Place them in indirect light in a sheltered spot for the first week. Like you, plants sunburn when exposed too long too early to direct sun. Gradually move them into brighter light. Don't be alarmed if some drop leaves their first week or two outdoors. The change of light has that effect on some, notably **ficus.**

Outdoors. Renew the mulch under newly planted trees before summer heat arrives.

 PRUNING

Prune to encourage dense branching to the ground in **pines, firs, spruces,** and other evergreens whose growth is initiated by candles (new candlelike growths at the ends of branches); cut the candles back by half when they appear at the branch tips. The ends of **hemlock** branches can be lightly pruned throughout the growing season. Prune **yews** and **junipers** anytime during their growth season.

Prune and shape up **crapemyrtles** you wish to grow as trees before they bloom. Remove dried flower clusters. To encourage a canopy to form, remove the branches a third of the way up the trunk. Remove branches rubbing across others and any growing into the center of the canopy. Prune unbranched limbs back to an outward facing bud.

Check fruit trees for an overabundance of tiny fruits and thin so that fruits are no closer than 4 to 6 inches.

Check the fruit trees for an oversupply of tiny fruits. In the next several weeks thin **apples, pears,** and **peaches** so that the fruits are no closer than 4 to 6 inches.

WATERING

Keep track of how often the soil in containers of the indoor trees moved outdoors needs watering, and plan a regular watering schedule.

Water outdoor trees growing in containers every two weeks, or when the soil seems dry.

For newly planted and transplanted in-ground trees, pour two or three 5-gallon bucketfuls of water around the roots once a week throughout spring unless you have rain.

FERTILIZING

Since frequent watering leaches nutrients from the soil, once a month give all the trees growing in containers a light application of a water-soluble organic fertilizer, seaweed or manure tea, for example.

CHANGE THE GRADE

Sometimes new landscaping or building plans require changing the grade of the land around an established tree. It can be done without killing the tree, if you avoid destroying the roots from at least half the distance from the trunk to the outer edge of the drip line. That means you must maintain the existing grade that far out from the tree trunk.

If you are lowering the grade, shore up the soil around the tree by building a retaining wall.

If you are raising the grade, arrange to channel downpours to avoid having water collect over the roots. Do not cover the roots with more than a few extra inches of soil. **Dogwoods** and **live oaks** are especially sensitive. If the change of grade is severe, surround the trunk and roots with a retaining wall, fill it with rocks, and cover them with chicken wire to keep the well from filling up.

PROBLEMS

Deer sightings may subside now that the woods are full of browsing material. Even so, continue to discourage them from visits to your yard looking for treats.

Woolly adelgid attack **Canadian hemlock** and can do severe damage. Spraying twice a year with horticultural oil is the preferred control. These lightweight botanical oils also control aphids, cankerworms, leafhoppers, leaf rollers, mealybugs, mites, psylids, scale, tent caterpillars, and webworms.

Caution: Spraying with horticultural oils can temporarily remove the blue color of blue **hostas** and **Colorado blue spruce.** Never spray during droughts, and always water deeply before applying.

Rake up weeds.

Late this month gypsy moths emerge. Spray trees with signs of infestations with a biological control such as *Bacillus thuringiensis.* Other controls are Sevin or malathion insecticide, pyrethrin, or rotenone.

Continue to look for and destroy the nests of bagworms.

JUNE

TREES

PLANNING

You can grow small ornamental trees in the limited space afforded by a rooftop, a balcony, or a deck by planting them in containers. The best subjects are small flowering trees, and dwarf, semi-dwarf, small, columnar, weeping, and slow growing forms.

Choose trees well within your cold hardiness range; the soil is more likely to freeze in pots than in the ground. Be aware that containers on rooftops are generally receiving more bottom heat than those on wooden decks or cement patios—not good in Zone 8 summers, but helpful in Zone 6.

Containers on rooftops must be raised three inches from the roofing material. Resting directly on the rooftop, a heavy container full of damp soil can create considerable damage to the ceiling below.

Use lightweight soil mixes to keep down the weight of pots that will require seasonal moving. André adds PermaTill®, an aggregate lighter than gravel, to soil mixes for very large containers. When you have to move a container, do it before watering.

Planters made of redwood are good for several years. Plastics hold moisture longer, and are okay if they have drainage holes. Clay containers are beautiful, and allow the plants to breathe, but they dry out more quickly especially in high, windy places.

PLANTING

You can plant even big container-grown trees—and entire landscaping projects—this month as long as you follow the watering practices recommended.

Many species of trees can be propagated from cuttings taken at certain times of the year. Softwood (new wood) cuttings of some **hollies** and **red maples** taken in June and July root fairly easily. **Witchhazels** root from softwood cuttings taken from trees three to five years old. **Juniper** cuttings taken during the winter will root. "Softwood" means new green branch tips whose bark has not yet begun to harden.

If you are interested in trying, turn to the section on Rooting Cuttings To Multiply Your Shrubs in June, Shrubs.

CARE

New trees. Make sure the mulch around new plantings is a full 3 inches deep before heat arrives.

PRUNING

As seasonal growth comes to an end, you can prune trees whose growth you want to slow or dwarf. Reducing the leaf surface reduces the sugar synthesized and translocated to the roots and limits next year's growth in the tree.

Even a rooftop garden can be landscaped with trees, shrubs, and turf.

Remove yellowing leaves and twigs beginning to crowd the crown of indoors trees, **ficus,** for example. Pinch out all but half a dozen or so tiny lemons developing on an **Improved Meyer lemon** tree.

SMALL TREES FOR CONTAINERS

- **American hornbeam,** *Carpinus caroliniana* (syn. *americana*) 'Fastigiata'
- **American smoke tree, chittamwood,** *Cotinus obovatus*
- **Amur maple,** *Acer ginnala* 'Flame'
- **Flowering autumn cherry,** *Prunus subhirtella* 'Autumnalis Rosea'
- **Flowering weeping cherry,** *P. s.* 'Pendula'; **double flowering weeping cherry,** *P. s.* 'Pendula Plena Rosea'
- **Carolina silverbell, wild olive,** *Halesia carolina*
- **Chinese dogwood,** *Cornus kousa* var. *chinensis*
- **Crapemyrtle,** *Lagerstroemia indica* x *fauriei* cvs.
- **English hawthorn,** *Crataegus laevigata* (syn. *oxyacantha*)
- **English holly, white-edged,** *Ilex aquifolium* 'Argenteo Marginata'
- **Flowering cherry,** *Prunus serrulata* 'Kwanzan', 'Shirotae'
- **Flowering cherry,** *Prunus yedoensis* 'Akebono'
- **Flowering weeping cherry,** *Prunus subhirtella* var. *pendula*
- **Fragrant snowbell,** *Styrax obassia*
- **Japanese flowering crabapple,** *Malus floribunda*
- **Japanese maple,** *Acer palmatum* 'Atropurpureum'; **moon maple,** *A. japonicum* and other cvs.
- **Japanese snowbell,** *Styrax japonicus*
- **Japanese tree lilac,** *Syringa reticulata* syn. *amurensis* var. *japonica*
- **Redbud, eastern redbud,** *Cercis canadensis*
- **Sargent cherry,** *Prunus sargentii*
- **Smoke tree,** *Cotinus coggygria* cvs.
- **Sourwood, sorrel tree,** *Oxydendrum arboreum*
- **Trident maple,** *Acer buergeranum*
- **Washington thorn,** *Crataegus phaenopyrum*
- **Southern black haw,** *Viburnum rufidulum*
- **Varnish tree, golden-rain tree,** *Koelreuteria paniculata*

WATERING

Maintain the soil moisture of the indoor trees moved outdoors for the season—**citrus, ficus,** and **palms.**

Water trees growing in containers once or twice every week or so, or when the soil seems dry. Since frequent watering leaches nutrients from the soil, once a month during the growing season, give the plants a light application of a water-soluble organic fertilizer—seaweed or manure tea, for example.

Pour two or three 5-gallon bucketfuls of water around new trees every week or ten days, unless you have a soaking rain.

FERTILIZING

Add a half-strength dose to the water for container trees and indoor trees growing outdoors at every second watering.

PROBLEMS

Early June is spray time for bagworms. Use *Bt*, Sevin, Neem, Permethrin, which is also effective against whitefly. If you spot bagworm tents, remove and destroy them now. Apply fungicidal formulations of copper to control powdery mildew, rusts, and bacterial diseases such as fire blight, bacterial leaf spots, and wilt.

JULY

TREES

PLANNING

In seashore gardens so close to the water they are within reach of salt spray, high tides, and brine-laden wind, plant only trees that tolerate salt. In coastal gardens that are out of the reach of salt water or salt spray, you can plant trees that do well in light, sandy soil.

At the shore, evergreens are the best plants for windbreaks. Your choices are varied; broad-leaved evergreens such as **privet,** and **American holly,** needled evergreens such as **Austrian black pine, hemlock,** and the **junipers.** The fast-growing evergreen **Leyland cypress,** x *Cupressocyparis leylandii,* is an excellent choice for windbreak, hedges, and screening. The bluish-green foliage is feathery and graceful, and the scaly reddish brown bark is handsome. 'Naylor's Blue', which has soft grayish-blue foliage accents, and 'Castlewellan', whose new growth is yellow, are colorful cultivars.

PLANTING

When filling containers for a seashore garden, use commercial potting soil rather than the sandy soil of the area. The humidity in the air reduces the need to water, but check the soil moisture often anyway.

To prevent plant damage from coastal storms, spray the upper and lower sides of the leaves with anti-desiccant; that coats them with a barrier against salt wind and spray.

You can plant container-grown trees this month and balled-and-burlapped shrubs, too. Don't buy B&B shrubs if they've been sitting unmulched and baking at a garden center since they were dug in early spring.

CARE

To help trees at the seashore recover from exposure to heavy spray and high winds after a storm, spray the foliage thoroughly with a hose to wash off as much salt as possible.

If a dangerously high tide is expected, it may be helpful to flood a stand of trees with sprinklers until the soil is so saturated it can't absorb much of the sea water that comes in. The damage will be reduced if the ground is wet when the salt water comes in.

PRUNING

Prune dead wood on evergreen conifers at any time.

Remove water sprouts and suckers from around the base, the trunks, and the branches of flowering fruit trees. The **flowering cherries** usually need repeated attention.

Study the shade enveloping your gardens. Where you are losing too much light to tree branches, mark limbs that can be removed to thin the canopy, and consider whether removing a few lower branches will help; late winter is a good time to remove them.

Use a string trimmer to keep down undergrowth in woodlands and groves. Leave the debris in place, and it will decompose and nourish the trees growing there.

WATERING

Maintain the soil moisture of the indoor tree moved outdoors for the season—**citrus, ficus,** and **palms.**

Water outdoor trees growing in containers every two weeks or when the soil seems dry. Since frequent watering leaches nutrients from the soil, once a month during the growing season, give the plants a light application of a water-soluble organic fertilizer—seaweed or manure tea, for example.

Established trees. They need watering in times of severe drought—more than two or three weeks without rain.

New trees. Water every week or ten days, unless you have a soaking rain. Slowly and gently lay down 1$\frac{1}{2}$ inches of water. Set a 1-pound coffee can under the sprinkler or the hose, and record how long it took to put 1$\frac{1}{2}$ inches in the can—then you'll know.

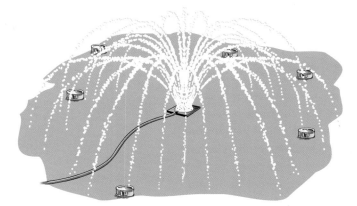

Measure how long it takes your sprinkler system to lay down 1$\frac{1}{2}$ inches of water.

FERTILIZING

At every second watering, add a half-strength dose of fertilizer to the water for indoor trees growing outdoors for the summer.

In-ground trees get all the fertilizer they need when you fertilize the surrounding lawns and beds.

PROBLEMS

Troops of Japanese beetles are at full strength right now. The creature is a beautiful metallic green and coppery maroon, and it chews the leaves and stems of many ornamentals. The grub stage is devastating to lawns and gardens, and while grub-proofing reduces the populations in your yard, it does not control the beetles that fly in.

Japanese beetle traps are effective, providing they are placed **far away** from the plantings you are trying to protect, not among them. If the infestation is minor, beetles can be picked off by hand. Insecticides containing Neem, rotenone, or Sevin insecticide help control this and other bad guy beetles.

Neem is an effective control for whitefly, mites, and bagworms. If you spot bagworm tents, remove and destroy them now. Apply fungicidal formulations of copper to control powdery mildew, rust, and bacterial diseases such as fire blight, bacterial leafspot and wilt.

TREES FOR THE COASTAL GARDEN

- **American holly,** *Ilex opaca*
- **Austrian black pine,** *Pinus nigra*
- **Black gum, sour gum,** *Nyssa sylvatica*
- **Eastern red cedar,** *Juniperus virginiana*
- **Hackberry,** *Celtis occidentalis* 'Magnifica'
- **Japanese black pine,** *Pinus thunbergii*
- **Japanese clethra,** *Clethra barbinervis*
- **Japanese pagoda tree,** *Sophora japonica*
- **Leyland cypress,** x *Cupressocyparis leylandii*
- **Live oak,** *Quercus virginiana*
- **London plane,** *Platanus* x *acerifolia*
- **Privet,** *Ligustrum* species
- **Red maple, swamp maple,** *Acer rubrum* cvs.
- **Red mulberry,** *Morus rubra*
- **Russian olive,** *Elaeagnus angustifolia*
- **Shadblow, serviceberry,** *Amelanchier canadensis*
- **Sweet bay,** *Magnolia virginiana*
- **Sycamore maple, planetree maple,** *Acer pseudoplatanus* cvs.
- **Thornless honeylocust,** *Gleditsia triacanthos* var. *inermis*
- **Washington hawthorn,** *Crataegus phaenopyrum*

AUGUST

TREES

PLANNING

A tree's winter assets are its silhouette against the sky, its bark, and its fruit. The symmetrical winter silhouettes of the **incense cedar,** the **white oak,** and the stylish **Serbian spruce** are arresting. The gnarly form of the **California sycamore** is high drama. The bark of most trees becomes more rugged and interesting with the years, and some species shed their bark in beautiful patterns. The peeling bark of **paperbark maple,** *Acer griseum,* reveals variations on its rich cinnamon color. The chalky white bark of the **lacebark pine** rivals the beauty of the **paper birch.**

PLANTING

You can plant container-grown trees this month. B&B trees, too, but don't buy B&B shrubs if they have been sitting unmulched and baking at a garden center since they were dug in early spring.

Evergreen trees do well moved August through October.

CARE

Don't leave orchard fruit lying on the ground. It attracts raccoons, skunks, possums, and yellow jackets. Not to mention deer.

PRUNING

Begin to prepare indoor trees summering outdoors for their return to winter quarters—**citrus, tropical hibiscus, flowering maples,** and the others. Deadhead, clear away yellowing foliage, and prune out branches that are crossing or crowding the crown.

WATERING

Maintain the soil moisture of the indoor trees moved outdoors for the season—**citrus, ficus,** and **palms**.

Water outdoor trees growing in containers every week or when the soil seems dry. Since frequent watering leaches nutrients from the soil, once a month during the growing season give the plants a light application of a water-soluble organic fertilizer, seaweed or manure tea, for example.

New trees. Water every week or ten days, unless you have a soaking rain.

Established trees. They need watering in times of severe drought—more than two or three weeks without rain.

FERTILIZING

Mid-month, stop fertilizing established outdoor trees growing in containers. Do continue to fertilize indoor trees summering outdoors at every second watering.

To make room for the leaves the trees will begin to shed next month, use up, or store, finished compost. Composting can happen in just one summer in our warm, humid regions if you have been keeping the pile watered and turned. (See Composting in this chapter's October pages.)

PROBLEMS

Bagworms and tent caterpillars are usually very active right now. If you spot bagworm tents, remove and destroy them now. You can also spray with a biological control such as *Bacillus thuringiensis* (Bt). Other controls are Sevin or malathion insecticide, pyrethrin, or rotenone.

Powdery mildew and rust turn up on susceptible plants. Sulfur controls both, as do fungicidal formulations of copper, which also control bacterial diseases such as fire blight, bacterial leafspot, and wilt.

TREES WITH COLORFUL FALL FOLIAGE

- **American smoke tree, chittamwood,** *Cotinus obovatus*
- **American sweet gum,** *Liquidambar styraciflua*
- **Amur maple,** *Acer ginnala*
- **Black gum, sour gum,** *Nyssa sylvatica*
- **Bradford pear,** *Pyrus calleryana* 'Chanticleer', 'Aristocrat'
- **Chinese dogwood,** *Cornus florida* hybrids; *C. kousa, C. x rutgersensis* Stellar Series
- **Golden larch,** *Pseudolarix amabile*
- **Japanese stewartia,** *Stewartia pseudocamellia*
- **Japanese zelkova,** *Zelkova serrata*
- **Katsura tree,** *Cercidiphylium japonicum*
- **Maidenhair tree,** *Ginkgo biloba*
- **Mountain ash, Korean mountain ash,** *Sorbus alnifolia*
- **Northern red oak,** *Quercus rubra*
- **Pistachio,** *Pistacia chinensis*
- **Red maple, swamp maple,** *Acer rubrum* 'October Glory', 'Red Sunset'
- **Sassafras,** *Sassafras albidum*
- **Scarlet oak,** *Quercus coccinea* 'Superba'
- **Sourwood, sorrel tree,** *Oxydendrum arboreum*
- **Sugar maple,** *Acer saccharum* 'Bonfire', 'Green Mountain'
- **Tatarian maple,** *Acer tataricum*
- **Tulip tree,** *Liriodendron tulipifera*
- **Washington hawthorn,** *Crataegus phaenopyrum*
- **Witchhazel,** *Hamamelis* x *intermedia* 'Diane'

A row of maple trees displaying brilliant fall colors.

TREES WITH EXCEPTIONAL BARK

- **American beech,** *Fagus grandiflora*
- **American sweet gum,** *Liquidambar styraciflua*
- **American sycamore,** *Platanus occidentalis*
- **American yellowwood,** *Cladrastis lutea*
- **Asian white birch,** *Betula platyphylla*
- **Beech,** *Fagus*
- **Chinese elm, lacebark elm,** *Ulmus parviflora*
- **Crapemyrtle,** *Lagerstroemia indica*
- **Dove tree, handkerchief tree,** *Davidia involucrata*
- **Franklin tree,** *Franklinia alatamaha*
- **Hawthorn,** *Crataegus viridis* 'Winter King'
- **Japanese larch,** *Larix kaempferi*
- **Japanese stewartia,** *Stewartia pseudocamellia*
- **Korean stewartia,** *Stewartia koreana*
- **Lacebark pine,** *Pinus bungeana*
- **London planetree,** *Platanus* x *acerifolia*
- **Paperbark cherry,** *Prunus serrula*
- **Paperbark maple,** *Acer griseum*
- **River birch,** *Betula* 'Heritage'
- **Sargent cherry,** *Prunus sargentii*
- **Shagbark hickory,** *Carya ovata*
- **Stewartia,** *Stewartia*
- **Whitebarked Himalayan birch,** *Betula utilis jacquemontii*

SEPTEMBER

TREES

PLANNING

Check out the changing color of the trees in your neighborhood and at public gardens, where the names of those you admire are sure to be available. Then look in your own garden for a spot just asking for a little red, coral, or yellow in the fall. Fall is one of the best planting seasons, and it's on its way.

Consider investing in a few trees that are especially beautiful in fall and winter to brighten corners that appear dull at this season. The **spruces** are gorgeous when they are outlined by snow, so plant one where you will see it from indoors. Even in a small garden you can find space for at least one deciduous specimen that has beautiful bark—the **river birch** 'Heritage', for example. Planted where it will shelter a big rock, a stand of grass that turns gold in fall, **ferns,** a few brilliant early **tulips** and **narcissus,** it will be a year-round destination.

PLANTING

When the leaves start to change color is the beginning of an excellent planting season for trees. Plant sales and pleasant September weather combine to make this a fine time to install a

It's never too late to start a compost pile; gather all your fall leaves to start one if you do not have one already.

hedge. You'll find suggestions for planting hedges under Planting in September, Shrubs.

If you've been wanting a too-expensive tree, a good-sized **Japanese maple** for example—take advantage of the seasonally discounted prices offered now. If you are buying a balled-and-burlapped tree, choose one that has just been dug rather than a tree that was dug in spring. Avoid B&B trees that have been unmulched and baking on the nursery lot all summer long.

CARE

In Zone 6, get ready to move outdoor trees growing in containers in exposed locations to more protected spots for the winter.

Before the end of the month move the indoor trees back inside for the winter. But first, hose them down, let them dry, and then spray the foliage lightly, top and undersides, with a horticultural soap.

You may need to wrap new trees as a protection from deer rubbing, critter nibbling, and sunscald this fall and winter. Plan to remove it come spring as wrappings eventually constrict the trunks and can cause cracking.

An easy way to prevent winter sun from injuring the bark of young trees is to paint the trunks with whitewash—calcium carbonate with resins in it.

As the leaves begin to fall, gather and save them for the compost pile. (See Composting in this chapter's October pages.) Dry leaves, along with grass clippings, are a major source of organic material for the compost pile.

PRUNING

Early this month, before preparing the indoor trees vacationing outdoors for their move back inside—**ficus, citrus,** and **palms**—groom them. Remove yellowing foliage and branches that are crossing so that the interior has air and light. Pinch off all but half a dozen or so tiny lemons developing on a **Improved Meyer lemon tree.**

Clear away spent flowers on late blooming flowering trees.

WATERING

Pour two or three 5-gallon bucketfuls of water around the roots of newly planted trees once every two weeks throughout fall. The earth remains warm even after leaves fall and the air cools, so roots continue to develop.

Check the soil moisture of the indoor trees you moved back indoors for the winter. Dry air indoors soon sucks the moisture out of the soil.

Indoors. Maintain the soil moisture for indoor trees, mist them, and air the room often.

TREES USED AS HEDGES

These are some beautiful trees that can be pruned to maintain a desired hedge height.
- **American arborvitae,** *Thuja occidentalis* cvs.
- **American hornbeam,** *Carpinus caroliniana*
- **American incense cedar,** *Calocedrus decurrens*
- **Canadian hemlock,** *Tsuga canadensis* 'Bennett', 'Jeddeloh', 'Jervis'
- **Crapemyrtle,** *Lagerstroemia indica* cvs.
- **European beech,** *Fagus sylvatica*
- **European hornbeam,** *Carpinus betulus*
- **European smoke tree,** *Cotinus coggygria*
- **Foster holly #2,** *Ilex attenuata*
- **Hinoki false cypress,** *Chamaecyparis obtusa*
- **Japanese cedar,** *Cryptomeria japonica* 'Yoshino'
- **Juniper,** *Juniperus* spp.
- **Leyland cypress,** x *Cupressocyparis leylandii*
- **Oleander, rose-bay,** *Nerium oleander*
- **Pine,** *Pinus* spp.
- **Privet,** *Ligustrum* spp.
- **Upright Atlas cedar,** *Cedrus atlantica* 'Fastigiata'
- **Washington thorn,** *Crataegus phaenopyrum*

FERTILIZING

In Zone 8, the last fertilization can be between the end of September and mid-October. In Zones 6 and 7, the time for the last application is between early September and early October.

Include mature trees that are doing poorly when you fertilize.

PROBLEMS

Fall tent caterpillars can be controlled by *Bacillus thuringiensis* (Bt). Other controls are Sevin or malathion insecticide, pyrethrin, or rotenone.

Treat the indoor trees, such as **citrus, ficus,** and **palms,** that have been summering outdoors for insects before moving them back inside for the winter.

Change whatever deer deterrents you are using. If bears have been reported in your area, do not put out bird feeders; they attract bears. See the section on Pests, Diseases, and Controls in the Appendix of the book.

Continue to search out and rake up weeds.

If you see signs of vole activity, bait the main runway with a rodenticide.

OCTOBER

TREES

 PLANNING

If there's no place in your yard for a compost pile, consider installing one of the many composters offered at garden centers and by mail-order. Or, compost in a black leaf bag; layer in it dry leaves, green weeds, chopped vegetable or fruit peelings, and then poke holes all over the outside. Wet the interior thoroughly, close the bag, and set it in a warm, out-of-the-way place to do its thing. Shake the bag, and turn it upside down often to speed the process.

 PLANTING

When the leaves start to change color you can dig and transplant trees. Now through November into early December is the perfect time for planting trees. The air is cold, but the earth still has warmth.

 CARE

Before adding leaves to an existing compost pile, gather the humus collected there, and use it or store it for use next year. Save the fallen leaves, and heap them in an out of the way place for composting, for insulation, or grind them to use as mulch. If you have only a few leaves, suck them up in a vacuum-blower, and blow the residue out over the lawn or the flower borders.

 PRUNING

You can prune out dead or diseased tree limbs, but delay any major pruning until later.

 WATERING

Indoors. Maintain the soil moisture of the indoor trees, mist them often, and air the room daily if you can.

Outdoors. Water newly planted trees and hardy trees in containers every week or ten days if the season runs dry.

 FERTILIZING

In Zone 8, the last fertilization can be between the end of September and mid-October. In Zones 6 and 7, the time for the last application is between early September and early October. See Understanding Fertilizers in the Introduction to the book.

PROBLEMS

Check trees for signs of scale, aphids, mealybug infestations, and control with ultrafine horticultural oil, horticultural soap, Neem products, or Permethrin.

Voles are most active October to March. If you see vole activity, bait the main runway with a rodenticide.

Change the deer deterrents you are using; they disregard deterrents they become accustomed to. See the section on Pests, Diseases, and Controls in the Appendix. If bears have been reported in your area, do not put out—or do remove—bird feeders.

In Zone 8, continue to rake away weeds.

COMPOSTING

Dead leaves become an asset when you use them to make compost, the soillike substance remaining when nature reduces organic material to humus.

Compost is called "black gold" because a 1-inch layer mixed into the soil every month releases its nutrients as the plants grow. Compost also replaces the organic content lost to healthy plant growth. It improves drainage, soil structure, aeration; sustains the microbial activity essential to healthy soil; encourages big root systems; buffers soil temperatures; and reduces the need for watering—100 pounds of humus holds 195 pounds of water.

Along with dry leaves, the other materials used in building a compost pile are grass clippings, chopped vegetable and fruit peels, healthy weeds, and plant debris. Never compost disease or insect-infested plant materials.

Your compost pile will deliver finished (ready to use) compost sooner if you break up the leaves with a blower/vacuum or a leaf shredder before putting them on the pile. Or, run a mulching mower over them. Or, pile them into a garbage can, and churn them with a string trimmer.

Here's the basic approach to building a compost pile:

1. Heap dry leaves in an out-of-sight place with access to a hose. Outline a base for the compost pile that is about 4 feet wide by 4 feet long. As the ingredients become available, build onto this base a 4 foot high pile of layers of any of the following four combinations of organic materials:

3 parts dry leaves (Carbon)
- 3 parts fresh grass clippings (Nitrogen)

2 parts dry leaves (Carbon)
- 2 parts straw or wood shavings (Carbon)
- 1 part manure (Nitrogen)
- 1 part fresh grass clippings (Nitrogen)
- 1 part fresh garden weeds/harvested plants (Nitrogen)
- 1 part kitchen food scraps (Nitrogen)

6 parts dry leaves (Carbon)
- 3 parts kitchen scraps (Nitrogen) (no meat or fish)
- 3 parts fresh grass clippings (Nitrogen)

3 parts dry leaves (Carbon)
- 1 part fresh garden weeds/harvested plants (Nitrogen)
- 1 part fresh grass clippings (Nitrogen)
- 1 part kitchen food scraps (Nitrogen)

2. As you build the pile, sprinkle over each layer about an inch of garden soil and/or compost to encourage microbial activity. Or, sprinkle on a microbial activator to speed up decomposition. Compost starter, activators, and/or inoculants hasten the composting. To make a compost rich in nitrogen, add dustings of bone meal for the phosphorus and calcium it contains, blood meal, or a high nitrogen garden fertilizer. To make it high in potassium, calcium, and carbon, and to reduce acidity, dust fireplace ashes onto the layers. If you wish to help reduce soil compaction and enhance aeration, dust on gypsum, which also adds calcium and sulfur.

3. Keep the pile moist, and turn it weekly, or as often as you can, with a pitchfork to hasten decomposition. Depending on the season, your climate, and how often you turn it, the pile will become compost in a few months (warm regions), or in year or two (cooler areas).

NOVEMBER

TREES

PLANNING

Hollies are very successful here and a joy at holiday time when the spiky leaves are ornamented by the bright red berries that tell us the holidays are just around the corner. Try one; you'll enjoy harvesting your own **holly** branches to make Christmas swags and holiday arrangements.

The most durable **holly tree** is the 40- to 50-foot pyramidal **American holly,** *Ilex opaca*, which is hardy in Zones 5 through 9 and tolerates urban pollution. The bright red berries mature in October and persist through winter. André's favorite varieties are 'Merry Christmas', 'George Hart', 'Xanthocarpa', and 'Old Heavy Berry'. Other fine **tree hollies** are **longstalk holly,** *I. pedunculosa,* and **English holly,** *I. aquifolium*. Slender 25-foot **Foster's holly #2,** a pyramidal tree 15 to 25 feet high with small toothed leaves and masses of tiny red berries, does well even in cities.

American and **Foster's holly** make a handsome pair. **Hollies** are dioecious (see About Shrubs That Bear Berries in November, Shrubs). That means that most females require a male pollinator to fruit well.

PLANTING

November and into early December is a still a good time to plant trees.

If you are planning to have a live Christmas tree, choose a permanent home suited to the tree's mature width and height, and dig the planting hole now. Improve the soil from the hole (see with Soil Preparation and Improvement in the Introduction to the book), and put it back in the hole. Cover the area with 12 to 18 inches of leaves held down by evergreen boughs to keep them from blowing.

CARE

Apply an anti-desiccant spray to the foliage of newly planted **hollies** growing in exposed positions, or wrap them in Reemay or burlap.

In snow country, move hardy trees growing in containers to a sheltered corner out of the wind for the winter, or store them in a garage or shed.

American Holly 'Canary'

PRUNING

Don't be concerned for their health when evergreens show some yellow in the interior of the branches—**pines, arborvitae, juniper,** and **yews** among them. It's most likely normal. The plants we call evergreens lose some of their older leaves at more or less regular intervals, but they look green all year because, except for the **golden larches,** they don't drop them all at the same time. Every plant must renew its foliage as part of its life cycle. Some **pine** species lose needles every fifteen to eighteen months, some **hollies** drop their leaves at four-year intervals. So when yellow shows up in an evergreen, chances are that it is a normal part of a cycle and not a problem.

WATERING

The earth remains warm even after leaves fall and the air cools, so roots continue to develop. That's why watering is recommended when fall runs dry.

POLLARDING AND PLEACHING

Europe's pollarded trees and pleached allées are the result of severe pruning. The process is lengthy, labor intensive, and interesting, and the results are elegant.

Pollarding is a form of pruning where the branches of a tree are cut back every year or so almost to the main trunk. The result is that you get branches that are long, thin, and flexible, and a tree whose crown is ball-shaped. In Europe, **willows** were commonly pollarded to produce whips used in basket-making.

Pleaching is a system of shearing trees (or tall shrubs) that are closely planted alongside a broad garden path or walk—**lindens, maples, sycamores** are often used. Set side-by-side, the branches are encouraged to grow together overhead. Shearing trains the top growth into a thin hedge overhead. Because a pleached allée takes forever to achieve and is time-consuming to maintain, you're likely to see this only in public gardens and arboreta. There's a pleached allée in one of the lower garden rooms at Dumbarton Oaks in D.C.

Maintain the soil moisture of indoor trees—**citrus, ficus,** and **palms**—mist them often, and air the room daily if you can.

Water outdoor trees growing in containers every two weeks or when the soil seems dry. Water thoroughly before the ground freezes so the plants don't go into winter dry.

FERTILIZING

Do not fertilize trees at this season, indoors or out.

PROBLEMS

Deer will eat **holly** leaves when they are starving, and young trees are especially susceptible. See the section on Pests, Diseases, and Controls in the Appendix the book.

Bait vole runs approaching trees with a rodenticide.

DECEMBER
TREES

PLANNING

Cut Christmas trees. The **Douglas fir** and the **balsam fir** (*Abies balsamea*) stay fresh longest, so they are popular. **Balsam fir** looks like **spruce,** the traditional evergreen with short, stiff needles.

Live Christmas trees. André recommends the **Colorado blue spruce,** *Picea pungens glauca,* and its varieties 'Thompsonii' and 'Hoopsii'. An 8-foot ceiling can't take a tree taller than 7 feet. Before buying, give the plant a health check. Is the rootball moist? Do needles drop when you shake it?

PLANTING

If you're planning on a live Christmas tree, prepare a planting hole for it (see November Planting).

CARE

Remove the lower branches to make room for the tree holder, and cut at least 1 inch off the bottom so it can more easily take up the water, which should contain Christmas tree preservative. Keep the tree in a shaded location. Before bringing the tree indoors, to keep the needles fresh longer, spray the tree with an anti-transpirant like biodegradable Wilt-Pruf. One application before decorating the tree should last. After the holidays, recycle the tree as mulch or wood chips.

Keep a live tree indoors no more than two weeks. Before it comes in, keep it outdoors in a sheltered spot with good light; spray needles with an anti-desiccant to help prevent drying out, water the soil well, and let it drain. If it's a B&B tree, place it in a leak-proof tub. Stand the tree far from radiators, fireplaces, and other heat sources. Keep the temperature under 65 degrees Fahrenheit if, or when, possible. Don't fertilize, and water only if the soil feels dry. Air the room, and mist the air around the tree—not the tree itself because of the ornaments and the lights—daily. If you cannot plant your live tree when you move it outdoors, place it in a sheltered spot with good light, and heap leaves, or bags filled with leaves, 14 to 18 inches deep all around the rootball.

Spray an anti-desiccant on young evergreens in exposed positions. Protect them from winds with a burlap screen.

PRUNING

Lightly harvest mature evergreens with cones and berries to use in holiday decorations—**pines, fir,** and **hollies.**

WATERING

Cut Christmas tree. Keep the stand filled with water containing floral preservative; fresh **fir** trees drink lots; **pine** trees drink some; **spruce** don't take up much water at all.

Maintain the soil moisture of the indoors trees—**citrus, ficus,** and **palms**—and mist them and air the room often. If there's no snow or rain, water all new outdoor plantings thoroughly.

FERTILIZING

Make a New Year's resolution to stick to non-polluting fertilizers and biodegradable controls. Decades of nursery experience have convinced André and Mark that trees that are inherently healthy, planted in suitable climate, in soil properly prepared (see Understanding Fertilizers in the introduction to the book), and given all the water they need the first years, are strengthened by normal stresses.

PROBLEMS

Trees growing indoors come under attack from mealybugs and spider mites. Frequent showers, and spraying with horticultural soaps discourages them.

VINES, GROUND COVERS, & ORNAMENTAL GRASSES

Vines, ground covers, and ornamental grasses solve landscaping problems by speedily greening barren areas with low-maintenance plants. Because they're speedy, all three types of plants also tend to be weedy so some maintenance is necessary.

VINES

Caution. Even cultivated vines can be as invasive as weed vines—so plant even the vines we recommend only where they won't escape and invade other plants including other native plants.

Perennial vines. Generally deep-rooted, the perennial vines grow vigorously and thrive for years rooted in a modest planting hole or a large planter or tub. Which is better—evergreen or deciduous? An evergreen vine—ivy or euonymus (*Euonymus fortunei* var. *radicans* for example)—is a good choice when you want year-round greening and screening. A deciduous vine is a better choice when you want summer screening coupled with access to sun in winter—clematis for the sake of its extraordinary flowers, or Dutchman's pipe for screening a porch or a pergola for outdoor dining.

GROUND COVERS FOR PROBLEM SITES

Lawn substitute. Four ground covers are commonly used as substitutes for turf lawns. They are evergreen and can be walked on occasionally without being damaged.

English ivy, (*Hedera helix*). An evergreen with tough glossy dark-green leaves on woody vines. Lots of interesting variegated types.

Vinca, Periwinkle (*Vinca minor*). Small, dainty, shiny dark green leaves on slim trailing stems 2 to 3 feet long. Lavender-blue flowers in early spring.

Pachysandra, Japanese Spurge (*Pachysandra terminalis*). Low-growing, wide-spreading, formal ground cover. Short green-white flower spikes in early spring.

Wintergreen, Checkerberry (*Gaultheria procumbens*). Evergreen shrubby ground-hugging mat with aromatic foliage and bright berries.

Under trees. Tree shade and root competition are hard on turf grass. These ground covers do well under trees.

Bugleweed, (*Ajuga reptans)*. Semi-evergreen rosettes of leaves and flowering spikes in blue or white in spring.

Hosta. Small colorful hostas like 8-inch 'Gold Edger'; 3-inch 'Venusta'; 7-inch *H. helemoides*; 15-inch 'Purple & Gold'.

Lilyturf, (*Liriope muscari*). Grasslike, and 12 to 18 inches high. Flowering spikes in blue, purple, lavender, or white in late summer.

Spotted Deadnettle, (*Lamium maculatum*). Semi-evergreen, low-growing, silver-white-green variegated foliage lightens the shadows. Pink or white florets in May and June.

Barrenwort, (*Epimedium* sp.). Deciduous, heart-shaped green foliage carpets the earth and turns reddish or gold in the fall. Dainty spurred yellow, pink, white, red florets in early to mid-spring.

Golden Moneywort, (*Lysimachia nummularia* 'Aurea'). Deciduous, lime-green, low-growing, and spreads rapidly in moist soil. In early summer, it bears masses of small cup-shaped yellow flowers.

Lily-of-the-valley, (*Convallaria majalis*). Deciduous, lovely 6- to 8-inch high ground cover ideal for open woodlands. The flowers are exquisitely fragrant.

The top of a vine will be up in the wind, so you want to make sure it will withstand the coldest winters your region can throw at it. If a vine's cold-hardiness is doubtful, place it where it will have the protection of a north-facing wall at its back.

Annual Vines. The annual vines grow at the speed of light and produce beautiful flowers. They're often used for summer screening, and they're good choices to clothe walls and fences that will need repainting periodically. Most annual vines need only light support. Many are easily grown from seed planted in spring. Where the growing season is short, the annual vines are usually started indoors early or purchased as seedlings.

Tropical and semi-tropical vines. They're great accent plants for patios and porches. They can

live through winter in a greenhouse or a bright window as house- plants. In Zones 6 and 7, they are not likely to survive wintering in their pots in a shed or garage unless some heat is provided.

TRAINING, PRUNING, AND TRANSPLANTING

Training. Vines need supports. How a vine climbs—the plant parts it uses to hold itself to advancing positions—dictates the type of support it needs. When you are choosing a vine, that's an important consideration. Carolina jessamine climbs by twining itself around its support. Chinese trumpet vine uses aerial rootlets to attach itself to its next position. Clematis holds on with twisting leaf-stalks (petioles). Before you buy or stake a vine, make sure you know the type of support it requires and

have figured out how you will prune it when it gets up there.

Pruning. Vines need a regular schedule of pruning to lead the branches in the direction you want them to grow, and to contain their usually exuberant growth. Those vines that flower on last year's growth—spring bloomers usually—should be pruned as soon as they finish blooming, late spring or early summer. Flowering vines that bloom on new wood are pruned before they begin to grow, late winter or early spring; they usually bloom late in the season. See About Pruning Vines in the February pages.

Transplanting vines. You can transplant a vine planted a year or two ago fairly easily. Before you dig it up, cut the stems back to within 2 or 3 feet from the crown, and tie them together. Then proceed as described for moving established shrubs under Planting, in the February pages of Shrubs. If the vine is a flowering plant, move it shortly after it bloomed to avoid cutting off next year's blooms.

GROUND COVERS

Ground covers are low-maintenance plants used to carpet the earth where lawn turf and ornamental plants are impractical or undesirable. Any fast-growing plant that spreads and grows without much attention can be used as ground cover, such as daylilies in the sun, hostas in shade. Many vines also fit the job description. But the plants specifically designated as ground covers spread rapidly and grow so thickly they keep out weeds even when they die down in fall.

Caution: The plants designated as ground covers, like weeds, spread rapidly.

The toughest evergreen ground covers are ajuga, pachysandra, myrtle (*Vinca minor*), and English ivy. All four can be walked on some and can be used as replacement for a lawn. Ajuga and myrtle bear sweet little flowers in early spring. Ivy can take a few years to get going, but once started spreads irresistibly. All four are seen by environmentalists as a potential threat to native plants so use them responsibly. Don't plant a ground cover where it might invade stands of native plants or woodlands.

PLANTING AND MAINTENANCE

To get a ground cover off to a fast, successful start, provide a well-prepared bed and humusy fertile soil. Dig the whole area to be planted, and improve the soil just as completely and care-

---

ABOUT VINES AND THEIR SUPPORTS

How a vine attaches itself to its support is stated in the table of plants in this chapter. How it climbs tells you what type of support it will need. That tells you whether a vine is suited to the job you have planned for it. There are variations, but here's the general idea:

Twining stems. For vines that climb by twining stems, Carolina jessamine, for example, suitable supports are narrow—a slim post, a pipe, wires, or strings.

Tendrils (twisting petioles). Vines that climb by twisting tendrils—clematis, for example—require a structure of wires, or wire mesh to climb on.

Clinging aerial rootlets. Vines that climb by aerial rootlets that secrete an adhesive glue, like English ivy, need only a rugged surface, such as a brick or stucco wall, or a rough, unpainted fence, for support.

However they climb, vines that eventually will be very heavy—like climbing hydrangea, bittersweet, trumpet vine, and wisteria—need supports built of heavy timbers, or even a dead tree, to hold them up.

Vines hold a lot of moisture. It is essential that the lumber you buy to create their support be pressure-treated.

fully as you do a bed for perennials. If you are installing an invasive ground cover such as ivy, vinca, or ajuga, plan to edge it with a 6-inch metal barrier to prevent it from overrunning neighboring plantings.

Planting through a mulch cover will minimize weeding chores, which can be burdensome in the season or two the ground cover will need to thicken enough to keep invaders out.

The first season of growth, a newly installed ground cover will need watering any time the perennial bed needs watering, weekly or every ten days unless you have a soaking rain. In the following years it should need watering only if the leaf tips are wilting.

An occasional pruning keeps a ground cover neater and stimulates branching and new growth—pachysandra, plumbago (Ceratostigma plumbaginoides), and ivy when fully mature will benefit from shearing every few years.

In fall, clear ground covers of fallen leaves only if they have matted down.

You fertilize a bed of ground covers twice a year, just as you do perennials. (See Fertilizing and Fertilizers in the introduction to Perennials.)

ORNAMENTAL GRASSES

The ornamental grasses add grade notes to the garden in summer, fall, and winter. On hot summer days the foliage sways and whispers in the slightest breeze, and when the flowers are gone, the airy flower heads (inflorescences) dance in the wind. In winter the dried foliage turns to gold in winter and binds mounds of snow at its feet.

In choosing a grass, consider the size first. Size is judged by the end-of-season height and width of the foliage. Best for the front of a flower border are grasses under 2 feet, like the little sedges (Carex species), mosquito grass (Bouteloua gracilis), Japanese blood grass (Imperata cylindrica 'Red Baron'), and blue sheep's fescue (Festuca amethystina var. superba).

Grasses 2 to 5 feet tall are ideal for the middle and back of a flowering border and can be used as a transitional ground cover. Some we like are the arching silver grasses (Miscanthus sacchariflorus and company), bold plants with broad, grassy, gracefully arching leaves. We also favor switchgrass, Panicum virgatum, and the pennisetums, whose graceful arching foliage is topped at the end of the summer by flower spikelets that have conspicuous bottlebrush bristles.

The very tall grasses—6 feet and up—are often used for screening and to enhance bare walls. Northern sea oats, a medium-tall, narrow, upright woodland grass is an excellent ground cover, especially lovely growing on a slope where the seedheads are backlit in early morning or late afternoon. Silver grass is a large landscaping grass to use boldly, in big spaces.

After the six footers, the sizes go on up to the very, very invasive Phragmites australis, an enormous reed 19 feet tall that grows wild in wetlands, brackish or fresh, everywhere. The fluffy, tannish seedheads swaying on rigid golden stalks are lovely, but invasive it surely is. A better choice where a very tall grass is needed is ravenna grass, Erianthus ravennae (Zones 6 to 9), a magnificent architectural plant 9 to 12 feet tall with broad, arching silvery leaves.

Each species of grass adds a distinct form and texture to the garden. Chinese silver grass is very erect; maiden grass arches; the foliage of the pennisetums fountains. The texture of the leaves and their color impacts the garden design—fine, coarse, bold, bluish, greenish, reddish, gold, striped, and variegated. We like contrast, so we recommend combining both upright and fountaining forms, fine and coarse-textured grasses, and green and variegated forms.

CHAPTER NINE

PLANTING AND MAINTENANCE

Like the perennial flowers, ornamental grasses begin to fill out the second year. They can be started from seed in spring, but the seedlings will take two years to gain any size. Planting root divisions is far more satisfactory.

Soil. Most of the ornamental grasses thrive in the fertile humusy soil best for most perennials. Most need a well-drained site, but some can handle, and a few need, moist soil.

Maintenance. In the grass garden at the National Arboretum, the plants are allowed to develop throughout the year without pruning, staking, spraying, or deadheading. Seedheads ripen and stand through fall and winter. In late winter or early spring, as new foliage begins to emerge they are cut back to within a few inches of the ground, mulched, and fertilized.

Most ornamental grasses need annual fertilization. The time for it is when signs of new growth appear. Apply a slow-release organic fertilizer such as Holly-tone or Espoma Organic Lawn Food. In prolonged droughts, water slowly and deeply.

Once installed, ornamental grasses are not expected to require division for at least five to ten years.

PESTS AND DISEASES

The vines, ground covers, and grasses we recommend are vigorous plants with no particular pest or disease problems.

JANUARY
VINES, GROUND COVERS, & ORNAMENTAL GRASSES

PLANNING

Take your garden catalogs to a window with a view of the garden—consider whether plantings of vines, ground covers, and ornamental grasses can solve problems and make some tired old things new.

Vines. Imagine a vine blooming on a garage corner, the garden shed, hiding a tree stump, covering an unsightly structure. Try the idea by plant a fast-growing annual climber. The three best are the purple-podded, scented **hyacinth bean** whose beautiful beans are edible; white-flowered **moonvine;** and **morning glory,** *Ipomea tricolor* 'Heavenly Blue'.

Ground covers. If drought plagues your lawn—or your lawn plagues you—consider replacing outlying portions of the grass with a ground cover.

Ornamental grasses. Dream a grass garden. Low-growing species add a texture and movement to the front of flower beds. Mid-height grasses are the natural transition plant to a woodland or water, and, in combination with native wildflowers, make a beautiful flowering meadow. The recommended ratio for a sunny meadow garden is one-third flowers to two-thirds ornamental grasses for sunny places; one-third grasses and two-thirds flowers for shade. Grasses 6 feet and up can replace a high-maintenance espalier fronting a masonry wall by growing into a low-maintenance screen.

PLANTING

Outdoors. This month or in early February, sow seeds outdoors of vines that need to be stratified (chilled) in order to germinate. This way you can multiply **trumpet vine,** which also can be sown in fall.

The Planting section of November, Perennials, describes how stratification is done.

CARE

Winter winds are going to keep blowing for weeks, so check and adjust the ties and supports of mature vines. Tie down branches whipping in the wind. Free branchlets burdened by snow or ice, including any lower branches buried in snow.

GROOMING

Ornamental grasses. In Zone 8 check established cool season grasses for signs of new growth. If the tips of new shoots are visible, cut the old stalks back to within a few inches of the crown.

WATERING

If the winter has been short of snow or rain, check the soil moisture of vines growing under overhanging structures. If the ground is dry and not frozen, water.

Water vines wintering in containers in a shed or garage often enough to keep the soil slightly damp.

FERTILIZING

It's too early to fertilize.

PROBLEMS

Repair and/or renew deer deterrents on vines. Check and adjust burlap covers and chicken-wire cages.

Spray **euonymus** with a dormant oil to keep scale away.

If vole runs appear near vines, bait the main runway with a rodenticide.

BARBERING ORNAMENTAL GRASSES

Allowing the grasses to stand through winter adds to your pleasure in the view, but you can cut them down anytime they lose their looks. Late in the season the stalks flop over providing some winter protection for the new shoots—not so nice looking. But you must give them an annual haircut *before* those new shoots get much growth, or you will be in danger of trimming the newbies with the golden oldies.

The best time to barber is just before or as new growth begins, so knowing when to check for growth is helpful.

The low-growing grasses and new plantings of the big grasses can be trimmed with hand shears. When a big grass matures, simplify the annual haircut by roping the leaves together with sisal twine. Tie them all the way to the top so they end up looking like a telephone pole. Then saw the top off a few inches above the crown. If you use a chain saw, take care not to catch the twine in the teeth!

Cool Season. The cool-season grasses shoot up in late January or February unless the winter is exceptionally cold. So check now to see if they are ready for the barber.

These grasses are a good choice when you are looking for plants that will be highly visible—the main show—starting early in the growing season.

Warm Season. The warm-season grasses begin to grow later—March or April. That's when you want to check their progress, shears in hand.

A warm-season grass is a good choice when you are combining grasses and flowers.

Early spring-flowering bulbs come into bloom after the grass's annual haircut and make the garden pretty while the grass is growing up. As the grass grows it will hide the ripening of the bulb foliage.

233

FEBRUARY

VINES, GROUND COVERS, & ORNAMENTAL GRASSES

 PLANNING

Place your order for mail-order catalog plants now.

You want to be ready to start planting in early March in Zone 8 and the Tidewater, mid-March in Richmond and Zone 7, and the end of March in Zone 6.

The ground around the ornamental grasses always seems bare before the grasses get their growth, but it doesn't have to be. Plan in June to order lots of the small early bulbs to plant around the grasses. In early fall, over-plant the area with some of the big showy flowers recommended in To Plant with Ornamental Grasses on the September pages of this chapter.

 PLANTING

Indoors. Start seeds of annual vines late this month or next. **Morning glory, moonflower,** and **hyacinth bean** can be started eight to ten weeks before the out-door air warms to 60 degrees Fahrenheit. They and many of the perennial vines grow readily from seed.

If you plan to plant lots of orna-mental grasses, consider starting your own from seed. See Starting Seeds Indoors under Planting in January, Annuals.

Outdoors. This is the last month you can sow seeds outdoors of annual vines that need to be stratified (chilled) in order to ger-minate. The planting section in November, Perennials, explains stratification.

If you plan to move a vine, root prune it now to prepare it for the change. A vine that has been in the ground a year or two can be moved anytime before growth begins. Moving a mature vine is a two-year proj-ect. See February, Shrubs, under Planting.

 CARE

As winter relents, start cleaning up the ground covers; a light rak-ing will do, just enough to get rid of soggy patches of leaves, twigs, and such. Discard, don't compost the debris; it may be incubating pests and diseases.

Early in the month check new plantings of ground covers, vines, and ornamental grasses for signs of heaving. Gently press the crowns back into the ground. Replenish the mulch to stabilize soil temperatures.

 GROOMING

Ornamental grasses. Cool-sea-son grasses are likely to have started growing. As soon as you see new growth, cut the old stalks back to within a few inches of the crown.

In late winter or early spring, prune weak stems of big-flow-ered **clematis** like 'Dutchess of Edinburgh', and the Jackmanii group back to a healthy stem. Take dead stems back to the ground. Prune the remaining stems back to a pair of strong buds.

February is a good month to start seeds of annual vines.

WATERING

Indoors. Water transplanted seedlings started indoors when the soil is dry to the touch. Water vines wintering in containers in a shed or garage often enough to keep the soil slightly damp.

Outdoors. If the winter has been short of snow or rain, check the soil moisture of vines growing under overhanging structures, and water if it is dry.

FERTILIZING

Indoors. Fertilize transplanted seedlings when the appearance of two or three new leaves indicates the root system is growing again.

Every two weeks, fertilize all the seedlings that will remain indoors another six weeks or more with a soluble houseplant fertilizer at half strength.

Outdoors. Vines, ground covers, and ornamental grasses produce a lot of foliage and need regular fertilization. It can begin in Zone 8 towards the end of this month. See Fertilizing, in the March pages of this chapter.

PROBLEMS

Seedlings started indoors that are crowded and lack good drain-

---

ABOUT PRUNING VINES

All vines need pruning to develop a strong beautiful framework and to enhance production. But the rules vary with the vine. **Wisteria** needs pruning two or three times a year; **clematis** varieties have individual pruning requirements.

Here are some of the guidelines:

• Prune a newly planted vine lightly for a year or two to direct its growth so that it develops a graceful framework.

• Prune all vines to remove dead, extraneous, or weak wood now and then throughout the growing season.

• Prune large, fast-growing rampant vines like **trumpet-creeper** and **sweet autumn clematis** severely in spring and again as needed. Timing depends on the plant.

• In late winter and spring, prune flowering vines that bloom on new wood. These typically bloom late in the season. Anytime just after the coldest part of the season and before growth begins is good. Cut back shoots that bloomed last year to a strong bud or buds near the base of the shoot, leaving the framework of the vine intact.

• In late spring and early summer, prune flowering vines that bloom on wood produced last year right after the flowers fade. These mostly bloom in spring. Cut branchlets that have flowered back to strong replacement shoots or buds; they will carry the next year's flowers. That gives the plant time to mature the wood that will flower the following year.

• In summer, prune vines grown for their foliage—like **ivy** and **Virginia creeper**—right after the major thrust of seasonal growth. It's best to avoid pruning vines in fall. The wounds heal more slowly, and pruning may stimulate growth, which could come too late to harden off before the first frosts.

---

age and air may show symptoms of damping off. It rots stems near the soil surface. Discard affected plants, reduce watering, and increase light and fresh air. If the problem reappears, mist the seedlings with a fungicide such as Thiram (Arasan).

Before buds on vines suspected of insect infestation break open into flowers, spray them with horticultural oil. The oil smothers insects and their eggs.

To keep rabbits, woodchucks, and other rodents away from shrubs, try chemical fungicide formulations such as Thiram (Arasan) and hot pepper wax.

MARCH
VINES, GROUND COVERS, & ORNAMENTAL GRASSES

 PLANNING

Vines hold moisture, so make sure the lumber you acquire to make a support for a vine is pressure-treated; untreated wood rots in the presence of constant moisture.

 PLANTING

In Zone 8 and the Tidewater, gardeners can start planting in early March; in Richmond and Zone 7, in mid-March; in Zone 6, at the end of March.

Ready string supports for **sweet peas,** and plant the seeds. They can take a lot of cold. We grow them in the kitchen garden.

Planting vines. A vine is a shrub with a boarding-house reach—so think shrub, and look in the Shrubs chapter for basic how-to information.

• Site the planting hole within reach of the support it will climb, but allow room for the roots to mature without crowding the wall, pole, or whatever.

• Keep an air space of 3 inches or more between vine foliage and a house wall. Vines need air circulation all around; moisture can cause damage to and through even masonry walls.

• If it's destined to climb a wall that will need maintenance, train a vine on a hinged trellis (that can be lowered for access to the wall) or a framework of wires attached to nails driven into the wall. You must leave 3 inches of space between the vine and the wall for air circulation. That keeps the vine healthy, and saves the wall (inside and out) from the moisture damage.

• For walls and fences that need regular painting, choose annual vines. **Dutchman's pipe's** big, heart-shaped leaves create a dense screen in a single season.

• Avoid planting vines within reach of trees, large shrubs, windows, or shutters.

• After planting, lead or tie the longest stems to the support with an soft, unobtrusive twine.

 CARE

Indoors. Pinch out the growing tips of seedlings that are becoming leggy.

Outdoors. After the late winter fertilization described below, top the mulch off to maintain a 2- to 3-inch layer.

 GROOMING

Ornamental grasses. Check warm season grasses for new growth. If it's happening, cut the grasses back to a few inches above the crown.

Ground covers. Some ground covers benefit from shearing in early spring before growth begins, among them **liriope, mondo grass,** and **plumbago.**

Vines. Early this month prune back vines that flower on shoots that will grow this year. Remove crowded shoots of **sweet autumn clematis** and **trumpet vine** (*Campsis radicans*); they bloom on new wood late in the growing season.

 WATERING

Indoors. Continue watering seedlings started indoors. Water vines wintering in containers in a shed or garage often enough to keep the soil slightly damp.

Outdoors. Water new plantings if it does not rain for more than a week or ten days.

 FERTILIZING

Indoors. Fertilize transplanted seedlings when two or three new leaves appear. Every two weeks fertilize seedlings that will remain indoors another six weeks with a water-soluble houseplant fertilizer at half strength.

Outdoors. Spring clean ground covers, vines, and ornamental grasses:

1. Check and adjust the soil pH.

2. Apply Rich Earth humate and fertilize:

• If you are using organic fertilizers, apply them four to six weeks before growth begins.

• If you are using chemical fertilizers, apply them just before growth begins.

• If you are using time-release fertilizers, wait just before growth begins apply an eight month formulation.

PROBLEMS

Indoors. Damping off is a fungus that rots stems of young seedlings near the soil surface. Discard affected plants, reduce watering, and increase light and fresh air circulation. If the problem persists, mist the seedlings with a fungicide, such as Thiram (Arasan).

Outdoors. About the time the **forsythia** petals fall, treat the ground covers with a pre-emergent weed killer whose label says it won't harm perennials,

annuals, shrubs, and so on. It will kill seeds and control established weeds.

In deer country, apply a new and different spray to vines they come to browse.

Voles are very active eating plants October to March. If you see vole runs, bait the main runway with a rodenticide. See Pests, Diseases, and Controls in the Appendix.

ABOUT CLEMATIS

Clematis species and hybrids have a lot of give. The vines are deciduous and climb by attaching leaf petioles (stalks) to their supports. Once established, clematis species expand at a rate of 5 to 10 feet in a single season and will cover other vegetation, walls, trellises, posts, fences, and arbors. The big beautiful flowers of the clematis hybrids are especially lovely planted with **climbing roses.**

Site. Clematis vines need to have their heads in the sun, but the roots need to be in cool, moist earth. If the roots aren't in shade, mulch heavily. A site with protection from strong winds is best; avoid hot, dry, airless sites. **Soils.** A pH between 6.5 and 7.5 is best, but clematis tolerates somewhat acid soils. **Support.** Provide a structure of twine or wire for support; use twine or wire to lead the vines to a fence, a tree, or other support. **Pruning.** Pruning affects the way clematis blooms, and the timing is important. When you buy a clematis, ask for pruning instructions.

To have masses of small fragrant flowers in spring, prune clematis that blooms on new wood—for example, **anemone clematis,** *C. montana* hybrids rosy-red 'Rubens' and white 'Alba'—immediately after flowering. This reduces the bulk and size of the plant and controls its growth.

To have spectacular flowers in the summertime, in late winter or early spring prune back large-flowered hybrids like 'Dutchess of Edinburgh', a double white; 'Henryi', a large single white; 'Jackmanii Superba', dark purple; and 'Nellie Moser', a mauve pink. These bloom on old and new wood. Prune weak stems back to a healthy stem. Take dead stems back to the ground. Prune the remaining stems back to a pair of strong buds.

To keep its growth in check, in early spring remove congested shoots of **sweet autumn clematis,** *C. terniflora* (formerly *C. maximowicziana*), a rampant vine that bears a froth of tiny, fragrant, whitish flowers on new wood.

APRIL
VINES, GROUND COVERS, & ORNAMENTAL GRASSES

PLANNING

Record in your garden log the dates the flowering vines bloomed as a prompt for next year's pruning dates.

PLANTING

Indoors. Transplant seedlings started indoors that are outgrowing their containers to larger pots.

Outdoors. Now until mid-May are excellent planting times for vines, ground covers, and ornamental grasses.

CARE

Mulch the ground under **sweet peas** to keep the earth cool and so prolong their flowering.

GROOMING

Indoors. Pinch out the tips of leggy seedlings, and transplant the bigger ones to larger pots if the weather is still too cold for transplanting out to the garden.

In Zone 6, warm season grasses should be showing new growth now, so plan for their annual haircut.

Liriope should be cut back to just above the ground about now to keep it full and enhance blooming.

Hand prune winter-damaged leaves of **barrenwort** (*Epimedium*) and **lamium.** Cut back wandering strands of **vinca**.

Prune **wisteria, Carolina jessamine,** and other spring-flowering vines after the flowers fade.

WATERING

Indoors. Continue to water seedlings. Water vines wintering in containers in a shed or garage often enough to keep the soil slightly damp.

Outdoors. New plantings need rain often enough to maintain soil moisture.

FERTILIZING

If you are using chemical fertilizers which are quickly available, such as 5-10-5, fertilize vines, ground covers, and ornamental grasses every six weeks from beginning to end of the growing season. How often you need to fertilize depends on the type of fertilizer you are using; it's explained in Planting A Ground Cover, on the facing page.

PROBLEMS

Hoe and rake weeds away now. Weed beds of **lily-of-the-valley** when the flowers are in full bloom—that way you can breathe in their perfume.

Check **clematis** hybrids for signs of whiteflies, spider mites, and scale, and apply the controls recommended in the Pests, Diseases, and Controls section of the Appendix.

Continue preventive measures to protect your garden from deer.

Cats and dogs investigate new plantings; ground covers are particularly vulnerable. Dog urine is high in nitrogen and burns. Squirrels dig up new plantings because they are sure you have hidden nuts in the hole. Try animal deterrents to keep them away.

If cats are the main problem, apply diatomaceous earth. It's dusty, and cats are fastidious and hate dust on their paws. It doesn't bother dogs, but some of the animal deterrents offered by garden centers do.

The more environmentally sensitive we become, the more we are going to allow wildlife to share our gardens. The more information we share on getting along with our furred and feathered friends, the more pleasure we'll have in them and our gardens.

PLANTING A GROUND COVER

A new ground cover takes off and fills out most rapidly when you start with rooted cuttings and plant in fertile, improved soil.

1. If you will be replacing turf, in early spring or in fall when the soil is dry, spray the bed with Round-Up®, or remove the top layer.

2. Cover the area with the amendments recommended in the Introduction to the book under Soil Preparation and Improvement, and add 2 or 3 inches of compost, decomposed leaves, or peat moss.

3. Rototill all this 8 inches deep and three times over a two-week period. If you are installing an invasive ground cover such as **ivy** or **ajuga,** bury a 6-inch metal barrier along the border to keep it from overrunning neighboring plantings.

4. To keep weeds out, plant through a cover of 3 inches of mulch. If even minimum weeding will be difficult, plant instead through a porous landscape fabric; push the edges of the fabric sheet into the ground, and weight them with rocks, or heel them in. Make rows of X-shaped slits in the fabric, and insert the plants through the slits with a trowel. Landscape fabric slows the rooting of the aboveground branches, so plant densely.

5. Working in even rows and starting at the widest end, scoop out a row of evenly spaced planting pockets 8 to 14 inches apart. If you are planting on a slope, dig the holes so the slope side is lower to keep water from escaping down the slope. Set the cuttings in the hole, and firm them into place.

6. Position the second row of plants zig-zag between those of the row above. Row three repeats row one; row four repeats row two.

7. Put down 1 1/2 inches of water right after planting. Set an empty 1-pound coffee tin or other container under your sprinkler and record how long it takes to accumulate 1 1/2 inches of water so you'll know for the future. Newly planted ground covers need 1 1/2 inches of gentle rain every ten days to two weeks; if the sky fails, run your sprinkler or the irrigation system long enough to lay down 1 1/2 inches of water.

8. Keep the mulch topped up until the ground cover has grown dense enough to keep weeds from growing. Meanwhile, keep the bed weeded. Very importantly, do not allow weeds to grow up and go to seed the first year or two; getting rid of them will be daunting. Plan on at least two years for the plants to grow enough to keep weeds down.

9. Plan to fertilize the bed just as you do perennials—twice a year if you are using organic fertilizers. The first application is before growth begins in spring and the last application is as growth slows at the end of the growing season.

If you're using organic blends, such as Holly-tone or Plant-tone, fertilize six weeks before growth begins in spring, and then again toward the end of the growing season.

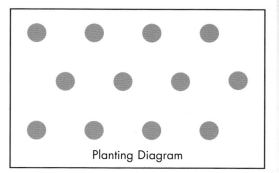

Planting Diagram

For time- or controlled-release chemical fertilizers apply just before the plants start to grow, and repeat according to the formulation. A nine-month formulation should carry you through the whole growing season.

MAY

VINES, GROUND COVERS, & ORNAMENTAL GRASSES

PLANNING

Keep a record of the year you plant ornamental grasses. They will benefit from dividing every five to ten years.

If you are looking for a great accent plant for your garden, patio, or porch, look over some of the beautiful tropical/semi-tropical vines—like **glory bush,** *Tibouchina urvilleana,* **mande-villa,** and **bougainvillea**—offered in late spring already blooming in big pots.

Mandevilla 'Alice du Pont'

PLANTING

Early this month, move seedlings started indoors to a protected shaded spot outdoors to harden off for a week or so, and then transplant them to the garden.

If you would like to add fragrance to the garden without having, or giving up, a lot of garden space, plant a fragrant vine. Here are some of our favorites:

Moonflower, *Ipomoea alba.* A tender perennial with huge leaves, it opens fragrant pure white flowers up to 6 inches across toward evening and closes them about noon the next day. It climbs by twining stems and needs strong support, such as a sturdy fence or pergola.

Sweet pea, *Lathyrus odoratus.* A sweetly scented annual, in cool spring weather it bears masses of small blooms that range from purple to pale lavender, ruby red, pale pink, white, and bicolors. It climbs by climbing tendrils and needs either a set of training strings or wires—or to be allowed to clamber over rocks and walls.

Carolina yellow jessamine, *Gelsemium sempervirens.* A perennial, it's a fast-growing woodland vine with dainty foliage that in late winter covers itself with small fragrant, golden flowers. The plant climbs by twining around anything handy, including fencing, porches, or trellises. Sun or shade.

Anemone clematis, *Clematis montana* hybrids like rosy-red 'Rubens', and white 'Alba'. Perennials, they bear masses of have small fragrant flowers in spring.

Japanese wisteria, *Wisteria floribunda* 'Longissima Alba'. This perennial bears long, drooping clusters of lightly scented, pastel-colored single or double blooms. It climbs by wrapping strong, slim stalks around anything handy.

Sweet autumn clematis, *Clematis terniflora.* This perennial blankets itself with tiny, sweetly scented flowers in September and October. **Clematis** climbs by attaching leaf petioles (stalks) to the support provided.

CARE

Vines are growing vigorously now. When you go to the garden, carry twine with you, and tie up new shoots in the direction you want them to follow.

Early this month move tropical and semi-tropical vines that have wintered in a shed or garage back to their spot outdoors. Remove the top 2 inches of soil in the pot, and replace it with compost and a slow-release fertilizer in an eight-month formulation.

GROOMING

Prune **anemone clematis,** *Clematis montana* hybrids, immediately after flowering to reduce the bulk and size of the plant and to control its direction.

Check the new shoots on all vines; cut back to the main framework all shoots not headed in the direction you intend.

Root out seedlings of ground covers that are stepping out of bounds. If you need new plants, pot up the rogues and coddle them until they are growing lustily, then transplant them to bare spots.

Prune—deadhead and pinch back—vines that have finished blooming.

Keep **sweet pea** flowers picked to keep the plants producing.

WATERING

Maintain the moisture in beds planted in seeds and seedlings. Water is essential to the unchecked growth that will develop root systems strong enough to bloom and withstand summer heat. If you do not have a good soaking rain every week to ten days, water planted beds gently and slowly long enough to lay down 1 1/2 or 2 inches.

ABOUT VINES AND THEIR SUPPORTS

How a vine attaches itself to its support is stated in the table of plants in this chapter. How it climbs tells you what type of support it will need. That tells you whether a vine is suited to the job you have planned for it. There are variations, but here's the general idea:

Twining stems. For vines that climb by twining stems, **Carolina jessamine,** for example, suitable supports are narrow—a slim post, a pipe, wires, or strings.

Tendrils (twisting petioles). Vines that climb by twisting tendrils—**clematis,** for example—require a structure of wires, or wire mesh to climb on.

Clinging aerial rootlets. Vines that climb by aerial rootlets that secrete an adhesive glue, like **English ivy,** need only a rugged surface, such as a brick or stucco wall, or a rough, unpainted fence, for support.

However they climb, vines that eventually will be very heavy—like **climbing hydrangea, bittersweet, trumpet vine,** and **wisteria**—need supports built of heavy timbers, or even a dead tree, to hold them up.

Vines hold a lot of moisture. It is essential that the lumber you buy to create their support be pressure-treated.

Check the moisture level in soil of vines growing in containers even if it rains; their foliage keeps the rain from the soil beneath.

FERTILIZING

If you are using only chemical fertilizers, such as 5-10-5, which are quickly available to the plants, then you will need to fertilize garden and container plants every six weeks.

Scratch in organic or time-release fertilizers if you haven't done it yet.

PROBLEMS

Weeds are flourishing; use a scuffle hoe or rake to get rid of them.

Apply or change whatever deer deterrents you are using. See the Pests section in the Appendix.

Early spraying with fungicidal formulations of copper will help to save susceptible plants from blackspot, powdery mildew, rusts, and bacterial diseases such as bacterial leaf spots and wilt.

Depending on your zone, gypsy moths may begin to appear. The Problems section in May, Trees, describes controls.

JUNE
VINES, GROUND COVERS, & ORNAMENTAL GRASSES

PLANNING

Good sized container-grown vines, ornamental grasses, and ground covers may be on sale this month, so if you are in the market for new plants, make a point of visiting the garden centers.

PLANTING

If you are thinking of planting a large transitional area in ornamental grasses, consider starting seeds now for transplanting in September or early October. (If the grasses you are interested in are named varieties—**blue switchgrass** 'Heavy Metal' for example, not just the original **blue switchgrass** species—then it's best to plant divisions, as cultivars do not reliably come true from seeds.)

Coddling the seeds and monitoring the germination will be easy if you start them in trays or flats kept indoors or in a cold frame. When the seedlings are 2 or 3 inches high, transplant them to an empty row in your kitchen garden, or to a sheltered spot in the flower beds. When the rains return in September, transplant the seedlings to permanent homes in the garden.

Provide a strong support for heavy vines such as clematis.

CARE

As new vines grow, every few weeks tie the new shoots to their supports.

Top up the mulch around your vines. Make sure the roots of the **clematis** vines have enough mulch to stay cool. The heads can be in sun, but the roots need to be cool. André uses fine grade hammermill bark and also recommends pine and hardwood bark, West Coast fir bark, cedar bark, and cypress. Compost and leaf-mold (decomposed leaves) are beneficial mulches, but weeds and roots grow into them, and they decompose quickly in heat.

GROOMING

As the blooms fade, lightly prune stems and shoots of vines that have finished blooming.

Sweet pea vines are likely to be yellowing—pull the roots up, and compost them. The vines add nitrogen to the soil—as do all legumes. A leafy annual vine, **Dutchman's pipe** for example, would be a good follow-on plant for **sweet peas**, or seedlings of large **marigolds.** If you grow **sweet peas** in the kitchen garden, a good follow-on crop would be a leafy vegetable such as **kale.**

Run control patrol on established ground covers, and root out and pot up or discard stragglers headed for far pastures.

WATERING

Keep track of the soil moisture of seedlings and newly planted ground covers. Unchecked growth is the name of the growing game, and that requires sustained moisture. If June has little rain, water the garden slowly and deeply every week to ten days. Apply $1^1/_2$ inches of water measured in a 1-pound coffee tin or rain gauge.

Check the moisture level in vines growing in containers even if it rains; their foliage keeps the rain from the soil beneath.

FERTILIZING

If you are using only chemical fertilizers, such as 5-10-5, you need to fertilize every six weeks. If you have already applied an organic fertilizer, you won't need to repeat until fall.

PROBLEMS

Renew deer deterrents ar sprays.

Check vines for lacebug damage. The leaf surfaces will be dull, speckled, pale, and the undersides will show specks of insect excrement. Spray the foliage with horticultural oil or insecticidal soap as directed on the package.

Whitefly and spider mite damage shows up as spotted and blanched leaves. Remove dead or severely infected shoots, and spray with Neem at the intervals indicated on the package until the infestation is gone. See Pests, Diseases, and Controls in the Appendix.

Watch out for aphids, and mites.

Handpick Japanese beetles—they're sluggish in the cool of early morning. Drop them into soapy water, and flush them down a drain. If they multiply, spray the plants with Neem, which will discourage feeding by adults. Try placing Japanese beetle traps far from the plantings you wish to protect, not among them. Insecticides containing Neem, rotenone, or Sevin insecticide are controls.

Keep the beds clear of weeds. Weeds that mature and go to seed will be followed by an army of offspring.

Slugs and snails are good climbers. Diatomaceous earth, a natural control, works in dry soil but isn't effective on moist soil. Instead, do them in with iron phosphate (Sluggo), slug and snail bait, and traps. You can make your own slug trap by pouring a little beer in shallow aluminum plates or empty tuna fish cans.

JULY

VINES, GROUND COVERS, & ORNAMENTAL GRASSES

 PLANNING

Assess your ground covers, vines, and ornamental grasses, and note in your garden log what you plan to put there next year.

Check garden centers for bargain plants that could meet your needs, and go through the garden catalogs for ideas for companion plants for vines and ornamental grasses that can be planted in September and October.

 PLANTING

Plant tall containers planted in colorful summer-flowering bulbs—**lilies**, for example, or **dahlias**—among beds of ornamental grasses to improve the view while waiting for the grasses to come into their summer/fall glory period.

 CARE

Prune, and retie new shoots of **clematis, trumpet creeper,** and other vines to keep the plants growing in directions that will improve the framework.

 GROOMING

Wisteria needs pruning two or three times a year to keep its exuberant growth in bounds and to make it produce a sumptuous show of flowers. The time to do it is soon after the blooms begin to fade. Prune both to establish the framework of the vine, and to encourage flowering. Cut the long lateral (side) branches back to about two or three buds. You will need to prune again in fall.

Many vines, including **wisteria** and **trumpet vine** can be multiplied by rooting cuttings taken this month. Rooting cuttings is described in June, Shrubs.

 WATERING

Vines that are sheltered from rain benefit from being hosed down now and then in summer—but don't hose a vine when it is coming into, or is already in, bloom, as that may bruise flowers that are open, or make them soggy.

Check the moisture level in vines growing in containers even if it rains; their foliage keeps the rain from the soil beneath.

Ornamental grasses once established are pretty well drought-tolerant. They only need watering in prolonged droughts. You can tell they need water because the edges of the leaves curl up. Water slowly and deeply, making sure you're laying down at least an inch and a half of water.

 FERTILIZING

If you are using only chemical fertilizers, such as 5-10-5, you will need to fertilize every six weeks.

If you have already applied an organic fertilizer, you won't need to repeat until fall.

PROBLEMS

Continue preventive measures to protect your garden from deer.

Continue Japanese beetle patrol and control.

Whitefly, mealybugs, scale, spider mites, and aphids multiply in hot, airless spots and will spoil the leaves even if they don't do permanent damage. Spray infestations two or three times with some form of Neem, *Pyrethrum*, or horticultural soaps—they won't harm the environment. You can also use horticultural oils. See the section in the Appendix for Pests, Diseases, and Controls.

Rust loves **lily-of-the-valley.** Control rust by avoiding overhead watering and by cutting out and disposing of infected foliage. Twice a month spray with a horticultural oil, Mancozeb, manzate, sulfur, or copper.

Continue weed patrol and control of ground covers and other plantings.

Aphid nymph

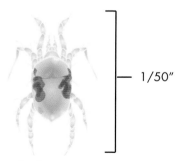

— 1/50"

Spider mite

Euonymous scale

SPRING-FLOWERING BULBS ARE GREAT COMPANION PLANTS

Many of the spring-flowering bulbs offered at good prices in the bulbs catalogs you receive this time of year are excellent companion plants for ornamental grasses and low-growing ground covers. The small early bulbs carpet the earth with color while the grasses are still dormant. The larger bulbs bloom above ground covers such as **pachysandra, myrtle, ivy,** and **ajuga.** They also show up well against the emerging growth of the grasses, which later masks their ripening foliage.

These small spring bulb flowers are very effective planted in front of the taller ornamental grasses—they appear in about this order:
- **Early crocus,** *Crocus* spp. and cvs.
- **Daffodils,** *Narcissus* miniatures and early varieties
- **Snowdrops,** *Galanthus*
- **Winter aconite,** *Eranthis*
- **Squill,** *Scilla tubergeniana*
- **Glory-of-the-snow,** *Chinodoxa luciliae*
- **Bluebell,** *Hyacinthoides non-scripta*
- **Grape hyacinth,** *Muscari* spp. and hybrids
- **Botanical/species tulips,** *Tulipa turkestanica*
- **Giant snowflake, summer snowflake,** *Leucojum aestivum*

These large-flowering bulbs are attractive planted here and there among ground covers, and add early color to beds of ornamental grasses:
- **Yellow daffodils**
- **Lily-flowered tulips**
- **Red parrot tulips**
- **Fosteriana tulips** 'White Emperor', 'Orange Emperor', 'Red Emperor'
- *Tulipa greigii* 'Sweet Lady', 'Goldwest', 'Oriental Splendour'
- **Foxtail lily,** *Eremurus stenophyllus*
- **Giant onion,** *Allium giganteum*
- **Indian lily,** *Camassia quamash*

AUGUST
VINES, GROUND COVERS, & ORNAMENTAL GRASSES

 PLANNING

Spend some time in the early morning or late afternoon asking your plants for progress reports.

Summer heat and drought reveal the vulnerabilities of plants, sites, and your annual soil maintenance program. Young vines whose leaves are showing crisped edges here and there may need more consistent watering. Patches of ground cover that are wilting when others do not may need more mulch or more humus added to the soil when you fertilize and refurbish the soil early next year.

Patches of **pachysandra** that are dying may be getting too much sun in winter when the leaves fall, or suffering from volutella leaf and stem blight. Consider replacing problem patches of **Japanese pachysandra,** *Pachysandra terminalis,* with **Allegheny pachysandra,** *P. procumbens.* It is native to the Southeast, and more tolerant of heat.

 PLANTING

In spite of the heat and drought, container-grown vines, ground covers, and the smaller ornamental grasses can be planted successfully this month as long as you water them every week

or so, and hose them down with a gentle spray if they wilt on hot days.

 CARE

After summer thunderstorms, check the vines, and make sure they are securely fastened to their supports.

GROOMING

By now, aggressive vines like **autumn clematis, Carolina jessamine, trumpet creeper,** and **wisteria** will have made a lot of new growth; prune to thin excess growth and to keep the main stems developing the framework.

 WATERING

Now and then hose down vines that are sheltered from rain. Check the moisture level in vines growing in containers even if it rains; their foliage keeps the rain from the soil beneath.

This month is usually dry, so expect to replace the missing rain by watering ground covers, vines, and ornamental grasses two or three times this month, every week to ten days. The ideal is to put down $1^1/2$ inches of water at each session.

Overhead watering is fine as long as you water deeply. There's less waste if you water before the sun reaches the garden in the early morning or late afternoon or evening. In hot dry periods, daytime overhead watering lowers leaf temperatures and reduces stress. Don't water more than three or four times in a month.

André doesn't recommend electrically timed mechanical watering systems that ignore the weather and water too often and shallowly. But he does believe they can do a good job if they are set up with the correct low-pressure nozzles, and timed to run long enough and to water gently and deeply every week or ten days in periods of drought.

 FERTILIZING

If you are using chemical fertilizers, you should be fertilizing every six weeks or so.

If you have already applied an organic fertilizer, you won't need to repeat until fall.

If vines fertilized with a timed-release chemical fertilizer are failing to grow as expected, supplement it with foliar feedings of water-soluble organic or fast-acting liquid fertilizers.

PROBLEMS

Change deer deterrents and sprays around in the garden.

Clear the ground covers and other beds of all weeds; don't let them grow up and go to seed!

High humidity and heat encourages powdery mildew. Avoid overhead watering, and apply sulfur, ultrafine horticultural oil, copper fungicide, Immunox, or Bayleton.

Check for fungal leaf spot, and apply a fungicide if needed. If you see continuing signs of mites, hose the plant down regularly, and spray with insecticidal soaps, or ultrafine horticultural oils.

SPACING FOR GROUND COVERS

Pachysandra

To know how many plants you will need to plant an area in a ground cover, divide the square footage of the bed by the amount of space each plant will need.

To figure out how many plants you will need, start by measuring the area to be planted. Outline the bed with marking paint or a hose, and then measure the length and the width. Multiply the length by the width, and that gives you the square footage. To get the approximate size of a free-form shape, outline the area with a hose, and then shape the hose into a square or a rectangle that encompasses the area, measure, and multiply the length by the width.

Then divide the spacing required for the plant you have chosen into the square footage of the area to be planted. The answer is the number of plants you will need.

Some growers' tags indicate how many plants to set out per square yard; Blooms of Bressingham tags recommend for the **barren strawberry** 'Red Ruby Strawberry' three to four plants per square yard. A square yard is 9 square feet. Dividing 9 (square feet) by four (plants) yields 2.2—one plant for every 2.2 square feet.

Most plant tags recommend you allow a certain distance between plants. Typical spacing for crowns of **Japanese painted fern** is 24 inches apart; for **lavender** 'Munstead', 15 inches; for **dusty miller,** 8 inches apart. The number of inches "apart" means "all around." To get the square inches needed for one **dusty miller** plant, multiply 8 times 8, which gives you 64 square inches. Divide 64 into the square footage of the area multiplied by 12, the number of inches in a foot. That tells you how many plants you will need.

Small ground covers that spread are planted one to four per square foot—four for upright plants like **pachysandra;** one to two for vining plants like **vinca**—two plants if it is rooted in a small pot, one if it is rooted in a large pot.

Closely spaced, these ground covers fill in the area in about a year and a half. More widely spaced, the plants will need two years to fill in.

SEPTEMBER
VINES, GROUND COVERS, & ORNAMENTAL GRASSES

 PLANNING

September begins an excellent planting season.

The best planting, dividing, and transplanting dates for Zone 6 are September 1 to 15; for Zone 7, September 1 to mid-October. In the warm Tidewater, the soil cools after Thanksgiving, so gardeners can plant, divide, and transplant as late as November 1.

 PLANTING

Consider reducing the amount of hand trimming around deciduous trees by planting a maintenance-free all-season ground cover like **ajuga, lamium,** or **vinca**—plants that take shade in summer and sun in winter. Next month is ideal for the project:

1. To avoid disturbing tree and shrub feeder roots located in the top 12 inches of the soil, remove the turf by hand, or kill it with RoundUp®.

2. Starting 4 to 5 inches from the trunk, add 4 to 5 inches of topsoil, and top that with 2 to 3 inches of humus—compost, partially decomposed leaves or seaweed, or other decomposed organic material.

3. Over every 100 square feet (an area 10 by 10 feet) spread the following—available at any garden center.

Holly-tone: 4 to 7 pounds
Superphosphate: 3 to 5 pounds
Greensand: 5 to 10 pounds
Clay soils only: gypsum 5 to 10 pounds
Osmocote® four-month: 2 pounds
Rich Earth Humate: 1 pound

4. Fork all this into the bed by hand.

5. Rake the bed smooth, and plant your ground cover. Mulch 2 to 3 inches deep.

6. Water slowly and gently to put down about 1 1/2 inches of water.

7. Water every week to ten days if you run into a dry spell.

8. In the following years, fertilize an evergreen ground cover with lawn fertilizer when you fertilize the lawn. Fertilize a flowering ground cover twice annually with Holly-tone.

 CARE

When temperatures head below 60 degrees Fahrenheit, move winter tender and tropical vines to a greenhouse, or try them as houseplants. Or, move them to a frost-free shed or garage.

 GROOMING

You can divide to multiply established stands of **blue fescue, blue oat grass,** and **feather reed grass** and many other grasses and ground covers this month.

Wisteria benefits from pruning two or three times a year. Give it its second trim now or in October. Cut the laterals back again leaving only two or three buds to each shoot.

 WATERING

If your vines are sheltered from rain, even when rainfall is plentiful make sure the soil doesn't dry out.

 FERTILIZING

If you are using organic blends, such as Holly-tone or Plant-tone, then you will need to fertilize the last time about six weeks before the end of the growing season.

The growing season slows in Zones 6 and 7 early September to early October. In Zone 8, Richmond and the Tidewater areas of Virginia, the last fertilization can be between the end of September and mid-October.

If you are using only chemical fertilizers, such as 5-10-5,

Wisteria (*Wisteria sinensis*)

the last fertilization for garden and container plants will be six weeks before the end of the growing season.

Weed around vines and ornamental grasses, scratching up the soil so fall rains can give the plants a deep watering.

 PROBLEMS

Change the deer deterrents you are using.

Give new ground covers a radical weeding. Check and remove ground covers creeping outside their boundaries.

OCTOBER
VINES, GROUND COVERS, & ORNAMENTAL GRASSES

 PLANNING

The Friendship Garden at the U.S. National Arboretum peaks this month. A brilliant example of a grass garden suitable for the average ranch home, it covers a one-third acre front yard.

The plants develop throughout the year without pruning, staking, spraying, or deadheading. In late winter, they are cut back to the ground, mulched, and fertilized as growth begins. Watering is by underground or surface irrigation system. Seedheads ripen and stand through fall and winter. Fruiting and berrying plants promote a healthy ecological balance that encourages birds and does not exclude insects. (A majority of insects are beneficial.)

Color, texture, and unfolding growth are present in all four seasons. In spring, naturalized flowering bulbs carpet spaces between the cut-back ornamental grasses. **Tulips** in exotic forms with **narcissus** and **species iris** work wonderfully well here. In summer, easy-care flowering perennials like **black-eyed Susan** and **Russian sage** bloom along the walks and among the half-grown grasses.

From early summer to fall, the dominant grasses lift tall, light-catching inflorescences to the wind. The tallest grasses and a few **hollies** shield the gift shop from the road. Smaller species grow closer to the building. A few well-placed trees and flowering or fruiting shrubs mimic a meadow's variety. Additional seasonal color comes from big tubs of annuals, vegetables, and herbs.

In fall, sweeps of **sedum** turn russet-pink-coral, then fade to brown, and the fruiting trees color red and orange. With cold weather, ornamental grasses come into their own—rustling, tossing in the wind, and eventually binding snow at their feet.

Through all its seasons, the broad paths and comfortable stopping places invite meditation. For the birds there are banquets of seeds, insects, worms, as well as nesting spaces and materials in this garden where chemical controls are never needed.

 PLANTING

Continue to plant spring-flowering bulbs and big, low-maintenance showy perennials with the ornamental grasses.

 CARE

In fall, clear your ground cover of fallen leaves with a leaf blower.

 GROOMING

Limit pruning to dead or diseased material.

 WATERING

Check vines sheltered from rain, and keep the soil moderately damp. The roots are still growing even if the air is cold, and water is essential.

 FERTILIZING

In Zones 6 and 7, the growing season slows between early September and early October. In Zone 8, Richmond and the Tidewater areas of Virginia, the growing season slows between the end of September and mid-October.

If you are using fertilizers that are organic blends such as Holly-tone or Plant-tone, you can fertilize for the last time about six weeks before the end of the growing season.

If you are using only chemical fertilizers, such as 5-10-5, the last fertilization should be four to six weeks before the end of the growing season.

If you are using time-release fertilizers, a spring application of a nine-month formulation should carry the plants through the end of the growing season—no fertilizer need be added at this time.

PROBLEMS

Apply or change whatever deer deterrents you are using. See the section on Pests, Diseases, and Controls in the Appendix.

If vole runs appear around shrubs, bait the main runway with a rodenticide. André's winter bait station is a pair of paper cups scented with apple juice, with a dose of the bait in the bottom, set under a half tire. Another way is to nestle the baited cups in straw held down by plywood and topped with a brick or a big stone.

GROUND COVERS: THINKING OUTSIDE THE BOX

If you are considering planting a slope with a ground cover, think outside the box. Consider, for example, **forsythia.** Most species and varieties are upright and fountaining, but *Forsythia* x *intermedia* 'Arnold Dwarf' roots where it touches, can withstand drought, and needs only periodic trimming. A lovely complement for a **forsythia** hill is naturalized bulbs— **daffodils, narcissus,** and lemon-yellow **daylilies.**

Another attractive ground cover good for steep grades is the ground-hugging **memorial rose,** *Rosa wichuriana.* The white flowers, which are typical of wild roses, are succeeded by modest reddish fruits. The branches trail and root when they touch moist soil, producing thick mats of glossy foliage that is evergreen in mild regions.

A new series of ground cover roses won Gold Medals in 1996 from rose societies in Australia, Britain, and America. These bloom continuously, are immune to pests and diseases, and do not need deadheading. The plants are 2 to 2^1/$_2$ feet tall by 4 feet across. The star is **flower carpet rose,** whose blooms are lavender pink and spicily perfumed. 'Jeeper's Creepers' is a white variety, and 'Baby Blanket' is a light pink.

Flower Carpet Red

NOVEMBER
VINES, GROUND COVERS, & ORNAMENTAL GRASSES

PLANNING

Gather the seedheads of the most beautiful grasses before the wind gets to them. Tie them loosely in bunches, and hang them to dry upside down in a dark, dry, warm place.

To keep feathery grasses from shedding, spray them with hair spray or a spray varnish.

Snip off the heads of **oat grass,** and bind them with florist's wire to make "ornaments" for holidays trees and decorations. Make a wreath from strands of **clematis,** by pruning away small shoots, and twining the stem into a circle.

PLANTING

Sow seeds that will benefit from stratification in the garden.

It's late to be planting container plants in Zones 6 and 7. If you have unplanted containers of vines, ground covers, or grasses, water them thoroughly, and sink the pots up to the tops of their rims in empty rows in the kitchen garden or elsewhere. With a winter mulch of evergreen boughs they should still be good to go in late winter when the ground dries enough for planting.

CARE

Rake matted leaves away from the ground cover.

GROOMING

Run control patrol on ground covers like **ajuga** and **vinca,** and use an edger to root out escapees. Pot offsets and plantlets for later use.

WATERING

Before the first anticipated hard freeze, water all your vines, ground covers, and ornamental grasses slowly, deeply, and thoroughly.

FERTILIZING

There is no need to fertilize this month.

PROBLEMS

In deer country, wrap susceptible evergreen vines with Reemay, or if they have been attacked in the past, circle them with bird netting or chicken-wire cages. Change whatever deer deterrents you are using. See the section on Pests, Diseases, and Controls in the Appendix to the book.

Dig up any young dandelions sprouting in new ground cover beds or around vines or ornamental grasses; they are still small enough to pull if you are careful. Any scrap of root left will consider itself a cutting and start a new plant, so dig carefully.

If vole runs appear around shrubs, bait the main runway with a rodenticide. See Pests, Diseases, and Controls in the Appendix.

Use an edger to prevent ground covers from "escaping" from their bed.

MULTIPLY BY DIVIDING

Now that the season is over, consider what you want for next year. If you need more, plan to multiply your plants.

VINES

Cuttings. Many vines, including **wisteria** and **trumpet vine,** can be multiplied by rooting cuttings. The process is described in June, Shrubs.

Stratification. Annual vines and some perennial vines will grow from seed. Some need stratification (chilling) to germinate. Seeds of **trumpet vine** sown in the fall will germinate some months later. The Planting section in November, Perennials, describes the process of stratification. Seeds to be stratified this time of year are sown out in the garden.

GROUND COVERS

Some ground covers can be started from seed, including **common myrtle** (Vinca minor) and **plumbago.** When seeds are available, starting the plants yourself from seed is the most cost-efficient way, but remember that named varieties may not come true from seed, as we explained in the Planting section of this chapter's June pages.

Most ground covers root easily from cuttings or root division. Those that multiply by means of aboveground runners like **ajuga** and **vinca** you can divide by simply cutting the plantlet from the parent and pulling it up.

Ivy is easy; you can divide a densely rooted clump in spring, but rooting cuttings taken in late summer or fall is easier. **Lamium** cuttings root easily in spring; divisions of the plant root easily in spring or early fall. Rampant growers like **creeping Jenny** (Lysimachia nummularia) can be grown from cuttings taken in spring or divisions planted in fall. **Pachysandra** will root from cuttings almost all year-round. Division is best in early spring before the plants start to grow or in early fall. Dig it by the shovelful including the dirt it is growing in.

Ferns are usually propagated by root division in spring. Plants that clump, like **liriope,** are multiplied by dividing a mature crown; use a spading fork to lift and gently break the clump apart, or use a spade to cut the clump apart.

ORNAMENTAL GRASSES

You can buy seeds for some ornamental grass species (not hybrids or cultivars), including **blue fescue,** Miscanthus sinensis, and the **pennisetums.** To get a head start, sow the seeds indoors early next year. Starting Seeds Indoors under Planting in January, Annuals, explains the process.

Like perennials, the ornamental grasses don't fill out until the second season, so if you are a hurry-up-and-grow gardener, you will be happier planting root divisions. André Viette and other nurserymen ship grasses bare root in spring, and potted rooted divisions spring, summer, and fall.

The grasses are not likely to need division for at least five to ten years. However, once a grass has filled out, you can divide the crown every year. Use a spading fork to lift and gently break the clump apart, or use a spade to cut the clump apart. The important thing is to be sure that each division has at least one growing point.

Most grasses are best divided in spring, before new growth begins, including **Japanese blood grass, fountain grass, Chinese silver grass,** and **switchgrass.** The smaller grasses can be divided in spring but also in fall, including **blue fescue, blue oat grass,** and **feather reed grass.**

DECEMBER
VINES, GROUND COVERS, & ORNAMENTAL GRASSES

 PLANNING

If you find turf grass high-maintenance, or have a problem with the grass under trees, consider a ground cover.

 PLANTING

If the weather remains mild, and soil temperatures are warm, you can still plant deciduous vines the first days of this month.

In Zone 8, some winters are mild enough to plant all winter long.

 CARE

Use evergreen boughs to provide winter protection for **European ginger,** the **hellebores,** and other ground covers that suffer in cold weather. A discarded Christmas tree provides greens to cover them.

 GROOMING

Prune **wisteria** laterals back again leaving only two or three buds to each shoot.

WHAT YOU NEED TO KNOW BEFORE BUYING ORNAMENTAL GRASSES

- Height and width at maturity
- Form—upright or fountaining
- Texture—fine or coarse
- Color—solid green, variegated, or striped
- Drainage—most need a well-drained site, but a few are excellent choices for moist spots
- Light—full sun for nearly all
- Cold hardiness—almost all the popular ornamental grasses survive winters in the Mid-Atlantic, so for most cold hardiness isn't crucial. One beautiful grass not likely to winter over in Zones 6 and 7 is tall **pampas grass,** whose plume-panicles are luminous. The compact variety, *Cortaderia selloana* 'Pumila', does winter over here.

 WATERING

Keep the soil for tropical and semi-tropical vines wintering indoors moderately damp.

 FERTILIZING

Nothing to fertilize this month.

 PROBLEMS

The scent-carrying oils in deer deterrents don't volatilize in cold air. If you are concerned, wrap clinging **hydrangea** and other still-green vines in Reemay for the winter.

If vole runs appear around shrubs, bait the main runway with a rodenticide.

Ginger

WATER & BOG PLANTS

A water garden is a living biological organism that exhibits an exquisite beauty and intelligence if you take the time to get to know the components and their life cycles.

Water, the flowers and fish, the submerged plants that help to clean and oxygenate the water, and the snails that graze on the dark green algae fuzzing the sides of the pond—each element plays a vital role and the whole makes a healthy, delightful garden ornament that is at least as easy to maintain as a small flower bed. A balanced complement of aquatic plants and livestock, with or without a pump and filtering system, makes it a garden, and keeps the water fresh and clear. **Water garden containers.** A water garden consists of a container, water, plants, and fish. It can be as small as a wall fountain, as simple as a Chinese water pot, or a half-barrel out on your patio. Preformed plexiglass liners in sizes up to about 10 by 10 feet are used to contain smaller inground ponds. Larger and free-form inground ponds are waterproofed by relatively inexpensive flexible rubber liners or some form of cement or gunnite.

Fountains, streams, and waterfalls. To enjoy sparkle and splash, you will need to add a pump that pushes the water through a bubbler or a fountainhead. Upgrading the pump and adding a filter to the system improves aeration. To return the water to the pond via a stream or a waterfall you will need a more powerful pump.

ABOUT WATER LILIES

Water lilies are the stars of the water garden. They come into bloom and fade away over a period of three to four days. There are two types:

Hardy water lilies are perennial in the Mid-Atlantic. Set out after the chill of very early spring but before growth gets under way, hardy water lilies may produce blooms the first summer, but they need two to three years to reach their peak. The flowers are open only during the day.

Tropical water lilies bloom where temperatures stay above 80 degrees Fahrenheit for three to four weeks. In Zone 8, they begin to bloom in May. In Zone 6, in June. They open the year they are planted. To keep them for another year, collect and store the tubers in a frost-free location for the winter (see October Planting). There are day- and night-blooming varieties. Day bloomers are sweetly fragrant; night bloomers are headily scented, open as the stars come out, and stay open until late morning. They're likely to continue to bloom after the hardy water lilies have shut down for the season.

One of a pond owner's few chores is removing yellowing foliage; a lily pruner makes the job easy. Removing closed four-day old blossoms seems to speed the rate at which water lilies present new flower buds.

Recirculating bog gardens. An interesting and environmentally friendly way to filter the water and return it to the pond is via a recirculating liner-proofed garden of bog plants and a pebble-lined stream.

You can have a beautiful pond without pump or filter. The magic formula given in the April pages is a combination of plants and fish that does a pretty good job of keeping the pond's biosystem in balance. Richard Koogle, Director of Operations at Lilypons Water Gardens®, recommends including in pond care the use of a supplemental bacterial product that controls algae by speeding the decomposition of waste from fish and plants. This is especially important if you are not using a pump or filter.

An inground water garden comes together in three basic steps:

1. You prepare the physical container, the excavation for the pond and other features you have decided on—recirculating bog garden, streambed, waterfall. You waterproof the system and add water. If you are using a recirculating pump and a filter, they go in next.

2. You set containers of water garden plants under the water in the pond. Some may need to be raised on platforms, which can be pots, bricks, or stones. Plants for a recirculating bog garden are rooted in the gravelly mix at the bottom of the bog.

3. You release fish, snails, and other livestock to help control pests and unwanted algae—and for the pleasure of learning more about them.

PLANTING

Like land plants, water garden plants respond to fertilizing and have active and dormant seasons. Some are hardy, surviving frost-belt winters; others are tropical and need winter protection in the frost belt. The containers for pond plants have no drainage holes.

There are three groups, 1. Submerged or oxygenating plants, 2. Aquatics, and 3. Bog plants.

1. The submerged plants (also called oxygenating plants) are leafy stems that grow up from containers at the bottom of the pond. They're there to take up nutrients that otherwise fuel algae

growth that makes water murky, and to add oxygen to the water.

2. The aquatics are large-leaved floating plants, and small-leaved floating plants. The stars are the water lilies and the lotus. They bear exotic blossoms and spread out big beautiful leaves that provide the fish with cool shade and a refuge from predators.

The small-leaved floating plants are mainly for contrast. They trace delicate green patterns between the lily pads and the lotus leaves. Some bear tiny flowers. The prettiest are perhaps white and yellow snowflake, the sweetly fragrant species of *Nymphoides* whose flowers are 3/4 of an inch across and centered by yellow stamens. They flower abundantly spring through fall. Another popular little floater is Australian water clover, *Marsilea mutica*, a dainty little plant that looks just like its nickname, four-leaf clover.

3. The bog plants, also known as marginal plants because they are placed at the margins of a water garden, are upright forms that thrive in partially submerged containers or in a bog's mucky soil or gravel. Some are narrow-leaved, like water-loving varieties of irises, and others are broad-leaved, like elephant's ear. These linears provide contrast with the flat, floating forms of the aquatics.

Bog plants can also be planted in a naturally wet spot. But before planting in any area big enough to be considered a wetland, consult your local environmental authorities.

CARE

Here's a quick look at year-round maintenance for a water garden:

Spring. Clear organic debris from the pond, the bog area, stream, or waterfall. Groom and fertilize the plants. In the frost belt, start the pump; in frost-free regions it would have been on through winter. Add a supplemental bacterial product to speed the decomposition of waste from fish and plants, especially if you are not using a pump and filter. Resume feeding the fish. Clean the filter as needed. Maintain the water level.

Spring/Summer. Clean the filter. Remove fading foliage and blooms. Feed the fish. Every thirty days add a pellet to kill mosquito larvae. Anytime plants and livestock are in the pond, it is necessary to keep up the water level. Wind and hot dry weather can evaporate so much pond water you might think the liner is leaking, especially if it is running over a waterfall and over a bog garden and/or streambed.

Fall. Keep the pond clear of leaves and dead plant material. Clean the pump. In the frost belt, shut the pond down for winter. If the pond is small and less than thirty inches deep, fish may be safer indoors in a fish tank for the winter. Empty and clean the pond, then refill it. Maintain the water level.

Still in the frost belt, if the pool is large, discard or bring indoors for the winter the frost-tender tropical water lilies and tender pond bog plants. In frost-free regions, you can keep the pump and filter working through the winter.

Winter. If ice threatens a pond where fish and plants will winter, put a de-icer to work.

PESTS

If predators are plentiful in your area, make the sides of the pond excavation vertical. That makes fishing harder. You might also place a few cinder blocks in the pond to give the fish hiding places.

JANUARY
WATER & BOG PLANTS

PLANNING

January is a fine time to plan a water garden. Study your garden from indoors to determine where you'd like to see a pond, keeping in mind a water garden's need for light, good drainage, and so on.

Potential locations. On flat land, a pond in the curve of a flower border is quite lovely. A stone wall or a fence can be an appealing backdrop. A sloping yard invites an installation of small ponds spilling into each other and makes it easy to establish a recirculating bog garden and a stream. If you are home mostly in the evening, or wish to grow the fragrant night-blooming **tropical water lilies,** look for a spot where the pond surface will reflect sunsets and moonrises.

If the yard is tiny, you might pave it and install a fountain splashing water back into a basin. For a deck, the water garden could be a Chinese water pot with a miniature **water lily** surrounded by potted plants or a wall fountain planted with a single small floating-leaved plant.

Light, power, water, maintenance. Light influences the blooming of aquatics. For **water lilies** and **lotus** to bloom fully, they must receive at least six hours of direct sun daily. Small tub and wall fountains need shade at noon to avoid overheating. If your pond is to be aerated by a sun-powered fountain, the site must be in full sun.

If you plan to have an electrically run pump to move water, the pond must be close enough to a power source and also within reach of a hose. For low maintenance, avoid sites that collect blown debris and leaves.

If your pond is to be an in-ground installation, make sure the site isn't home to buried electrical, gas, or water lines.

Drainage. Good drainage is necessary. Do not site a pond where puddles collect during wet periods because it may be heaved when the water table rises—with spring thaw and after big storms.

Where a site is lower than the surrounding land, be prepared to grade the area to avoid runoff water that will bring mud, grass, and weeds into the pond and contaminate it with residues from chemically treated trees and grounds, roofing, spouting (new copper in particular), and petroleum from driveways.

Or, be prepared to create diversion channels to conduct the runoff away from the pond.

Land level matters. Site your pond on ground that is or can be leveled. A rock ledge can be a

problem, but if it juts well above ground you may be able to use it as the base for a waterfall (see December).

Protection from predators. When choosing a site, avoid places popular with predators, notably raccoons. Scrambling for fish, they'll upset the plantings, not to mention the fish. They love *escargots naturel;* they pick the meat out, and leave the shells in a row on the edge.

PLANTING

You have time now to carefully study water garden plants and equipment in water garden catalogs. An album of aquatic plants and materials—liners, pumps, bubblers, fountains, and other accessories—comes in handy when choosing plantings for

A waterfall in a water garden is a great extra feature.

the pond. Make one up from catalog pages, and take it when you are shopping for pond materials at local garden centers.

CARE

Established pond. Check on and maintain the moisture of the **tropical water lilies** and bog plants wintering indoors. Discard plants showing signs of rot.

GROOMING

Established pond. Rake dead leaves and other debris away from the edges of the pond to avoid having anything blow into the water.

Break ice forming on the surface of the pond—gases from the pond must have an escape route.

WATERING

Established pond. In warm areas, ponds kept active throughout the cold season may need additions of water as the weather turns mild.

FERTILIZING

There is no fertilizing to do during this season.

ABOUT FILTERS

A water garden that includes a pump usually—but not necessarily—has some sort of filtering device. Some small pumps handle solids without the help of a filter. Others you can encase in a homemade mesh basket to keep out larger bits of debris.

You need a filter if you are returning water to the pond via a fine spray nozzle and for larger ponds. How frequently the filter will need cleaning should be a consideration when you are choosing one. There are three main types:

1. **Mechanical filters.** For a small pond (say under 5 by 8 feet and holding 300 gallons of water), a small, inexpensive combination pump-and-filter is sufficient. These filters slip off and on easily for cleaning, likely to be a daily occurrence in hot weather. For ponds twice that size, a popular filtering system consists of a small pump connected by tubing to a velcro-fastened filter. This type likely needs cleaning every one to five days.

Pumps for large ponds (say 16 by 26 feet and holding 4,000 gallons of water) usually push the water through large filters outside the pond and may return it via a waterfall, a streambed, and/or a recirculating bog garden. These filters are likely to need maintenance every two to seven days.

2. **Biological filters.** A biological filter needs cleaning only a few times a month. The filter is a large or small gravel-filled cylinder installed outside the pond and screened by a waterfall, plantings, or decorative fencing. Filtering is done by bacteria that colonize layers of gravel. Though not inexpensive, costs balance out as biological filters are powered by inexpensive pumps and use less electricity.

3. **Recirculating bog garden.** The most effective filtering system for a large pond is one that pumps the water to a biological filter outside the pond and returns the water via a shallow recirculating bog garden and streambed or waterfall.

PROBLEMS

If you see signs of scale or whitefly on the tender **aquatics** you brought indoors for the winter, rinse the stems and foliage at weekly intervals until the condition clears.

FEBRUARY
WATER & BOG PLANTS

PLANNING

When the weather permits, visit sites you like for your water garden and try to visualize a shape that will be just right.

If your architecture and landscaping are formal, then consider a symmetrical shape form—an oval, a circle, a triangle, a square, or a rectangle. Plan to include a pump and to return the water to the pond through classical statuary—the human form or stylized metal frogs, for example. A tall stream of water also makes a formal statement.

If your architecture is casual and the landscaping naturalized, then consider an asymmetrical or a free-form pond design. In nature there's hardly a perfect curve or a straight line anywhere. Returning the water via a pump tumbling over piled-up rocks, a stream, or a bog garden would enhance the natural look.

Inground ponds. When you have settled on a shape for your water garden, the next decision is size. The surface area and depth govern the number of gallons a pond will hold. That influences the size of the pump and filter and the number of plants and fish you can have.

Calculating the size of the pond. The pond size many find about right aesthetically and for maintenance is between 10 by 10 feet to 10 by 15 feet. Outline the shape you have chosen on the site with a hose or a string. Then measure the length and the width. Multiply the length by the width and that gives you the square footage of the surface. With that number you can figure out how many gallons it will hold (see Calculating Pond Measurements on the facing page), and the number of gallons it holds influences many other choices.

To get the approximate size of a kidney-shaped or a free-form pond, outline it with a hose, then shape the hose into a square, a rectangle, or a combination of these shapes that encompasses the area, and measure the length and the width.

The usual pond depth is between 18 to 30 inches. Anything deeper may be classified as a pool and local regulations may require that you fence it. Bog gardens and streambeds are about a foot deep.

In Zone 6, fish are considered safe to overwinter in a pond 24 inches deep. In a large pond, the depth can be as little as 18 inches. In Zone 7, the fish are okay for winter in a pond 18 inches deep. In Zone 8, the fish stay all year, even in a small pond 18 inches deep.

Most pumps for inground ponds push or pull the water through a cleansing filtering system (see January). The number of gallons of water in the pond dictates the size of the filtering system and the power of the pump, and the number of gallons is determined by surface size. The farther and higher the water has to be pushed by the pump, the more powerful the pump needs to be. And, the more powerful the pump, the more it costs to buy and to operate.

Calculate the size and depth of your pond and the gallons it will hold, and your supplier will help you to choose suitable equipment.

PLANTING

Take cuttings or divide tender bog plants overwintering indoors.

CARE

In warm regions where the pump may have been running all winter, take it out and clean it.

GROOMING

Established pond. Plants over-wintering in the pond may be showing winter damage. Clear away damaged and dead foliage.

WATERING

Established pond. Continue to monitor the moisture in pond plants stored indoors last fall and replenish it if needed.

FERTILIZING

Established pond. When pond plants wintering indoors show signs of growth, fertilize them at half strength.

PROBLEMS

Continue to check tender **aquatics** wintering indoors for signs of scale or whitefly. The remedy is to rinse the stems and foliage at weekly intervals until the condition clears.

ABOUT RECIRCULATING PUMPS

The sound and movement of a water garden is created by a pump. The pump returns the water via a bubbler or a fountain and that aerates it. Or, the pump returns the water via a filter, a waterfall or streambed, and/or a recirculating bog garden.

The larger the pond and the farther the water has to be pushed, the more powerful the pump needs to be, and the more costly it will be to buy and to operate.

Small floating fountains powered by the sun are the easiest to install and maintain, ideal for small water features like wall fountains and tubs. They rest on islands of wiring encased in watertight containers. Solar power turns them on and sends up sprays or showers 8 to 24 inches high, depending on the strength of the unit. The largest solar fountains can move 60 gallons an hour!

The downside to this free energy and beauty is that when the sun doesn't shine, sun-powered pumps don't perform. You can't count on a sun-powered floating fountain to make magic in the moonlight.

CALCULATING POND MEASUREMENTS

To Calculate the Square Footage of the Pond Surface
- **Rectangle** length x width = square feet of surface
- **Circle** 3.14 x {$^1/_2$ the diameter x $^1/_2$ the diameter} = square feet of surface

To Calculate the Cubic Feet of Water in a Pond
- **Rectangle** length x width x depth = cubic feet
- **Circle** 3.14 x {$^1/_2$ the diameter x $^1/_2$ the diameter} x depth = cubic feet.

TO CALCULATE THE GALLONS A POND HOLDS

There are 7.5 gallons of water per cubic foot, so the number of cubic feet multiplied by 7.5 gallons = the number of gallons in the pond.

March

WATER & BOG PLANTS

 PLANNING

You can install a good-sized in-ground pond in one weekend with just one helper. And if you have four or five strong backs and pairs of willing hands, you can do it in one day. This month invite likely helpers to a mid-May pond installation picnic. Plan to have the equipment delivered before the date chosen.

If you are planning to enhance your pond with a stream, a waterfall, or a flowing bog garden, prepare these elements before you buy the equipment.

Electrical source. To accommodate the line from the pump to its source of electricity, dig a trench 12 inches deep from the pond edge to the outlet. It must be at least 6 feet from the edge of the pond.

Have a licensed electrician install a weatherproof outlet for the pump. Any standard three-prong household electrical outlet will do, but it must have a ground fault circuit interrupter.

The electrical circuit must have reserve amp capacity beyond what is needed for the operation of the pump. This is especially important with pumps using more than 8 amps. Overload can cause the circuit breaker to turn off the current.

Equipment. Water garden kits simplify installation. Otherwise, for the day of the installation, plan to have on hand: the pond liner, pump and filter, and tubing to take the water from the pump to its point of return—bubbler, fountain, bog garden, waterfall, and stream. If the liner is flexible rubber, it will need an underlay (old carpeting will do) and coarse builder's sand to level the liner. If you plan to edge the pond with flat coping stones, be sure to provide the stones and mortar to cement them in place;

in the frost belt, you'll also need metal reinforcing strips or wire for the cement. Before you order the equipment, outline the pond on the site and take final measurements to make sure there will be no problems when the great day comes.

Preformed pond. With a string and stakes, outline the pond, adding 2 inches all around to allow for the sand that will buffer the liner. At either end, dig holes to make sure there are no hidden obstructions.

Flexible liner. At the site, outline the pond with string and stakes. For a rectangular or a square pond, use a carpenter's square to get the angles just right; for a circular pond, use a string tied to a central stake to outline the circle.

To determine the width of the liner, measure the outline at the widest point then add twice the depth to allow for the sides, plus 2 feet more to cover the

When constructing a water garden, arrange for different heights so bog and water plants can be situated properly.

edges of the ground around the pond. To determine the length, measure the maximum length, then add twice the depth, plus 2 feet more.

PLANTING

Established pond. As the weather permits, clean up any flower beds around the water garden and plant hardy perennials.

Prepare for planting the **tropical water lilies** you overwintered. See Planting in the October pages for details.

CARE

Established pond—frost belt. Clean the water garden pump and turn it on. Fertilize the soil in the containers of the perennials in the pond, and return them to their places in the water.

GROOMING

If you are not using a pump and filter, as the weather warms add a supplemental bacterial product to speed the decomposition of waste from fish and plants and to prevent the growth of detrimental algae. Read the container directions and make a mental note about the timing of additional doses.

ABOUT POND LINERS

You can create a water garden in any almost container that is watertight and nontoxic, from a wall fountain to a half barrel to as large as you please.

The smallest container that is a suitable home for plants and fish is a round or oval kettle about 3 feet in diameter by 18 inches deep. That's enough to accommodate a couple of snails, two or three goldfish, one pretty little **water lily**—such as 'Dauben' or the white pygmy 'Ermine'—and the lovely bog plant we call **sweet flag.** A small electric pump and a bubbler would add a musical dimension and aerate the water.

Next in size are inground ponds waterproofed by preformed fiberglass pond liners that start at about 4 by 6 feet. They accommodate enough livestock and vegetation to keep a pond in balance; the snails, the fish, submerged plants, and a pair of **water lilies** like white 'Gonnere' and 'Albida', along with a small floating-leaved plant, and one or two marginal or bog plants.

The most popular water garden is an inground pond waterproofed by a sheet of flexible rubber about 10 by 10 feet. It accommodates snails, fish, five **water lilies,** one space-eating **lotus,** a few small-leaved floaters, and a few marginals.

Larger ponds, free-form ponds, bog gardens, and streams are all waterproofed with flexible rubber liners or fish grade PVC (polyvinyl chloride) rubber. Black pond liners give the pond a natural look; black reflects the sky and shows off the flowers and the fish.

WATERING

Continue to monitor moisture in bog plants wintering indoors and the water levels over the **tropical water lily** tubers.

FERTILIZING

As the fish become active (when water temperature exceeds 44 degrees Fahrenheit), resume feeding them.

PROBLEMS

Wild creatures are getting restless; keep an eye out for raccoons in a fishy mood.

APRIL

WATER & BOG PLANTS

PLANNING

Mail-order suppliers deliver aquatics at about the right moment to plant them in your area; they must be stored in a cool shady place and kept wet. Most except **lotus** will hold for at least two weeks.

The formula on the facing page gives the proportions of living elements needed to keep a pond in balance. A 10-by-10-foot pond with 100 square feet of surface (see February) can have sixty to seventy percent floating cover. A 20-by-50-foot pond is more beautiful with only a third of its surface covered.

This "magic formula" for stocking a pond and keeping it in balance was developed by Charles Thomas, former President of Lilypons Water Gardens, in Buckeystown, Maryland. You can substitute a **lotus** for one large **water lily**.

PLANTING

Suppliers sell aquatics and bog plants already planted in pans or pails; catalogs often ship them bare root packed in moist materials. Plant hardy aquatics anytime after the pond water is warm enough to work in comfortably, about 55 degrees Fahrenheit. Plant **tropical water lilies** after

the pond water stays above 69 degrees Fahrenheit (see July, The Magnificent Lotus).

Plant the rhizomes and tubers in pans 6 to 8 inches deep that hold 9 to 20 or more quarts of soil, the larger the better. Extra growing room encourages multiple crowns and more flowers. Heavy garden soil, which garden centers sell bagged, is good for aquatic plants. Keep it free of peat, manures, vermiculite, and anything light that floats. Avoid commercial mixes. Optimum pH is 6.5 to 7.5. Push a fertilizer tablet for aquatics into the soil of each container.

Set tubers and rhizomes so the growing tips are just above the soil; set plants with crowns so the crown is an inch below the soil level. To keep the soil in place, cover it completely with $1/2$ inches of rinsed gravel $1/2$ to $3/4$ inches in diameter. Soak the planted containers, and keep them in bright shade and wet, until you are ready to place them in the pond. Be sure to pack the garden soil tightly into the container, so that once the potting is completed and the container has been topped with gravel it is brim full. Otherwise, when you submerge the container and the air in it is displaced with water, you'll end up with a pot half full of soil, which isn't enough for the plants to perform to their greatest potential.

CARE

Established pond. Check the pH of the water, and if needed, adjust it to between pH 6.5 to 7.5, as recommended in the introduction to this chapter.

Lift and clean the filter, pump, and air pump, and return them to the pond.

Don't be alarmed if the pond water gets murky as air temperatures rise. Pond plants and critters will soon become active, and the water will clear.

GROOMING

Established pond. Lift out the hardy perennials and groom them. Check aquatics and bog plants that have been in their containers for two or three years and if they are crowded, divide them. Plants growing in large tubs can wait twice as long to be divided.

Prune and groom the submerged plants and repot them.

WATERING

Established pond. When the water level falls below normal, top the pond. When adding tap water that includes chlorine, chloramine, or chlorine dioxide, follow label directions on a neutralizing agent to get rid of these elements.

CONTAINERS FOR AQUATIC PLANTS

Aquatics and bog plants for a water garden (but not those for a flowing bog recirculating system) grow in soil in pans, pails, and tubs placed in the pond. The container sizes are measured in inches and quarts. Containers for aquatics do not have holes for drainage. When you are planting bog plants for the pond in containers for aquatics, make one or two nail holes in the bottoms.

FORMULA FOR EVERY 1 TO 2 SQUARE FEET OF POND SURFACE

- 1 bunch (6 stems) submerged/oxygenating plants
- 1 black Japanese snail
- 2 inches of fish for fish up to 6 inches long
- $1/10$ of a small, or medium-size, **water lily** (that is, 1 lily per 10 to 20 square feet)
- $1/3$ of a marginal or a small, floating-leaved plant (that is, 1 bog or marginal plant or 1 small-leaved floater for every 3 to 6 square feet)

Here's a "for instance" for planting and stocking a pond about 10 by 10 feet, that is, 100 square feet of surface:
- 50 to 100 bunches of submerged/oxygenating plants
- 50 to 100 black Japanese snails
- 100 to 200 inches of fish in assorted sizes up to 6 inches long
- 5 to 10 **water lilies**
- 18 to 33 marginal and/or floating-leaved plants, 3 each of each variety chosen

FERTILIZING

Established pond. Push a bar of aquatic fertilizer into the soil in each container. Use a nitrogen-phosphate-potash formulation (NPK) of 10-14-8.

As fish become active, resume feeding them. If your water garden does not have a pump and filter, add a supplemental bacterial product to speed the decomposition of waste from fish and plants.

PROBLEMS

Established pond. With spring warmth, insects become active. Moving water and hungry fish discourage insect development, and so do frogs. Add tadpoles if you foresee insect problems.

MAY

WATER & BOG PLANTS

 PLANNING

Before your pond installation party, review the pond equipment you have ordered, and lay out digging tools, a crowbar for rocks, shears, a tarp for the excavated soil, a 2-by-4-inch board the width of the pond, a carpenter's level, a tape measure, and cement blocks, bricks, slate, or treated wood to help level the edges.

Installation. The installation procedure goes about like this:

1. **Digging the pond:**

Preformed pond. Following the outline created earlier (see March), excavate a hole that will fit the preformed liner.

Flexible liner. Following the outline created earlier (see March), dig a hole 15 to 30 inches deep and in the center create a trough 1 inch deep and 18 inches across. If the soil is firm, slope the sides at a 75 degree angle; if it crumbles, slope the sides at a 45 degree angle.

2. **Leveling the excavation:**

Flexible liner and preformed pond: Center a 2-by-4-inch board across the hole and check the level of the rims, then make them even. Flatten high spots. Use sand to raise spots that are low by less than 2 inches. To raise areas more than 2 inches low, use cement blocks, bricks,

slate, or treated wood covered with sand.

3. **Creating a pond rim:**

Preformed pond and flexible liner. To prepare for the edging that will be installed later, cut the sod around the pond into strips 10 inches wide and 12 to 15 inches long. Without detaching the strips from the lawn, roll them up gently away from the pond.

4. **Placing the liner:**

Preformed pond. Line the bottom of the excavation with an inch of sand. Place the pond so the rim is just above ground level. Check and adjust the level of the rim to within 1/4 inch.

Flexible liner. Line the bottom of the excavation with an inch of sand, then cover the sand with the underlayment. Open the liner, and gently spread it over the underlayment. If you find the liner heavy, fold it in fourths and unfold it from inside the excavation. Smooth the liner, pushing the excess up over the rim of pond.

5. **Filling the pond:**

Preformed pond. Begin filling the pond, and as the water level rises, pack sand (or soil) behind the sides of the form. Keep the pressure inside and outside similar by adding sand or soil at a rate matching the rise of the water level so the form does not buckle.

Liner pond. Fill the pond to within 1 inch of the top. Cut the surplus liner off leaving an overlap of 6 to 12 **extra** inches all around. Smooth the overlap over the dirt around the pond, and nail it firmly in place using 4- to 6-inch spike nails (no other kind).

6. **Edging the pond:**

If you'd like to edge the pond with sod, scratch up and fertilize the soil you stripped of sod in Step 3, then roll the grass strips back and firm them in place.

If you plan to edge the pond with coping stones (stones used for the flat topmost layer of a stone wall), cut off and discard the sod strips. To protect the liner, place the coping stones so they extend 1 to 2 inches over the rim of the pond. Use mortar to keep them in place. In the frost belt, use metal reinforcing rods or wire inside a 2- to 3-inch mortar base. Use as little mortar as possible so the stone looks natural. Check the level of the stones often as you work.

After the mortar has dried, clean the stones with a stiff brush and a mixture of 1 part ordinary vinegar to 1 part water or muriatic acid and water, and rinse thoroughly. Drain the pond, and refill it with fresh water.

PLANTING

Instructions for planting and stocking the pond are given in June, Planting.

CARE

Established pond. Clear the filter as often as suggested by the manufacturer.

GROOMING

You can help keep the pond healthy if you promptly remove yellowing and dying vegetation, as well as spent blooms.

WATERING

Restore the level of the pond water anytime it shows a measurable dip.

FERTILIZING

As long as the water temperature remains under 75 degrees Fahrenheit, fertilize **lotus** and **water lilies** monthly.

ABOUT SUBMERGED/ OXYGENATING PLANTS

Submerged plants are included among pond plantings to gobble the nutrients feeding undesirable algae and to add oxygen. Four available from most suppliers are: **Anacharis** (*Elodea canadensis* var. *gigantea*); **dwarf saggitaria** (*Sagittaria subulata*); *Myriophyllum* species; **Washington grass** (*Cabomba caroliniana*).

The plants are usually sold in bunches of six stems about 6 inches long. Growing in sand-filled pans set on the pond bottom, they quickly develop stems 2 to 3 feet long. Allow 6 square inches of container surface for every bunch of submerged plants, and use a separate container for each variety. To plant, take off the rubber bands, and gently press the ends of each bunch 2 inches into the sand. Add sand to within an inch of the rim, and top that with rinsed gravel. Water the containers to displace trapped air. Never fertilize—their job is to take nutrients from the water.

Koi and goldfish over 6 inches can nibble the submerged plants to death. Cover the pans with plastic mesh domes; the plants grow through the mesh and the fish graze without harming the roots. You can make your own dome using a plastic mesh sold by aquatics suppliers.

Take care not to get lawn chemicals and clippings into the pond when you are fertilizing and mowing.

PROBLEMS

If you do not have a pump and filter to help keep an excess of algae from developing, apply a supplemental bacterial product to speed the decomposition of waste from fish and plants.

Fish should be enough to keep insects to a minimum. If not, add tadpoles. Pesticides and herbicides aren't recommended around ponds.

Control grass and weeds growing into the pond from the edging.

Add a pellet to kill mosquito larvae.

JUNE
WATER & BOG PLANTS

PLANNING

The beauty of your water garden depends in part on its setting. Here are some suggestions:

Pot, tub, or barrel water garden. Surround the container with potted plants of different heights.

Formal pond. Plant **boxwood, roses,** or **Japanese maples** in the background of a pond that is symmetrical, oval, circle, triangle, square, or a long narrow rectangle. Repeat the dominant color of the pond flowers in the plantings around it.

Naturalized pond. Use native plants found near water in the setting—**reeds,** native shrubs, **dogwoods,** and, in shaded areas, **ferns, Solomon's-seal,** and green **mosses.**

Free-form pond. Use Japanese-style garden ornaments with a kidney-shaped or free-form water garden—a **dwarf ornamental cherry, dwarf azaleas, Siberian irises, quilted hostas, ferns, mosses,** and forest flowers.

PLANTING

Before placing fish and other wildlife in a new pond, allow a couple of weeks for the water to de-chlorinate and warm.

The plants can go into the pond anytime after it is filled. Aquatics need a specific amount of water overhead, and the amount is indicated in mail-order catalogs and on plant tags. Some can rest on the bottom of the pond, while others will need to be raised on platforms that can be made of stones, clean bricks, and weathered cement blocks. Avoid new cement blocks because they raise the water pH. When wet, plant containers can be heavy, so slide and float them to their destinations.

The submerged plants are set out first, at a depth of 1 to 2 feet. Next, set out the large floating-leaved plants. Allow several feet between **water lily** and **lotus** containers. Place the small floaters next. Group the pond **bog plants** on the far side of the pond 1 to 2 feet apart.

Plant the plants for a recirculating bog garden in the gravel on the bottom, with a ball of soil around the roots and about $1/2$ to 1 inch of water overhead.

CARE

Clear the filter as often as necessary to keep the pump free. If the filter becomes clogged, the water flowing back to the pond will slow or stop.

If you do not have a pump and filter, add a supplemental bacterial product to speed the decomposition of waste from fish and plants.

Keep fertilizer carts and lawn mowers far from the pond rim to avoid getting chemicals and grass clippings into the water.

New pond. If you have mortared the coping stones around the pond rim, check the pH of the water, which may be affected by runoff from the mortar. If the pH is way up, particularly after the first couple of rains, adjust it as directed in the introduction to this chapter.

GROOMING

Remove yellowing leaves and dead flowers, leaving nothing to decay.

If strands of the submerged plants elongate and become puny, raise the containers to positions where they receive more direct sunlight. When they're 8 inches tall and growing well, you can cut them back or divide them and make more plants. Just break off the top 5 or 6 inches, press the ends into a container filled with sand, and place it in the pond.

 WATERING

Maintain the water level of the pond.

 FERTILIZING

When the water temperature is over 75 degrees Fahrenheit, fertilize **lotus** and **water lilies** twice monthly. Fertilize the pond bog plants monthly, if they are not growing well. Do not fertilize the plants in the recirculating bog system or the submerged plants; their job is to starve out the nutrients that feed unwanted algae.

 PROBLEMS

Weed around and between the coping stones.

Add a pellet that kills mosquito larvae. Avoid using pesticides and herbicides around the pond.

A large water feature offers more opportunity for landscaping with water and bog plants.

JULY
WATER & BOG PLANTS

PLANNING

Ask your aquatics supplier to recommend a biological or microbial product to suppress **algae** that turn the water a murky green or green-brown. These products control **algae** by speeding up the decomposition of the fish and plant waste on which unwanted algae feed.

Algae can be beneficial, but some are not. The three main **algae** are a good-guy, moss-like clinging algae, and two other not-good guys—a floating surface type and a drifter. The good-guy clinging algae mosses the stones and the sides of the pond with beautiful deep-green filaments, and fuzzes plant stems and snail shells. Welcome it. You can control the unwanted floating type by raising the water level and pushing the floating algae off the surface with a broom. Biological products keep them all in check.

PLANTING

The sun changes positions throughout the year, and it can happen that your pond ends up with more shade at certain times than you anticipated. Shade may be the culprit if **water lilies** and **lotus** are failing to bloom up to expectation. You can solve the problem by replacing sun-lovers with **water lilies** that bloom with 4 to 6 hours of direct sun. Among them are the very popular **hardy water lilies** 'Charlene Strawn', which is yellow, 'Virginia', a white, and red 'James Brydon'.

A few **tropical water lilies** also bloom with less sun. Along them are: 'Albert Greenberg', a rose-tinged gold that does well in any pond over 4 feet and blooms longer than other tropicals; 'Director George Moore', a compact tropical with magnificent deep blue flowers; and 'Panama Pacific', blue tinged with red, which grows small or large according to the space available.

Several tropical bog plants also succeed in partial sun, including **elephant's-ear** and **taro,** species of *Colocasia,* and several species of **papyrus,** *Cyperus,* including **umbrella plant.** These are all tender perennials in our region.

CARE

Clear the filter. If you do not have a pump and filter, add a supplemental bacterial product to speed the decomposition of waste from fish and plants.

When thunderstorms come close, turn off the pond pump to avoid attracting lightning.

Pinch off yellowing leaves and dead flowers as they occur. **Water lilies** are continually putting out new leaves and stretching them outward as more arise. As they fade, get rid of them.

GROOMING

Deadhead the flowering plants, and immediately remove yellowing and decaying vegetation.

WATERING

Now that the high heat of summer is here, check and adjust the water level of your pond daily, especially when the day is hot, dry, and windy.

If your water is heavily chlorinated, and you are adding as much as 10 percent to the volume of the pond—if it's down as much as 2 inches, for instance—add a 10 percent solution of a de-chlorinator when you top it.

Lawn sprinklers have little effect on pond water unless their spray drips into the pond from foliage that's been treated with herbicides or pesticides. You want to avoid that.

THE MAGNIFICENT LOTUS

The **lotus** is an extraordinary plant. The large pointed bud rises above the water on a stem 2 to 6 feet tall, and unfolds an enormous perfumed blossom. Colors are lush shades and combinations of white, pink, red, yellow, and cream. For three days the **lotus** blossom opens mornings before the **water lilies,** and closes at tea time. The third day the petals fall, leaving the seedpod that is sought after for dried arrangements. It looks like the spout of a watering can, or ET, the movie character.

Lotus

Mail-order suppliers ship **lotus** tubers bare root the few weeks in spring when the rootstock is in tuber form. Later the tubers send out runners and atrophy, which makes planting impossible. They can be planted as soon as the water temperature is in the 40s or above.

Use pans 16 to 24 inches in diameter, 9 to 10 inches deep, for standard **lotus**; miniatures make do with half to two-thirds this size. Set the tubers 2 inches under the soil with the top half inch of the growing tip above the soil (see April, Planting). Place the pans in the pond with 2 to 3 inches of water overhead; they bloom sooner in shallow water.

Two or three weeks after being planted, a **lotus** sends up a first set of floating leaves. They look like **lily pads** without the notch. A second set of leaves rises and opens high above the water. The leaves of **miniature lotus** are 6 to 16 inches across, and the stems are 2 to 3 feet tall; **standard lotus** leaves can be 2 feet wide, and the stem the height of a tall person—6 feet.

FERTILIZING

When the water temperature rises above 75 degrees Fahrenheit, fertilize the **water lilies** and the **lotus** twice monthly.

PROBLEMS

Add a pellet that kills mosquito larvae.

Get rid of grass and weeds growing into the pond from the edging, but avoid pesticides and herbicides near the pond.

AUGUST
WATER & BOG PLANTS

PLANNING

Goldfish usually live ten to fifteen years unless they encounter a predator. When you go on vacation, you won't have to plan to have the fish and other pond creatures to be fed in your absence. In a balanced pond (see the April sidebar), the fish feed on the submerged plants, on the moss-like **algae** on the sides of the pond, and on the insects and larvae you do want to be rid of. Your pond might be clearer when you come back because you haven't been feeding the fish.

PLANTING

Now that your pond plants are maturing, watch for those that can be, or need to be, divided.

You can plant or transplant container-grown and rooted **hardy water lilies,** and many bog plants, from early spring until a few weeks prior to the first killing frost. **Water lilies** that are moved while blooming just sulk a bit.

Water lilies need dividing when they become crowded. The blossoms of **water lilies** like 'Virginia' and 'Charlene Strawn' usually stand an inch or two above the water; when their pads also are held high (and the rhizomes are 12 or more inches under water), that's a sign the plants will need dividing next spring before growth begins.

Lotus tubers are shipped bare root in spring in plastic bags containing moist materials. They're almost as easy to grow as **water lilies,** but they can be transplanted only during the few weeks in spring when the rootstock is in tuber form. When the rootstock puts out runners, the tubers atrophy, and transplanting is virtually impossible.

Irises can be divided anytime after they bloom, including **Japanese irises,** such as *Iris kaempferi, I. laevigata* 'Variegata,' the big **yellow flag,** *I. pseudacorus* and the **Louisiana hybrid irises.**

CARE

When thunderstorms threaten, turn off the pump.

Clean the filter consistently. It's apt to clog more often this time of the year. If you do not have a pump and filter, add a supplemental bacterial product to speed the decomposition of waste from fish and plants.

Monitor the pond as the trees begin to shed their first leaves,

Yellow Flag Iris

and remove leaves and debris from the pond daily.

GROOMING

The submerged plants may need pruning and division. If you are losing the open water to the summer growth of small- and large-leaved floating plants, cut it back enough to keep about a third of the water surface clear.

Deadhead consistently, and remove yellowing and decaying foliage.

WATERING

When the water level of the pond falls below its normal height, top the pond. If you are adding more than an inch of tap water to the pond—water that includes chlorine, chloramine, or chlorine dioxide—add a de-chlorinating chemical according to the label directions for neutralizing these elements.

FERTILIZING

Fertilize **water lilies** and **lotus** in ponds in Zones 7 and 8 early this month.

Hardy plants rooted in a recirculating bog should be taking all the nutrients they can use from the water. However, some may be more aggressive than others; cut these back, and push a half-strength dose of fertilizer into the soil of the containers of less successful plants.

In Zone 6, aquatics will be shutting down soon and should not be fertilized after August 1.

PROBLEMS

Add a pellet that kills mosquito larvae.

ATTRACTING WILDLIFE

In a city, a pond 2 feet by 3 feet is enough to attract songbirds, butterflies, and dragonflies, though it's minimal space for frogs.

In less urban settings, a secluded pond 10 by 10 feet and up attracts small animals such as deer, fox, raccoons, possums, and uplands game birds. In wild mountain terrain, a large pond will draw in all sorts of native animals.

Site your pond where you can watch nervous visitors and not be seen. Stock the pond with native minnows and small goldfish rather than showy koi, which attract predators, especially raccoons. If you want showy fish, do without a filter that keeps the water clear. Or, add a black dye (see November), which is used to limit visibility and make the water look deep and inviting; there are no bad side effects.

Make the area safe for birds. If there are cats around, provide a high observation post 6 to 8 feet from the pond for the birds. It can be a tree, or shrubbery that screens them from hawks. Birds like a clear a path to the water—a high-up branch far away, then one closer and lower, then a landing site at the pond, a broad stone for example. Plant berried shrubs, and let **pines** and **hemlocks** grow tall to provide nesting places, materials, and safe perches.

If your aquatic plants begin to have a chewed look at the edges, look for little brown snails, and remove them by hand.

Pull out grass and weeds growing into the pond from the edging.

If night raiders are visiting your pond, cover it with screens at night. Or, install a grid of broad mesh fencing that the fish can dive through to evade marauders. Less colorful fish attract fewer predators.

273

SEPTEMBER
WATER & BOG PLANTS

 PLANNING

In our region, fall is an important planting season. Make time now to evaluate the effect of the plants in your water garden and around the pond. Consider additions that will increase your pleasure in your pond. For inspiration, study the album of aquatic plants you made from the pages of mail-order catalogs back in January.

 PLANTING

You can divide spring-blooming hardy bog perennials successfully anytime during the next few weeks.

In the beds that create the setting around your pond, hardy perennials can be divided up to a month before the ground is expected to freeze and in early spring before new growth begins. The rule of thumb for autumn-flowering perennials is to divide them in early spring, before any sign of growth appears.

Most perennials benefit from division. If you want more plants to fill out or enlarge the beds, check out those that been in the ground two years—if they are growing well it's okay to divide them.

The next four to six week are first rate for planting and transplanting trees and shrubs. Consider adding an evergreen to the setting for your pond. **Gold-dust tree,** Aucuba japonica, gets tall enough here to make a handsome backdrop. The **weeping hemlock** is a dark evergreen that stays low for years. For fun, add three baby **boxwoods** pruned to globe shape.

Deciduous trees and shrubs add structure and a more open look to a pond setting. A **Sargent crabapple** (6 to 10 feet high) in bloom beside a pond is lovely. For summer bloom, plant a miniature **crapemyrtle** such as 'Chickasaw'; for late summer bloom plant the **hardy hibiscus** 'White Chiffon'. You can keep the **crapemyrtles** and **shrub althea** at shrub height by trimming them back before growth begins in early spring.

 CARE

Continue to keep the pond filter clear. If you do not have a pump and filter, add a supplemental bacterial product to speed the decomposition of waste from fish and plants.

Remove leaves that fall into the water at once. If there are deciduous trees near the pond, when the first leaves begin to fall, cover the surface with bird netting. Keep the netting in place until all the leaves have fallen and been cleared away.

When the water temperature falls below 55 degrees Fahrenheit, any tubs, half-barrels, and water gardens less than 30 inches deep are likely to become too cold for the fish. You have two solutions; set the fish free in a large pond, a stream, or a lake; or bring them indoors to a fish tank for the winter. In any case, stop feeding them (see October).

 GROOMING

Continue to deadhead flowering pond plants, and clear away yellowing and dead foliage as soon as you spot it. Rotting foliage may incubate pests and diseases over the winter months.

Keep an eye on the annuals and discard them when they are played out.

WATERING

Keep track of the water level in your pond, and bring it back to normal as often as it falls.

FERTILIZING

Monitor the changing water temperature—when it falls below 75 degrees Fahrenheit, stop fertilizing the plants.

PROBLEMS

Where fall is warm, if mosquitoes are a concern, add a mosquito larvae control pellet.

As the foliage in the pond collapses with the cold, colorful fish become more obvious to predators. The bird netting recommended in the Care section of this month to keep leaves out of the pond also affords some protection for the fish and snails.

ATTRACTING BUTTERFLIES AND HUMMINGBIRDS

It takes just a few nectar-bearing plants in the pond area to attract butterflies and hummingbirds, and fall is a good time to plant those that are hardy perennials.

Butterflies fly down to showy plantings of brilliant blooms—purple, yellow, orange, and red. They hover over flowers that have flat-topped or short, open-mouthed tubular blossoms that make landing platforms. Single rather than double flowered types make gathering nectar easier for them.

The number one attraction for butterflies is the **butterfly bush,** *Buddleia davidii.* It bears graceful flower spikes on new wood, so if it doesn't die to the ground in your climate, before growth begins in early spring, cut it back. Other butterfly magnets are **butterfly weed,** *Asclepias tuberosa,* a sweetly scented perennial, and *Lantana camara,* which is grown as an annual in our cooler regions. **Passion flower,** *Passiflora,* a flowering tropical vine, is popular with these beautiful flying acrobats.

Hummingbirds spend their days looking for the food necessary to fuel their amazing energy output. Their primary diet is nectar, rounded out with tiny insects. They rely on sight, not scent, to locate nectar, and go to many of the flowers that attract butterflies. Some that do well in part sun are **pentas, impatiens, red cardinal flower,** and **beebalm.**

Butterfly Bush

275

OCTOBER
WATER & BOG PLANTS

PLANNING

In frost-free regions, a water garden in a sheltered spot can likely go right on all winter without missing a beat—pump, fish, plants, and all, although there will be fewer flowers.

In the frost belt as the thermometer plummets, the foliage and flowers of the pond plants begin to subside, a signal the season is over. Now you must evaluate what to discard and what to keep. If the growth of the small floating-leaved plants is invasive, discard a few. At the end of the season, many pond owners discard the less costly cold-tender pond bog plants, saving limited indoor winter storage space for the most valuable.

If your **tropical water lilies** grew from tubers you saved last year, decide now whether their performance this year makes saving them worth the effort.

PLANTING

When nights are below 65 degrees Fahrenheit, bring the most valuable tender pond bog plants indoors to save them for next year. They thrive set in pans filled with an inch of wet pea gravel in a big south-facing window. Keep the soil moist. During the darkest months of the year, supplement the daylight with fluorescent light.

In the frost belt when the **tropical water lilies** stop blooming many owners discard them and start fresh next year. But it's possible to collect and save the tubers. Here's how:

1. A week or so after a killing frost, lift the rootstock, and gently wash off as much soil as you can.

2. Pick off one or more tubers, air dry them for two days, and then remove the remaining soil.

3. Store them in jars of distilled water, in a cool closet at about 55 degrees Fahrenheit.

4. In late winter, two months before the pond water temperature will warm to 70 degrees Fahrenheit, bring the tubers out and set them to sprout in a pan of water in a sunny window.

5. When the pond temperature reaches a constant 69 degrees Fahrenheit, replant the tubers and return them to the pond. They should bloom two to three months later.

CARE

To keep falling leaves from getting into the pond, cover it with bird netting. It's black and not very visible.

A biological filter (see January) needs a thorough cleaning at the end of the growing season.

Discard played-out annuals. Cut back the submerged/oxygenating plants. Clear away fading vegetation. Dying organic matter in the pond will decay producing toxic levels of methane gases that harm the fish and the hardy perennials staying on for winter.

In the frost belt, slide the cold-**hardy water lily** and the pond bog plant containers to the deepest spot in the pond for the winter. The water will be warmest there.

GROOMING

Keep any plants still in the pond clear of decaying foliage and spent flowers. Cut back the submerged plants.

WATERING

Maintain the water level of the pond for the sake of the fish and the plants overwintering there.

FERTILIZING

There is no fertilizing to do at this season.

PROBLEMS

When raccoons and other little mammals are getting ready to nap for winter they become very interested in food. With the vegetation fading or gone from the pond, the fish are more visible. If you see a lot of critter activity, cover the pond with bird netting to discourage fishing expeditions.

FEEDING THE FISH

Fish gobble larvae and insects and nibble plants, so it's not necessary to feed them. But they're fun to feed. Once they know you they will come as you approach and make their interest in food obvious.

The fish in a well-balanced pond may not need feeding, but fish that aren't fed remain wild. They will hide when you are there, by vanishing behind submerged plants or under **lily pads**. Feeding creates a relationship fairly rapidly with the goldfish and koi—golden orfe are less responsive.

To make friends with your fish, the first days they are in a pond, let them find their own food. Then, at a time of day you can come regularly to the pond, relax next to the water and lean over the pond for a minute or so. Then gently drop a pinch of fish flakes onto the water. The first few times you drop in food they'll wait till you are gone to come up for it. But eventually they'll come when you are there and even be at the surface before you feed them.

Feed fish only as much as they eat in five minutes. Extra fish food and waste loads the water with more nutrients than the plants can absorb. The result is a green growth called algae bloom that uses up nitrogen then dies, consuming oxygen faster than the water can absorb it from the air. Lacking oxygen, the fish die. The bigger fish die first. Smaller fish tolerate water with low oxygen content longer.

Fish eat more in hot weather and again in the fall as they stoke up for winter dormancy. When the water temperature drops to 55 degrees Fahrenheit, their body processes slow as they become dormant and they can no longer digest the food.

November

WATER & BOG PLANTS

PLANNING

As winter approaches, plan to find time to prepare the pond for the cold season. If the pump is not hard-wired into its electrical source, unplug it and lift it. Clean it and store it indoors. If it can't be unplugged, take the pump out of the pond, flush it with clean water, and return it to the pond. In warm regions, you can turn it back on.

In the frost belt the pump must not go on in winter. Here's why: in summer the coolest water is at the bottom of the pond, but in winter the warmest water is in the bottom and that's where fish gather. If the pump goes on, the bottom will get cooler and the fish will suffer.

A large pond benefits from cleaning every two or three years. Small pond and water features need annual cleaning. Plan to begin after the pond plants have subsided and all the tree leaves have been cleared away.

1. Begin by filling a large container with pond water as a temporary home for the pond livestock. Use the pump and a hose to spill the water out over nearby garden plants; it's rich in nutrients.

2. When the water is almost gone, net the fish, snails, and other livestock and place them in their temporary home. Cover it to keep the fish from jumping out.

3. Slide the plant containers from the water, and cover them with moist newspaper.

4. Use a plastic scoop to remove the organic waste from the pond bottom. Use a hose and sponges to clear algae and clean the sides.

5. Refill the pond. If the water includes chlorine, use a dechlorinating agent to prepare the water for the return of the critters.

6. Gradually blend enough of the fresh pond water into the fish container to bring its temperature down so the fish will have acclimated to the new temperature in the pond before you return them to it.

7. Clean and groom the plants. If you are in a frost-free region, fertilize the pond plants and return them to their accustomed places.

8. If you are in the frost belt, slide the winter-hardy plants to the deepest spot in the pond and submerge them.

PLANTING

In the frost belt, **hardy water lilies** stored in water below ice level can live through winter. If the winter is hard and the pond isn't deep enough to escape ice even its lowest point, move the **water lilies** in their pans to a frost-free garage or a root cellar. Cover each with damp newspaper, and wrap it in a plastic bag. Check the rhizomes now and then—don't let them dry out.

FROGS IN THE POND

Frogs are a water garden's very good friends and charming ornaments. In the tadpole stage, they do a fine job of clearing up leftover fish food and undesirable algae. Those that make it to froghood are a huge help with mosquito control.

Frogs sleep in winter buried in mud around the edges of your pond. If your water garden includes a recirculating bog garden, they likely will winter in the gravelly bottom muck.

The only trouble with frogs is you get fond of them, and they are independent creatures that may not stay, especially when rainy weather invites them to venture abroad. But if they are happy in your pond, they will make babies and in time may provide a frog chorus that will add greatly to your evening pleasure.

BLACK WATER IS BEAUTIFUL

A black dye sold by water garden suppliers is the magic that gives a velvety black look to the water gardens in many public gardens, including the National Aquatic Gardens at the U.S. National Arboretum in Washington, DC. The inky surfaces mirror the sky, mask the algae, and the **water lilies** stand out beautifully while the fish seem to float in and out of a mysterious deep.

The vegetable-based dye doesn't kill the algae, but it does hide it.

The label on the dye container tells how much to use. The proportions don't change with regional temperature or the contents of the water. After you've used the dye a few times, you'll know how much you want to put in. It's safe for pets and wildlife that may come there to drink.

 ## CARE

If you have covered the pond with bird netting to keep falling leaves out, you can remove it as soon as they all have fallen and been removed. But keep the netting on if the pond is attracting the attention of wild visitors like raccoons and herons.

In the frost belt if fish are going to winter in your pond, stop feeding them when the thermometer drops to 45 degrees Fahrenheit. They will go dormant and can winter safely in the deepest part of ponds 30 inches deep. If they are disturbed, they'll swim a bit, then go back to their rest.

 ## GROOMING

In warm regions where water garden plants may remain active over the winter, it is necessary to continue to deadhead the few flowers that bloom and to remove decaying foliage. In the frost belt, groom bog plants wintering indoors.

 ## WATERING

Anytime the water level of the pond falls below its normal height, top it.

 ## FERTILIZING

There's no fertilizing to do at this season.

 ## PROBLEMS

Raccoons spend winter in a den, sleeping but not hibernating. Be aware that in warm periods they're up and about, and they're good fishermen.

DECEMBER
WATER & BOG PLANTS

 PLANNING

Now, with the gift-giving season near, is a fine time to plan ways to make your water garden more interesting next year.

If you put together an album of catalog pages showing garden equipment such as liners, pumps, bubblers, fountains, and other accessories, look through it for inspiration. Santa may be pleased to know of your interest.

Adding a waterfall. If you're considering changing the configuration of the pond, perhaps by adding a waterfall, this is a good time to start it.

 PLANTING

In warm regions where there is still a month before the first frosts are expected, there's time to divide **hardy water lilies** and pond bog plants.

 CARE

In frost-free regions, keep the pump and filter in place and working through the winter. At the coolest moment in winter, give the biological filter a thorough cleaning.

In the frost belt, if your pond is likely to develop a thin coat of ice now and then and you are keeping fish and plants there for the winter, plan to cover the pond until the danger of frost is past.

You can offset frosts by covering the pond with a couple of 2-by-4 boards with a tarp or canvas over them. If you don't think that will be enough to stop the surface from freezing, cover the tarp with a 3-inch layer of leaves held in place with netting. Secure the edges with rocks so the arrangement can withstand winter winds. Allow a small open space on the down side of the prevailing winds for ventilation. Don't seal the pond. Gases from the pond must have an escape route, and fresh air must be available.

Where it is likely ice will cover the pond surface for more than three or four consecutive days, install a floating deicer. A little ice isn't bad, but ice that covers the surface for days on end keeps the pond from breathing. The surface of the water takes from the atmosphere the oxygen your pond creatures need and disperses gases released by organic decay and carbon dioxide wastes built up by animal life. The exchange can't take place while ice covers the surface.

A deicer is a simple heating element attached to a flotation device. The best deicers are equipped with thermostats so they turn themselves on only when warmth is needed. The most popular are rated at 1500 watts. Float the deicer only during the weeks or months that it is needed and always in conjunction with a ground fault circuit interrupter.

 GROOMING

In warm regions, continue to deadhead and clear dying foliage from **lilies** and bog plants throughout the winter.

 WATERING

Keep track of the water level in your pond, and bring it back to normal as often as necessary.

 FERTILIZING

There's no fertilizing to do at this season.

 PROBLEMS

Raccoons and other intrepid fishermen are the only likely pests this time of the year.

PESTS, DISEASES, & CONTROLS

COMMON INSECT PESTS AND CONTROLS

Many factors play a role in how light or heavy your insect problems will be:

1. The presence of natural parasites and predators cuts down on pests and diseases.
2. Dry or wet seasons encourage certain problems.
3. Very cold winters can reduce insect populations.

By choosing pest- and disease-resistant plants that thrive in our climate, and by being faithful to the healthy garden practices we recommend, you can avoid many of the most common problems in the Mid-Atlantic—spider mites, whitefly, Japanese beetles, blackspot, mildew, rust, and nematodes.

What you can't avoid, try to control. Identify the problem and apply controls early in the developmental cycle, not late. The development stage of each species is affected greatly by warm early seasons and cool late seasons. Just as the growth of the plant on which an insect or disease preys is delayed or stimulated by the weather, so is the insect affected.

Keep an eye on plants that hosted problems in previous years. The colder the zone and the season, the later the infestation will come. Blackspot, mildew, mites, whitefly, Japanese beetles appear earlier in gardens in Zone 8 of Tidewater Virginia than in yards in Zones 6 and 7. Gardeners in the warmer climates may face more broods of insects per year.

Various controls are appropriate for certain stages in the development of various pests and diseases. Here's an outline:

• With aphids, crickets, earwigs, grasshoppers, leafhoppers, scale, thrips, and similar insects, the metamorphosis to adulthood is simple: All stages of larvae and adults are similar to each other and all feed on the host plant. The egg hatches and there is a series of nymphs, which shed their skin (molting), getting larger each time until the final adult stage. A little cricket molts and molts, and becomes a large adult cricket. You use the same control from beginning to end of the cycle.

• For other creatures, metamorphosis requires an egg stage, a larval stage, a pupal stage (resting stage), and then there is a miraculous transformation into a very different adult.

• With some insects such as beetles, the grub stage feeds on the roots of plants, and the adult beetle feeds on the leaves, stems, and flowers of the host plant.

• In the case of moths and butterflies, nectar feeds only the adult butterfly. For the larval stage—the caterpillar—most butterfly species must locate a specific host plant because the caterpillar would die rather than eat anything else. After mating, a female butterfly flutters slowly near plants, touching down and tasting them through organs on her front legs. When she finds a plant acceptable for her kind, she will deposit one or more eggs, and then wander off looking for other host plants.

Here is a list of insect pests and their controls:

Aphids. Aphids attack a wide range of plants. Small, pear-shaped insects, they have piercing, sucking mouthparts, and in some cases can transmit diseases. The symptoms of aphid damage are stunted and deformed leaves and stems. Aphids produce enormous amounts of a sugary, sticky, honey-like substance called honeydew. A black fungus quickly spreads on the honeydew and slows down photosynthesis. This fungus is called sooty mold. **Controls:** *Aphids usually can be sprayed off with a strong jet of water from a hose. Repeat if they return. If they persist, try a soap-based insecticide or products with malathion or pyrethrin. Some biological controls are green lacewings, lady beetles, and aphid lions. Some natural controls are applying rubbing alcohol with cotton swabs, horticultural soap, and ultra-fine horticultural oil.*

Beetles. Beetles and weevils belong to a group called *Coleoptera.* Weevils, or curculios, are beetles that have jaws at the end of long snouts. Some have a larval stage that feeds on plants. Black vine weevil, which is most destructive to garden plants, is an example. Many other species of beetles, including the June beetle and rose chafer, affect garden plants. The Japanese beetle, a metallic green and coppery maroon insect, is one of the most destructive pests east of the Mississippi. They chew the leaves and stems of some 200 species of perennials, ruin roses, basil, and other favorites. The grub stage is devastating to lawns and gardens. Grub-proofing lawns and gardens reduces the population already existing in your yard, but does not control those beetles that fly in. **Controls:** *Japanese beetle traps are effective, providing they are placed far away from the plantings you are trying to protect, not among them. If the infestation is minor, beetles can be picked off by hand. Insecticides containing, Neem, rotenone, or Sevin insecticide control many of the negative beetles.*

Bugs. This is a term sometimes used loosely to describe all insects. True bugs belong to the *Hemiptera* family and do their damage by piercing and sucking. Examples are squash bugs, stink bugs, and the tarnished plant bug. **Controls:** *Products containing Sevin insecticide, or are best, along with Pyrethrin or malathion. These are most effective when the bugs are in an early stage of development.*

Caterpillars. Caterpillars are the immature stage of moths and butterflies. Their mouthparts chew holes in the leaves, stems, and flowers of most everything. Caterpillars may be smooth or fuzzy, and range in size from very small to the huge tomato hornworm. They include leaf rollers and tent makers. Also in this group are other destructive pests such as the gypsy moth and tent caterpillar. **Controls:** *One of the best ways to get rid of a minor infestation is to pick the critters off by hand. The other way is to spray with a biological control such as Bacillus thuringiensis. Other controls are Sevin or malathion insecticide, Pyrethrin, or rotenone.*

Leafminers. Leafminers can be the larval stage of small flies, moths, and beetles. Over seven hundred kinds of leafminers affect plants in North America. There can be as many as four life cycles in warmer climatic zones. Leafminers burrow between the upper and lower epidermis of the leaf, making irregular serpentine tunnels. **Controls:** *Spray with a product containing malathion or Pyrethrin. Sprays must be applied before the larvae hatch out and enter the leaf. Once inside, the only effective control is a leaf systemic insecticide. An alternative is to cut off the affected foliage; columbine and some plants affected by leafminers generally grow back healthy.*

Mealybugs. Mealybugs are one-eighth of an inch long and have a mealy, waxy covering. They lay eggs on the undersides of leaves and affect stems, roots, and foliage. Like aphids, they exude honeydew. The presence of sooty mold is an indicator that mealybugs, aphids, or soft scale are present. Mealybugs affect a wide range of hosts, including ferns, ficus, and African violets. **Controls:** *Lady beetles are a predator control and are available from biological companies. Spraying with horticultural soaps and ultra-fine horticultural oils controls mealybugs.*

Scales. Soft and hard scales have piercing, sucking mouthparts. The crawler stage is mobile.

After that the insect becomes stationary. Hard scales resemble tiny oyster shells and occur in great numbers. Soft scales are larger, more cup-shaped, and are especially destructive to house-plants. **Controls:** *Ultra-fine horticulture oils and horticultural soaps are effective controls.*

Whiteflies. These tiny whiteflies erupt into clouds of insects when the plant is touched, and then settle back. Their piercing, sucking mouthparts stunt and yellow the host plant. Sooty mold may follow. **Controls:** *The most effective control is to spray four times with an insecticide, five to seven days apart. Ultra-fine horticultural oil or insecticidal soaps may be used. Pyrethrin and malathion are also effective. The undersides are where whiteflies cling, so be sure to spray there most thoroughly. Insecticidal soap can handle small infestations. For persistent infestations, use insecticides based on seeds of the Neem tree.*

BOTANICAL AND NATURAL INSECT PEST AND DISEASE CONTROLS

Copper. Use fungicidal formulations. **Use to control:** *Blackspot, peach leaf curl, powdery mildew, rusts, and bacterial diseases such as fire blight, bacterial leaf spots, and wilt.*

Crab Shells. Crab shells (Chitin) is the crushed shells of crabs, crab meal. A source of nitrogen must be provided, such as dried blood or cotton-seed meal. **Use to control:** *Harmful nematodes. Apply crab meal at the rate of 5 pounds per 100 square feet.*

Diatomaceous earth. This is a powdery substance mined from fossilized silica shells. Physical contact destroys soft-bodied insects. Rain and high humidity may render it less ineffective. **Use to control:** *Ants, aphids, caterpillars, cockroaches, leafhoppers, slugs, snails, and thrips.*

Horticultural oils. These are botanical oils sprayed on eggs and immature stages of insects to smother them. **Use to control:** *Woolly adelgids (which do so much damage to Canadian hem-locks), aphids, cankerworms, leafhoppers, leaf rollers, mealybugs, mites, psylids, scale, tent caterpillars, webworms.* **Note:** *Spraying with horticultural oils can temporarily remove the blue in blue hostas and Colorado blue spruce. Never spray during droughts, and always water deeply before applying.*

Horticultural soaps. This control dates back to the late 1800s. **Use to control:** *Aphids, fruit flies, fungus gnats, lacebugs, leafhoppers, mealybugs, phyllids, scale crawlers, scale, spittle bug, thrips, whiteflies.* **Note:** *Water deeply before using. Do not use on plants under stress, especially drought. Do not use plants you have just set out, nor on delicate plants such as ferns and lantana.*

Neem. Derivatives of various parts of the Neem tree, *Azadirachta indica,* Neem is a broad-spectrum repellent, growth regulator, feeding inhibitor, contact insect poison, and is partial systemic. The most effective formulation is made from the extract of Neem seeds. It also controls certain diseases. **Use to control:** *Aphids, leafminers, gypsy moths, loopers, mealybugs, thrips, mites, crickets, mosquitoes, face flies, flea beetles.*

Pyrethrin. This is an extract of the flowers of *Chrysanthemum cinerariifolium.* **Use to control:** *Many piercing, sucking and chewing insects, such as ants, aphids, beetles, cockroaches, coddling moths, grasshoppers, Japanese beetles, leafhoppers, leafminers, loopers, Mexican bean and potato beetles, spider mites, stink bugs, ticks, thrips, weevils, whiteflies.*

Rotenone. Rotenone is a very old botanical pesticide, first used in the mid-1800s. It is prepared from the roots of the tropical plant *Lonchocarpus.* **Use to control:** *Aphids, beetles, caterpillars, Colorado potato beetle, thrips.*

Ryania. This is a powdered extract from the roots and stems of the South American shrub, *Ryania speciosa. Use to control: Caterpillars, corn earworms, European corn borer, leaf beetles, thrip.*

Sabadilla. Sabadilla is made from the grinding of the seeds of the *Sabadilla* plant. **Use to control:** *True bugs, caterpillars, Mexican bean beetle thrips.*

Sulfur. This is a mined mineral. **Use to control:** *Blackspot, leaf spot, mites, powdery mildew, rusts, and other plant diseases.*

Ultra-fine horticultural oils. These are dense refined oils, some based on petroleum and others on vegetables such as cottonseed and soybeans. Sprayed on, they smother insects in the egg and immature stages, and they control certain diseases. **Use to control:** *Blackspot, mildew, and certain insects including adelgids, aphids, leafhoppers, mealybugs, mites, scale.* **Note:** *A Cornell University control for mildew is to spray with a solution consisting of 1 tablespoon of ultrafine oil and 1 tablespoon of baking soda (soda bicarbonate) dissolved in 1 gallon of water.*

CHEMICAL CONTROLS FOR COMMON INSECT PESTS AND DISEASES

Carbaryl (Sevin). **Use to control:** *Beetles, caterpillars, Japanese beetles, mealybug, thrip.*

Mancozeb, manzate. Use to control: *Fungal diseases (especially rust on asters and hollyhocks), anthracnose, botrytis blight.*

Sevin (see Carbaryl).

Malathion. Use to control: *Aphids, beetles, leafhopper, leafminer, mealybug, spider mites, thrips, whitefly.*

Parzate (see Mancozeb, Manzate).

Permethrin. Use to control: *A wide range of insects, including whitefly.*

COMMON NON-INSECT PESTS AND CONTROLS

Nematodes. Nematodes are microscopic wormlike creatures. Some feed on roots, others feed on foliage. Endoparasitic nematodes enter the root, causing galls. An example is root-knot nematode. Others are cyst nematodes, such as the golden nematode of potatoes. There are ecto-parasitic forms that feed on the outside of the roots. Symptoms are a yellowing and stunting of the plant, lack of vigor, and wilting during hot weather. **Controls:** *Growing orange French marigolds for three months and tilling into the soil before planting has been effective. Also effective is the application of ground crab shells, which are commercially available.*

Spider mites. Spider mites are more closely related to spiders than to insects. So tiny you need a magnifying glass to see them, spider mites can attack all parts of a plant but are most prevalent under the leaf. These piercing, sucking pests cause a yellowing of the plant, and finally result in a rusty and sometimes silvery look to the leaf. For a positive identification shake the plant onto a white pad, and if little dots move on the paper, you have spider mites. Roses, indoor plants in hot dry conditions, and evergreens in dry airless corners, are especially susceptible. **Control:** *Hosing the plant down regularly discourages spider mite activity. Insecticidal soaps, ultrafine horticultural oils, and miticides can be used.*

Slugs and snails. These plant pests feed on lush foliage, leaving holes in the leaf. Irregular shiny, slimy trails are a telltale sign. Complete defoliation can occur on some lush-leaved annuals and perennials, hostas, for example. **Control:** *Diatomaceous earth, iron phosphate (Sluggo), slug and snail bait, beer in shallow aluminum plates or tuna fish cans, or commercially available traps.*

COMMON DISEASES AND CONTROLS

Bacterial disease. Bacteria is not a fungus, and although the symptoms may be similar, in order to control the causative agent, you must use a bacteriacide such as copper fungicide. **Controls:** *Copper fungicide, Kocide 101, Agri-Strep.*

Botrytis grey mold (Botrytis Blight). Symptoms are a grayish-to-brown powdery covering on

buds, leaves, and stems. This disease affects many perennials, including peonies. **Controls:** *Sulfur, Daconil 2728.*

Foliar diseases. Symptoms are leaf spots and blight on perennials that can be bacterial or fungal in origin. **Controls:** *Sulfur, copper fungicides, Daconil, Mancozeb, Immunox.*

Leaf spots. Most gardeners encounter this as blackspot. They are caused by bacterial or fungal agents. Examples are blackspot of roses and leaf spot on tall bearded iris. **Controls:** *Copper fungicide, Daconil, horticultural oil, Immunox, sulfur.*

Powdery mildew. This fungus covers buds, stems, and leaves with a white-gray powdery substance. High humidity increases the severity of powdery mildew. If you water often with underground sprinkling systems you may find this disease difficult to control. Powdery mildew is commonly found on asters, monarda, and phlox. **Controls:** *When buying new plants, go for those advertised as mildew resistant. Roses, phlox, lilacs, and many other garden favorites are susceptible. Wide spacing for good air circulation and air movement helps. Apply sulfur, ultrafine horticultural oil, copper fungicide, Immunox, Bayleton.*

Root and stem rot. Symptoms are the wilting and rapid death of the plant. The plant crown or rhizome may be wet or slimy. The cause may be bacterial or fungal. **Controls:** *For fungal causes, use Terrachlor or Mancozeb. For bacterial causes, use copper fungicides, Kocide 101, Agri-Strep.*

Rust disease. This form of fungus may be a single or double host disease. The first indication is yellow or pale spots on the upper surface of the leaf, with powdery orange spores visible on the bottom of the leaf. Asters, chrysanthemums, lily-of-the-valley, and hollyhocks are common hosts. **Controls:** *Fungicidal controls labeled for rust, sulfur, copper fungicide, Daconil, Immunox, Mancozeb.*

Viral diseases. These diseases are not fungal or bacterial in origin, but in fact are minute particles of protein and genetic material seen only with an electron microscope. Piercing sucking insects commonly spread viral diseases. Viral diseases may be difficult to diagnose and have no known control. Symptoms are a mottling or mosaic discoloration of the leaf or ring spots. **Control:** *No known control except removing the infected plant.*

COMMON ANIMAL PESTS AND CONTROLS

Deer. The most destructive of all the wild creatures that visit our gardens is the deer. New repellents for deer come on the market every season, but at this writing we know of none that are *permanent.*

When deer really want what you've got, they come on in and get it in spite of flashing lights, jets of water, ultra sound devices, evil smelling egg and protein sprays, predator odors, bitter Bitrex, hot pepper wax, garlic, and systemic repellants. Deer-Off® can be used on fruits and vegetables as well as flowers, trees, and shrubs. Tested by Rutgers University, it lasted for up to three months. Some nurseries successfully protect clients' plants with their own deterrent spray versions. Some gardeners have luck by hanging old pantyhose containing human or canine hair around the property. Most deterrents of this type fail to keep deer away once they get used to it. Here are approaches that have some effect:

• *Don't invite deer by planting Class A fatal attractions:* Apple or pear trees. If you have fruit trees, be sure to harvest the fruits daily before the deer get to them. Arborvitae, rhododendrons, and broadleaved evergreens are winter favorites, along with shrub althea and hydrangeas. Hostas and other big, lush leaved plants, phlox, 'Autumn Joy' and other *Sedum spectabile* varieties, tomatoes, peas, beans, and other leafy vegetables, are summer favorites. Roses, raspberries, and other members of the *Rosa* family—deer relish them all.

• *Protect small endangered plantings,* beds of hostas and daylilies for example, by screening them with enclosures of deer fencing or chicken-wire supported by wooden or metal stakes. Deer generally avoid small, enclosed spaces that could be traps. Protect large plantings with bird netting.

• *Enclose your property or gardens with a single strand of electric wire 30 inches high* with a stake every 20 feet and baited with peanut butter can be effective. Close the peanut butter into a square of tinfoil, and crimp it on to the wire every 20 feet. The deer nibble the peanut butter and, without being really hurt, learn to avoid the fence.

• *Enclose your property with a deer fence 8 to 10 feet high* supported by a post every 40 feet. This high tensile steel fencing is unobtrusive.

• *Train a dog* to run deer off your property.

• *Discourage visits by positioning a variety of alarming and distasteful smells* where deer customarily enter your grounds, and change the smells often. For example, hang at the height of a deer's nose tubes of crushed garlic, or predator urine, or Irish Spring or lavender soap, or human hair dampened with odorous lotions. Place a different scent at each entry point. And, this is crucial, change each deterrent every four to six weeks while the weather is warm enough to volatilize scents.

• *For winter, wrap rhododendrons, arborvitae, and other species in burlap or chicken-wire.*

• *Choose new plants from those on the list of deer-resistant plants* at André and Mark Viette's site, **www.inthegardenradio.com.**

Moles and Voles. You think "moles" when you see tunnels heaving the lawn, and blame them when perennials disappear and bulbs move around. But they are innocent. Moles eat bugs, grubs, and worms only. The culprits are voles, *Nicrotus* species. Often called pine or meadow mice, these small rodents are reddish-brown to gray, 2 to 4 inches long, and have short tails, blunt faces, and tiny eyes and ears. They live in extensive tunnel systems usually less than a foot deep with entrances an inch or two across.

Protecting the plant is easier than getting rid of voles. They dislike tunneling through coarse mate-

rial. André keeps them away by planting with VoleBloc or PermaTill, which are bits of non-toxic, light, long-lasting aggregates like pea gravel with jagged edges. The stuff promotes rooting.

Established plantings: Dig a 4-inch-wide, 12-inch-deep moat around the drip line of perennials under attack, fill it with VoleBloc, and mulch with VoleBloc.

New plantings: Prepare a planting hole 2 inches deeper than the rootball(s), and layer in 2 inches of VoleBloc. Set the rootball in place, and backfill with VoleBloc. Mulch with more VoleBloc.

If vole damage appears in winter, bait the main area around the plants with a rodenticide, and pull the mulch apart, spray the crown lightly with a repellent, and put the mulch back in place.

Bears. Where bears may be a problem, they may come to bird and hummingbird feeders. They harvest berries and sometimes your pets. If there are bear sightings near you, take in bird feeders and other attractions.

Birds. Our feathered friends are beautiful, lovable, inspiring, and useful in that they eat insects, some good and some bad. They also eat berries and fruit, your kind as well as theirs; seeds you give them and seeds you don't; and sunflowers.

• A bird mesh cover is the almost only way to protect fruit birds want to eat.

• Cover ponds with bird netting to keep the fish safe from herons and other expert fishermen.

Rabbits, woodchucks, raccoons, and other rodents.

• Try chemical fungicide formulations such as Thiram (Arasan) and hot pepper wax.

• Fence gardens with 6 feet high chicken-wire that starts 24 inches underground. If you have woodchucks to deal with, leave the chicken-wire loose and floppy, not stiff enough to climb. Keeping raccoons out of the vegetable garden requires enclosing your garden overhead as well; keeping them from fishing in your water garden may require covering the pond with netting.

PUBLIC GARDENS & RESOURCES

ROSE GARDENS

Delaware

Hagley Museum and Library
298 Buck Road East
P. O. Box 3630
Wilmington, Delaware 19807
Phone: 302 658 2400

District of Columbia

Dumbarton Oaks
1703 32nd Street NW
Washington, D. C. 20052
Phone: 202 339 6401

The George Washington University
2033 G Street NW and 730 21st Street
Washington, D. C. 20052
Phone: 202 994 4949

United States Botanic Garden
245 First Street SW
Washington, D. C. 20052
Phone: 202 225 8333

Maryland

Brookside Botanical Gardens Rose Garden
1500 Glenallen Avenue
Wheaton, Maryland 20902
Phone: 301 495 2503

Ladew Topiary Gardens
3535 Jarrettsville Pike
Monkton, Maryland 21111
Phone: 410 557 9466

Maryland Rose Society Heritage Rose Garden
The Clyburn Arboretum
4915 Greenspring Avenue
Baltimore, Maryland 21209
Phone: 410 396 0180

William Paca Garden
1 Martin Street
Annapolis, Maryland 21401
Phone: 410 263 5553

Virginia

Bon Air Memorial Rose Garden
Bon Air Park
850 North Lexington Street
Arlington, Virginia 22205
Phone: 703 228 6525

Confederate Cemetery
401 Taylor Street
Lynchburg, Virginia 24501
Phone: 434 847 1465

Norfolk Botanical Garden Bicentennial
   Rose Garden
6700 Azalea Garden Road
Norfolk, Virginia 23519-5337

River Farm—American Horticulture Society
7931 E. Boulevard Drive
Alexandria, Virginia 22308
Phone: 703 768 5700 or 1 800 777 7931

Woodlawn Plantation
9000 Richland Highway,
Alexandria, VA 22309
Phone: 703 780 4000

PUBLIC GARDENS

Delaware

Hagley Museum's E. I. Du Pont Restored Garden
298 Buck Road East
P. O. Box 3630
Wilmington, Delaware 19807
Phone: 302 658 2400

Mount Cuba Center for the Study of
   Piedmont Flora
Barley Hill Road
Greenville, DE 19807
Phone: 302 239 4244

Nemours Mansion and Gardens
1600 Rockland Road
Wilmington, DE 19803
Phone: 302 651 6912

District of Columbia

Bishop's Garden
Washington National Cathedral
Massachusetts & Wisconsin Avenues, NW
Washington, DC 20016
Phone: 202 537 2937

Dumbarton Oaks
1703 32nd Street
Washington, DC 20007
Phone: 202 339 6401

PUBLIC GARDENS & RESOURCES

Hillwood Museum & Gardens
  4155 Linnean Avenue, NW
  Washington, DC 20008
  Phone: 1 877 HILLWOOD
United States Botanic Garden and Conservatory
  245 First Street SW
  Washington, DC 20024
  Phone: 202 225 8333
United States National Arboretum
  3501 New York Avenue, NE
  Washington, DC 20002
  Phone: 202 245 2726
The George Washington University
  2033 G Street and 730 21st Street NW
  Washington, D. C. 20052
  Phone: 202 994 4949

Maryland
  Clyburn Wildflower Preserve and
    Garden Center
  4915 Greenspring Avenue
  Baltimore, MD 21209
  Phone: 410 396 0180
  Brookside Gardens
  1500 Glenallan Avenue
  Wheaton, MD 20920
  Phone: 301 949 8230
  Ladew Topiary Gardens
  3535 Jarretsville Pike
  Monkton, MD 21111
  Phone: 410 557 9570
  McCrillis Gardens
  6910 Greentree Road
  Bethesda, MD 20817
  Phone: 301 365 5728
  William Paca Garden
  186 Prince George Street
  Annapolis, MD 21401
  Phone: 410 263 5553

Virginia
  André Viette Farm & Nursery
  994 Long Meadow Road
  P O Box 1109
  Fishersville, VA 22939
  Phone: 800 575 5538
  www.inthegardenradio.com
  Ashcroft Hall
  4305 Sulgrave Road
  Richmond, VA 23221
  Phone: 804 353 4241

Colonial Williamsburg Foundation
  PO Box C, Horticulture Department
  Williamsburg, VA 23187
  Phone: 804 229 1000
Community Arboretum at Virginia Western
    Community College
  Colonial Avenue
  Roanoke, VA 24014
  www.vw.vccs.edu/arboretum
Green Spring Gardens Park
  4603 Green Spring Road
  Alexandria, VA 22312
  Phone: 703 642 5173
Gunston Hall
  10708 Gunston Road
  Lorton, VA 22079
  Phone: 703 550 9220
Kenmore
  1201 Washington Avenue
  Fredericksburg, VA 22401
  Phone: 540 373 3381
Lewis Ginter Botanical Garden
  1800 Lakeside Avenue
  Richmond, VA 23228-4700
  Phone: 804 262 9887
Maymont
  1700 Hampton Street
  Richmond, VA 23220
  Phone: 804 358 7166
Monticello
  Thomas Jefferson Foundation
  PO VA 53
  Charlottesville, VA 22902
  Phone: 804 984 9822
Montpelier Gardens
  James Madison's Home
  11407 Constitution Highway
  Montpelier Station, VA 22957
  Phone: 540 672 2728
Mount Vernon Estate & Gardens
  South End of George Washington
    Memorial Parkway
  Mount Vernon, VA 22121
  Phone: 703 780 2000
Norfolk Botanical Garden
  Airport Road off of Azalea Garden Rd
  Norfolk, VA 23518
  Phone: 804 441 5830
Oatlands Plantation
  200850 Oatlands Plantation Ln. US 15
  Leesburg, VA 20175
  Phone: 703 777 3174

PUBLIC GARDENS & RESOURCES

River Farm
American Horticultural Society
7931 East Boulevard Drive
Alexandria, VA 22308
Phone: 703 768 5700

Virginia House
4301 Sulgrave Road
Richmond, VA 23221
Phone: 804 353 4251

ROSE ORGANIZATIONS
American Rose Society
P. O. Box 30000
Shreveport, Louisiana 71130-0030
Phone: 318 938 5402
For local rose societies
web site: www.ars.org
E-mail: ara@ara-hq.org
District Rose Societies
Colonial District
Delaware, Maryland, Virginia,
   Washington, D. C.
Nita Bowen
2703 Pony Farm Court
Oakton, VA 22124

MAIL-ORDER SOURCES for Natural Controls for Pests and Diseases
Earlee, Inc.
2002 Highway 62
Jeffersin, IN 47130
Phone: 812 282 9134

Gardens Alive!
5100 Schenley Place
Lawrenceburg, IN 47025
Phone: 513 656 1482

Natural Gardening Company
217 San Anselmo Avenue
San Anselmo, CA 94960
Phone: 707 766 9303

Nature's Control
PO Box 35
Medford, OR 97501
Phone: 503 899 8318

Peaceful Valley Farm Supply
PO Box 2209
Grass Valley, CA 95945
Phone: 916 272 4769

Safer, Inc.
9959 Valley View Road
Eden Prairie, MN 55344
Phone: 800 423 7544

NURSERIES with Good Plant Selections
Behnke Nurseries
11300 Baltimore Avenue
Beltsville, MD 20705
Phone: 301 937 1100

Homestead Gardens
Route 214
743 West Central Avenue
Davidsonville, MD 21035
Phone: 800 300 5631

Merrifield Garden Center
12100 Lee Highway
Fairfax, VA 22030
Phone: 703 968 9600

Merrifield Garden Center
8132 Lee Highway
Merrifield, VA 22116
Phone: 703 560 6222

MAIL-ORDER SOURCES for Perennials, Daylilies, Peonies, Irises, Hostas, and Grasses
André Viette Farm & Nursery
994 Long Meadow Road
P O Box 1109
Fishersville, VA 22939
Phone: 800 575 5538

Bluestone Perennials
7211 Middle Ridge Road
Madison, OH 44057
Phone: 800 852 5243

Borbeleta Gardens
15974 Canby Avenue
Faribault, MN 55021
Phone: 507 334 2807

Caprice Farm Nursery
10944 Mill Greek Road SE
Aumsville, OR 97325
Phone: 503 749 1397

Kuk's Forest Nursery
10174 Barr Road
Brecksville, OH 44141-3302
Phone: 216 546 2675

Kurt Bluemel Inc.
22740 Greene Lane
Baldwin, MD 21013
Phone: 800 248 7584

Mellinger's Inc.
2310 W South Range Road
North Lima, OH 44452-9731
Phone: 800 321 7444

PUBLIC GARDENS & RESOURCES

Milaeger's Gardens
4838 Douglas Avenue
Racine, WI 53402-2498
Phone: 800 669 1229

Plant Delights Nursery Inc.
9241 Sauls Road
Raleigh, NC 27603
Phone: 919 772 4794

Prairie Nursery—Wild Flowers
P O Box 306
Westfield, WI 53964
Phone: 800 476 9453

Roslyn Nursery
21 1 Burrs Lane
Dix Hills, NY 11746
Phone: 516 643 9347

The Fragrant Path
P O Box 328
Fort Calhoun, NE 68023

Thomas Jefferson Center for Historic Plants
RD Box 316
Charlottesville, VA 22092
Phone: 800 247 7333

K. Van Bourgondien & Sons
245 Route 109, RD. Box 1 000
Babylon, NY 11702-9004
Phone: 800 552 9916

White Flower Farm
P O Box 50
Litchfield, CT 06759-0050
Phone: 800 503 9624

MAIL-ORDER SOURCES for Flowers, Annuals, Perennials, Wildflowers, Vegetables, Herbs, Rare and Antique Seeds

W. Atlee Burpee & Co.
300 Park Avenue
Warminster, PA 18991
Phone: 800 888 1447

Franklin Hill Garden Seeds
2430 Rochester Road
Sewickley, PA 15143-8667
Phone: 412 367 6202

Gurney's Seed & Nursery Co
110 Capital Street
Yankton, SD 57079
Phone: 605 665 1930

Harris Seeds
60 Saginaw Drive
PO Box 22960
Rochester, NY 14692-2960
Phone: 716 442 0410

Johnny's Selected Seeds
955 Benton Avenue
Winslow, ME 04901-2601
Phone: 207 861 3900

Nichols Garden Nursery
1190 N. Pacific Highway
Albany, OR 97321
Phone: 541 928 9280

Park Seed
1 Parkton Avenue
Greenwood, SC 29647
Phone: 800 845 3369

Pinetree Garden Seeds
P O Box 300
New Gloucester, ME 04260
Phone: 207 926 3400

Primrose Path
921 Scottsdale-Dawson Road
Scottsdale, PA 15683

Seeds of Change Heirloom Seeds
P O Box 15700
Santa Fe, NM 87506
Phone: 888 762 7333

Seeds of Distinction
P O Box 86
Toronto, Canada M9C 4V2
Phone: 416 255 3060

Select Seeds
180 Stickney Hill Road
Union, CT 06076
Phone: 860 684 9310

Seymour's Selected Seeds
PO Box 1346
Sussex, VA 23884-0346
Phone: 803 663 3084

Shepherd's Garden Seeds
30 Irene Street
Torrington, CT 06790
Phone: 800 482 3638

R H Shumway Seedsman
P O Box 1
Graniteville, SC 29829
Phone: 803 663 9771

Southern Exposure Seed Exchange
PO Box 460
Mineral, VA 23117
Phone: 540 894 9480

Stokes Seeds Inc.
P O Box 548
Buffalo, NY 14240
Phone: 800 263 7233

PUBLIC GARDENS & RESOURCES

Thompson & Morgan Inc.
P O Box 1308
Jackson, NJ 08527
Phone: 800 274 7333

Wildseed Farms
P O Box 3000
Fredericksburg, TX 78624
Phone: 800 848 0078

MAIL-ORDER SOURCES for Tender Perennials, Annuals, Tropicals, Houseplants, Bromeliads, Bougainvilleas, Cactus, Orchids, Pineapples, Begonias, Gesneriads, and African Violets

Banana Tree, Inc.
715 Northampton Street
Easton, PA 18042
Phone: 610 253 9589

Davidson-Wilson Greenhouse, Inc.
RR2, Box 168
Crawfordsville, IN 47933
Phone: 317 364 0556

Glasshouse Works
Church Street
Stewart, OH 45778
Phone: 614 662 2142

Going Bananas
24401 SW 197 Avenue
Homestead, FL 33031
Phone: 305 247 0397

Good Scents
RR2, P O Box 168
Crawfordsville, IN 47933
Phone: 765 364 0556

Kartuz Greenhouse
P O Box 790
Vista, CA 92085
Phone: 760 941 3613

Lauray of Salisbury
493 Undermountain Road, RT 41
Salisbury, CT 06068
Phone: 860 435 2263

Logee's Greenhouse, Ltd
141 North Street
Danielson, CT 06239
Phone: 860 774 8038

Lyndon Lyon Greenhouse, Inc.
P O Box 249
Dolgeville, NY 13329
Phone: 315 429 8291

Stokes Tropicals
P O Box 9868
New Iberia, LA 70562
Phone: 800 624 9706

Sunshine State Tropcials
6329 Alaska Avenue
New Port Richey, FL 34653
Phone: 813 841 9618

MAIL-ORDER SOURCES for Roses

Chamblee's Rose Nursery
10926 US Highway 69 North
Tyler, TX 75706-8742
Phone: 800 256 7673

David Austin Roses Limited
15059 Highway 64 West
Tyler, TX 75704
Phone: 800 328 8893

Edmund's Roses
6235 SW Kahle Road
Wilsonville, OR 97070-9727
Phone: 888 481 7673

Hardy Roses for the North
Box 2048
Grand Forks, BC Canada VOH 1HO
Phone: 604 442 8442

Heirloom Old Garden Roses
24062 NE Riverside Drive
St Paul, OR 97137
Phone: 503 538 1576

High Country Roses
P O Box 148
Jensen, UT 84035-0148
Phone: 800 552 2082

Historical Roses
1657 W Jackson Street
Painesville, OH 44077
Phone: 216 357 7270

Jackson & Perkins Co.
1 Rose Lane
Medford, OR 97501-0702
Phone: 800 292 4769

Lowe's Own-Root Roses
6 Sheffield Road
Nashua, NH 03062
Phone: 603 888 2214

Meilland Star Roses
P O Box 249
Cutler, CA 93615
Phone: 800 457 1859

Nor'East Minature Roses, Inc.
P O Box 307
Rowley, MA 01969-0607
Phone: 800 426 6485

PUBLIC GARDENS & RESOURCES

The Antique Roses Emporium
  9300 Lueckemeyer Road
  Brenham, TX 77833
  Phone: 800 441 0002

MAIL-ORDER SOURCES for Trees, Shrubs, and Evergreens

Arborvillage Farm Nursery
  15604 County Road CC
  Holt, MO 64048
  Phone: 516 643 9347

Arrowhead Nursery
  5030 Watia Road
  Bryson City, NC 28713
  Phone: 440 466 2881

Camellia Forest Nursery
  125 Carolina Forest Road
  Chapel Hill, NC 27516
  Phone: 919 968 0504

Collector's Nursery
  16804 NE 102nd Avenue
  Battle Ground, WA 98604
  Phone: 706 356 8947

Fairweather Gardens
  P O Box 330
  Greenwich, NJ 08323
  Phone: 800 548 0111

Forest Farm
  990 Tetherow Road
  Williams, OR 97544
  Phone: 503 543 7474

Foxborough Nursery Inc.
  3611 Miller Road
  Street, MD 21154
  Phone: 360 574 3832

Girard Nurseries
  P O Box 428
  Geneva, OH 44041
  Phone: 919 967 5529

Greer Gardens
  1280 Goodpasture Island Road
  Eugene, OR 97401
  Phone: 609 451 6261

Porterhowse Farms
  41370 SE Thomas Road
  Sandy, OR 97055
  Phone: 409 826 6363

Roslyn Nursery
  211 Burrs Lane
  Dix Hills, NY 11746
  Phone: 541 846 7269

Wayside Gardens
  1 Garden Lane
  Hodges, SC 29695
  Phone: 800 845 1124

MAIL-ORDER SOURCES for Water Plants and Ponds

Lilypons Water Gardens
  6800 Lilypons Road
  Buckeystown, MD 21717
  Phone: 800 999 5459

Gilberg Farms
  2172 Highway O
  Robertsville, MO 63072
  Phone: 636 451 2530

Springdale Water Gardens
  P O Box 546
  Greenville, VA 24440-0546
  Phone: 800 420 5459

BIBLIOGRAPHY

A Garden of Herbs, Eleanor Sinclair Rohde

A-Z of Annuals, Biennials & Bulbs, Reader's Digest

The American Horticultural Society A - Z Encyclopedia of Garden Plants, Christopher Bricknell and Judith D. Zuk

The American Horticultural Society Flower Finder, Jacqueline Hériteau and André Viette

America's Garden Book, Brooklyn Botanic Garden, Howard S. Irwin

André Viette Gardening Guide, Viette Staff

Annuals 1001 Gardening Questions Answered, Editors of GardenWay Publishing

Annuals & Bedding Plants, Nigel Colborn, Trafalgar Square Publishing

Annuals for the Connoisseur, A-Z Horticulture

Annuals, Sunset Publishing Corp.

Armitage's Manual of Annuals, Biennials, and Half-Hardy Perennials, Allan M. Armitage

Botanica, R. G. Turner, Jr.

The Brooklyn Botanical Garden: America's Landscaping Book, Louise and James Bush Brown and Howard Erwin

The Brooklyn Botanical Garden Illustrated Encyclopedia of Horticulture Volumes A-Z, Thomas H. Everett

Burpee, America Gardening Series, Annuals, Suzanne Fruitig Bales

Cathey Wilkinson Barash's Edible Flowers, Cathey Wilkinson Barash

Check List of Pyracantha Cultivars, Donald R. Egolf and Ann O. Andrick

The Complete Guide to Texas Lawn Care, Dr. William E. Knoop

Conifers for Your Garden, Adrian Bloom

Designing with Perennials, Pamela J. Harper

Discovering Annuals, Graham Rice, Timber Press

Diseases of Annuals and Perennials, A. R. Chase, Margery L. Daughtrey, Gary W. Simone

Eastern Butterflies, Peterson Field Guides

Easy Care Ground Covers, Donald Wyman

Encyclopedia of Organic Gardening, J. I. Rodale and Staff

The Exotic Garden, Designing with Tropical Plants in Almost Any Climate, Richard R. Iverson

Eyewitness Handbook, Herbs, Lesley Bremness

Eyewitness Handbook, Ornamental Grasses, Mary Hockenberry Meyer

Fern Growers Manual, Barbara Hoshizaki

Ferns And Fern Allies of Shenandoah National Park, Peter F. Mazeo

Ferns of Eastern Central States, Jesse M. Shaner

Ferns to Know And Grow, Gordon Foster

Field Guide to Ferns and Other Pteridophytes of Georgia, James Bruce and Lloyd Snyder

Field Guide to North American Trees, revised (Grolier)

For Your Garden Ornamental Grasses, Rick Darke

The Gardener's Guide to Growing Hardy Geraniums, Trevor Bath and Joy Jones

The Gardener's Guide to Growing Hellebores, Graham Rice and Elizabeth Strangman

The Gardener's Illustrated Encyclopedia of Trees and Shrubs, 2000 Varieties, Brian Davis

Gardening with Climbers, Christopher Grey-Wilson, Victoria Matthews

Gardening with Grasses, Michael King, Piet Oudolf

Gardening with Herbs for Flavor and Fragrance, Helen Morgenthau Fox

Gardening with Perennials Month by Month, Joseph Hudak

Garlic, Onions & Other Alliums, Ellen Spector Platt, Stackpole Books

Genus Hosta, W. George Schmid

Glorious Gardens, Jacqueline Hériteau

Good Housekeeping Illustrated Encyclopedia of Gardening, Hearst Publishing

Growing and Decorating with Grasses, Peter Loewer

Hardy Geraniums, Peter F. Yeo

The Hearst Garden, Annuals, Ted Marston, Editor

Heirloom Flowers, Tovah Martin and Diane Whealy

The Herb Society of America Encyclopedia of Herbs and Their Uses, Deni Brown

Herbaceous Perennial Plants, Allan M. Armitage

Herbaceous Perennials' Diseases and Insect Pests, Margery L. Daughtrey and Morey Semel

Herbaceous Perennials, Volume 2, Leo Jellito, Wilhelm Schacht

BIBLIOGRAPHY

Herbs And Things, Jeanne Rose's Herbal Herbs, Their Culture and Uses, Rosetta E. Clarkson

Hollies: The Genus Index, Fred C. Galle

Hortus Third, Staff of L. H. Bailey Hortorium, Cornell University

The Hosta Book, Paul Aden

Illustrated Encyclopedia of Conifers, Two Volumes, D. M. van Gelderen and J. R. P. van Hoey Smith

Illustrated Encyclopedia Houseplant Identifier, Peter McHoy

Indoor Greenhouse Plants, Volumes 1 & 2, Roger Phillips, Martyn Rix

Index Hortensis, Volume 1 Perennials, including Ground Covers and Ferns, Piers Threhane

Index of Common Garden Plants, Mark Griffiths, RHS

Japanese Iris, Currier McEwen

Jekka's Culinary Herbs, Jekka McVicar

Landscape Plants of the Southeast, R. Gordon Halfacre, Anne R. Shawcroft

Landscape Plants: Their Identification, Culture and Use, Ferrell M. Bridwell

Lawns: Your Guide to a Beautiful Lawn, Nick Christians with Ashton Ritchie

Manual of Cultivated Conifers, P. Den Ouden, Dr. B. K. Boom

The Manual of Woody Landscape Plants, Michael A. Dirr

Michigan Gardener's Guide, Tim Boland, Laura Coit, Marty Hair, Cool Springs Press

Mid-Atlantic Gardener's Guide, André and Mark Viette with Jacqueline Hériteau, Cool Springs Press

Morning Glories and Moonflowers, Anne Halpin

Naamlijist Van Vaste Planten, vander Laar, Fortgens, Hoffman and Jong

National Gardening Association Dictionary of Horticulture, The Philip Lief Group, Inc.

The National Arboretum Book of Outstanding Garden Plants, Jacqueline Hériteau, H. M. Cathey, and the Staff of the National Arboretum

The New York Botanical Garden Illustrated Encyclopedia of Horticulture, Thomas H. Everitt, Volume 10

North Carolina Gardener's Guide, Toby Bost, Cool Springs Press

Ornamental Grass Gardening, Reinardt, Reinardt, and Moskowitz

Ornamental Grasses: The Amber Wave, Carol Ottesen

Ortho's Complete Guide to Vegetables, Jacqueline Hériteau

Pennsylvania Gardener's Guide, Liz Ball, Cool Springs Press

Peonies, Allan Rogers

Perennial Garden Plants, Graham Stuart Thomas

Perennial Ground Covers, David S. MacKenzie, Timber Press

Perennials for American Gardens, Ruth Rogers Clausen and Nicolas Ekstrom

Plants and Their Names, A Concise Dictionary, Roger Hyam and Richard Pankhurst

The Plant Finders Guide to Tender Perennials, Ian Cooke

Plants That Merit Attention, Volume 1, Trees, Janet M. Poor

Poppies, Christopher Grey-Wilson

The Pruning of Trees, Shrubs and Conifers, George E. Brown

Rhododendrons of the World, David G. Leach

Rodale's All-New Encyclopedia of Organic Gardening, Rodale Press

Rose Gardening, Elvin McDonald, Meredith Books

Shrubs and Vines for American Gardens, Donald Wyman

Siberian Iris, Currier McEwen

Southern Living, Annuals and Perennials, Lois Trigg Chaplin, Editor

Tender Perennials, Ian Coors

Tennessee Gardener's Guide, Judy Lowe, Cool Springs Press

Thyme on My Hands, Eric Grissel

Timber Press Dictionary of Plant Names, Allen J. Coombes

The Time-Life Complete Gardener: Perennials, André Viette, Stephen Still

The TriState Gardener's Guide, Ralph Snodsmith

Tropical Flowering Plants, Kristen Albrecht Llamas

Tropical Gardening, Fairchild Tropical Garden

Tropicals, Gordon Covetright

The Vegetable Gardener's Bible, Edward C. Smith, Storey Books

Virginia Ferns & Fern Allies, A. B. Massey

Water Gardens, Charles Thomas and Jacqueline Hériteau

The Well-Tended Perennial Garden, Planting & Pruning Techniques, Tracy DiSabato-Aust

Wyman's Gardening Encyclopedia, Donald Wyman

The Year in Trees, Timber Press

BOTANICAL INDEX

BOTANICAL INDEX

COMMON NAME INDEX

INDEX

INDEX

INDEX

INDEX

INDEX

INDEX

SCARLET HILTIBIDAL

ANXIOUS

FIGHTING ANXIETY WITH
THE WORD OF GOD

Lifeway Press®
Nashville, Tennessee

Published by Lifeway Press® • © 2021 Scarlet Hiltibidal
Reprinted September 2021

ISBN: 978-1-0877-3386-9
Item: 005829921
Dewey decimal classification: 152.4
Subject heading: FEAR / ANXIETY / PEACE

To order additional copies of this resource, write Lifeway Resources Customer Service; One Lifeway Plaza; Nashville, TN, 37234-0113; FAX order to 615.251.5933; call toll-free 800.458.2772; email orderentry@lifeway.com; or order online at lifeway.com.

Printed in the United States of America

Lifeway Resources
One Lifeway Plaza
Nashville, TN 37234-0152

EDITORIAL TEAM, LIFEWAY WOMEN BIBLE STUDIES

Becky Loyd
Director, Lifeway Women

Tina Boesch
Manager, Lifeway Women Bible Studies

Sarah Doss
Team Leader, Lifeway Women Bible Studies

Sarah Doss
Content Editor

Erin Franklin
Production Editor

Lauren Ervin
Graphic Designer

TABLE OF CONTENTS

DEDICATION

For Kaye Geiger, who led me through Bible studies on her living room floor, who discipled me without me knowing it by letting me come through the unlocked garage door, and who helped me laugh and cry and pray and learn.

ABOUT THE AUTHOR

Scarlet Hiltibidal is the author of *Afraid of All the Things* and *He Numbered the Pores on My Face*. She writes regular columns for *ParentLife Magazine* and devotionals for *She Reads Truth* and enjoys speaking to women around the country about the freedom and rest available in Jesus. Scarlet has a degree in biblical counseling and taught elementary school before she started writing. She and her husband live in Southern California where she loves signing with her three daughters, eating nachos by herself, writing for her friends, and studying stand-up comedy with a passion that should be reserved for more important pursuits.

Session
One

INTRODUCTION—
ANXIOUS TO BE HERE

I HAVE TOLD YOU
THESE THINGS SO THAT
**IN ME YOU MAY HAVE
PEACE.** YOU WILL HAVE
SUFFERING IN THIS WORLD.
BE COURAGEOUS! **I HAVE
CONQUERED THE WORLD.**

John 16:33

INTRODUCTION

We live in a broken, sad, scary place. There is plenty to be anxious about:

- dying;
- black holes;
- cancer;
- the fact that our phones have cameras on them that just sort of turn on sometimes;
- hurricanes;
- failing as a mom/friend/wife/employee/intermittent faster.

And the world is full of insufficient solutions for our anxiety:

- food;
- clothes;
- friends;
- medicine;
- hobbies;
- achievements;
- _____.

Here's the thing. Nothing really works every-moment-all-the-time-perfectly-and-forever, right? Have you gotten to that point? That point where the counselor's advice just doesn't seem to stop the mind spiral quickly enough? Your closet is full of clothes, but your heart is still full of worry? You get the promotion, win the award, and achieve the goal, but instead of the peace it promises, you only find more fears? The bottom of the queso cup appears alarmingly fast, and you're left asking yourself, maybe out loud, *AM I JUST MORE MESSED UP THAN EVERYONE ELSE?*

I've been in that place so many times. I've been a slave to my panic, planning and avoiding and doing everything I could to insulate myself from pain and discomfort. But none of it worked.

So I made my life quiet. Isolated. "Under control."

I thought that would make me peaceful.

It didn't. Isolation and "control" might produce a quieter life, but peace isn't a quiet life; peace is a quiet soul. Peace is the gift of Jesus through the work of Jesus that we can have no matter what is going on in our living rooms or our in-boxes or our Instagram® feeds. The loudest of lives can't overwhelm the quiet that comes from Christ.

True peace comes when we learn to hold God's Word up to what worries us. There, we learn we can't fix ourselves; we can't protect ourselves. Instead, the Bible tells us we can rest, knowing Jesus walked into the broken, sad, scary place to rescue us and love us. He is the One who fixes. His is the only protection that matters.

When we fear the Lord rather than fearing the brokenness in our world, we can take hold of the perfect peace that is only available in Him.

The peace we are looking for is found in the already finished work of Christ (more on that later) revealed to us over and over again in God's Word, through prayer, and with our Christian community. When those of us who live with tornado awareness and constant cancer concern see the power of Jesus in the pages of the Bible, we can say with certainty, "The LORD is on my side; I will not fear. What can man do to me?" (Ps. 118:6, ESV).

WHERE ARE WE HEADED?

In this study, we'll look at different people in the Bible and what we can learn from them about anxiety. We'll discover how to live in freedom by clinging to God's Word and God's gospel in community and in prayer. This Bible study book will challenge you to study Scripture as you fight your worries. It will help you put some spiritual disciplines in place that will aid you in keeping your eyes on the cross of Christ (even if you've just seen an article show up on your Facebook® feed about the real-life dangers of black holes).

HOW DO I USE THIS STUDY?

This study is meant to be used in a small group setting. You are welcome to do this book on your own, but the study is designed to be done with others. Fighting anxiety alone is a lot like fighting an army alone. Imagine walking onto a battlefield by yourself while surrounded by enemies with bigger guns and stronger muscles. Actually, don't imagine that. This is supposed to help you with your anxiety, not add to it.

Every person should have her own Bible study book, a Bible, a pen, and some snacks.[1] In this book, you'll find personal study that you can do individually and a memory verse that you can learn on your own (and review together as a group). Also, flip to pages 186–187 in the Appendix to keep some of my favorite on-the-go, anxiety-blasting Scriptures handy! Then, when you come together, you'll watch a video and discuss your answers from the week's work as a group. **You'll find detailed information for how to access the teaching videos that accompany this study on the card inserted in the back of your book.**

During the final session of this study, we'll dive into what God's Word says about fighting anxiety together—why it is important and how the body of Christ is so vital in our approach to combating the lies anxiety tells us. I hope this study helps you as you engage with Scripture personally, and I hope you can use your personal study and experiences to encourage the other people in your group when you meet together.

So grab your five nearest neighbors. Or text your twelve closest coworkers. As a last resort, call your grandma and your sister and the lady that knows your order at the local Starbucks® and ask them to join you.

1. Snacks are not required but strongly recommended.

You'll find detailed information for how to access the teaching videos that accompany this study on the card inserted in the back of your Bible study book.

WHAT IF I NEED MORE THAN A BIBLE STUDY?

This study probably won't fix all your problems.

In 2004, Tim Keller preached a sermon called, "The Wounded Spirit." It had such an effect on me that I shared a good portion of it in the book I wrote about my personal fight with fear—*Afraid of All the Things*.

The thing is, I've been on anxiety pills. I've sat across from Christian psychiatrists while they offered big-word diagnoses to explain my particular version of anxiety.

I lived years feeling shame and fear over my mental weaknesses. I thought if my friends really knew how I struggled in my mind, they would reject me.

This sermon changed that for me. In it, Keller talked about different sources that might contribute to our woundedness and weakness. He didn't say, "Why are you so messed up? Just pray more!" He said, ". . . you know what the biblical answer is? It's complicated."[2]

That's what I want you to hear from me as you walk into this study. Your brain is complicated. Your anxiety could be rooted in an existential issue, or maybe for you, it's mostly physical. Maybe you have a bum thyroid. (I had mine taken out last year and the hormonal imbalance it causes can absolutely lead to anxiety and depression.) Maybe, as Proverbs 28:1 says, you flee "when no one pursues" (ESV) because you are intentionally walking in wickedness. In that case, a pill or a therapy session won't fix you like repentance will.

That's the driving message of Keller's sermon. There are many contributing factors. We must rely on prayer and God's Word, but we can do so while knowing that we might be dealing with physical sources or sin sources or emotional sources or existential (the BIG questions, like *What is life?*) sources. It's important to recognize these things as you fight your personal battle in your own personal way.

This study will not replace thyroid hormone medication or any other prescribed and necessary medication or weekly meetings with a Christian counselor or taking care of your health and well-being. Pursuing those outside resources, if and when needed, is wise and wonderful. Rather, this study is designed to help you, wherever you're at and whyever you're at it, to pursue Jesus in His Word, give you a better understanding of who He is, and learn how to set your mind on the things above (see Col. 3:2) and how to live your life consumed by the ultimate peace and joy of walking with Christ. If you find yourself needing a bit more support than this study offers, I encourage you to reach out to your local church or some trusted friends. I can look back on so many times in my own life that I needed help, and my Christian community, friends, and counselors definitely held me together during those times.

WILL IT ALWAYS BE THIS WAY?

About that "ultimate peace." I've never written from the stance of "I've overcome anxiety and so can you." If you're looking for ten easy steps, you won't find that here. In our broken world, it's a constant temptation to find a final fix. We hope to check the box and expect smooth sailing from then on. We will absolutely have smooth sailing someday. Just not in this world. The seas of this world have hurricanes. But the Lord has reminded me again and again, through His Word and His Spirit, that ultimate peace is our hope someday, but abundant life is available today.

Forever peace is coming, but present peace must be pursued.

We must learn to expect and accept the suffering Jesus promised us—"In this world you will have trouble . . ." (John 16:33, NIV)—all the while straining to see through all the sad and scary to the second half of the verse. There is Jesus, who tells us, ". . . take heart! I have overcome the world" (v. 33, NIV).

My hope is you'll walk into this study not looking for magic words that make fear disappear from your life forever but rather looking to and leaning on Jesus, who has already overcome everything that makes you anxious.

As you begin, give each member a Bible study book. Make sure to watch the video and go through the introductory material so everyone knows what to expect from this study. This week, you will complete the personal study for "Session Two: Anxious David." When you get back together next week, you will watch a video on Session Two and discuss your answers. As for this week, just watch the Session One video and use the discussion guide below to get to know one another.

WATCH

Write down any thoughts, verses, or things you want to remember as you watch the video for Session One of *Anxious*.

DISCUSS

Share names, family information, favorite restaurants, educational/vocational backgrounds, and current favorite things.

Do you struggle with anxiety? What does that battle look like in your life today?

Have you seen anxiety affect others in your community? Explain.

What are some ways you have tried to fight anxiety in the past? What helped? What didn't?

What are you hoping to take away from this study at the end of the eight weeks?

PRAY

As a group, take turns sharing prayer requests and figuring out how you want to pray for one another throughout the week. Maybe someone wants to take notes and send out a weekly email. Maybe you could all write your requests in a notebook. Find out what works for your group and make sure you have a way to touch base throughout the week. Close in prayer.

To access the teaching sessions, use the instructions in the back of your Bible study book.

ANXIOUS DAVID

JESUS IS OUR SHIELD IN
THE FIGHT AGAINST ANXIETY

MANY SAY ABOUT ME,
"THERE IS NO HELP FOR
HIM IN GOD." *SELAH*.
BUT YOU, LORD, ARE
A SHIELD AROUND ME,
MY GLORY, AND THE ONE
WHO LIFTS UP MY HEAD.

Psalm 3:2-3

PRETEND INSANITY

1 samuel 21:10-15 and Psalm 34

I have a lot of great conversations with myself while boiling water. When I'm doing tedious household things, my mind tends to wander to hypothetical relational problems. *What if there's assigned seating at my step cousin's baby shower in two months, and what if her former roommate/friend is there and we're seated right next to each other, and what if she asks if our kids can get together for a playdate, which should be no big deal, and I guess the normal answer is "Sure!," but last time our kids got together, her kids taught my kids how to break into a car and start it with a bobby pin. So what am I going to say if she asks about that playdate? Maybe I just shouldn't go to the baby shower.*

I'm exaggerating, but please tell me I'm not the only one who practices conversations for uncomfortable scenarios that don't actually exist yet.

> **Check one.**
> ○ **You're the only one who does this.**
> ○ **You too? This is exactly why I don't boil water.**

It sounds crazy when I think about it, but that's what my brain does. Sometimes I'm afraid of people and the potential problems that come with people, and I think I can conversation-practice my way to peace. Let's see what David did when he was worried about potential relational conflict.

> **Read 1 Samuel 21:10-15. How did David act in the face of a threat to his safety? Write any observations in the space below.**

Today, in 1 Samuel, we read about when David was so afraid of how King Achish might treat him that he pretended to be a crazy person. Pretty brilliant, right? It is amazing how our worries can lead us to behave. Maybe you tend to get tense and angry when you feel anxious about how others think about you or what they might say or do to you. Maybe you get defensive. Maybe you, like David, behave in ways that will scare people away. I mean, lion- and giant-slaying King David, of God's own heart, literally scribbled and drooled. Or maybe you isolate and put your phone on airplane mode so the texts and expectations can just stop for one minute, please!

How do you tend to struggle when it comes to relational anxiety?

Read Psalm 34.

Psalm 34 was actually written by David about this very time in his life—when he pretended to be a crazy person in the presence of Abimelech (probably the same guy mentioned earlier as "King Achish" in 1 Sam. 21:10-15).[1] David clearly knew what it was like to be anxious when he wrote this psalm.

Now let's focus on verses 1-4 of Psalm 34 for a second. How would you describe David's posture as he shared this message?

Sometimes, when I'm afraid, I forget how to pray. I forget how to think like a daughter of God. I panic and don't know what to say.

What do your prayers to the Lord sound like when you're stuck in a panic?

In verse 4, David said he "sought the LORD." Read the verse again and write what the Lord did as a result.

What do you think it means to seek the Lord?

What does verse 5 say is a result of looking to God?

When was the last time you felt joyful and void of shame? What was your relationship with God like at that time?

Read verse 8 from the CSB translation online. What emotion does the Bible say people who take refuge in God have?

On a scale of 1 to 10, how "happy" does your heart feel right now? (If you looked it up in a different translation, you may have seen the word *blessed*.) What do you think would move you closer to a 10?

| 1 | 2 | 3 | 4 | 5 | 6 | 7 | 8 | 9 | 10 |

Not too happy.   The happiest.

Take the next few minutes to think about what it means to take refuge in the Lord. What are some things you find refuge in, apart from the Lord? What do you need to cut from your life or add to it to help you seek Him when you feel anxious?

In verse 11, David talked about teaching "the fear of the LORD." Fear is not a bad thing when it is focused on our Father. It's when we fear the wrong things that we feel anxiety.

What does God's Word say the fear of the Lord leads to? Look up the following verses and write the answer beside them.

Psalm 25:14 _____

Psalm 33:8 _____

Proverbs 9:10 _____

Proverbs 14:26 _____

Proverbs 14:27 _____

Proverbs 19:23 _____

Proverbs 22:4 _____

Luke 1:50 _____

When we fear the Lord, we gain. When we fear the Lord, it is easier not to worry about the things the Lord has already defeated. When we fear the Lord, we remember He is our shield and protector.

Read Psalm 34:9.

When we fear the Lord, what do we lack?

What are some misplaced fears you have right now? How does the work of Jesus impact those worries?

I'm not into war movies or battle-y things in general, but the idea of being shielded sounds awesome to me. If I could just be shielded, at all times, from danger, from conflict, from sadness—my heart longs for that. When I'm doing the boiling-water-conversing thing I told you about, what I'm really doing is trying to prepare and protect myself. David's interpersonal conflicts were much more murder-y than mine tend to be, but it's convicting and inspiring to me that he sought protection and refuge in the Lord.

Close out this time asking God to help you rest in the reality that He is eternally shielding you from the things that would harm your soul.

DAY TWO
DOEG IS NOT COOL
1 Samuel 22 and Psalm 27

I sat in a therapist's office last week and used my fifty allotted minutes to detail every relational conflict I could recall being involved in for the past fifteen years. My counselor wanted to know what my goal was—why I was seeking counseling and why I wanted to talk about closed-door conflicts from years past.

I said, "I feel haunted by my relational failures. I feel shame over the times I felt misunderstood. I just want to feel peace even though there are people from my past who might not think happy thoughts when they think of me."

Sometimes, I feel trapped by anxieties, stuck with thoughts of those I've been at odds with at one point or another. Maybe I've not had the same kinds of enemies, who carried swords and sought to kill, that David had, but I've had people who weren't for me. To one degree or another, we've all experienced enemies. It sure can feel like you have an enemy when you lose a friend. It sure can feel like an enemy when things don't go as planned and you're walking through a divorce you never thought would happen, or when, yet again, an attempt to reconcile with an estranged family member ends in tears.

Enemies. No matter what form of conflict they bring to our lives, what do we do with them, and how can we find peace?

I'm really encouraged when I read about how David responded in prayer over his enemies. We're going to take a look at a psalm he wrote that theologian Charles Spurgeon thought was likely about a particular enemy of his named Doeg.[2] But first, let's get a little background on Doeg and how his life intersected with David's.

Read 1 Samuel 22 and answer the following:

What did Doeg tell Saul about what he witnessed between David and Ahimelech?

What did Saul command be done to Ahimelech and his priests for protecting David? Who carried out Saul's command?

Psalm 52 was written by David about the whole Doeg ordeal. It's definitely worth a read. But the Psalm I want you to open up to and focus on is Psalm 27. Though uncertain, Spurgeon believed David wrote this Psalm about Doeg as well.[3] And regardless of the motive, it is a powerful song for those of us who struggle with anxieties about enemies.

Read Psalm 27.

Write out the first phrase of each sentence in Psalm 27:1. Also, write out the two questions David posed in this verse.

David asked whom he should fear and whom he should dread, but he answered those questions even while asking them. What is the answer?

When the LORD is your light, salvation and stronghold, there is nothing else to fear. "LORD," or Jehovah, is the proper name of the one and only God of the universe. LORD means "The Existing One."[4] That means God doesn't just exist, but that He must exist. The LORD is the One from whom everything else that exists gets its existence. We may have enemies, but we also have the LORD. The ENT office receptionist who said you talked too fast, or the hurricane headed toward your coast, or even the hotdog you are scared to eat because your esophagus seems to be hotdog-shaped—everything and everyone is at the mercy of The Existing One. Your enemies are never more powerful than your LORD.

He is the stronghold of our lives. He is our light and our salvation. He is our source of true protection. We don't get to finish reading this page in this book without Him giving us the breath in our lungs, the sight in our eyes, and the clarity of our minds to do it.

What are some things/people/situations you sometimes fear rather than fearing the Lord?

Now back to Psalm 27. Reread verses 1-4. How do these verses help you get your mind off of your enemies and onto Jesus?

The Bible, the Old and New Testaments alike, are about the work of Jesus. When we read the first four verses of this psalm, as Christians living after the resurrection, we can see Jesus as the ultimate fulfillment of David's hope and the ultimate reason our enemies shouldn't cause anxieties. Through the work of Christ on the cross, we have received salvation forever. At the cross, our greatest enemies stumbled and fell. We can be confident, as David was, because we have a Jehovah who is also our Rescuer and proves our enemies are no match for Him. See "Becoming a Christian" on page 184 in the Appendix for more information about the Christian faith and how to commit to being a Christ-follower.

What was David wanting and asking of the Lord in verse 4?

What other verses can you think of that remind you that the God whose power dwarfs enemies like Doeg and Satan and everyone else is also whom we should most desire and whom we can most be satisfied in?

Our Lord, the conqueror of enemies, isn't just "The Existing One." He is our good Father and the giver of joy.

Copy the following verses below each of them:

For you did not receive a spirit of slavery to fall back into fear. Instead, you received the Spirit of adoption, by whom we cry out, "*Abba*, Father!"

ROMANS 8:15

You reveal the path of life to me; in your presence is abundant joy; at your right hand are eternal pleasures.

PSALM 16:11

When you're stuck worrying about your enemies, are you able to worship? If you can, get alone in this moment and sing God one of your favorite songs of praise.

If you don't feel like you can worship, and I know sometimes this happens to us, would you consider taking a moment to write an honest prayer to God below? Or reaching out to a trusted Christian friend with your struggle? God wants to know the truth of what's happening in your heart and mind and so does your faith family.

The last verse in Psalm 27 says, "Wait for the LORD; be strong, and let your heart be courageous. Wait for the LORD" (v. 14). The word *wait*, in the original Hebrew, means "to wait, look for, hope, expect."[5] When we look for, hope in, and expect our God to come through, we can be people of courage, even those of us (Hi!) who tend to lean more into worry.

What are some ways you can "Wait for the LORD" as you battle your fear of people?

God is able to shield us from pain because He went to the cross and took the pain. There is now no barrier between us. In Christ, there is a shield for us who trust Him. He is on our side. He is our defender. We don't need every human in the world to understand us when the God who made us and knows us—our best parts and the very worst ones—loves us that much.

At the end of the therapy session I mentioned earlier, my counselor helped me realize I was longing to tie up a bunch of loose, frayed ends in a world where not everything can have beauty and closure. Some things remain unfinished, unsaid, unheard, untied, unraveled. But see, we have a Shield. Not to protect us from all pain, but to protect us from pain that lasts forever. God is the only relational being who can love us perfectly and forgive us fully, and He does. The more I meditate on that, I know my eternity ends finished, tied, heard, and beautifully held together. Then it is easier for me to make peace with today's loose ends.

> **Close out this time asking the Lord to help you feel forever peace in a world that's lacking it.**

DAY THREE
WHEN PRAYER TIME WAS THE WORST

Psalm 61

When I was nineteen, I was a hostess at a local restaurant known for its great salads. I started dating my husband who was a church planter/worship pastor and quickly left the great salad place to join the small church staff as the administrative assistant.

I'm embarrassed to admit this, but my least favorite part of our staff meetings was the prayer time.

Once a week, we'd all sit on the floor in our pastor's office and take turns praying. I'd listen to our pastor pray, then my husband, then the youth pastor, and, at that point, my heart would be beating out of my chest.

I hated prayer time.

Of course I understood the value of staff prayer. And of course I wanted to talk to God. But all I could think about while sitting in that little warehouse office space was what my words would show the other people in that office about how unspiritual I was. I wasn't in the prayer time to worship and to seek the Lord on behalf of the people we were serving together. I just hoped to say something that would garner a "Yes, Lord" or a nice, dramatic "Mmmm" from someone else in the room. I worried my prayers wouldn't seem potent enough for the people listening. But David modeled for us that prayer isn't something to worry about; rather, it is a weapon we can use against our worries.

Psalm 61 records one of David's prayers. It was definitely not the kind of prayer that might be said under duress in a church warehouse office space. David's prayer is earnest and needy and beautiful.

Scholars believe this psalm was written after David had come to the throne and was likely when his son, Absalom, was rebelling against him (which you can read about in 2 Sam. 15–18).[6] It was certainly a time when anxiety would be understandable.

Read Psalm 61:1-4 and reflect on David's tone with the Lord. Do you approach the Lord similarly?

When I read those first two verses, it struck me that David was pretty direct. He was so serious. He didn't say a bunch of words out of tradition or compulsion, as I did in the church office and still sometimes do today, but rather, he talked to God like he was talking to a real person.

Spurgeon noted that David's tone "was in terrible earnest." Then he said, "Pharisees may rest in their prayers; true believers are eager for an answer to them: ritualists may be satisfied when they have, 'said or sung' their litanies . . . but living children of God will never rest till their supplications have entered the ears of the Lord God of Sabaoth."[7]

Take a minute to read that over again. That convicted me so hard. I don't want to be a person who worriedly chants religious phrases in order to feel satisfied or make other people think I'm holy. I want to know and speak to the living God. Don't you?

Verse 2 says, "I call to you from the ends of the earth when my heart is without strength."

During seasons of anxiety or fear, we can approach the Lord in prayer and find Him to be a "refuge" and "rock" and "strong tower" as David described Him in verses 2-3. But anxiety often keeps us from that. It keeps us stuck in our own loop of fears—whether they are, *What will this church staff think of my prayer?* or *What will happen if my husband loses his job?* or *What is this lump under my arm?*

What's your first course of action when feeling anxious? Is it prayer? Is it TikTok®? Is it chips and queso?

Reread Psalm 61:4.

How do you think it helped David to pray this while dealing with exile?

Have you ever found comfort in your eternal destination while dealing with right-now suffering? What made that possible for you?

I just love verse 4. In fact, I think it is worthy of a nice "Mmmmmm." In that verse, we witness David doing the most wonderful and biblical thing, which I imagine crushed the anxiety he was facing. He, as Colossians 3:2 tells us to do, "set [his mind] on things above, not on earthly things."

In the following space, write down some right-now anxiety-inducing things in your life. And beside each one, find a Bible verse that helps you "Set your mind on things above" in regard to that struggle.

Now, read Psalm 61:5-8. Notice the change of tone.

Commentary writer Matthew Henry said, "David, in this psalm, as in many others, begins with a sad heart, but concludes with an air of pleasantness—begins with prayers and tears, but ends with songs of praise."[8]

That is so beautiful to me because I've experienced it. We can look at David's prayer in Psalm 61 and model our own anxious prayers after it. We can speak to the Lord directly and earnestly without pretense. We can set our minds on the eternal hope He offers, and we can conclude our prayers experiencing real peace, real hope, and real communion with the Father who loves us.

Below, write a prayer from your own heart and try to model it after Psalm 61. Be honest, reflect on eternity, and praise the Lord who is bigger than your worries!

DAY FOUR
CHASED AND HECKLED
2 Samuel 16:5-14 and Psalm 3

The heading for Psalm 3 in the CSB translation says, "Confidence in Troubled Times." When do you feel confident? Do you usually feel confident in "troubled times"?

My answer is certainly NO. When we lost our first baby in an ectopic pregnancy, I barely left my bed for months. When we adopted our middle daughter, who appeared to have significant physical and cognitive developmental delays, I barely left my bed for days. I've often buried myself under blankets in troubled times.

How do you usually react when times are troublesome?

Before we get any further, I want to say that making space to grieve is important. And we can turn toward God, even in our grief. He wants to sit with us in it, to carry us in it. All clear? Great. Back to Psalm 3.

The Bible tells us this was "A psalm of David when he fled from his son Absalom." You may remember from yesterday's study that this is the same time period scholars believe David penned Psalm 61.[9]

The events that led to the writing of this psalm are found in 2 Samuel 15–18 when David was betrayed by Absalom and others in his life. Absalom was leading a rebellion against his dad, the king. People who were at one time his friends turned against him. It was an undoubtedly troubled time in the life of David. It was, what some theologians might call, a "where's my blanket" moment.

Read 2 Samuel 16:5-14. Now, let's look more closely at verses 5-8. Who was Shimei, and what was he doing?

Read verses 11 and 12 again. What emotion do you pick up on from David? How did his response reflect a trust in the God of justice?

In verses 13 and 14, David moved on down the road, going his way while Shimei went on cursing him. Then it says, David "refreshed himself" (v. 14, ESV). It's really crazy to me that David was able to experience peace given his circumstances. Remember—he was on the run from his own son! His son, who should have been in his corner. And then, he was being heckled by this Shimei guy. And somehow, "he refreshed himself." There's no way unless God was helping him, right?

Now, flip to Psalm 3 and read the whole chapter. Take a closer look at verses 1 and 2.

I wonder if his "refreshing himself" was similar to the prayer we find in Psalm 3?

In Psalm 3:3, David called God his shield, his glory, and the lifter of his head. Below, next to these powerful names for God, explain how these terms were refreshing for David in his time of trouble and how they might be of help to you.

SHIELD

GLORY

LIFTER OF
MY HEAD

God is our protector (shield). Nothing can get to us without first getting through God. God is our source of significance (glory). We can fight anxiety knowing the things we worry about could never truly jeopardize the value we have because we are approved by God through Jesus. God is the lifter of our heads. God is the one who leads us to look up from our sorrows and worries and reminds us we can have joy and hope through our friendship with Him.

Which of these three descriptions of God's work in our lives means the most to you right now? Why?

Take another look at verses 5-6.

In these verses, David slept. It can be hard to sleep when you feel anxious (even if you rarely leave your bed). I love the idea of praying psalms like this one when your mind and body aren't cooperating.

Revisiting verses 7-8, what words or phrases show that God is for you in these verses?

How do you need God to fight for you right now as you battle anxiety and troubled times?

Close your time today thanking God for saving you and blessing you. Thank Him for rising up, in Jesus, to strike the enemies of sin and death and failure and fear. You belong to Him, and He has overcome. Ask Him to help you see Him as your shield, glory, and hope. Ask Him to help you sleep and not be afraid.

DAY FIVE
SHEPHERD AND SHIELD

Psalm 23

In Psalm 23:1, David wrote, "The LORD is my shepherd; I have what I need."

I have what I need. What if we really believed that?

Oftentimes when I'm anxious, my worry is rooted in feeling like I'm lacking something. My mind tells me, *If I just had this . . .* or *If that circumstance would just line up the right way . . . THEN, I'd have what I need.*

> **What is it, right now, that your mind is telling you that you need to have peace?**

Read Psalm 23.

> **Look at verse 2 and highlight the phrase "he leads."**

I heard an illustration from Elisabeth Elliot about Psalm 23 in which she talked about getting lost in the car and needing directions. Updating her example a little, imagine using your iPhone GPS to get somewhere, but then, while you are traveling, your phone dies, and you don't have your charger.

Maybe you pull over and ask someone how to get to where you're going, and he/she starts giving you a long, detailed, confusing explanation. But then imagine how you would exhale if someone were to simply drive ahead of you and lead the way. Elliot said, ". . . isn't it a relief if somebody just says, 'Follow me.'"[10]

There's no doubt that an anxious mind complicates a simple thing. Sure, we've all got complicated, painful relationships. Sure, we're juggling lots of responsibilities and wearing lots of hats and dealing with lots of incoming problems. And of course, you, if you were really smart, might be building a tornado shelter right now. But let's just remember this truest of true things. We are sheep, and we have a Good Shepherd who loves us and who leads us.

> **Read the following verses and write down the phrase Jesus kept saying to His people: Matthew 16:24; Mark 1:17; Mark 10:21; Luke 5:27.**

When we think about the role of a shepherd, we remember that a shepherd takes care of his sheep, provides for them, leads them, and protects them.

> **What are some examples from your own life of when your Good Shepherd has taken care of, provided, led, and/or protected you?**

Psalm 23:4 in the CSB translation uses the phrase, "darkest valley," but I love the imagery used in the ESV translation—"valley of the shadow of death." I used to think of that phrase as reflective of the very worst horrors life has to offer—things like disease and abuse. But, truly, this whole life is the "valley of the shadow of death," right? We are all dying every day. Some days are filled with pleasantries, and some days are filled with pain, but we live every moment in the shadow of death.

> **Even though we are all walking toward death, we can "fear no evil" (v. 4, ESV). Why?**

Verse 6 refers to the day we will dwell in the house of the Lord. Is there a home you love to visit? Maybe it is your childhood home? Or maybe your own childhood home was filled with dysfunction, but every time you visited that one aunt or grandma or that one friend, you were met with warmth and food and comfort and love?

Describe that setting in the space below.

All week, we've been looking at David. There's so much of his life we didn't have time to cover. Have you ever heard about the time he was a scrawny young boy who slayed the giant, Goliath, with a sling, some stones, and without physical armor (1 Sam. 17)? Or, you know, that time he sinned against Bathsheba and then had her husband killed (2 Sam. 11–12)? I mean . . . David lived a *life*.

He had lots of great days and lots of bad ones. Based on his life events, he likely experienced the anxiety of being the victim and the anxiety of being the bad guy. But he was a bad guy with faith in a good God. He was often a bad guy whose prayer life demonstrated that he sought forgiveness and protection, not through an earthly shield (not even when fighting a giant) but an eternal One. God protected David from his fears and from following his sin to destruction. God guarded and guided His child through all kinds of circumstances we can hardly imagine.

Now skip over to the New Testament and read about when God, the Good Shepherd, was walking the earth in flesh. Read John 10:1-11. What did Jesus call Himself in verse 7?

What did Jesus call Himself in verse 11?

Look at Psalm 23 and read through it again, but every time you see the phrases "the LORD" or "He," say, "Jesus."

Jesus is my shepherd;
I have what I need.
Jesus lets me lie down in green pastures;
Jesus leads me beside quiet waters.
Jesus renews my life;
Jesus leads me along the right paths
for his name's sake.
Even when I go through the darkest valley,
I fear no danger,
for Jesus is with me;
Jesus' rod and his staff—they comfort me.

Jesus prepares a table before me
in the presence of my enemies;
Jesus anoints my head with oil;
my cup overflows.
Only goodness and faithful love will pursue me
all the days of my life,
and I will dwell in the house of Jesus
as long as I live.

Here's the thing. Because of Jesus, we have access to the Shepherd. Because of Jesus, we have access to safety and satisfaction. Because of Jesus, we are sheep who don't need to be afraid of the lingering wolves in our lives. He leads us. He loves us. He is with us.

We are like David in that we fail, but Jesus doesn't. We worry, but Jesus understands. Jesus knows this world is broken, sad, and scary. But when we hold up what we are anxious about next to the good news of the gospel, we see that we actually can rest because He has already handled everything on our behalf. We are His, and He has won, is winning, and will win forever. It's not a onetime thing. It's an everyday opportunity to sit at His feet and in His Word, to claim His promises, think on His help, and believe in His power.

What can you do this week to remember the truth—that Jesus, your Shepherd, is with you—loving you, comforting you, leading you, holding you, and protecting you?

This past week, you completed the Session Two personal study in your books. If you weren't able to do so, no big deal! You can still follow along with the questions, be involved in the discussion, and watch the video. When you are ready to begin, open up your time in prayer and push play on Video Two for Session Two.

WATCH

Write down any thoughts, verses, or things you want to remember as you watch the video for Session Two of *Anxious*.

FROM THIS WEEK'S STUDY

As a group, review this week's memory verse.

Many say about me, "There is no help for him in God." *Selah*. But you, LORD, are a shield around me, my glory, and the one who lifts up my head.

PSALM 3:2-3

REVIEW SESSION TWO PERSONAL STUDY

From Day One: In Psalm 34:11, David talked about teaching "the fear of the LORD." What are some things we learned that the fear of the Lord leads to (include your favorite references from the chart on p. 21)?

From Day Two: Which Bible verses remind you that the God whose power dwarfs enemies like Doeg and Satan and everyone else is also whom we should most desire and whom we can be most satisfied in?

From Day Three: Do you approach the Lord similarly to the way David did in Psalm 61:1-4?

What's your first course of action when feeling anxious? Is it prayer? Is it TikTok®? Is it chips and queso?

From Day Four: Which of these three descriptions of God's work in our lives means the most to you right now? Why?

From Day Five: What are some examples from your own life of when your Good Shepherd has taken care of, provided, led, and/or protected you?

#AnxiousBibleStudy

DISCUSS

What is the most interesting thing you worried about this week? ☺

What have we learned about who God is through our look at some of the anxiety-inducing events in David's life?

How have David's prayers helped you?

When David was fleeing from Absalom, he prayed, "But you, LORD, are a shield around me" (Ps. 3:3a). Share about a time in your life when the Lord was your shield.

Back in Day One, we looked at verses all over the Bible that show us what happens when we fear the Lord. Which of these benefits resonates with you? If you're comfortable doing so, share a testimony of that experience in your group.

PRAY

Take turns sharing anxieties you're dealing with right now and have your group talk about how the gospel speaks to those worries. Spend the remainder of your time in prayer for each other.

To access the teaching sessions, use the instructions in the back of your Bible study book.

ANXIOUS JONAH

JESUS IS OUR KING IN
THE FIGHT AGAINST ANXIETY

BUT SEEK FIRST THE
KINGDOM OF GOD AND
HIS RIGHTEOUSNESS, AND
ALL THESE THINGS WILL
BE PROVIDED FOR YOU.
THEREFORE **DON'T WORRY
ABOUT TOMORROW**,
BECAUSE TOMORROW WILL
WORRY ABOUT ITSELF.
EACH DAY HAS ENOUGH
TROUBLE OF ITS OWN.

Matthew 6:33-34

DAY ONE
RUN!

Jonah 1

I grew up in a time of old. In a time before GPS was a thing. A time when one could get "lost" in the city she lived in and have to drive around until something looked familiar.

Terrifying, I know.

The absolute worst was when I'd be riding in the backseat of the car with my mom behind the wheel and I'd see her shoulders tense up and hear her mumble, "We're lost . . . and this . . . is . . . a bad . . . neighborhood."

I was very aware of "bad neighborhoods" and all that they entailed because my adoptive dad worked the night shift as a SWAT cop/helicopter pilot in Miami-Dade. We were, at the time, the second most crime-ridden county in America. I know these things, because of course I do. So, as you might imagine, his answers to, "How was work last night, Daddy?" were . . . intense.

I remember regularly sliding out of my seatbelt and becoming one with the floorboard of the car. My large fear of being killed by bad guys overpowered my medium fear of dying in a car accident without a seatbelt on.

So I definitely identify with Jonah and his caution/fear/aversion/panic over "bad neighborhoods" and the "bad people" there. I identify with running away from a scary place. Let's look at his situation in the Book of Jonah.

Read Jonah 1.

Now, take a look at verses 1-3.

What did God tell Jonah to do?

How did Jonah respond?

Here's what you need to know about Jonah and Nineveh. Jonah was an Israelite. Nineveh was the capital of Assyria, which was Israel's worst enemy. One thing commentators say that made them so scary was that the Ninevites had an established reputation for treating their enemies badly.[1]

In other words, Jonah's fear was warranted. It would be like if you'd asked me, during my one-with-the-floorboard moment, to go for a nice jog by myself on the same street where my dad had been shot at by murderous drug lords during his last shift. Jonah's fear was rational, but that didn't mean he couldn't be obedient.

Can you think of a time in your life when you "pulled a Jonah" and did the exact opposite of the thing you felt the Spirit prompting you to do because you were scared?

Read Jonah 1:4-17.

How did God respond to Jonah's disobedience?

In *The NIV Application Commentary*, James Bruckner, reflecting on Jonah telling the men of the boat to throw him overboard, wrote, "The captain hopes what Jonah already knows, that his God is compassionate."[2]

And then, as the story goes on, we see God's creative and perfectly timed compassion in the form of a big fish.

In verse 17, Jonah was eaten by a fish. I used to think of this part of the story as a punishment because . . . gross. But what mercy! God was saving Jonah's life. A big fish and a dark place brought a second chance.

> **Can you think of a time in your own life when God gave you a fresh opportunity or a second chance? Describe it below.**

Maybe you grew up in church and the whole fish-eating-a-man-and-man-surviving thing sounds totally normal to you. But maybe you're more like, *This is the weirdest, most ridiculous religious story ever.*

If you're more in that second camp, I found this really fascinating. Have you ever heard of *Encyclopedia Britannica*? Well, apparently, if you were to reach out to them to request research about Jonah being swallowed by a whale, they would send you information that not only scientifically proves the possibility that a man could be swallowed and survive in a whale, but they'd include an actual article about an event that transpired in 1891. A large sperm whale swallowed a sailor named James Bartley. In time the whale was captured, and his stomach was opened the next day. The sailor was found in the stomach, unconscious, but alive. He survived.[3]

Good luck ever going in the ocean again, but I love that God allowed that to happen. What a horrible few days for that dude, but what a helpful story for skeptics. God is supernatural, working within this natural world He created, and He reaches in and rescues again and again, creatively and redemptively.

This week, we're talking about Jonah and how Jesus is our King in the fight against anxiety. Often, in my life, my fears are king. My doubts are king. But it is so huge to remember the power of the real King.

God didn't just make a giant fish swallow Jonah; He made the giant fish. Out of nothing. And He didn't just make the giant fish in the vast ocean; He made the vast ocean. The King of your heart can make worlds and move whales to help His kids take the right next step.

What is a next right step of obedience for you? What is something you've sensed the Spirit leading you to?

Read Jonah 1:17 again.

"The LORD appointed" can be such a comfort.

What is the situation you fear most right now?

How would you ask God to help if you really believed He's an ocean-making, whale-moving King?

Close this day out reflecting on ways you've seen God's hand in situations in which you were initially scared. Or write out a prayer asking the Lord to help you respond to the circumstances you face with faith instead of fear.

DAY TWO
STUCK IN A FISH
Jonah 2 and Romans 8:26-30

For several years in my young adulthood, I lived as a slave to a secret eating disorder. My food dysfunctions and the lengths I took to hide them completely ruled me. My anxiety surrounding my big secret was crushing. See, I wasn't just a person. I wasn't just a Christian. I was a church secretary. I was a young pastor's wife. I was a Bible college student. I was all these very super-Christian-y things, and I was certain that if I came clean about my sins, I'd lose everything.

So I fought in secret. I prayed and cried and quietly begged God for healing. My prayers didn't seem to go far though, and it was because my heart was full of pride. I was unwilling to be obedient to the Spirit's leading. My sin was the king in my life, and as much as I wanted to worship the real King, I felt like my fears kept me stuck. God kept bringing me to Proverbs 28:13— "The one who conceals his sins will not prosper, but whoever confesses and renounces them will find mercy."

But I was too afraid. I was afraid that if I obeyed, if I confessed, I would lose everything. I thought I'd destroy my reputation. I thought my husband would leave me. I thought my family would be disgusted and disown me.

What fears do you have that keep you from obedience when you encounter a command in God's Word or direction from the Holy Spirit?

My worries kept me stuck in sinful patterns for three-and-a-half years. But when I finally confessed my sin to others, God took my one, weak moment of obedience, and He healed me. My desire to be dysfunctional with food evaporated, and I never struggled with it again. It was maybe the most miraculous thing I've ever experienced.

The disclaimer I always give when I tell this story is that there are things I've been praying for my entire life that are still unresolved. I know God doesn't always give miraculous overnight healing, but sometimes He does. Jonah and I have that in common. God is capable of orchestrating major, miraculous deliveries.

Do you have a story like mine? A time you hit rock bottom/the end of yourself and felt stuck in something you couldn't get out of? Did you run to the Lord for help or run from Him? Share a little bit about your experience below.

Commentator James Montgomery Boice said the following about this point in Jonah's story:

> To concentrate so much on what happened inside the great fish that we miss noting what happened inside Jonah is to make a great mistake . . . So we must now turn to Jonah's prayer to God from inside the monster. As we read it we discover that the prayer reveals the truly great miracle. It shows that though Jonah had been brought to the depths of misery within the fish, he nevertheless found the mercy of God in his misery. He discovered that though he had forsaken God, God had not forsaken him, though it seemed that he had. In brief, Jonah found salvation even before the fish vomited him up on the land.[4]

Chills, right?

A human heart receiving God's mercy is a miracle.

Jonah didn't pray magic words that bought him a second chance. His heart shifted. His fear stopped ruling his actions, and he spoke to God with humility and desperation. That's a miracle.

> **In the space below, write about a time in your faith life when you experienced the miracle of a heart shift—an upward posturing—a moment when you stopped pursuing self and started pursuing the Savior. If you have never experienced anything like this, write about what you feel is holding you back. Is it fear? Is it pride? Is it a desire to hold onto control?**

Read Jonah 2.

Until studying this passage, I never realized that Jonah's recorded prayer is referencing an earlier prayer. From the belly of the big fish, in verse 2a, he said, "I called out to the LORD, out of my distress, and he answered me . . ." (ESV) referring to whatever prayer of desperation he prayed when he was thrown overboard, facing death.

Here's what's cool to me. There's no way that in that moment, as he was flung from the boat into the storm, Jonah said a thoughtfully worded and perfectly crafted petition to the God who was in control of the storm. I wonder if his prayer was a simple "AHHHHHHHHH!" or "Heeeeeeeelp meeeee!" or "GOOOOOOOOOOOOOD!"

In some of my lowest moments, my prayers were less about words and more about desperation. One of the countless beautiful mysteries about the Holy Spirit is that when He lives in you, He intercedes for you. He helps you pray when you don't know what to say.

Read Romans 8:26-30.

How are you weak right now?

In light of your weakness, what do you think the Spirit might pray on your behalf?

In just that small Romans passage we not only have the Holy Spirit interceding for us but also the Father working all things for our good and the Son showing us how to live in the promise of being justified and glorified.

Whether you are alone on your couch right now or being flung over the railing of a storm-shaken ship, you have an incredible King in the fight against anxiety. You have a King who prays for you even as He promises you He'll make sure you win.

Look back at Jonah 2, specifically verse 9. What do we see as part of Jonah's prayer here?

I'm going to tell you the answer. ☺ It's gratitude. I've heard it said that thanksgiving is the remedy to anxiety. It's hard to be scared when you know why you're grateful. Remember the miracle of God's mercy and surrender your worry.

In the space below, write out a prayer of thanksgiving and ask God to deliver you from what you're anxious about today or help you give up whatever might be holding you back from following the Holy Spirit's leading in your life.

BIG CITIES AND SACKCLOTH AND MOST LIKELY TO BE MUGGED

Jonah 3; Luke 11:11-13 and John 3:16

I presently (and since the beginning of time) get anxious when visiting big cities. *Will I be able to figure out how and where to park? Will I get mugged? Probably most carjackings happen in big cities, right? If I survive the attempted muggings and jackings, will I remember where I parked?*

At this point, we've already established that God was sending Jonah to a place called Nineveh and that there were scary people there. And, guess what, there are still scary people there. Nineveh is now called Mosul, Iraq, which might be the number one country you don't want to visit if you're a Christian. In 2019, the *BBC* put out an article titled "Iraq's Christians 'close to extinction.'"[5]

Thinking about such dangers helps me have compassion for Jonah when reading his story. Jonah went to a big city with scary, violent people because God asked him to go.

I know this is scary to write out on paper, but what is a place you would have a hard time being willing to go to if you felt God leading you there? Why?

I've always hated questions like the one I just asked. Some broken part of me sometimes forgets the kindness of God and assumes He is out to get me.

Like, I better not tell God what I don't want to do because then He will for sure make me do it.

> **Does your head ever sound like that?**
> ○ **Yes**
> ○ **No**
>
> **Read Luke 11:11-13. To worry God is out to get us is to forget what kind of Father He is. List some of the "good gifts" God has given you in the space below.**

Now let's look at Jonah 3. Perhaps the craziest part of this story is that when Jonah finally did go visit his literal worst, most violent enemies, they actually listened.

> **Read Jonah 3:5-10. How did the people of Nineveh respond to Jonah's message, and what did God do?**

In ancient times, fasting and wearing sackcloth was a sign of mourning. Verse 5 begins by saying the Ninevites "believed God." The fasting and wearing of rough, goat-hair clothing was a response to their recognition of sin. They mourned their sin. Belief came first. Followed by repentance. Followed by the mercy of God. It's so amazing and simple, but this is another way worriers can get it wrong. It can actually be frustrating and scary to read an instance like that.

My brain, for instance, can easily read chapter 3 and think, *But how do I perfectly posture my heart? How do I ensure my repentance is enough? Is sackcloth Prime® eligible?*

However, it should be so much easier for us to repent and rejoice and rest in the forgiveness of God than it was for the Ninevites. We don't just have the message of Jonah; we have the actions of Jesus.

Read John 3:16 (or just recite it to yourself).

Now underline, circle, highlight, or burn this next sentence into your brain—*Jesus is enough.*

Jesus' perfection, not your sin, His sacrifice on the cross, not your sackcloth, His power, not your weakness, is what God sees and approves and why God loves without stopping and forgives without going back.

When we get so caught up in "our part," that's where the anxiety kicks in. As the old hymn says,

> Turn your eyes upon Jesus,
> Look full in His wonderful face,
> And the things of earth will grow strangely dim,
> In the light of His glory and grace.[6]

Inside the following graphic, make a list of "I believe . . ." statements about God and back them up with Scripture references. Here are some places to look:

ROMANS 6:22	2 CORINTHIANS 3:17	EPHESIANS 2:8-9
2 TIMOTHY 1:7	1 PETER 2:16	1 JOHN 1:9

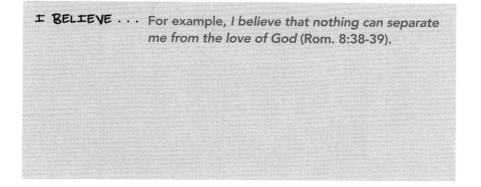

I BELIEVE . . . For example, *I believe that nothing can separate me from the love of God* (Rom. 8:38-39).

Here's the thing. When we believe in the goodness of God, we won't care as much where He asks us to go. When we remember we too were the Ninevites and God responded to our repentance with grace and more grace, we can worry less about the cities we hope to never see or the fact that we've never owned sackcloth. The King who leads us loves us.

He wants us to have a vibrant, ever-growing relationship with Him. He wants us to experience the joy of trusting and obeying.

In the space below, write out a prayer. Ask the Lord to set you on a mission that helps you grow more and more aware that He is on the throne, that He is good, and that your anxieties don't have the power to rule over you.

DAY FOUR
WHEN PREFERRING DEATH

Jonah 4

A few years after we brought our sweet Joy home from China, I made myself a counseling appointment. I sat down in my counselor's office with a problem—I didn't feel what I thought I should feel. To echo the apostle Paul's sentiment in Romans 7, I didn't feel the way I wanted to feel. I felt a way I hated.

I wanted love to be the cure-all in our adoption story. I wanted the bonding to happen more quickly—instantaneously, even. I mean, aren't Christians supposed to come chock-full of supernatural love for others? How could I, new mother of this miracle, feel anything other than awe and gratitude? Why was I so easily frustrated with our child—a former orphan—when she didn't behave correctly or even when she couldn't do things easily? What kind of monster feels anything but compassion and affection for a child with disabilities?

I bring this up because, if reading Jonah 4 through the lens of my old, pious church-lady self, I'd be like, *Hang on. Jonah just got a second shot at loving his enemies—and they actually listened? And they turned to the Lord? Mission accomplished. Jonah was safe. Um . . . why does chapter four start the way it does?!*

I'm getting ahead of myself, aren't I?

Go ahead and read Jonah 4.

How does verse 1 tell us Jonah felt on the heels of all the great stuff God had just used him to do?

Do you, at all, resonate with Jonah here? Can you think of a time you knew how you ought to act/feel/believe but found yourself in the wrong?

If you're honest, I think you have to say yes. We long to be in control—little gods of our own universe—making the plans and calling the shots. Jonah was so angry that God had mercy on the evil Ninevites that he literally asked God to let him die (v. 3). Wow.

What is the last thing Jonah is recorded to have said in the Bible book named after him (v. 9b)?

Those are some pretty intense last words for a book of the Bible. It was not Jonah's best moment. Probably not the words he'd want on his gravestone, or, I don't know, at the very end of his titular book in the HOLY SCRIPTURES.

But here's what's cool. Jonah is not the hero of this book.

Even the WHALE, the accurately vomiting rescuer, is not the hero of this book. Author and Bible teacher Priscilla Shirer said it like this, "These four little simple chapters are not really about the whale; they're about our God."[7]

Read Jonah 4:10-11. What does the end of this book tell you about God?

There is so much to learn from Jonah's story. We learn that God is gracious and slow to anger. We learn that God's plan is redemption when our plan might be revenge. Jonah reacted wrongly to seeing God spend His mercy on the people of Nineveh, the same mercy that had saved Jonah again and again. He could have been moved and grateful for the compassion of God in His own life and the compassion of God for his enemies. But he wound up bitter and miserable.

Two things I don't want us to pass by here: 1. Jonah missed out on the joy he could have experienced being used by God in the redemption of the Ninevites. 2. Even when Jonah was feeling angry and hopeless, God continually tried to engage with him. God didn't leave him alone in his bad attitude. And God does the same for us. He engages our hearts, even when our hearts are hard.

> **When you look at the circumstances and struggles in your own life, do you focus on the role others play? Do you focus on your own part? Or do you look for God? Do you look for the hope—the healing, the redemption, the restoration project—that Jesus is working on?**

> **In the space below, list out some of the circumstances you're currently struggling to sort out. Where is God? What do you think your King is doing?**

I don't have the full picture, but I can already see so much of God's presence and power in the story of Joy and this adoptive family He's put her into. When I struggled to feel the right things, I was comforted by another adoptive mom who shared she'd felt the same things too. When God allowed us to walk through various medical issues with Joy, I was astounded by how He used those situations to bring us closer together as a family. I don't get how the whole thing works, guys. But I know God blesses us with the most amazing gifts. Gifts like healing. Gifts like growth. Gifts like the ability to lay our heads down at night without feeling the weight of our burdens. Gifts like having hearts that are able to say, "God, this hurts, but thank You for it." God knows how to love as He leads.

DAY FIVE
JONAH, NINEVEH, AND YOU!
Matthew 6:25-34 and Matthew 12:38-41

Last night, I had a dream about recording the videos for this Bible study. Brace yourself, because I know nothing is more riveting, interesting, and helpful than hearing the details of someone's super weird dream. ☺

So it was the first day of shooting the videos for this study (about fighting anxiety with the Word of God). In my dream, I got to the set, and everything I was wearing or had brought to change into was stained, pilling, and had huge holes in it. Then, the producer walked up and said, "Scarlet, we want you to wear this Anna costume—so you'll be dressing like the princess from Frozen® while you teach the Bible, OK?" And then I nodded and stepped into the changing room to learn that the costume was sized for a toddler. It was all a tragedy.

This just goes to show you where my mind was. *HOW CAN I TEACH A BIBLE STUDY WITHOUT THE RIGHT OUTFIT ON!?*

OK. Now, make me feel better by answering this next question, please.

> **When is the last time you fixated on a super non-important aspect while preparing for an important thing?**

> **What was important in that situation and what were you focused on instead?**

It's really sad that Jonah, even after failing to obey God in his fear, even after his second chance, even after obeying and being used by God in such a clear way, lost focus. Jonah was essentially the toddler-sized-Anna-costume wearer of the Old Testament. Throughout this story, we see an anxious and cowardly Jonah turn into an angry and bitter Jonah, but all throughout the story, his eyes were on the wrong prize.

Both anxiety and anger usually reveal a heart that is focused on the wrong things.

So what are we to do? We're often anxious, angry, bitter, and resentful, aren't we? Or we are too busy stuffing our faces or our Amazon® carts to notice we are. So what's the cure? Who is our hope? How can we have peace and be people who are consumed by love instead of fear? How can we avoid an ending like Jonah's?

It's certainly not by trying harder and doing better and faking it till we're making it.

Let's read Matthew 6:25-34. What does the heading in your Bible say right before verse 25? If your Bible doesn't have a heading, what do you think the heading could be?

Looking at my version, the CSB (Christian Standard Bible), it says, "The Cure for Anxiety." Before you continue reading Jesus' living words in Matthew 6, I want you to pray that the Spirit will remove any cynicism or disbelief that leads you to think there's not real hope. Jesus says there is. Let's believe Him.

Now look at verse 25. Would you agree that "life [is] more than food and the body [is] more than clothing"? Why or why not?

It's easier to agree to than it is to believe. Maybe you agree life is more than food and clothing, but your actions say otherwise. Maybe you followed God to Nineveh, but your emotions don't line up with your mission. Maybe your focus is on shaky things because your heart is doubting what is solid.

So what's at the root of our anxiety? The *ESV Study Bible* says, "To be anxious . . . demonstrates a lack of trust in God, who promises that he will graciously care for 'all these things.'"[8]

Read verses 26-34. Jesus told us to consider the birds and the flowers. What else can we consider, not listed in this passage, that Jesus cares for and sustains? List as many things as you can in the space below.

We see Jesus here, in His infamous Sermon on the Mount, telling us why we're anxious. We worry about food and clothes and video shoots and getting even and getting rewarded, and it all boils down to ME-ME-ME-ME-ME-ME-ME!

So what do we do? Copy Matthew 6:33 in the space below.

What does "all these things" refer to?

"All these things" are the things we chase. Food. Clothing. Status. Security. The secret is that it's only when we pursue the King that we find our needs and, more importantly, our souls satisfied.

Jesus is our King in the fight against anxiety. He has to be.

> **Read Matthew 12:38-41. Even sinful, anxious, bitter Jonah was used by God. List some of the ways God used him to point people to Himself.**

The most important thing about Jonah is that he points us to Jesus. "Something greater than Jonah is here" (v. 41). Thank God! Jonah knew how to preach repentance, but then he whined when it worked. Jesus preaches repentance, but then when we turn and call on His name, He forgives. Guys, Jesus forgives us! He forgives us when we're too anxious to obey. He forgives us when we obey with poor motives. He forgives us when we lose focus and fail to trust Him and make our fears our temporary king. King Jesus can take care of us. King Jesus is going to take care of us.

> **Do you meditate on this reality? Do you preach the good news of Christ's death and resurrection to your heart when you're feeling anxious, or do you rehearse, reflect, and ruminate on things that lead to bitterness? Practice writing a three- or four-sentence gospel sermon to your anxious heart below.**

This past week, you completed the Session Three personal study in your books. If you weren't able to do so, no big deal! You can still follow along with the questions, be involved in the discussion, and watch the video. When you are ready to begin, open up your time in prayer and push play on Video Three for Session Three.

WATCH

Write down any thoughts, verses, or things you want to remember as you watch the video for Session Three of *Anxious.*

FROM THIS WEEK'S STUDY

As a group, review this week's memory verse.

But seek first the kingdom of God and his righteousness, and all these things will be provided for you. Therefore don't worry about tomorrow, because tomorrow will worry about itself. Each day has enough trouble of its own.

MATTHEW 6:33-34

REVIEW SESSION THREE PERSONAL STUDY

From Day One: What did God tell Jonah to do, and what was his response? How did God respond to Jonah's disobedience?

From Day Two: What fears do you have that keep you from obedience when you encounter a command in God's Word or direction from the Holy Spirit?

From Day Three: How did the people of Nineveh respond to Jonah's message, and what did God do?

From Day Four: What does the end of the Book of Jonah tell you about God (Jonah 4:10-11)?

From Day Five: Other than the birds and the flowers, what else can we consider that Jesus cares for and sustains?

DISCUSS

In this session, we looked at the Book of Jonah and studied the story of God mercifully and creatively offering Jonah a second chance. If you're comfortable with it, share about a time God gave you a second chance.

This session's main idea is "Jesus is our King in the fight against anxiety." What are some things you've made "King" in your life that contribute to anxiety? Why is Jesus a better King than those things?

What verses from this session have stuck with you and helped you as you fight to make Jesus King of your life and battle against your fears?

This week's memory verse is about seeking the kingdom. Try to recite the verse together as a group. Then, talk about what God might have you pursue individually or as a group for His kingdom this week.

PRAY

Take turns sharing prayer requests and thanking God for the power of His forgiveness and the power He gives us to forgive others. Spend the remainder of your time in prayer. Maybe, if you sit in a circle, each woman can pray for the woman on her right—that she will be able to seek first God's kingdom and find freedom from her worries.

To access the teaching sessions, use the instructions in the back of your Bible study book.

ANXIOUS JONAH   67

ANXIOUS
MOSES

JESUS IS OUR STRENGTH IN THE
FIGHT AGAINST ANXIETY

BUT MOSES SAID TO THE PEOPLE, "**DON'T BE AFRAID**. STAND FIRM AND SEE THE LORD'S SALVATION THAT HE WILL ACCOMPLISH FOR YOU TODAY; FOR THE EGYPTIANS YOU SEE TODAY, YOU WILL NEVER SEE AGAIN. THE **LORD WILL FIGHT FOR YOU**, AND YOU MUST BE QUIET."

Exodus 14:13-14

DAY ONE
WHEN THE BABY BASKET ISN'T SO CUTE

Exodus 3; Isaiah 6:1-8 and 1 John 3:1

In school this week, my five-year-old daughter did a "Baby Moses Craft." She colored a little baby, glued it to a basket picture, and stuck the whole thing to a sponge. Then she was supposed to put the sponge in a bowl of water and watch it float like baby Moses. Yippee! It floated! Adorable! Fun!

Right?

Here's some other words I think of when I look at this sweet little craft:

- drowning;

- separation-anxiety;

- trauma;

- genocide;

- slavery;

- general horribleness.

I have to confess something. I don't love crafts. But my daughter did love the craft. It's just that I felt less "Yippee!" and more disconcerted by the image. When you're little and cutting a piece of sponge to put a baby picture on, it's harder to imagine the gravity of that historical account than when you're a mother with babies of your own.

Here's the thing. The reality of that little sponge craft represents a real time when baby boys were being taken from their mothers' arms and slaughtered.

The sponge craft rested on a rough situation.

When we were in the process of adopting our daughter, Joy, we watched hours of video training and read required books detailing the trauma a child goes through when he/she is separated from his/her birth mother. We were told again and again that every international adoption is a "special needs adoption." We learned about how, when a mother instinctively rocks her baby, his/her inner ear is stimulated, which allows him/her to learn and helps his/her brain make connections. We learned about the mental and physical distress an infant goes through when he/she is unable to be with his/her mother.

I say all this to tell you Moses' experience with anxiety probably didn't start when he saw an on-fire bush not burning. It probably didn't even start when he killed an Egyptian and ran. It more likely started when he was a baby, separated from his mother and put into a basket into a river—by himself.

All adoptions are special needs adoptions birthed out of trauma. So here we are at the outset of Exodus 3. Up until this point, Moses had spent his life in a foreign family, discovered he was adopted, found out his people were mistreated slaves, and fled after killing an Egyptian. And now there's a bush on fire that's not burning up, and a voice is coming out of it.

Read Exodus 3. Draw a picture of what happened to Moses in this chapter.

Look at verse 1. What mundane and faithful thing was Moses doing when the angel of the LORD appeared to him in the burning bush?

It's often in the mundane moments of faithfulness that the Spirit will break through and prompt us, speak to us, move us, call us to action.

What are some parts of your life that feel mundane right now?

When the Lord called my family to adopt, I was active in a small group and walking in obedience in small, unseen, mundane ways. As I told you in the Session Three teaching video, the Spirit broke my heart over abandoned girls in China with special needs while I drove to the grocery store because I'd forgotten to pick up dishwasher detergent.

There's nothing like experiencing the supernatural, all-powerful God while you go about your natural, powerless-looking life—picking up detergent or taking care of sheep.

Reread verses 2-6.

How did Moses respond to God in verse 6?

What does Moses' response to God tell us about him and his feelings?

The way Moses responded, covering his face and feeling "afraid" (v. 6), as the Bible tells us, reminds me of when Isaiah entered the Lord's throne room in Isaiah 6 "and the train of his robe filled the temple" (v. 1b, ESV).

Real quick, flip to Isaiah 6 and read verses 1-5. How did Isaiah respond to what he saw?

He was terrified, "undone" (v. 5, NKJV), sharply aware of his unworthiness as he stood in the presence of the One who is Holy.

> Read Isaiah 6:6-8. What led the undone Isaiah to go from "I am ruined" (v. 5a) to "Here I am. Send me" (v. 8b)?

God is merciful.

Looking back at Moses' story, here's something cool. Once God had his attention with the bush, He said Moses' name twice. Apparently, in ancient Jewish culture, saying someone's name twice was a way to show friendship, affection, and endearment.[1]

How beautiful that even as He revealed His impossible-to-comprehend power and commanded Moses to do a hard/scary/terrifying/life-threatening thing, He addressed Moses lovingly—as a friend, as beloved.

> Do you ever read God's Word or hear about it in church and feel afraid, like Moses did, by what you encounter? Are there specific verses in the Bible that cause you to feel afraid?

The Bible isn't warm and fuzzy, and God isn't a teddy bear. I've often neglected the Lord because I was afraid of Him. I'd read the words of Jesus to His disciples, as He told them about the cost of following Him. Sometimes, Christian persecution overseas will break into my mind, and I long for comfort, fluff, and ignorance.

But that's because I forget how He speaks. Yes, He has the power to destroy all life with a flood or fire or just His voice. But that's not how He talks to His own. He calls me "daughter." He says, "Scarlet, Scarlet . . ."

Read 1 John 3:1. How should this reality affect our fear of God?

Because we're loved children, we can fear God with awe but approach Him as Dad. We can walk in obedience, knowing He doesn't promise us an easy life, but He promises us His love and presence and His strength as our own.

Read Exodus 3:7-11.

What did God ask Moses to do and how did Moses respond?

What does God's assignment for Moses tell us about His character and His purposes?

The compassion and care of the Lord is so evident in these verses. He told Moses that He heard the cries and saw the pain of His people and that He was going to rescue them. And He wanted to use Moses to do it. How crazy is that?

Read Exodus 3:12 and copy it down.

In the space below, I want you to write out the things you're afraid God could ask of you. Then write, "I will certainly be with you" after each one. God doesn't send us alone. When we go, we go in His care, His strength and His name. Whatever your worry, ask God to help you trust Him.

WHY FEAR ACTUAL SCARY THINGS WHEN YOU COULD FEAR CONVERSATION?

Exodus 3:13-22 and John 8:56-58

I know, OK? I know we live in a world of legitimate problems. I know there are countless things a normal person should fear. There's no need for me to make a list of them because you know what they are. The grown-up realities. We can worry about evil, abuse, pain, and death. Those are the real scary things. So why is it that my number one anxiety often goes like this:

If I say this, and she says that, then what do I say? And if I do say that, will I say it the right way? What will she say? If she says something I don't think she'll say, then what should I say? What if I just don't say anything? But what if she's super upset because I don't say anything? What if Jesus could just come back right now and say something before I have to say something or not say something?

Maybe you're rolling your eyes because you would never be anxious about a situation so silly. But I'm sure you worry about other things that aren't exactly life or death.

Most of us do it. And I would argue that neglecting the actual scary things and instead worrying over relational awkwardness or other small concerns is a very human, very timeless way to respond to bigger problems. Most of the times I'm afraid of silly things like conversations that don't exist, I've got much more serious stresses in the back of my mind.

Spoiler alert—you're about to read about Moses doing exactly this.

Read Exodus 3:13. God told Moses to go lead the Israelites, who, mind you, had been slaves for four hundred years, out of Egypt. If God told you to do something of that magnitude, what would your first questions be?

God told Moses to return to a place where he was known as a murderer-runaway and rescue a nation of slaves. And if you read the conversation, it sounds a lot like, *If I say this . . . and they say this . . . what do I say next?*

Anxiety can lead us to focus on the wrong things. The little things.

Imagine you're standing in the middle of the road on a hill and a speeding car is coming right toward you. The normal-fear response would be to fear the imminent danger and respond by getting out of the way. The best response to that situation would be for your legs to start moving out of the path of the car. But what if you focused on smaller worries? *Hold on. What are you going to do if your insurance doesn't cover this hospital bill? If you dive out of the way and lose your phone, who will call the police? Please don't ruin your favorite jeans.*

When a car is about to hit you, you don't have time for anxiety. You get out of the way of the danger. You don't worry about insurance or cell phone placement.

Moses did the same things we do. He focused on problems when what he needed to do was remember God called him to this and God would carry him through this.

Do you find Moses' imperfect faith comforting? Why or why not?

We can take comfort knowing the heroes of the faith were shaky people like us. People who questioned God's plan. People who probably had anxiety rather than feeling awe and confidence in their interaction with the great "I AM."

Read Exodus 3:13-22.

In verses 13-14, Moses basically asked God His name, and God gave a seemingly strange answer. What did God say His name is?

What did He mean? Do a quick Google® search or look inside of a study Bible to see what you find about this name for God. Record your findings in the space below. (And share some with your group when you meet together!).

I AM tells us God exists. In fact, "I AM WHO I AM" means God must exist. God is the one and only Necessary Being. That leads us to the truth that nothing can exist without God giving it existence. I AM WHO I AM. God can't *not* exist. And everything else can't exist without Him. But perhaps the most significant application of this name God gave Moses is that God has, as John Piper put it, "drawn near to us in Jesus Christ."[2]

Read John 8:56-58. In verse 58, we see Jesus said something very powerful. What did He say, and what does it have to do with God's name in Exodus 13?

Jesus was claiming the name of the great "I am." Jesus was telling the world that He isn't just a teacher, or just a healer, or just a worker of miracles. He is I AM. He is God. He is existence itself in a human body, come to save the world.

That's who Moses had on his team and that's who we have forever. We don't have to be anxious because Jesus is I AM. I AM existed before anything else did and everything that is, *is*, because He is. He can handle your awkward conversation no matter how it goes down.

I AM came into this broken, sad, scary place to live and die and rise again. He is more powerful than even death.

When we look at Moses' life, we see a weak man used powerfully by a strong God. Isn't that a relief? God doesn't need us to "be awesome." He's awesome. He wants us to love Him and obey Him—even when we don't feel brave, even when we fumble over our words and prayers and responses to His leading in our lives.

In the space below, list a few of God's awesome attributes that are on display in this story and thank Him for being so good.

DAY THREE
A BROKEN THYROID AND A GOD WHO SEES

Exodus 14:1-14

The year before writing this Bible study, I had a drawn-out season of HARD.

I began suffering mysterious symptoms that lasted for months. I was bounced around to different doctors and machines, ultimately leading to tumors at the end of whatever is the opposite of a rainbow. The doctors thought I had cancer, but they weren't sure. It was a rough run. I knew that because of my relationship with Christ, I could have (and should have) "count[ed] it all joy" when I experienced "trials of various kinds" (Jas. 1:2, ESV). But the thing is, I wasn't joyful. I wasn't thankful. Instead, I was sad and lonely. Scared and weak. I didn't understand why God was allowing my health to fail me. He was allowing a big heap of painful and scary and hard things, and I had more questions than answers.

What questions did you ask God in your last drawn-out season of HARD?

Read Exodus 14:1-4.

What did God tell Moses to do here?

What did God tell Moses Pharaoh would do?

The first handful of verses in Exodus 14 are striking. We've skipped ahead a little, but what's happened, in a nutshell, is God did as He said He would, and He used Moses to free the Hebrews from slavery. Moses then led them through the wilderness toward Canaan, "the promised land," where they would be free to flourish.

But then the story takes a turn. In chapter 14, we see that while God's people were probably still exhaling, trouble was coming again. Pharaoh changed his mind about freeing them and wanted to take them back as slaves. And, prepare yourself, it was GOD'S PLAN. What?!

Can you think of a time in your life when you felt God was causing or allowing something hard or negative to happen to you? What were the circumstances?

God, the Creator and Sovereign I AM, is so involved and in control of what's going on in the world that He hardened Pharaoh's heart and led him to pursue the Israelites with his army. And it wasn't because He's mean or wanted to scare anyone. He wanted, as He told Moses here, to "receive glory" (v. 4). His plan was to break through time and space, as He has done so many times and still does and still will do, to remind humanity that He is BIG and sea-splittingly trustworthy.

Now let's look at verses 5-12.

What happened to the Israelites in these verses?

How did the Israelites respond? (See verses 10-12.)

How do you think you would have responded in this situation?

If you've taken a good look at the darkness inside your own heart, you'll nod in understanding to the response of God's people.

How many times have you seen this play out in the movies, in the lives of your friends, in your own family? It's human nature to want to return to familiar problems rather than face an unknown danger. We often return to what we know, even when we understand it's bad for us.

What do you think was at the root of the Israelites' response to the danger they faced?

In his book, *The Knowledge of the Holy,* A. W. Tozer wrote, "What comes into our minds when we think about God is the most important thing about us."[3]

What comes into your mind when you think about God?

I look at this story and wonder what I'd be thinking and feeling if I were an Israelite. Depending on how well I'm understanding or trusting God at the time, I might have felt shocked or angry with God. I may have doubted His goodness and provision. I may have, like the Israelites, blamed the guy/girl/institution leading me.

Look at Moses' response to the people in verses 13 and 14 and copy it in the space below.

When I had my thyroid taken out last year, I went into that surgery expecting to wake up to a cancer diagnosis and a mortality rate. But God healed me. There was no cancer, and once my broken thyroid was out, He restored my health and most of my energy.

God is able on the days full of joy. God is able even when you get the hard diagnosis. God is able no matter what circumstance you find yourself in. "Stand firm and see the LORD's salvation" (Ex. 14:13). The God who allows cancer can kill cancer. The God who allows pharaohs to chase can drown them in the sea. But we'll get to that tomorrow.

> As you go about the rest of your day, meditate on Moses' response to the people at the end of today's passage. "Don't be afraid. Stand firm and see the LORD's salvation that he will accomplish for you today . . . The LORD will fight for you, and you must be quiet" (Ex. 14:13-14).

BUT WHAT IF MY DAUGHTER DIES?

Exodus 14:15–31 and Matthew 6:34

I went through a season of major anxiety when my oldest daughter was about three. I became obsessed with the thought that I could lose her. I was constantly aware that she could die.

There were days it was all I could think about. I had bouts of hyperventilating and said no to anything fun if it sounded remotely dangerous. It was not a good phase.

How has your family had to deal with your anxiety in the past? How have your worries impacted them, and how have they responded?

Charles Spurgeon once said, "The worst evils of life are those which do not exist except in our imagination. If we had no troubles but real troubles, we should not have a tenth part of our present sorrows. We feel a thousand deaths in fearing one."[4]

In Matthew 6:34 (remember this verse from last week?), what did Jesus say NOT to worry about? Why?

Now read Exodus 14:15-18. In verses 17-18, God was explicit about *why* He was doing what He was doing. What is the reason He gave?

Sometimes, I experience suffering, and I can see glimmers of good in the midst of the bad. I see, as it's happening, some of the *why* God allows it. But other times, I don't see anything. There are situations in our lives that seem only evil and painful and hopeless. But this is exactly why we know not to look only at our own lives.

What you are doing right now, getting to know the character and greatness of God in His Word, is preparing you to trust God when you think you only see hopelessness. God's Word helps you fight with truth when you only feel fear. The Bible teaches you to recognize glory when, otherwise, you might only see pain.

Write down just three reasons God is worthy of glory at all times.

1.

2.

3.

All over the Old Testament, we see God in the stories of these heroes of the faith, like Moses, and we learn the way God acts and thinks.

All over the New Testament, we see Jesus sharing and showing His power. We learn that Jesus is the way to hope. That He brings redemption. He makes all things new. God's glory is displayed all over the place, and the more we see it the more we understand that as God is getting glory, He is bringing about our good.

Read Exodus 14:19-31.

Try to draw a picture of the miraculous things that happened.

What is your favorite part of this miracle? Why?

Read verse 31 again. How did God's people respond to what God did?

God parted the sea and led His people to safety. The result was that instead of fearing the unknowns and potentials for pain, they feared the Lord.

Anxiety crushes us because it makes us fear the wrong things.

What are some of the wrong things you're fearing right now?

When we fear the Lord, when we recognize He is worthy of our fear, awe, and glory, the smaller things that make us "feel a thousand deaths" are swallowed in the sea.[5]

When I focus on the glory of God, I don't find myself praying in a panic that my daughters won't die. I find myself praying for their souls, for their understanding of God's love, for their future callings to make Him known to their generation.

God is doing miracles all the time. And He uses regular, flawed, cowards like us. When we look to Him, see His power, and trust His plan, we find freedom from our fears.

> **Make a list in the space below. What would you like to see God do this week? Think of the people in your life who don't know Him—who don't know freedom and peace. Commit to praying for them this week and see what God will do. Ask the Lord to help you fear Him rather than the unknowns in your life.**

DAY FIVE
IS THAT A FIRM NO?
Exodus 4:10-13 and Hebrews 3:1-3

I have this thing with my husband. I know husband-wifery is a team thing, but the problem is, I really like things to go my way.

Sometimes I want one thing, and he wants something else. I don't really want to be the boss. I don't want to do anything that will bankrupt us or ruin our kids. I just want everything I want to always happen immediately. Is that so much to ask? ☺

There are times, if you can believe it, I have a clearly amazing idea he should definitely be on board with, and he says, NO.

But then I ask, "Is that a firm no?"

I question his answer, in hopes it might change. (It works a lot by the way.)

Read Exodus 4:10.

In Exodus 4:10, Moses questioned God in hopes the plan might change.

What was Moses' excuse for not wanting to do what God told him to?

Look at verses 11-12. How did God respond?

Moses was persistent in his resistance. How did he respond to God in verse 13?

The story of Moses is a beautiful picture of God's faithfulness in the midst of our fear and hesitation. Moses was a worrying, doubting, God-questioning, messed up human, just like me and just like you, who did a really hard thing. And God was with him, just as He promised He would be.

Have you ever gotten to witness this in someone's life? When have you seen God use someone unlikely to do something impressively compassionate or miraculous?

Looking at and attempting to mimic Moses' obedience (no matter how fear-filled or questioning) is a wonderful idea. But the clearer, better way to move toward peace and obedience is by looking at and chasing after Someone else.

The story God was inviting Moses into wasn't actually about Moses. It was always about God.

Read Hebrews 3:1-3. Who is considered "worthy of more glory than Moses" (v. 3)?

In verse 3, the writer of Hebrews compared Jesus' superiority to Moses to a builder getting more honor than the house. What do you think this comparison tells us about God?

A created thing can't be better than the Creator. Jesus is the I AM, remember? Jesus is the builder of all things. Jesus created Moses and the stuttering, questioning, staff-raising miracles that came through him. Jesus is immeasurably greater than Moses.

What are some ways Jesus is better than Moses?

Moses confronted Pharaoh. Jesus confronted Satan, sin, and death.

Moses led from physical slavery to the promised land. Jesus leads from spiritual slavery to freedom.

Moses lifted up his staff to make a way for his people to cross the sea. Jesus lifted up His body to make a way for His people to cross from death to life.

Moses served, died, and was buried. Jesus served, died, was buried, left the grave behind, ascended to glory, lives forever, and rules the world every minute of every day.

So, yes, Moses was good, but Jesus is better.

Jesus is the reason anxious Moses could move forward and find freedom. Jesus is the reason anxious you can move forward into whatever God has planned. You are scared, but guess what? Jesus isn't.

What are some ways Jesus is better than you?

How do you need Jesus to be strong in you today?

As you go about the rest of your week, remember that you don't have to fight your way to peace. Jesus is your strength in the fight against anxiety. He will lead you through the waters, to the other side, to the promised land. And in the ways that matter most, He already has. He has saved you. In Jesus, you're on the other side of the sea, and it's time to rest.

This past week, you completed the Session Four personal study in your books. If you weren't able to do so, no big deal! You can still follow along with the questions, be involved in the discussion, and watch the video. When you are ready to begin, open up your time in prayer and push play on Video Four for Session Four.

WATCH

Write down any thoughts, verses, or things you want to remember as you watch the video for Session Four of *Anxious*.

FROM THIS WEEK'S STUDY

As a group, review this week's memory verse.

But Moses said to the people, "Don't be afraid. Stand firm and see the LORD's salvation that he will accomplish for you today; for the Egyptians you see today, you will never see again. The LORD will fight for you, and you must be quiet."

EXODUS 14:13-14

REVIEW SESSION FOUR PERSONAL STUDY

From Day One: Do you ever read God's Word or hear about it in church and feel afraid, like Moses did, by what you encounter? Are there specific verses in the Bible that cause you to feel afraid?

From Day Two: In Exodus 3:14, God told Moses His name was I AM. What did you learn about this name as you studied it this week?

From Day Three: Can you think of a time in your life when you felt God was causing or allowing something hard or negative to happen to you? What were the circumstances?

From Day Four: In Matthew 6:34, what did Jesus say NOT to worry about? Why?

From Day Five: Compare and contrast Jesus with Moses. What can we learn from Moses, and why is Jesus better than Moses?

DISCUSS

This week, we studied Moses. We saw him scared and sinful, but also obedient and faithful. He was fully a human and fully loved by God. He went through scary things, and He followed God to what looked like scary places in order to be used in accomplishing God's purpose for His people. If you're comfortable with it, tell your group about a time God asked you to do something hard or scary.

This session's main idea is "Jesus is our strength in the fight against anxiety." What are some things you lean on as "strength" that can't hold up under the weight of life? How is Jesus better?

What verses from this session have stuck with you from and helped you as you fight to make Jesus your strength as you battle against your fears?

PRAY

Take turns sharing prayer requests and thanking God for His strength that lets us rest. Thank Him for showing us how to walk with Him and for being merciful when we forget that it's His strength we depend on. Spend the remainder of your time in prayer. Pray specifically that you, as a group, would rely on the strength of the Spirit as you seek to love the people you've been scared to love and do the things you've been scared to do. Ask the Lord to unite your group and remove all anxiety that is keeping you from service to Him and peace in His Spirit.

To access the teaching sessions, use the instructions in the back of your Bible study book.

ANXIOUS MOSES   91

session
Five

ANXIOUS
ESTHER

JESUS IS SOVEREIGN IN OUR
FIGHT AGAINST ANXIETY

IF YOU KEEP SILENT AT
THIS TIME, RELIEF AND
DELIVERANCE WILL COME
TO THE JEWISH PEOPLE
FROM ANOTHER PLACE,
BUT YOU AND YOUR
FATHER'S FAMILY WILL BE
DESTROYED. WHO KNOWS,
PERHAPS YOU HAVE COME
TO YOUR ROYAL POSITION
FOR SUCH A TIME AS THIS.

Esther 4:14

DAY ONE
A HAND-ME-DOWN BARBIE DREAM HOUSE AND A *VERY* ROMANTIC LOVE STORY

Esther 1–2 and Colossians 1:16–17

When I was in fifth grade, a neighbor from down the road gave me a hand-me-down Barbie® DreamHouse™. Pretty much all I remember from that year is locking myself in my room and playing out what I thought was the ULTIMATE romantic situation, over and over again.

I know this is what you're here for, so let me explain.

Barbie and Ken™ are at a party. Sorry, I meant to say a ball. They're at a ball. They're talking, laughing, waving goodbye to people. They both happen to be walking backward when they bump into each other and fall on the floor. Both clearly annoyed, they argue, in unison, "How dare you! Where do you thi–" And then, they pause. This is the moment that they both realize their whole lives have been leading up to this moment. And that they're destined for love.

That's the magic of playing dolls. Two lives (plastic dolls), led by the hands of destiny (tweenage Scarlet) to find each other, fall for each other, and "enjoy" a lengthy, awkward plastic doll kiss.

Would you believe this is a way I've taught my daughters about sovereignty? They have their own hand-me-down Barbie house (thanks Autumn) and their own plans for romantic doll destiny, and I want them to trust the powerful guidance of a loving God.

Now, God is not a preteen, and we're not brainless plastic dolls, but we can take comfort in the fact that He exists outside of our world, outside of time itself, and is in total control of every situation we experience. We are anxious Kens and worrying Barbies. But God is sovereign all the time.

As we study Esther this week, we're going to look at the sovereignty of God that exists even when life looks impossibly bad or scary, and we'll remember why and how that can nudge us toward peace.

Look up the word *sovereignty* in a dictionary, and write down the definitions you find in the space below.

As much as I'd like to be sovereign over my home and my life the way I was sovereign over my Barbies, I'm just not. To be sovereign is to possess supreme or ultimate power. I don't have power over the behavior of the people in my life, over the cells in their bodies doing what they're supposed to do, over their safety, or even their happiness.

When God allows pain I don't understand, probably nothing is more comforting to me than to remember He has ultimate power over all things.

Let's look at this idea through some of the scarier situations that went down in the life of a woman named Esther.

Read Esther 1–2 and try to see if you can find any mentions of God. Did you find any?

Esther is the only book in the Bible that doesn't mention God one single time. How strange is that? How is there a book in the Bible, authored by God, all about God, that fails to mention God? In reading commentaries on this book, I learned that not only is God not mentioned, but neither are there any recorded prayers or references to the Torah (the first five books of the Hebrew Bible) or the temple.[1]

So why is this book here? As we'll see, it's all about sovereignty.

Esther was a Jew living in Persia being raised by her cousin, Mordecai. During those days, the Jews were in exile. They were religious minorities in a God-opposing culture led by an absolute monarch.

So in the first chapter of Esther, we learn that King Ahasuerus (you've probably also heard him called by his Greek name, Xerxes) was getting rid of his queen, Vashti, and looking for a new one. That's the kind of thing he could just do without any consequences.

Look back at Esther 1:10-12.

Why was the king mad at Queen Vashti?

What did the king's advisers encourage him to do? (See verses 13-21.)

Esther 2:10 says Esther didn't reveal her ethnicity because Mordecai told her not to. Have you ever experienced anxiety over being different than people around you, whether it was because of physical, socioeconomic, ethnic, or racial differences? If yes, what happened?

Have you ever experienced anxiety because of someone in power who was doing things you disagreed with? Explain.

How do you tend to cope with this sort of anxiety?

King Ahasuerus had absolute earthly power. That's scary. When there are employers or presidents or family members whom we don't agree with in any position of power, it can lead us to feel insecure, especially when politics or racism are involved, like what we see in Esther's story.

When we see people in power who are making sinful decisions, it's tempting to believe God's gone missing.

> Read Colossians 1:16-17. Write the following in your own words, "He is before all things, and by him all things hold together" (v. 17).

The story of Esther, the story of Colossians, and the story of the universe itself is that God never goes missing. Whether you're struggling with a circumstance, a relationship, or a person, you can fight your anxiety by holding on to the truth, the reality, that God is before all things. He is powerful over all powerful people. He doesn't need to be named, but He can't be ignored because He holds life itself together. When life looks like bad decisions and chaos and a big mess we can't control, we don't have to control. The sovereign God is leading the way.

> In the space below, list the situations in your life that look bad. Surrender them to the Lord and trust He will hold you together. He will hold everything together. You can trust He will sustain His people just like He sustained the Israelites through Esther and Mordecai.

DAY TWO
A SNIFFLE, A SURGERY, AND A GIANT TOOTH

Esther 3:1-11; Psalm 4:8; Psalm 121:2-4; Romans 8:28 and 1 Peter 1:8

Recently, my daughter, Joy, had her last of three ear surgeries. I'd been up all night with another sick kid the night before and woke up to an alarm at 4 a.m. to take Joy to the hospital. My husband couldn't take her because he was also sick. That was already a less-than-ideal day, but while I was sitting in the waiting room, I felt a telltale sign of a dental abscess (not my first abscess rodeo—I've got troubled teeth). I called my dentist friend, drove to the dentist chair, and had to have my largest molar pulled out of my head for an hour and a half.

A few things:

1. Why does it take an hour and a half?

2. Always say yes to laughing gas. Always.

3. Expressions like "When it rains, it pours" exist for a reason.

4. The week of sickness, surgery, and emergency molar removal has filled me with more gratitude than I've had in a long time.

Isn't that weird?

We looked at this James verse earlier, but let's look again—James 1:2 says, "Consider it a great joy, my brothers and sisters, whenever you experience various trials."

I used to read that and feel panicked by it. I thought various trials were always coming for me—that failure, danger, and pillagement were around every corner and that if I didn't do every Christian thing just right, I'd miss the joy, ruin the moment, and experience all the things I was afraid of for no good purpose at all. I was missing the whole point.

Every living and active word of the Bible points us not just to the steps to take in trials, but to a sovereign Savior, whose perfection is completely given to us and whose power is always working.

Today, we follow more of Esther's story as she took steps in a terrifying trial as a great God worked behind the scenes.

Read Esther 3:1-11.

What do we see Haman attempted to do?

At this point, did it look like he would succeed in his objective?

Have you ever had one of those moments when it just felt like your whole life was falling apart? What is the hardest season you can remember in your life?

What did you do?

What did God do?

Look up 1 Peter 1:3-9. Focus on verse 8 and copy it in the space below.

We can see our problems, and they scare us. We don't physically get to see God right now, but we love Him. We believe in Him. We can rejoice, knowing He is at work even throughout abscess emergencies, political emergencies, and personal trauma we didn't see coming.

Turn to Romans 8:28.

What does God do in every situation for those who love Him?

What are some trials you're walking through right now that you can praise God for today, knowing He is at work and will use it for good?

God is sovereign, which means He's never not working.

Read Psalm 121:2-4.

Where does our help come from?

What is God called in verses 3 and 4?

What does verse 4 tell us God does not do?

When I was little, I couldn't fall asleep unless I heard my parents watching TV and puttering around. I didn't want to be awake when they were asleep because then I'd feel alone and scared. I sensed safety when I knew they were awake and could take care of me. I trusted them to protect me if something happened while I was off the clock. So I've always loved this truth—that my Protector, the only one who actually has real control over my safety, never sleeps.

Read and copy Psalm 4:8 in the space below.

Life with Jesus means hope for later and abundant life today. It means trials are temporary, and joy is eternal because we place our hope in His hands that run the world and never tire.

You might be having a less-than-ideal day, or week, or moment in your home, but you have a "let us not grow weary" hope in your heart (Gal. 6:9, ESV). You can have peace instead of panic because you have access to the God who is in control, even when it feels like your Hamans are going to win.

Write a prayer asking the Lord to help you trust He is working in situations that look hopeless. Ask that He will help you rest and trust and sleep, knowing He is awake, present, and loving.

DAY THREE
A SWAT REFLEX AND A BUNK BED RESCUE

Esther 4 and Romans 11:36

My most "for such a time as this" memory involves my SWAT officer dad. When I was twelve, my little sister was exploring the bedroom of a little girl named Beth. I was loitering around with the grown-ups waiting for dinner to be ready when our hosts asked if we wanted a tour of the house.

They took us from room to room and then we got to Beth's. Beth was four with a little blonde bob and a bunk bed. For whatever reason, right as we walked in, everything seemed to change to slow-motion as we watched little Beth dive headfirst from the top bunk toward the floor.

My adoptive dad and his SWAT muscles were, thankfully, in the room at that moment, and he calmly raised his hands and caught Beth by the ankles right before her head hit the ground.

It was a little bit like witnessing a miracle. The strong, trained officer was standing at the right place at the right time to save a little girl from breaking her neck. That's the type of providence we see in the life of Esther.

Read Esther 4. In verse 7, what did Mordecai share that he learned was to happen to the Jews?

In chapter 4, the messenger relayed information between Mordecai and Esther, ending on Mordecai's famous plea, "Who knows, perhaps you have come to your royal position for such a time as this" (v. 14b).

Mordecai suggested Esther's position and her opportunity to serve her people wasn't simply a coincidence. Mordecai, a believer, knew God orchestrated everything, and maybe He put Esther in this position of power so that she could save God's people.

Look up Romans 11:36 (CSB translation) and fill in the blanks.

For from _____ and through _____ and to _____ are all things. To _____ be the glory forever. Amen.

Guys, please never forget that God has all the power. He doesn't have some of the power. He doesn't have most of the power. From Him and through Him and to Him are all things.

Sometimes that means Paul Wessel is standing at the right bunk bed at the right time. Sometimes that means Esther is in the right court in front of the right king to save a people from genocide.

Read Esther 4:15-17. What brave action did Esther plan to take?

Courage like that looks impossible from the outside. We think only "super Christians" do super brave things. But the longer I live, the more I see that God takes anxious people with simple obedience to accomplish extraordinary things in His sovereignty.

How do you think Esther may have felt in the days of fasting and planning to go before the king?

The Bible doesn't tell us how she felt, but I bet she felt great anxiety. She couldn't know how it would go. She didn't know if she'd be killed or banished (like Vashti) or if lives would be saved. But she trusted in God's sovereignty.

Why is it comforting to read about Esther and all the uncertainty she walked through that led to freedom for her people?

Maybe you haven't recently witnessed a miraculous moment. Maybe life feels ho-hum, and God just feels far away, and maybe that makes you nervous. Take heart. God uses every season and every circumstance to draw us closer to Himself. (See Romans 8.) When life looks scary and faith feels hard, remember that God is sovereign as you fight to feel peace.

Try to list three situations you've witnessed or been through where you saw the sovereignty of God on display.

1.

2.

3.

Close out your study time today thanking Him for His power and care and asking Him to help you do what He's called you to today, trusting that He is working, He is present, and He loves you.

DID GOD REALLY FIND YOUR PHONE?

Esther 5 and Esther 7:1–6

When my oldest was six, she gave me the following pep talk:

> *Mommy, God knew this was going to happen.*
> *From the moment Adam and Eve sinned, He*
> *knew you were going to lose your phone.*

I thought it was hilarious and adorable and such a churched-kid thing to say. Obviously, I'd lost my phone. But I didn't think to involve God in the issue.

> *Like, "Hey God, I know You are probably busy*
> *caring for orphans and widows and listening to*
> *prayers about peoples' cancer and stuff, but*
> *can You just help me find my phone because I*
> *haven't checked Instagram in a few seconds?"*

I often live parts of life as if God's not involved. Sure, He's involved in big things. But, like, lost iPhones? It just seems like a job not for Him. In our fight against anxiety, we need to know everything is a job for Him.

Today, we'll continue to look at God's involvement in the details of Esther's story.

Read Esther 5.

What did Esther ask the king?

How did the king respond to Esther's request?

Once again, we witness a "coincidence" of good fortune for Esther.

I used to kind of giggle when older Christians would talk about how God answered their prayers about finding their missing car keys or keeping them safe on airplanes. I failed to recognize what those older saints knew to be true—God is in the details, the little ones and the big ones. Recognizing He is present and active in every circumstance is an excellent way to quiet anxiety.

Throughout the rest of the Book of Esther, we read about a banquet with the king and Haman. We see Esther requested another banquet and then a drunk Haman left and saw Mordecai. I'll say the horrifying part as unobtrusively as I can. Haman got mad and ordered that Mordecai be impaled on a big stake on top of having already ordered that all Jews be killed in chapter 3.[2] We good?

Read Esther 7:1-6. What was the first thing the king said to Esther in this chapter, and how did she respond?

The gist of it is, the night before, the king had trouble sleeping. (See Esth. 6:1.) While the royal chronicles were being read to him, he heard about how Mordecai saved his life. So in the morning when Haman was about to tell the king he wanted Mordecai dead, the king ordered the opposite. He made Haman honor Mordecai. You can read the rest of the story in Esther 8–10. Long story short, Esther and Mordecai worked with the king to save the Jews. There were celebration banquets; Mordecai became second in command; the Jews prospered. That's the story.

There's no amen. There's no prayer. There's no tell-all theological explanation in the Book of Esther. But let's read between the lines.

Let's move ahead to the New Testament. Look up the following verses and write what it says about God next to the reference. *Some of these verses may look familiar because we studied them earlier this week!*

Romans 8:28

_____

Ephesians 1:11

_____

Colossians 1:16-17

_____

1 Timothy 6:15-16

_____

Which of these verses is most encouraging to you and why?

What would you do differently this week if you totally believed these verses were true?

No king, no ruler, no evil of any kind can keep God from caring for His people. Remember this as you wait for your biopsy results. Remember this when you get frustrated with your colicky newborn. Remember this when you get ready to share Jesus with your neighbor. Remember God is there, and He is sovereign over every small, massive, and medium thing in your life.

I want to challenge you today to include God in the little things. Bring your small concerns and your big ones and trust He is working behind the scenes in ways you can't see. He is looking on you with favor as the king looked on Esther. The difference is you don't have to worry or wonder about it. You don't have to hope your King doesn't change. Your King is perfect and powerful and favors you forever in Jesus.

List some of the little things that are on your mind today.

Now list the big ones.

What do you hope to see God do in each circumstance you wrote down?

In the space below, pray about some of these little and big things and ask God to speak to you in the details. Ask Him for an awareness of His presence and His providence in your life and a faith that says "I trust You" when you can't understand what He's doing.

DAY FIVE
THE PSALM I LEARNED IN HIGH SCHOOL

Psalm 103 and Hebrews 11:1,6

In tenth grade, my teacher made us memorize Psalm 103. I'm thirty-four, and I could still say it in my sleep.

> Bless the LORD, O my soul,
> and all that is within me,
> bless his holy name!
> Bless the LORD, O my soul,
> and forget not all his benefits (vv. 1-2, ESV).

Read Psalm 103.

Look closely at verses 3-13. List what "his benefits" are below.

In the following blanks, personalize these verses a bit and list what God has done for you in each of these ways.

A sin of mine He forgave

A way He healed me

A time He showed me mercy

A way He renewed me

Which of those benefits is most meaningful to you right now, in this season of your life? Why?

The Book of Esther may not mention God, but we see so many of His behind-the-scenes benefits. We see Him redeem His people from the pit. We see Him execute acts of righteousness and give justice to the oppressed. We see His compassion and grace toward sinful people.

Read Psalm 103:19 and copy it below.

If I had to summarize the Book of Esther, I would do it by quoting Psalm 103:19. The Lord rules over all. That's it.

Paul Tripp spoke about the Book of Esther like this:

> This God who seems absent is actually working to protect and preserve His story. You shouldn't conclude, because you can't see the hand of God, that God isn't at work anymore [than] you should conclude that the sun isn't shining because you're in your basement and you can't see it. These are these moments where you have to do what Hebrews 11 says, "You must believe that God exists and He rewards those who seek Him." I'm not going to give way to belief in the functional death of my Redeemer even in moments where I do not see His hand.[3]

Do you ever feel like God is absent in your life? On the scale below, mark down how tangibly you're currently experiencing His presence.

1	2	3	4	5	6	7	8	9	10

I don't feel God near.   God feels close to me.

It's so difficult to walk through seasons of life when God feels absent. If you're a believer, you know He's there. But sometimes you sense Him, and other times, He feels far away.

What are some ways you can pursue communication with God when He feels far away?

Turn to Hebrews 11:6. What do we need to please God?

What *is* faith? (Look at Heb. 11:1 for the biblical definition.)

When I read the Book of Esther, I see proof after proof after proof that God is working. Look at your own life. Maybe it's been some time since your relationship with God felt ablaze, but look at His blessings in your life. Your life is hard, but has He provided? Your life is sometimes scary, but has He protected?

List some of the ways God met your needs during those harder seasons when He felt far off.

You can believe in a God you can't see. You can trust He's working in your life even if your life looks like a bunch of Hamans and unfair beauty contests and conversations that could ruin you.

Esther went through a lot, and she came through it prosperous—not because she was awesome, but because God is. He had a plan for her, for her cousin, and for His beloved people. And He has a plan for you too. You don't have to save the day. God has already saved it. He's saved you. He's so, so powerful and nothing can touch Him. "The Lord rules over all." You can rest.

Pray through your anxiety by praising God for the work He does that you cannot see. Thank Him for being faithful and above all things.

This past week, you completed the Session Five personal study in your books. If you weren't able to do so, no big deal! You can still follow along with the questions, be involved in the discussion, and watch the video. When you are ready to begin, open up your time in prayer and push play on Video Five for Session Five.

WATCH

Write down any thoughts, verses, or things you want to remember as you watch the video for Session Five of *Anxious*.

FROM THIS WEEK'S STUDY

As a group, review this week's memory verse.

If you keep silent at this time, relief and deliverance will come to the Jewish people from another place, but you and your father's family will be destroyed. Who knows, perhaps you have come to your royal position for such a time as this.

ESTHER 4:14

REVIEW SESSION FIVE PERSONAL STUDY

From Day One: Esther 2:10 says Esther didn't reveal her ethnicity because Mordecai told her not to. Have you ever experienced anxiety over being different than people around you, whether it was because of physical, socioeconomic, ethnic, or racial differences? If yes, what happened?

From Day Two: Have you ever had one of those moments where it just felt like your whole life was falling apart? What is the hardest season you can remember in your life?

From Day Three: Why is it comforting to read about Esther and all the uncertainty she walked through that led to freedom for her people?

From Day Four: How do you approach God with the little things? Did you see God in the smaller details of your life this week?

From Day Five: Which of God's benefits, as laid out in Psalm 103, is most meaningful to you right now, in this season of your life? Why?

DISCUSS

This week we studied Esther. We looked at a book of the Bible where God is harder to find. We read between the lines, and we learned that though life is scary and complicated and people are sinful and messed up, God is always working things together for the good of those who love Him.

Did you learn anything new about the story of Esther this week? Share with your group.

What are you going through right now that causes anxiety because you can't see God's purpose in it? What do you think God's purpose might be? Share with your group and ask them to lift you up in prayer.

Which Bible verse was most impactful to you this week? Why?

This session's main idea is "Jesus is sovereign in our fight against anxiety." What are some action steps you can take this week to help yourself remember God is in control and He is trustworthy?

PRAY

Take turns sharing prayer requests and thanking God for being above all things and taking care of us. Pray He might use you to help people find spiritual freedom the way He used Esther to redeem the Jews. Ask Him to give you compassion for others and to dwell on His goodness and power rather than on the brokenness you see in the world.

To access the teaching sessions, use the instructions in the back of your Bible study book.

session
six

ANXIOUS
PRAYER

PRAYER IS OUR POSTURE IN
THE FIGHT AGAINST ANXIETY

HUMBLE YOURSELVES, THEREFORE, UNDER THE MIGHTY HAND OF GOD, SO THAT HE MAY EXALT YOU AT THE PROPER TIME, **CASTING ALL YOUR CARES** ON HIM, BECAUSE HE CARES ABOUT YOU.

1 peter 5:6-7

DAY ONE
JESUS TOOK MY BIRD AND SAW AWAY

1 Peter 5:6-7

I have a bunch of snapshot memories of the year my parents were getting divorced. I was very young, but I know there was a barbeque. A trampoline. A secret rock in the yard with nooks where I would stash pennies. I remember being in a lawyer's office with a copy machine and colored Wite-Out®. There are images of Grandma Marlene coming to stay with us to take care of me for way longer than usual.

I didn't understand my family was splitting apart. I didn't know whether to be sad or scared yet.

Grandma Marlene was amazing. She'd sit me on her lap outside by the pretty yellow flowers and sing hymns. So many hymns.

> I'm so happy and here's the reason why;
> Jesus took my burdens all awayyy.
> Now, I'm singin' aaaas the days go byyyyy;
> Jesus took my burdens all away.[1]

I loved the songs. But that one confused me.

"Jesus took my burdens all away" sounded to me a whole lot like, "Jesus took my bird and saw away."

I didn't understand why Jesus wanted a bird and saw and why my Grandma was so happy He took hers.

I got older and figured out the lyric misunderstanding but remained confused about how, specifically, to give Jesus my burdens. I'd sit through church youth events as a teenager and hear adults plead, "Come forward and leave your burdens at the cross!"

And I'd obey and think as hard as I could, *BURDENS, HERE, I LEAVE YOU. AT THIS CROSS MURAL IN THIS HIGH SCHOOL GYMNASIUM. ABRA CADABRA! AND AMEN!*

I *so* wanted my burdens to go away. I so wanted God to help me. But goodness—I didn't know how to do my part. Maybe you've wondered about that too. We all have burdens. What can we do with them?

Write 1 Peter 5:6-7 in the space below and circle the first two words.

When I first saw that and realized that it came before the "cast your anxiety" command, I felt like I'd cracked a secret code! So THAT'S how you do it! That's how you cast your cares on God! You humble yourself!

Wait—oh no—another abstract-sounding command.

Look up the word *humility* in the dictionary and write down what you find.

In the original Greek, *humility* denotes "not rising far from the ground"[2] and *humble yourself* means "to make low, bring low."[3]

The season I read that, I actually started praying on my knees. I'd always had a bit of an aversion to on-my-knees praying because once I discovered God loved me, not because of what I do, but because of what Jesus did, I relished in my freedom to pray with my eyes open, to pray in the middle of a meal or the end instead of the beginning. *Freeeeedoooom!*

But when I read that, I wanted to physically lower my body when I was talking to God. To train my body to remind my brain that I am low, that I am aware of God's bigness and power and my own weakness and frailty.

It was an incredible season where I tasted supernatural peace more often than I ever had before.

> **Write some other practical ways you can think of to "humble yourself" before God.**

Here's the incredible thing. When I humbled myself, when I came before the Lord, lowly in Spirit, "casting my cares" on Him was a natural response. It just sort of happened. I remembered my status, as a created being, wholly dependent on a good, perfect, loving Father, and all those worries seemed to float to Him because I remembered He knows what to do. After I humbled myself, I was able to hum to "Jesus took my bird and saw away." (I don't think I did, but I could have!) After I humbled myself, I could smile, because I actually meant it, because I actually felt it.

I know this may not look exactly the same for each of us in our individual lives on our individual days, but God has promised to provide grace for each one of us as we humble ourselves before Him and cast our cares on Him.

Use this space to draw a picture of a time in your life when you felt free from burdens. How old were you? What was happening?

In Christ, we're born again. We can be like little children who have never been wounded by the big, bad scary world. Children who know our Dad is going to protect us. We can be like that because we are that.

If you've never considered that pride might be a big part of your anxiety, confess ways in which your heart has been prideful in the space below. It's hard to confess sin because it requires humility. But remember 1 John 1:9 says, "If we confess our sins, he is faithful and righteous to forgive us our sins and to cleanse us from all unrighteousness." And James 4:6 reminds us that God "gives grace to the humble."

Jesus isn't in the business of taking birds or saws away. He's a lover of souls and a lifter of burdens. When we communicate with Him through prayer, remembering the reality that He has that kind of power, we can echo Grandma Marlene (with the correct lyrics), singing, "I'm so happy and here's the reason why; Jesus took my burdens all away. . . ."[4]

DAY TWO
WEIRD NOSE-MOUTH-LIP-FINGER SEASON

Philippians 4:1-9

The first six months after I had my thyroid removed, my body freaked out a little. Weird stuff started happening. For example, I had a photo album saved on my phone titled, "Weird nose mouth lip finger thing" that I brought to doctors' offices all over Nashville.

I don't want to gross you out, but there was ample oozing and swelling and crusting involved. ON MY FACE. Itching and tingling and burning. Is that enough? I'm sensing that you, reading this in the future, are uncomfortable. I'll stop. After just one more descriptor—gook.

So I'd just gone through the thyroid ordeal. I'd had blood tests and CT scans and all sorts of testing. So I guess I should have taken solace in that. But, in my mind, every throat tickle and allergic reaction was a symptom of something bigger. A sniffle is never just a sniffle with me. A sniffle is nasal cancer. An itch is lymphoma. A stomachache is clearly internal bleeding.

Toward the end of my weird nose mouth lip finger thing (WNMLFT from now on), I saw a specialist and described my symptoms. I showed him photos of all the sores, and I gave him a detailed timeline of events. When I was finished, he said, "Some of the words you used to describe your condition . . . are you in the medical field?"

Here's the point I'm getting at: what you put into your mind—what you think on—what you pray for—matters. I spent so much time worrying about being sick that I sounded like a doctor.

Maybe you already have this week's key sentence down. Maybe prayer is already your posture as you fight your anxiety. But if your prayers sound like mine did during WNMLFT season, you might find yourself remaining anxious, even as you pray.

During WNMLFT, my prayers were extremely similar to all the words I typed into *WebMD's* Symptom Checker. It was kind of like:

God, does the tip of my tongue feel numb? Lord, why is it so smooth here and bumpy there? Is that normal? Isn't it supposed to be bumpy in all areas? And my ring finger on the left hand has been itchy for way more than a week. That can't be normal, right, God? Let's You and I see what Google has to say about this for the next two hours.

I don't know that I ever got to the "Amen" because my prayers weren't really prayers as much as they were obsessively-fearful-brainstorming sessions.

What you think on matters.

> **Read Philippians 4:1-9. What are some words in verse 1 that let you know how the author (Paul) felt about the people he was writing to?**

I point out that introduction because it is helpful as we apply the gospel to this passage. In the past, I've often attributed a *tone* to God's Word that just isn't there. This passage is not angry and obstinate. It's loving and helpful.

The Book of Philippians is Paul's letter to the people of Philippi, but it's also God's Word to us, today. God is not attacking us in this chapter for not thinking on the right things. He's lovingly helping us, just as Paul did with the Philippians, to think on the things that will bring life to our souls.

Read verses 4-7 again. What are the four things Paul said to do in these verses?

Which of these four things are you best at? Which do you need the most growth in?

In this letter, Paul was speaking to a church that was in the midst of persecution. So the "worry" these people were dealing with was valid, life-or-death fears.

Have you ever feared persecution for your beliefs? If so, what triggered that fear? If not, how do you feel when you consider persecuted Christians in the world today?

Look back at verse 9. What did Paul say is a result of following his instruction?

It's much harder to fear the broken, sad, and scariness of this world when you are experiencing the tangible presence of the more-powerful-than-ANYTHING God. Praying places your mind on God, and, when your mind is on God, your mind is on peace.

This next exercise might take you some time, but it will be worth it. Use Google (don't get side-tracked on *WebMD*) or a Bible dictionary to look up each of the terms in the chart. Then, write down something in each category that you are grateful for in the blanks beside the terms and back up your answers with a Bible reference. In the third blank, write down what that means for your battle with anxiety. I'll do the first one to give you an example.

	THING TO THINK ON	REFERENCE	WHAT THAT MEANS AS I FIGHT
WHAT IS TRUE?	"I am the way, truth, and the life."	John 14:6	Jesus is the Word, and His words are true, so when I'm afraid, I can remember that if He promises me hope and sharing in His glory for all eternity, I can be comforted by that.
WHAT IS HONORABLE?			
WHAT IS JUST?			
WHAT IS PURE?			

	THING TO THINK ON	REFERENCE	WHAT THAT MEANS AS I FIGHT
WHAT IS LOVELY?			
WHAT IS COMMENDABLE?			
WHAT IS MORALLY EXCELLENT?			
WHAT IS PRAISEWORTHY?			

Close out this day thanking Jesus for the blessings you listed. Ask Him to help your prayers be more worshipful and less doubting, more grateful and less anxious.

Oh, and by the way, it turns out WNMLFT was just an allergy to chapstick.

DAY THREE
WORLD'S MOST AMAZING PENCIL SHARPENER

Matthew 6:1-8

I don't know how extreme your teen angst was when you were in high school, but mine went deep. Pretty much everything I did in ninth grade was an effort to be seen/noticed/respected/admired by, well, every male that existed.

I remember sitting in my third hour class, making intense listening faces during lectures, asking the teacher what I considered to be thoughtful or funny or interesting questions, and getting up to sharpen my pencil with these thoughts in mind: *Are any of the three to seven boys that I'm in love with in this room looking at me, and, if so, are they daydreaming about how they will propose to me when I'm finished sharpening this pencil? And, if they do propose, what will I say? And if they ALL propose, whom will I choose?*

As you can tell, my early ideas about love were very much about, um, me. I was so extremely wrapped up in my desire to be loved that I didn't love other people very well. My whole life was some sort of weird performance art that was, with zero subtlety saying, *LOOK AT ME! LOVE ME! PLEASE, I BEG OF YOU!*

I was also the kid who volunteered to close nearly every class in prayer at my Christian school. Because, I mean, then the teachers and even GOD would love me more, right?

I was a classic example of what Jesus said not to do in today's passage.

Read Matthew 6:1-8.

What did Jesus tell His disciples not to do in verses 1-4?

Is there anything you do in life for the sole purpose of being noticed/praised?

Those first few verses we just read were about generosity—helping the poor and doing good. But the next few we're going to look at are specifically about prayer.

Reread verses 5-8. What do you think Jesus meant when He said that the hypocrites who love to pray in public have their reward?

A lot of us are wired to look for reassurance that we're doing things the right way. There's no anxiety quite like the anxiety that comes with wondering if you got what matters for ETERNITY right. These verses are a gentle reminder to me that prayer isn't a formula to earn something. Prayer is its own reward.

What do the following verses tell you about the benefits of prayer?

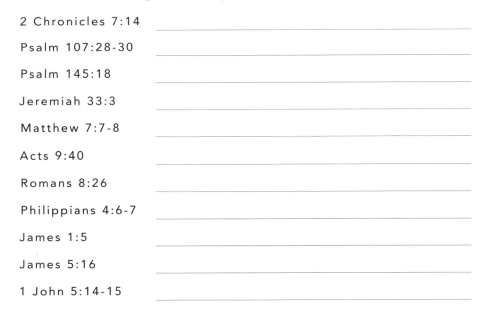

2 Chronicles 7:14

Psalm 107:28-30

Psalm 145:18

Jeremiah 33:3

Matthew 7:7-8

Acts 9:40

Romans 8:26

Philippians 4:6-7

James 1:5

James 5:16

1 John 5:14-15

People who pray falsely for attention don't get the reward of friendship, intimacy, and actual, experiential, back-and-forth conversation with their Creator. There's nothing more incredible, nothing more peace-giving, nothing more worth your time, than talking to God in secret.

Describe the best prayer time you can remember experiencing.

What are some practical ways you can organize your schedule and life to make time and space for one-on-one alone time with God in prayer?

Examine yourself today. Are you still walking up to pencil sharpeners, anxious to be approved by fellow flawed people? You don't need to impress Jesus with your words or actions or pencil-sharpening-prowess. You're loved because you're His. You're forgiven because He's merciful. Dwell on that today in your thoughts, in your prayers, and in your deeds.

DAY FOUR
THE WORST PRAYER
I EVER PRAYED

Matthew 6:9-13; Matthew 11:28-30 and
Romans 8:26-27

The worst prayer I ever prayed was on an operating room table. I was about to have the surgery that would save my life after an ectopic pregnancy left me with no baby, a quart of blood loose in my abdomen, and the worst pain I've ever felt.

The medical staff went from ultrasounding me to sprinting with my gurney in a single second. Papers that said things like "DNR" and "living will" were being shuffled near me, and nurses kept covering me with heated blankets because my teeth were chattering. I was going into shock.

When they transferred me from the gurney to the operating table, a stranger said, "Okay, I want you to count backwards from ten," and I knew I had less than ten seconds to tell God what might be my last words.

Silently, I prayed, *If I should die before I wake, I pray the Lord my soul to take . . .*[5]

What a tragedy. I'd been trying to walk with the Lord for a decade at that point, and my rhyme-y childhood prayer revealed that I was still anxious about my eternal security. Back then I'd had ten years of studying the Bible, praying, trying to pursue the things of the Lord, and, still, I wanted to just MAKE SURE if I'd "done it wrong" all those other times, I'd still make it into heaven.

God used that near-death tragedy in my life to give me assurance of my faith. And that prayer itself is an example of how that works.

Here's the beautiful thing. My worst prayer ever didn't change God's love for me. I could have sung my doubting nursery rhyme, died on the table, and woke up in His arms. It is not our skill that makes prayer powerful. It's the God we pray to. The weakest prayers have worth when we are children of God. And, amazingly, our Father not only makes prayer powerful, He helps us know how to do it.

Can you think of a time you prayed a "weak" prayer? What was happening? What about your prayer makes you consider it "weak"?

Read Matthew 6:9-13. Use it as a model and write your own prayer, verse by verse. For example, I might rewrite verse 9 ("Our Father in heaven, your name be honored as holy") by saying, "God, you are so much higher and bigger than I am. You are good and pure and clean and so different than me.")

Your Version:

Verse 9 _____

Verse 10 _____

Verse 11 _____

Verse 12 _____

Verse 13 _____

The Lord's Prayer here might sound very formal, but the point of Matthew 6 is that God doesn't want you to pray or talk or act to perform. Because of Jesus, God is our Dad. Because of Jesus, we don't have to feel guilty when we talk to Him.

I look at this prayer to help me when I'm not sure how I should pray. It reminds me to thank God for who He is and what He's done, rather than grow desensitized and forgetful. It teaches me I am fully dependent on Him to meet my every need.

Reread Matthew 6:9-13. What does Jesus' example of prayer teach you?

Remember what God does in our weakness? Review Romans 8:26-27. What does He do?

Here's a thing. I don't think God considered my "worst prayer" to be the worst. I don't think that's true, based on what I know of Jesus.

Flip to Matthew 11:28-30. What did Jesus say in these verses?

Isn't that crazy? Jesus is humble. Jesus is the only being who doesn't NEED to be humble!

He and the Father are one. But He lowers Himself. He associates with us, sinners. He has compassion for our weaknesses. We can pray weak prayers. We can pray silent prayers. We can pray frustrated or sad or joyful prayers.

Jesus loves us. It's that simple. And He knows it's hard to talk to someone we can't see. So He gives us this beautiful example. This beautiful reminder.

Close this day out thanking Him for showing us the way and for loving us when we do it wrong or when we feel too weak or anxious to do it at all. Ask Him to transform your prayer life and help you learn to pray in a way that glorifies Him and helps your heart toward peace.

DAY FIVE
JOY'S SECRET LANGUAGE

Matthew 10:22; John 10:10; John 15:18-27 and Romans 8:18-28

The doctors at Vanderbilt don't think our daughter Joy will ever be able to talk. She's such a miracle, but she had so much stacked up against her in those early years that as much as she tries and as much as she thrives, when she tries to vocalize, her sounds just don't come out as words.

People can't understand her.

It's something that was way harder to deal with at first. When we weren't all fluent in sign language, it would kill me to not know what she was saying. Sometimes she'd cry and get upset and make noises, and none of us could figure out what they meant.

Now, she signs, and we usually get it, but once in a while, we're all left scratching our heads, and she usually shrugs and signs, "Never mind—it was nothing," and she walks away.

It's a hard thing. It's a hard thing for her; I'm sure. And it's a hard thing, as her parent, to want to connect and understand what she's thinking and not be able to. Maybe you've experienced something similar when trying to communicate with someone who doesn't speak your language.

We humans, even those of us without any physical or mental special needs, are limited in our communication. Have you ever been speechless? Even people with the most sophisticated vocabularies sometimes find themselves in situations where they just don't have the words.

Read Romans 8:18-28. Which of these verses means the most to you today and why?

In verses 18-22, Paul reflected on how much different it will be when we are free from suffering, free from "labor pains" (v. 22). Can you even imagine it? During my most intense seasons of anxiety, my mind has made me feel like the suffering would never end.

What is a circumstance about which you "groan within" yourself (v. 23) today? What do you look forward to being relieved from?

For Christians, it can be tempting to look at today's passage and feel hopeless about today and like everything will be pins and needles and the wringing of hands until heaven. The gospel tells us this isn't true, though.

Read John 10:10 and copy the second sentence in the space below.

If you've been part of the church for a while, you may have heard the term *abundant life* thrown around. That term comes from this verse, when Jesus was explaining He has come so we can have life in abundance.

Some people misinterpret this and think Jesus is saying if you follow Him, you'll have all the good stuff of life. In reality, Jesus promised otherwise.

Read Matthew 10:22 and John 15:18-27. How did Jesus say our lives as followers of Him would be?

Life can be hard and still be abundant. Jesus told His disciples and is telling us now that joyful life is from Him. Life in abundance is only found when we pursue Him and His kingdom. Anything and everything else will leave us anxious and unsatisfied.

Have you tested that truth? Have you pursued peace and pleasure in things outside of Jesus and found they didn't work?

Share below about the things your flesh craves and where those roads lead.

So we pray. We pray, remembering the truth of Romans 8. We pray, remembering the truth of Jesus as our way to life and peace. We pray, remembering the reality that after this life, we will someday be in actual glory with everlasting peace that can never go anywhere. We pray that way, and it changes us right now.

We pray that way, and the casting of cares and releasing of burdens actually happens.

One day, my youngest asked me if Joy would be able to talk in heaven. It got me emotional. I'd never considered it. My communication with my non-verbal daughter is limited. But Philippians 3:21 tells me that at Christ's return, we'll get new bodies. Perfect ones where all the parts work and we won't fear them breaking down anymore. And Joy's ears and mouth will work. And we'll never wonder what she's saying as she praises her Maker with us around the throne.

What are you grateful for right now? Tell God about it. He's listening.

This past week, you completed the Session Six personal study in your books. If you weren't able to do so, no big deal! You can still follow along with the questions, be involved in the discussion, and watch the video. When you are ready to begin, open up your time in prayer and push play on Video Six for Session Six.

WATCH

Write down any thoughts, verses, or things you want to remember as you watch the video for Session Six of *Anxious*.

FROM THIS WEEK'S STUDY

As a group, review this week's memory verse.

Humble yourselves, therefore, under the mighty hand of God, so that he may exalt you at the proper time, casting all your cares on him, because he cares about you.

1 PETER 5:6-7

REVIEW SESSION SIX PERSONAL STUDY

From Day One: What are some practical ways you can "humble yourself" before God?

From Day Two: In Philippians 4:4-7, what four things did Paul say to do?

From Day Three: What are some practical ways you can organize your schedule and life to make time and space for one-on-one alone time with God in prayer?

From Day Four: What does Jesus' example of prayer teach you?

From Day Five: Which of the verses that you looked at from Romans 8 means the most to you this week and why?

DISCUSS

This week, we studied prayer. We talked about how to do it, how not to do it, and how we can cast our cares on Jesus. If you're comfortable with it, discuss your own experience with prayer. In which ways do you struggle? What are some disciplines you have put in your life to help you? Do you have any amazing stories of answered prayer?

What is one thing you have been anxious about this week? How can this group pray for you?

This session's main idea is "Prayer is our posture in the fight against anxiety." Are there any ways you now intend to pray differently when taking your burdens to the Lord? Discuss ideas with your group.

PRAY

This would be a great week to use most of your time to pray for one another. Consider praying through the Lord's Prayer (Matt. 6:9-13) together. Maybe take one verse at a time and add to it in the direction Jesus leads. Look back to Day Four and see how you changed each verse's example into your own words. Take turns praying like this and for one another's burdens.

To access the teaching sessions, use the instructions in the back of your Bible study book.

ANXIOUS PRAYER   135

ANXIOUS READER

THE BIBLE IS OUR WEAPON IN
THE FIGHT AGAINST ANXIETY

[THE ORDINANCES OF THE LORD] ARE MORE **DESIRABLE THAN GOLD**— THAN AN ABUNDANCE OF PURE GOLD; AND SWEETER THAN HONEY DRIPPING FROM A HONEYCOMB. IN ADDITION, YOUR SERVANT IS WARNED BY THEM, AND IN KEEPING THEM THERE IS **AN ABUNDANT REWARD**.

Psalm 19:10-11

DAY ONE
SO HOW'S LEVITICUS GOING FOR YA?

Hebrews 4:1-12

In 2008, a friend and I decided we were going to hold each other accountable to read through the Bible from Genesis to Revelation in one year.

It was a good goal to set, and the first few days of texting back and forth went really well.

The thing is, we both dropped off. One of us missed a day. One of us had a crisis. The texts stopped. The plan was thwarted. We never finished it.

I write this in the year 2020 and smile because every few years, she and I will check in with a text: "So . . . what are you on now . . . Leviticus?

Bible reading can be hard. The Bible was written in different languages across years and years to multiple audiences. It contains books like Leviticus and Revelation. Add to that complexity the reality that we have an enemy who comes "only to steal and kill and destroy" (John 10:10), and it should be no surprise that there are days Bible reading seems like work.

But the Bible isn't just a book from history; it is a book from heaven (Ps. 119:89). It doesn't just have old words; it has God's words (2 Tim. 3:16). It isn't just long; it is alive (1 Pet. 1:23). The Bible literally does supernatural work in your heart while you read it (Isa. 55:11).

Our own weakness, anxiety, selfishness, and sin, at times, make the Bible hard to read, but it is light and life itself (Ps. 119:130; Matt. 4:4). The Bible is our weapon as we fight to trust God and find the peace He gives.

What are some of the most common reasons you don't read your Bible?

I'll answer that question as well. One of the primary reasons I will ignore the Bible is because I sometimes bring my anxiousness filter into the text.

When my anxiety is fierce, I find I can misread Scripture and, instead of a loving God with an easy yoke, I see a judging One with a list of demands I can never adhere to. God's plan for us is peace, but it is possible to read the Bible and panic.

Read Hebrews 4:1-12. What does your heart and mind latch onto when you look at verse 1?

This is a great example of how anxiety can impact the reading of Scripture. Some of you probably saw "the promise to enter his rest remains" (v. 1) and thought *Yeeeeeeees.*

Others of you saw, "beware that none of you be found to have fallen short" (v. 1) and thought, *I'm dooooomed.*

Which reaction did you have? (Feel free to add your own write-in reaction. I've given you an extra box.)

○ *Yeeeeeeees.*
○ *I'm dooooomed.*
○ _____.

Both phrases are true. Here in Hebrews 4 is the hope of rest, as well as a warning about unbelief. It can be pretty scary to read if you're used to listening to the lies your anxiety tells you. But the perfect love of Christ "casts out fear" (1 John 4:18, ESV), so let's look, soberly, at this text and examine our hearts—not in a panic but as children of God.

Look at Hebrews 4:2-4.

What keeps people from entering the rest?

What are some things you do when you're trying to rest?

The Lord, the One who invented rest (see verse 4) when He created everything you know and see, knows how to satisfy your soul. He knows how to give you peace because He invented peace.

Our Hebrews 4 passage deals with several types of rest, among them are— ultimate rest in salvation, eternal enjoyment in heaven, and peace that we can experience even now on earth through Christ's provision.

How does the eternal rest promised by God through salvation in this passage form the way that you can rest your anxious heart even in the here and now?

Entering into the rest can be as easy as entering into His presence. If God's Word is alive and true and made to lead you to Him, time in God's Word should be a comfort, not a chore.

Now look back at verse 10. When we imitate God by resting, what is it that we are resting from?

It's exhausting trying to do everything right, isn't it? Because we fail! Eventually our working turns to worrying turns to wandering away. And if our hope and our peace and our rest is all tied up in us "doing good," we will be crushed when we have a bad day.

Reread verse 11. Rather than pursuing our own goodness, what does God's Word tell us to make an effort to do?

In verse 12, what are some things we learn the Word of God is able to do?

Isn't it crazy that a book can read your mind? I mean, it sounds crazy until you remember that the Bible is inspired, or "God-breathed." If God's Word is alive and active in that book, He is certainly able to know you and speak to you, shape you and teach you through those words. It's such a beautiful truth.

My friend and I or your friends and you can plan to try to read through the Bible in a year or three months or a weekend. And maybe you'll do it! But if you're doing it to earn God's approval, to check a box, or to stay out of hell (that was me), you're missing it. You're missing the rest. You're missing the magic. You're missing the gift that God's Word is to our anxious hearts. God wants you to read His Word and enter His rest here on earth and eternally.

Close out this day by thanking God for His Word, this gift, this weapon. In your prayer, reflect on a time God's Word was a weapon in your fight against fear, if one comes to mind.

DAY TWO
"GOOD PEOPLE" AND BIBLE READING

Psalm 19:1-11

Here's some of what I battle when it comes to Bible reading:

- I get anxious about "doing it right" or "doing it enough," and I forget that it is a living, active gift.

- I get distracted thinking about using the wrong kind of Bible. Do super Christians read the Bible on their phones? That's not as good, right? I need a big, worn study Bible. I need a Bible that doesn't have the Tiny Wings™ app on it. Man, Tiny Wings is great. Can you believe your daughter has gotten better than you at Tiny Wings? Unacceptable, Scarlet. Be better. Just be better. We're going to practice Tiny Wings today, and we will absolutely win the race to Island 4 tonight.

- I get anxious/frustrated when I read things I don't understand.

- I focus so much on potential dangers or problems I feel like I need to fix that I fail to look to the Lord.

It takes discipline to read the Bible regularly and well. What sort of rhythms have you put in place in your life to help you stay consistent?

Reading the Bible doesn't have to be a battle. Today, we're going to look at the first part of a psalm David wrote, and we'll reflect on what it tells us about the Bible. But first, let's look at the beginning of this psalm.

Read Psalm 19:1-6. In these verses, what is it that is declaring and proclaiming the glory of God?

General revelation is the phrase used to explain how God's glory and character are revealed to mankind through nature.[1] It's that thing when you stand at the ocean, speechless. The thing when you see a baby being born or you stand on top of a mountain or look out over a valley and just think, *Wow.*

The natural world tells us God is glorious. Creation, in its scope and life, reveals some of the beauty and grandeur of God.

But God doesn't leave us staring at trees and "Wowing" at seas while wondering what it all means.

Read Psalm 19:7-11.

Special revelation is supernatural communication between God and humanity.[2] Verses 7-11 are speaking directly to that.

What key words in this passage tell us these verses are about the Bible?

What words did David use in verses 7 and 8 to describe the Bible?

Read verse 11. What did David mean when he said, "in keeping them there is great reward" (ESV)?

When I was a teenager, I'd leave to hang out with my friends or go on a date, and my dad would stop me and say, "Scarlet, remember, all sin leads to heartache." He said that so many times.

He was giving me freedom. Freedom to go sit in movie theaters or go to parties with other seventeen year olds. But, a warning. His warning wasn't, "Don't do bad stuff, or I'll ground you." His warning was, "If you sin, you will hurt. I love you, and I don't want you to hurt."

That's what the Bible does for us so often! It is like God, leaning over the kitchen counter, saying, "This is how to live, child! Remember, sin leads to heartache."

The reward of "keeping" God's Word as a priority in your life is peace—joy—happiness! He doesn't give us rules to harm us. He gives us instruction to protect us. He is a good Father.

In the space below, write out some personal reasons you treasure God's Word.

DAY THREE
A LETTER WE CAN LEARN FROM

Matthew 16:25 and 2 Timothy 3:10-17

Paul, the apostle, (the guy who was also known as Saul—a serious big-time Jew who killed Christians, but then Jesus blinded him and revealed Himself and then he spent the rest of his life serving and preaching and writing Bible books—that guy) . . . well, let me just stop and take a breath. I'm just really proud of myself for that summary of Paul's life.

If you want the non-abridged version, read about his amazing conversion story in Acts 9.

Moving on. Paul wrote a bunch of Bible books—letters to churches and to people—letters that were written then and for then but that God designed to be applied to us today.

Author and Bible teacher Jen Wilkin did an Instagram Q&A, and I loved what she said about applying Scripture. She said, "All Scripture applies first to its original audience . . . This is important because how we apply it today must relate to how they applied it then. It can't mean something to us that it could never have meant to them then. Once you examine what it said to them-for-then, think about its message to us-for-always."[3]

So first, let's look at the "then" context of our 2 Timothy passage. Paul was writing this letter to Timothy, whom he met during a missionary journey.

In the chapter we're looking at today, he was encouraging Timothy not to lose heart during times of stress and suffering.

Read 2 Timothy 3:10-17.

What was Paul reflecting on in verses 10 and 11?

Who did Paul credit for his rescue from troubles?

What are some difficult circumstances you've endured recently?

Are you able to echo Paul in any similar ways? How did the Lord provide for you?

Reread verses 12-13. What did Paul say all who want to live a godly life will experience?

I used to get so caught up in verses like these. I'd think, *NO THANK YOU. I WANT A GOOD LIFE.* But I've lived plenty of seasons of "good life" and still been miserable.

I've lived fearful I'd lose what I had. Stressed over things that didn't matter. We can get caught up fearing the bad stuff of this life when we forget that we have a prize that can't be taken from us.

We think if we cling to the things we love in life, we'll save them. But the opposite is actually true.

Read Matthew 16:25.

What did Jesus say will happen to someone who gets caught up in "sav[ing] his life"?

Then, Jesus went on to describe a group that will find life. What are believers to do with their lives, according to Jesus?

If we are anxious to cling to anything in life other than Jesus, we'll find that we're never at peace. No matter how good we are at worrying, we aren't capable of holding on to anything. We don't have the power to keep life going and to keep jobs safe and to keep bodies healthy. When we "lose" our lives or surrender them, when we trust that Jesus knows better than we do, there is where we find the peace.

Read 2 Timothy 3:14-17.

What did Paul say Scripture gives us (v. 15)?

I love verses 16 and 17 so much. What a beautiful list of benefits. In the chart below, I want you to take each benefit and write down in the blank how that specific thing can help you as you fight your anxiety.

Teaching _____

Rebuking _____

Correcting _____

Training in
Righteousness _____

The Bible teaches us about the God who died to free us from slavery to fear. The Bible rebukes us when we are numb to sin and indulging in self-centeredness. The Bible corrects us when we look to the wrong things for comfort and security. The Bible trains us to live lives centered on enjoying the love we have in Christ and sharing it with others. The Bible reminds us that to lose our lives is to find our lives.

It really does equip us. It equips us to be happy, healthy children. It prepares us to be ambassadors—service-minded, fulfilled, contented people who bring their burdens to the only One who is strong enough to carry them.

Close this day asking the Lord what He wants to speak into your life in regard to your fears today. Ask Him. Read. Listen. Write it down below. Remember it. God is for You. He loves you. His Word is a gift and a weapon.

DAY FOUR
THE WORD IS A PERSON

Genesis 1:26; Matthew 24:35; Luke 21:33 and John 1:1-5,14

Remember in Day One when we talked about Hebrews 4:12 and how the Word of God can discern your thoughts and intentions? Well, I could barely wait to get here, to Day Four, because we are going to talk about why this book has such power. Why is this book able to change us and help us and even KNOW us? Today, we're looking at one of my favorite parts of the Bible—John 1. John 1 tells us who the Word is.

Read John 1:1-5. What do we learn about "the Word" from these verses?

Now, look down the Bible page to verse 14. If the Word is God, and the Word was made flesh and dwelt among us, who is the Word?

Commentator James Montgomery Boice wrote,

What do you think of Jesus Christ? Who is he? According to Christianity this is the most important question you or anyone else will ever have to face. It is important because it is inescapable—you will have to answer it sooner or later, in this world or in the world to come—and because the quality of your life here and your eternal destiny depend upon your answer. Who is Jesus Christ? If he was only a man, then you can safely forget him. If he is God, as he claimed to be, and as all Christians believe, then you should yield your life to him. You should worship and serve him faithfully.[4]

The reality that Jesus is God isn't just a fact you have to memorize to excel at the Christian faith. It's the basis of our faith. If Jesus isn't God, then we aren't forgiven. If Jesus isn't God, we still await punishment for our sins. If Jesus isn't God, we have no access to our Creator, no access to the joy we can only find in His presence, and no access to eternal life beyond the grave.

Jesus is God. Jesus has always been God and will always be God. But Jesus isn't only described as God. Jesus is "the Word." Jesus, our Rescuer, our Hope, our Peace, is alive in the pages of Scripture.

Now, look at Genesis 1:26. Are there any words in this verse that lead you to believe God the Father wasn't alone when He created the world? List them here.

John 1:2-3 affirms Jesus was there with God the Father, in the beginning. So in this little handful of verses, we learn that Jesus is called the Word.

We learn He is God—that He also, as God, created all things. Listen, maybe that makes your brain hurt. No problem. Just thank God He is smarter than us!

But it's really important as we seek to worship Jesus to recognize He isn't just a guy, and He isn't even "just" God. Jesus is revealed to us in the Bible. God is speaking through those pages.

Have you ever been reading the Bible and experienced Jesus? (By that, I mean, have you ever been reading the Bible and felt you were not just reading a book about God but that you were communicating *with* God through the power of the Holy Spirit?)

What are some specific passages He has used in your life? Share about them in the space below.

Look up Matthew 24:35 and Luke 21:33. What do these accounts tell us Jesus said?

Isn't it comforting to know that Jesus created us, that He is forever, that no matter what comes against them, His words are forever too? When you hear them, when you read them, when you commit them to memory, the Spirit stirs in your soul and helps you believe the truth—the truth that this scary world isn't forever, but Jesus is.

What is the most recent thing you've done when you felt overcome by panic?

Sometimes, I wake up in a panic. Maybe it's a bad dream, or, often, I just wake up to get water and a horrible thought crosses my mind. What if such and such happened to my husband? What if one of my daughters does this or that? What if-what if-what if-what if . . .

Often, I lie back down and either think of the Word or read the Word, or sometimes I just whisper the Word's name, "Jesus."

But if you only have one word, that's the one. He is the One. He is the Word.

Take the next few minutes to look through my list of favorite anxiety-fighting memory verses in the Appendix on pages 186–187. Pick out a verse that will give you some words to carry with you for the rest of the day. Write out the verse you picked that reminds you how loved and protected you are by the Prince of peace in the space below and try to memorize it.

If you read the Bible and don't experience Jesus, examine your heart and ask yourself what your motives are.

Try to answer these next few questions honestly by checking the one that best fits your response.

When you open the Bible, are you looking to experience God, or are you trying to "do what good people do"?
○ **Looking to experience God.**
○ **Trying to do what good people do.**

When you read the Bible, do you open it randomly and pull verses out not knowing what they mean and then close it, feeling like you've done your duty for the day?
○ **Yes.**
○ **Nah, not my style.**

If you don't understand something you've read, do you give up, or do you press in and research what it means?
○ **Throw in the towel.**
○ **Research is my middle name.**

A lot of our Bible frustrations exist because we forget that God meets us when we open the Bible. We read it because we should. Or we read it because that makes us feel like we're winning at life. Don't read the Bible like you're completing a homework assignment you don't want to do. Read it like you're on a coffee date with your best friend and what you're reading is what He's saying (and what He's saying are the words of life). Go to the Bible like what you're reading is His advice to you, His encouragement to you, His comfort for you.

Now, write out a prayer, worshiping and thanking God for giving us access to Himself through His Word.

DAY FIVE
WATCHING JOY PRAY
John 17:1-19

Watching Joy pray in sign language is one of the most rewarding things I get to experience as a mom. It's amazing, because when I met her, three years ago, she didn't have any language. She had no words. When she felt things or needed things, she didn't know what to do.

For a week and a half, while still in China, we actually didn't think she'd ever learn any words. She was so medically not ok. But our first glimmer of hope came at the buffet table when she realized that every time Daddy fed her a bite of vanilla yogurt, it was after he brought her fingers to her lips. The sign for *food*.

Next, she learned the word *drink*. Then, *cracker*. Sweet Joy was hungry. And those three words changed her life.

Now, she prays.

This week, I had a tooth pulled (my teeth hate me), and before I left for the dentist, I told the girls I was a little scared. My oldest offered to pray for me, and it was so precious. And then, Joy took over. She squeezed her eyes shut, and her hand went to work praying for every detail of what I was about to experience. She prayed that I wouldn't be afraid.

Read John 17:1-19.

In John 17:1-19, we read about Jesus, the Word made flesh, praying for His disciples. Two times in His prayer, He made requests in connection to the Word. What were those two requests?

In verse 13, Jesus desired for His disciples to have completed joy. Write about a time you have obeyed God's Word and felt joy.

In verse 17, Jesus asked that God sanctify His friends through the Word. Let's give this some attention. Look up the word *sanctify* in a dictionary and write out the definition below.

To be *sanctified* is to be separated from things that are evil, things that are not pleasing to God. When we talk about being sanctified, we are talking about living as followers of Christ. So, naturally, we see plenty of instruction about how Christians are to live in the Word.

We're not going to walk perfectly. But to be sanctified means to take steps of obedience and pursue the Lord through prayer and through His Word. That is how we become like Him. That is how we experience the joy of verse 13. This is how we learn to be less anxious people. The Word leads us toward sanctification and away from anxiety.

Think back to the most peaceful season of your life. What were you doing? What was happening?

Where were you in your relationship with Christ?

One of the most peaceful seasons of my life was when we were in the adoption process. We didn't have the money to do what we were doing. We didn't have medical answers or even hope that things would work out at all. But we knew we were walking the direction the Lord was leading. His Word comforted us when we were sad. It convicted us out of our fears. It humbled us when we forgot He was the only reason anything good ever happens to us.

Why does it matter that Jesus asked God to sanctify His friends through the Word? Because, essentially, what He was asking was that His friends would be safe—have peace—be happy. Safety, peace, and happiness are the opposites of anxiety. And God wants that for us. God wants that for you.

Copy this week's memory verse (found at the beginning of this lesson) in the margin. (I've shown you where). ➝

Now, let's look back at the memory verses we've already learned. See if you can fill in the blanks from memory without looking back. God's Word is a weapon. His Word is a comfort. His Word is a way to fight anxiety. Praise God.

SESSION TWO

Many say about me, "There is no _____ for him in God." *Selah*. But you, LORD, are a _____ around me, my _____, and the one who _____ up ____ _____.

PSALM 3:2-3

SESSION THREE

But seek _____ the kingdom of God and
his _____, and all these things will
be _____ for you. Therefore _____ _____
about tomorrow, because tomorrow will worry
about itself. Each day has enough _____ of its own.

MATTHEW 6:33-34

SESSION FOUR

But Moses said to the people, "Don't be _____.
Stand _____ and see the LORD's _____
that ____ will _____for you today; for the
Egyptians you see today, you will never see again. The
LORD _____ _____ for you, and you must be _____."

EXODUS 14:13-14

SESSION FIVE

If you keep _____ at this time, relief and _____
will come to the Jewish people _____ another
_____, but you and your father's family will be
destroyed. Who knows, _____ you have come to
your royal position for _____ a _____ as _____.

ESTHER 4:14

SESSION SIX

_____ yourselves, therefore, under the

_____ hand of _____, so that he may exalt

you at the _____ time, _____ all your _____

on _____, because he _____ about you.

1 PETER 5:6-7

This past week, you completed the Session Seven personal study in your books. If you weren't able to do so, no big deal! You can still follow along with the questions, be involved in the discussion, and watch the video. When you are ready to begin, open up your time in prayer and push play on Video Seven for Session Seven.

WATCH

Write down any thoughts, verses, or things you want to remember as you watch the video for Session Seven of *Anxious*.

FROM THIS WEEK'S STUDY

As a group, review this week's memory verse.

[The ordinances of the LORD] are more desirable than gold—than an abundance of pure gold; and sweeter than honey dripping from a honeycomb. In addition, your servant is warned by them, and in keeping them there is an abundant reward.

PSALM 19:10-11

REVIEW SESSION SEVEN PERSONAL STUDY

From Day One: What are some of the most common reasons you don't read your Bible?

According to Hebrews 4:2-4, what keeps people from entering the rest?

From Day Two: What sort of rhythms have you put in place in your life to help you stay consistent with your Bible reading?

From Day Three: What are some of the benefits of Scripture, as found in 2 Timothy 3:16-17?

From Day Four: Have you ever been reading the Bible and experienced Jesus? (By that, I mean, have you ever been reading the Bible and felt you were not just reading a book about God but that you were communicating *with* God through the power of the Holy Spirit?)

From Day Five: Think back to the most peaceful season of your life. What were you doing? What was happening? Where were you in your relationship with Christ?

DISCUSS

This week, we talked about fighting anxiety with the Word as our weapon. If you're comfortable sharing, discuss ways and circumstances in which you've used God's Word to fight your worries.

What are some ways you've struggled with your Bible reading? Since you're together as a group, this is a great opportunity for those of you who have walked with the Lord for a long time to share what has helped you in your pursuit of studying the Word.

Do you have a key Scripture passage you turn to when you're feeling afraid? Discuss that passage with your group.

Is there something you could do together as a group to hold each other accountable for time in the Word/Bible memorization? Brainstorm together.

PRAY

Today, challenge yourselves as a group to pray Scripture. Take five minutes to look through the Psalms or other parts of the Bible for some Scripture you can use in your prayer time together. Then spend the rest of the prayer time lifting up the needs of your group and asking God to help you as you encourage one another and fight, side by side, with the living and active Word as your weapon.

To access the teaching sessions, use the instructions in the back of your Bible study book.

ANXIOUS READER   159

ANXIOUS TOGETHER

COMMUNITY IS OUR LIFELINE IN
THE FIGHT AGAINST ANXIETY

AND LET US CONSIDER ONE ANOTHER IN ORDER TO PROVOKE **LOVE** AND **GOOD WORKS**, NOT NEGLECTING TO GATHER TOGETHER, AS SOME ARE IN THE HABIT OF DOING, BUT **ENCOURAGING EACH OTHER**, AND ALL THE MORE AS YOU SEE THE DAY APPROACHING.

Hebrews 10:24-25

DAY ONE
MEDICAL SHOWS, SNACKS, AND PLEASE, NO PEOPLE

Hebrews 10:19-25

Shortly after my near-death ectopic pregnancy experience, I got pretty dark.

I couldn't return to work for a month because I couldn't move. I was married without any kids yet, and my husband had gone back to work, so all there was in my life that month was the TV medical dramas I binged on, the snacks I binged on, and the deep sadness I weirdly relished.

I wanted to be sad. I wanted to be distracted. I wanted the world to leave me alone.

I remember my small group trying to invite me back into civilization, and I remember ignoring their calls. I remember Super Bowl party invitations I threw away. And I remember staying home from church on Sundays, even when I was well enough to go.

I didn't want to hear people telling me God had a reason for this. I didn't want people to smile sympathetically and say, "When are you going to try for another baby?" I didn't want people encouraging me to pray. I didn't want any of it. I just wanted to escape with my *Grey's Anatomy*, *House*, and my bedside bag of Hot Tamales®.

Have you ever experienced a season of discouragement?

What were the circumstances, and what were you feeling?

I pushed people away. I pushed God away. I didn't want to fake-smile or fake-talk or fake-pray. I just wanted to be distracted from my sadness, and I thought the way to do that was to isolate myself.

Deep down, I was afraid to approach God with my feelings because I knew my feelings were misguided. It felt wrong to be mad at Him for the circumstances I was in. So I stayed silent. I stayed away. And my soul started to shrivel.

> **Read Hebrews 10:19-25. Because of Jesus, what does verse 22 say our hearts will be full of?**

I think the enemy jumps at the opportunity when he sees a discouraged Christian. Since he can't take us out, he just tries to shut us out. If he can keep us from wanting to approach the throne of grace, he can keep us shriveling up.

The truth is, we can approach God with boldness, even if we're discouraged. Even if we're messed up and angry and at our worst. We can approach our Father and talk to Him and trust Him because of the blood of Jesus. (If this phrase is unfamiliar to you, flip over to pages 184–185 in the Appendix.)

Look again at verse 23.

> **Why is it that we can hold on to our confession of hope?**

> **In the space below, write out your own confession of hope in a couple of sentences. What has Jesus done for you?**

Read verses 24-25.

God created us for community. God created us to help each other and to remind each other that we have the same confession. What Christ did for one messed up, angry, sad, flawed human, He did for all of us. His sacrifice bought us access to the only One who can comfort us and heal us and assure us we are loved and okay, even when we don't feel like it.

He uses other believers to remind us of this.

> **Can you think of a time in your life when the body of Christ held you together when you were weak? Describe it below.**

Sometimes anxiety doesn't look like being scared of bad things. Sometimes it looks like being afraid of God, being anxious about asking Him the hard questions and being worried about letting other people help us and love us and see us at our worst.

The community of other Christians is our lifeline in the fight against anxiety. I don't know how I would have crawled out of my TV and candy crises if it hadn't been for Brandi and Nicole bringing me meals, Pastor Rick telling me the disciples struggled with doubting Jesus too, Toni telling me I could tell God how I felt even if my feelings were painful, and Jackie praying and fasting on my behalf and being a non-judgmental ear when I said I didn't want to pray. Those people brought me back to life with Jesus.

> **What can you do this week to lean on other believers or let them lean on you?**

DAY TWO
ON HATING HELPING
Acts 2:42-47

I've cycled through a lot of church-y anxieties. Maybe you can relate. I have often dreaded Sunday mornings in fear of:

- being asked to serve in children's ministry;

- being approached by eager, passionate mission trip leaders;

- being told unexpectedly that someone had a "word" for me (I'm not anti-"word," but it has, during anxious times, certainly caught me off guard).

I think, if you'd given me some sort of truth serum during the years I was a very young pastor's wife, I would have confessed something to the effect of, "I hate helping."

If you get anxious about other people placing expectations or demands on you, that's probably not something you'd like to admit on paper. So I won't ask the question, lest someone look over at your Bible study book when you're sharing answers. But I suspect you've sometimes felt the same way.

The church can, at times, feel like a steady stream of *DO MORE. HELP ME. GIVE THIS. BOY, DO I HAVE A CALLING FOR YOU.* At just the wrong time, it can send you over the edge.

As Christians, we want to please the Lord, so when we feel like we're not or feel like other people think we're not, it can lead us to run away from the people we need and the people who need us.

Let's compare this tendency to the activity of the early church.

Read Acts 2:42-47.

What were the early Christians devoted to?

How do these things compare to what you or the believers in your life are devoted to?

This next part is for those of you who are wired like me to read your own experiences and fears and failures into the text. Let me reassure you.

I don't want you to start breathing into a paper bag over this passage as I have in the past. We have to look at the cultural context of the early church. Just because they gathered daily doesn't mean you're out of the will of God if you don't have daily worship gatherings at your church.

On this note, Ajith Fernando wrote,

> Nowhere is it stated that Christians should continue to meet daily as they did in the first days of the Jerusalem church (v. 46). Considering the responsibilities one has in family life and in witness and vocation in society, it may not be a good idea for Christians to have a program in church every day of the week. History has shown that usually at the start of a revival there are daily meetings. After that it tapers off into a less frequent but regular pattern. Certainly it is helpful for new believers to be with Christians daily until they are more stable in their faith.[1]

All this to say, breathe in and breathe out if your small group isn't on a daily schedule. Don't throw away your traditional church programming experience because of this text. The early church was a community. They ate together. They helped each other. They worshiped, side by side.

In our culture, this might look like texting the family in your small group to see if they need help organizing meals after a surgery. It might look like giving your bag of hand-me-down toddler clothes to the young family that shares one car. (We were that family and my daughters still wear those clothes—thank you, Beverly!) It looks like making attendance and participation in your local church a priority. Not because you will be punished if you don't, but because you will be loved and able to love and encourage others when you do!

Look at verses 46 and 47. What two adjectives describe the hearts of the people in this early church?

I remember reading Acts 2 when I was in the I-hate-helping phase of my life and thinking, *OK, this sounds terrible. I don't want to have people in my house/room/world. I don't want to give away my stuff. I want to eat nachos by myself, thank you.* (I actually still stand by that one. Eating nachos alone is the only way to eat nachos.)

Our inherent selfishness can lead us to believe we will feel peaceful if we're alone with our nachos, detached from people's drama. But in the Spirit, we have everything in common. When we learn to let go of our other-people-anxiety, we can actually experience things like JOY, sincere love, and peace.

Share about a time you experienced joy in being there for a brother or sister in Christ.

There's so much beauty in being dependent on each other. There's beauty in needing other believers. When we approach the Lord and one another with the humility that says, "I need Jesus, and I need you," we find that we're not alone. When we're scared, we're held together and surrounded by a body of believers who share our hope and remind us of our hope and embody our hope in their actions.

I'm happy to report I don't hate helping anymore. That's because as I got a little older and a little more world-weary, I discovered how much I needed help. I've experienced the deep need for the sincere love and generosity of other believers. I've known the joy of being weak when others who were strong in the body of Christ comforted me and restored me and led me back to the peace I have because I am held by Christ.

Close out this day praying for the people in your life that you might be used by the Lord to love them and comfort them and assure them they are loved and safe. Ask the Lord to help you have the courage to imitate the early church and become a person who loves helping and being helped.

DAY THREE
WOULD YOU RATHER CHANGE DIAPERS OR LEARN SIGN LANGUAGE?

John 13:34-35; 1 Corinthians 12:12-26 and Philippians 2:8

Being part of the body of Christ feels a little bit like playing that game "Would You Rather?"

One of my favorite church moments happened while discussing a sermon with some friends. We'd been meeting together for a while, and we were a smorgasbord of people. There was a couple in their twenties—the husband a Christian musician and the wife in nursing school. There was a single guy, an older married couple, and a handful of other people in varying life stages and situations. We didn't have a whole lot in common besides Jesus.

So this one day, we started discussing what our pastor had taught and what his message was encouraging us to pursue. We went around the circle sharing what we felt personally called to.

One person said she wanted to sign up to rock babies in the nursery on Sundays. A newlywed couple said they had a heart to foster middle school boys from troubled homes. We talked about the struggles of communication we were experiencing in our adoption. And after a few minutes of sharing, we all started laughing.

We all felt called to such different things, and not a single one of us wanted anything to do with what the person next to us felt called to.

It was a happy moment because we all realized we were being the body, as God intended it.

I remember my husband saying, "I would never, ever want to rock babies on Sundays. That is the last thing I would sign up to do." And whoever said that laughed and said, "Well, I don't know how you all adopted a deaf daughter. That sounds impossible to me."

It was a really great reminder that surrendered people are called to serve in ways that lead to joy. We don't need to fear what God will ask us to do.

Anxiety can lead us to be scared of callings, but love leads us to pursue serving in ways that fit how we were made.

Read 1 Corinthians 12:12-26.

What are we, as believers, called in this passage?

What "body part" do you think you are, or could be, in the body of Christ?

What gifts or desires has God planted in you that led you to that conclusion?

Look at verses 15-24. Have you ever wished you were a different part in the body of Christ? Have you ever been envious of someone who was called to something different?

What did that person have that you felt you were lacking? How do you think Jesus would speak into that feeling?

God didn't design us to be a people who tear each other down and pursue someone else's calling. We are to work together in unity with concern for each other.

Read John 13:34-35.

How does Jesus command us to treat one another?

What will this you-first love show the world, according to verse 35?

Christ set the ultimate example for us in this. He certainly could have wanted an easier job. Instead, He humbled Himself.

How does Philippians 2:8 tell us Jesus humbled Himself?

Jesus left the majesty of heaven and came here as an infant. He lived His life meeting the needs of others, and He died that excruciating death that brought His people life.

When we delight in the Lord, we are able to delight in how He made us. We are able to use the gifts He's given us to love and to serve, and it's there that we find joy. It's there that anxiety disappears. It's there that we stop worrying about our comfort and safety because we're too busy being blessed serving the needs of our friends.

What are some ways in which you feel God has uniquely equipped you to be able to serve the body?

In the space below, think of three people who have been "the body" to you, suffering in your suffering, rejoicing in your joys and delighting in your honor. Make an effort to reach out to them and encourage them this week.

1.

2.

3.

Who can you serve this week? What can you do? Who has God called you to love right now?

If you're feeling anxious about your calling, use the space below to pray for God to grant you clarity of purpose and joy in giving yourself to the work of His kingdom. Pray for joy and peace and pray God uses you to help others see they are loved.

DAY FOUR
SCARY PEOPLE ON MONDAY NIGHTS
Romans 15:7-13 and 2 Corinthians 3:18

When I was pregnant with my youngest, I had aversions to meat and small groups. My husband was leading our group, and I was—um—vocally opposed to pregnant participation.

"I'm keeping a baby alive! How am I supposed to also be with people on Monday nights?" I would, of course, panic about it.

In my mind, small-grouping while with child was an impossible task. It meant babysitting-arranging and long-listening and people asking for help. I spent Monday afternoons worried someone on Monday night would need my help while I was trying to give all my energy and focus to baby growing. What horror!

Yep. That's me. That's your Bible study coach.

I'll never forget the night the group brainstormed about a service project we could do together.

I wanted to be transported to another planet. *What if they voted for us to go find murderers mid-murdering and tell them about Jesus? What if they asked us to gain the trust of the mid-murdering murderers by letting them babysit my newborn?*

I pondered excuses. I dreaded Monday nights.

And then, something happened. I sat beside other Jesus followers enough nights in a row that I started to love them. They answered study questions with Bible verses they had memorized. They held my baby (who was eventually born) when my arms got tired. They brought us meals when we'd had a rough week. This group loved my fear away, and their love made me want to love them back. Then, it made me want to love the whole world.

In fact, God called us to adopt Joy while we did life alongside those people.

Read Romans 15:7-13.

What does verse 7 tell us we are to do to one another as Christ has done for us?

What did Christ become on behalf of God's truth?

What did He confirm to the fathers?

In your own life, your own church, your own local body of believers, what unique opportunities do you personally have to be a servant to the people around you?

We, as the body of Christ, are able to imitate Christ by welcoming people into our lives, by serving them, by reminding them of God's promises. We do this for each other, and, as a result, we receive blessing.

What blessings does God fill us with as we believe? (See verse 13.)

"Now may the God of hope fill you with all joy and peace as you believe so that you may overflow with hope by the power of the Holy Spirit" (v. 13). That's it, guys. Welcome one another until your worries fall away. Serve until suddenly you are filled with peace. Be in the body. Please, be in the body, so that you may overflow with hope. We have such an amazing situation together in Jesus.

During my anti-small-group season of fear, I was so anxious about what people would burden me with, but it never felt like a burden. They were just people like me who pursued service in Christ, and, as a result, they had joy and peace, and it overflowed and changed me.

My anxiety evaporated when I was plugged in with those people. I felt strong around them because they were so good at meeting my needs, and I delighted in finding ways to meet theirs. It was just a natural overflow of the joy and peace I'd been given by God, through them.

It's what we are made for.

In the pie chart below, fill in what percentage of the time you feel like you are overflowing with joy and peace and what percentage of the time you are a slave to your fears.

overflowing with
joy and strength

slave to my fears

It ebbs and flows. But I believe our pie charts will look different in ten years. I believe that 2 Corinthians 3:18 is true.

> We all, with unveiled faces, are looking as in a mirror at the glory of the Lord and are being transformed into the same image from glory to glory; this is from the Lord who is the Spirit.

God is always transforming His children, and He often uses His other children to do it. What a gift. What a joy. We get to be part of the healing and hope and freedom of our friends.

A big contributor to anxiety is isolation. If you've been actively pushing people away from your pain, what can you do this week to bring people in?

Name another believer you can reach out to for prayer and support and help.

If you're not currently struggling, who can you support this week? Who can you encourage and support and remind that they are loved and that they are not alone?

DAY FIVE
A BALLET STUDIO, A BIOPSY, AND A BRAVE MOM

2 Corinthians 1:3-7

My mom and I were in the bathroom at my daughter's ballet studio when she told me she'd found a lump. It took my breath away. Cancer? The very worst of the bad, scary things? My mom?

It was a surreal year. She had surgery. She had chemo. She had radiation. She went bald. She was living out my worst nightmare.

The first time I went to go see her during her chemo treatment, I was struck by my surroundings. She was at the end of a long, white, sterile hallway. In every room I passed, I saw bald women with sad faces and tired faces and scared faces.

All I could think was, *This is the valley of the shadow of death.*

And then I got to my mom's room, and there she was. Curly rainbow-colored wig. Venti Frappuccino®. Her laptop on the table and her big Bible in her lap.

"My baby!" she chirped.

There she was, at the end of the valley, showing me how to walk through it. My mom was being comforted by the Word of God, and she was able to comfort me with her testimony.

Years later, when I walked through a cancer scare, I thought of her and her faith and her peace. I remembered the hope we share in Jesus, and the surgeries and the waiting weren't as scary.

Read 2 Corinthians 1:3-7.

Anyone would agree that the cancer patient who is currently having red poison infused into her bloodstream is the one who needs comfort. But, through the power of Christ, God is able to use the afflicted to reveal His power. The power He has gives us peace when life is the opposite of peaceful.

What did Paul call God in verse 3?

Commentator David E. Garland said, "Here he identifies him as the Father of all mercies and God of all comfort and implies that mercies and comfort are brought to realization through Christ."[2]

This is important because through Christ, God is able to comfort us since Christ defeated sin and death. Christ broke the curse so that all this broken-sad-scariness we live with will one day be gone. God can comfort us because He is the only One with the power to comfort us. His comfort isn't false or temporary. It's powerful. It's eternal. It's shareable.

According to verse 4, what are we able to do with the comfort God gives us in our affliction?

Verses 4-5 tells us the comfort of Christ overflows out of us as believers. A Christian comforting another Christian isn't just a "there, there" with a pat on the back. A Christian is a Spirit-filled messenger, sharing tears and sharing hope that one day, as Sally Lloyd-Jones put it, "everything sad will come untrue."[3]

What are some ways other believers have comforted you when you were feeling anxious or afflicted?

You can't be convinced the world is caving in while being convinced that the world is being made new. Anxiety is complicated. And there are so many reasons for it and so many biological and emotional factors. But when we bring our fears and our doubts into the light, when we do life alongside other believers, we see that though they walk through scary things, like cancer, they also walk with hope and comfort. That stuff is contagious. The hope, not the cancer. Praise God.

My mom's peace poured out in that infusion clinic when she was having her cancer treatments. It touched me, and it touched nurses, and it touched doctors, and it touched other people suffering the same sickness.

Her joy made people think, *Why? What is this hope? Where is this comfort coming from?*

In the space below, ask God to comfort you in the areas of your life that trigger anxiety. Ask Him to use that comfort not just to remind you of your soul's safety and hope, but to spill onto others who are anxious too.

Alone, we're anxious. Alone, we're convinced this world is going to eat us alive. But together, we're walking reminders, we're walking proof, that though Jesus was right when He said, "In this world you will have trouble" (John 16:33, NIV), He was also right when He said we can "take heart!" because He has overcome the world.

I wish I had the words and the power to end this study promising you that completing this book would help you overcome anxiety. I can't make that promise though. I'm powerless; I'm sinful; and I'm so often scared too. But I know God made us to bring Him glory. I know He is glorified when anxious people remind other anxious people of the truth. The truth that raises dead people to life and gives hopeless people hope. This truth that is so powerful, it changes us from self-centered, isolated, insulated people into joy-filled, purpose-driven, ambassadors of peace. We live in a scary place, and we are weak. But that's not all. We are held together by a Savior who has won and is winning and will win forever over every anxious thing.

Cling to His Word. Cling to this thrilling hope. Cling to others who are held together by Him and rejoice with me that we are loved, that we are free, that we are safe in all the ways that matter most, and that one day we'll be safe forever.

This past week, you completed the Session Eight personal study in your books. If you weren't able to do so, no big deal! You can still follow along with the questions, be involved in the discussion, and watch the video. When you are ready to begin, open up your time in prayer and push play on Video Eight for Session Eight.

WATCH

Write down any thoughts, verses, or things you want to remember as you watch the video for Session Eight of *Anxious*.

FROM THIS WEEK'S STUDY

As a group, review this week's memory verse.

And let us consider one another in order to provoke love and good works, not neglecting to gather together, as some are in the habit of doing, but encouraging each other, and all the more as you see the day approaching.

HEBREWS 10:24-25

REVIEW SESSION EIGHT PERSONAL STUDY

From Day One: Have you ever experienced a season of discouragement? What were the circumstances, and what were you feeling?

From Day Two: According to Acts 2:42-47, what were the early Christians devoted to? How do these things compare to what you or the believers in your life are devoted to?

From Day Three: Have you ever wished you were a different part in the body of Christ? Have you ever been envious of someone who was called to something different?

From Day Four: What does Romans 15:7 tell us we are to do to one another as Christ has done for us?

From Day Five: According to 2 Corinthians 1:4, what are we able to do with the comfort God gives us in our affliction? What are some ways other believers have comforted you when you were feeling anxious or afflicted?

DISCUSS

This week, we looked at how God created us for community. He created us to comfort and encourage each other. He created us to hold each other together in this often scary and unpredictable life. Allow time for anyone who wants to share a testimony of God comforting them in a way that comforted others or of them being comforted by God through others.

Do you tend to isolate or seek community when you feel anxious? If you isolate, who will you ask to hold you accountable, to reach out, to make sure you're not trying to fight alone when you're struggling?

Reflect on what God has taught you about fighting anxiety throughout this week. What have you learned that helped you the most? Which Scriptures have been most comforting? What will you do differently going forward as you fight the good fight and finish the race (2 Tim. 4:7)?

PRAY

Close out your time together in prayer, thanking God for what He's done, thanking Him for being our source of comfort and hope in a world full of scary things. Lift up the specific requests of your group members to the Lord in faith, believing He is sovereign and working all things together for the good of those who love Him and are called according to His purpose (Rom. 8:28).

To access the teaching sessions, use the instructions in the back of your Bible study book.

ANXIOUS TOGETHER   183

APPENDIX
BECOMING A CHRISTIAN

Romans 10:17 says, "So faith comes from what is heard, and what is heard comes through the message about Christ."

Maybe you've stumbled across new information in this study. Maybe you've attended church all your life, but something you read here struck you differently than it ever has before. Or maybe you are exhausted from wrestling with anxiety, and you are looking for the rest and peace that can only come from casting your cares on Jesus, who cares for you. If you have never accepted Christ but would like to, read on to discover how you can become a Christian.

Your heart tends to run from God and rebel against Him. The Bible calls this sin. Romans 3:23 says, "For all have sinned and fall short of the glory of God."

Yet God loves you and wants to save you from sin, to offer you a new life of hope. John 10:10b says, "I have come so that they may have life and have it in abundance."

To give you this gift of salvation, God made a way through His Son, Jesus Christ. Romans 5:8 says, "But God proves his own love for us in that while we were still sinners, Christ died for us."

You receive this gift by faith alone. Ephesians 2:8-9 says, "For you are saved by grace through faith, and this is not from yourselves; it is God's gift—not from works, so that no one can boast."

Faith is a decision of your heart demonstrated by the actions of your life. Romans 10:9 says, "If you confess with your mouth, 'Jesus is Lord,' and believe in your heart that God raised him from the dead, you will be saved."

If you trust that Jesus died for your sins and want to receive new life through Him, pray a prayer similar to the following one to express your repentance and faith in Him.

Dear God, I know I am a sinner. I believe Jesus died to forgive me of my sins. I accept Your offer of eternal life. Thank You for forgiving me of all my sins. Thank You for my new life. From this day forward, I will choose to follow You.

If you have trusted Jesus for salvation, please share your decision with your group leader or another Christian friend. If you are not already attending church, find one in which you can worship and grow in your faith. Following Christ's example, ask to be baptized as a public expression of your faith.

SCARLET'S FAVORITE FEAR-FIGHTING VERSES

Put these in your pocket. Tape them to your mirrors. Write them on your childrens' faces! This is truth. These words have power. This is how we fight.

Be strong and courageous. Do not fear or be in dread of them, for it is the LORD your God who goes with you. He will not leave you or forsake you.
DEUTERONOMY 31:6 (ESV)

Have I not commanded you? Be strong and courageous. Do not be frightened, and do not be dismayed, for the LORD your God is with you wherever you go.
JOSHUA 1:9 (ESV)

I sought the LORD, and he answered me and delivered me from all my fears.
PSALM 34:4 (ESV)

When I am afraid, I put my trust in you.
PSALM 56:3 (ESV)

You will keep the mind that is dependent on you in perfect peace, for it is trusting in you.
ISAIAH 26:3

Fear not, for I am with you; be not dismayed, for I am your God; I will strengthen you, I will help you, I will uphold you with my righteous right hand.
ISAIAH 41:10 (ESV)

Therefore I tell you, do not be anxious about your life, what you will eat or what you will drink, nor about your body, what you will put on. Is not life more than food, and the body more than

clothing? Look at the birds of the air: they neither sow nor reap nor gather into barns, and yet your heavenly Father feeds them. Are you not of more value than they? And which of you by being anxious can add a single hour to his span of life? And why are you anxious about clothing? Consider the lilies of the field, how they grow: they neither toil nor spin, yet I tell you, even Solomon in all his glory was not arrayed like one of these.
MATTHEW 6:25-29 (ESV)

Therefore, since we have been justified by faith, we have peace with God through our Lord Jesus Christ. Through him we have also obtained access by faith into this grace in which we stand, and we rejoice in hope of the glory of God. Not only that, but we rejoice in our sufferings, knowing that suffering produces endurance, and endurance produces character, and character produces hope, and hope does not put us to shame, because God's love has been poured into our hearts through the Holy Spirit who has been given to us. For while we were still weak, at the right time Christ died for the ungodly.
ROMANS 5:1-6 (ESV)

For our sake he made him to be sin who knew no sin, so that in him we might become the righteousness of God.
2 CORINTHIANS 5:21 (ESV)

Do not be anxious about anything, but in everything by prayer and supplication with thanksgiving let your requests be made known to God. And the peace of God, which surpasses all understanding, will guard your hearts and your minds in Christ Jesus.
PHILIPPIANS 4:6-7 (ESV)

For God gave us a spirit not of fear but of power and love and self-control.
2 TIMOTHY 1:7 (ESV)

There is no fear in love; instead, perfect love drives out fear . . .
1 JOHN 4:18a

ENDNOTES

SESSION ONE

1. Snacks are not required but strongly recommended.

2. Tim Keller, "The Wounded Spirit," *Gospel in Life*, December 5, 2004, accessed February 18, 2021, https://gospelinlife.com/downloads/the-wounded-spirit-5389/.

SESSION TWO

1. Bible scholars say that Abimelech was sometimes used as a proper name but was also a common title for a Philistine king. So, as explained in the *Holman Illustrated Bible Dictionary* (p. 9), Abimelech may have been King Achish's title. It is likely they are the same dude.

2. C. H. Spurgeon, "Psalm XXVII" and "Psalm LII," *The Treasury of David*, Vol. II (New York: Funk & Wagnalls, 1885).

3. Ibid.

4. "Jehovah Rapha (The Lord Who Heals)," *Blue Letter Bible*, accessed February 23, 2021, https://www.blueletterbible.org/study/misc/name_god.cfm.

5. Strong's H6960, *Blue Letter Bible*, accessed February 22, 2021, https://www.blueletterbible.org/lang/lexicon/lexicon.cfm?Strongs=H6960&t=CSB.

6. *Holman Old Testament Commentary: Psalms 1–75*, Steven J. Lawson, ed. (Nashville: Broadman & Holman Publishers, 2003).

7. C. H. Spurgeon, "Psalm 61," *Treasury of David, Blue Letter Bible*, accessed February 22, 2021, via https://www.blueletterbible.org/Comm/spurgeon_charles/tod/ps061.cfm?a=539001.

8. Matthew Henry, "Commentary on Psalms 61," *Blue Letter Bible*, accessed on February 22, 2021, via https://www.blueletterbible.org/Comm/mhc/Psa/Psa_061.cfm?a=539001.

9. Ibid, *Holman Old Testament Commentary: Psalms 1–75*.

10. Elisabeth Elliot, "The Lord is My Shepherd," *Series: Elisabeth Elliot Speaks About*, accessed February 22, 2021, https://www.blueletterbible.org/audio_video/elliot_elisabeth/misc/Elisabeth_Elliot_Speaks_About.cfm#The_Lord_Is_My_Shepherd.

SESSION THREE

1. Joshua J. Mark, "Assyrian Warfare," *World History Encyclopedia*, May 2, 2018, accessed February 25, 2021, https://www.ancient.eu/Assyrian_Warfare/.

2. James Bruckner, *The NIV Application Commentary* (Grand Rapids, MI: Zondervan, 2004).

3. James Montgomery Boice, *The Minor Prophets, Vol. I* (Grand Rapids, MI: Baker Books, 1983.

4. James Montgomery Boice, *About The Minor Prophets (Hosea–Jonah): An Expositional Commentary,* Vol. I (Grand Rapids, MI: Baker Books, 2002).

5. Frank Gardner, "Iraq's Christians 'close to extinction,'" *BBC*, May 23, 2019, accessed March 1, 2021, https://www.bbc.com/news/world-middle-east-48333923.

6. Helen Howarth Lemmel, "Turn Your Eyes Upon Jesus," 1922, accessed March 1, 2021, https://hymnary.org/text/o_soul_are_you_weary_and_troubled.

7. Priscilla Shirer, *Jonah: Navigating a Life Interrupted*, video (Nashville, TN: Lifeway Christian Resources, 2010), https://www.youtube.com/watch?v=-Vb19mJcb48.

8. Note on Matthew 6:25, *ESV Study Bible* (Wheaton, IL: Crossway, 2008).

SESSION FOUR

1. Douglas K. Stuart, *The New American Commentary: Exodus,* Vol. II (Nashville: B&H Publishing Group, 2006), 113–114.

2. John Piper, "I Am Who I Am," *desiringGod*, September 16, 1984, accessed March 3, 2021, https://www.desiringgod.org/messages/i-am-who-i-am.

3. A. W. Tozer, *Knowledge of the Holy* (New York: HarperCollins, 1961), 1.

4. Charles Spurgeon, *God Always Cares* (Shawnee, KS: Gideon House Books, 2017), 33.

5. Ibid.

SESSION FIVE

1. Karen H. Jobes, *The NIV Application Commentary* (Grand Rapids, MI: Zondervan, 1999), 19–21.

2. Some translations actually say *hanged* (CSB, ESV, KJV) and others (NIV, NLT) say *impaled.*

3. Paul Tripp, "018. Esther Summary," *Paul Tripp Ministries: The Gospel One Chapter At a Time,* September 2, 2019, accessed March 8, 2021, https://www.paultripp.com/bible-study/posts/esther-summary.

SESSION SIX

1. Stanton W. Gavitt, "I'm So Happy And Here's the Reason Why," Singspiration Inc., 1936.

2. Strong's G5011, *Blue Letter Bible*, accessed March 30, 2021, https://www.blueletterbible.org/lang/lexicon/lexicon.cfm?Strongs=G5011&t=CSB.

3. Strong's G5013, *Blue Letter Bible*, accessed March 11, 2021, https://www.blueletterbible.org/lang/lexicon/lexicon.cfm?Strongs=G5013&t=CSB.

4. Gavitt, "I'm So Happy And Here's the Reason Why."

5. John Cotton, *The New-England Primer* (Aledo, TX: WallBuilder Press, 1991, reprint, originally pub. 1777).

SESSION SEVEN

1. Don Stewart, "What Is General Revelation," *Blue Letter Bible*, accessed March 17, 2021, https://www.blueletterbible.org/faq/don_stewart/don_stewart_370.cfm.

2. Don Stewart, "What Is Special Revelation," *Blue Letter Bible*, accessed March 17, 2021, https://www.blueletterbible.org/faq/don_stewart/don_stewart_1196.cfm.

3. Jen Wilkin, "Q&A: Applying," Instagram story, September 2020, accessed March 17, 2021, https://www.instagram.com/jenwilkin/?hl=en.

4. James Montgomery Boice, *The Gospel of John: The Coming of the Light (John 1–4)*, Vol. I, (Grand Rapids, MI: Baker Bookos, 1985,1989).

SESSION EIGHT

1. Ajith Fernando, *The NIV Application Commentary: Acts* (Grand Rapids, MI: Zondervan, 1998), 125.

2. David E. Garland, *The New American Commentary: 2 Corinthians*, Vol. 29 (Nashville: B&H Publishing Group, 1999), 59.

3. Sally Lloyd-Jones and Sam Shammas, *The Jesus Storybook Bible Curriculum*, 2011, https://www.sallylloyd-jones.com/wp-content/uploads/2014/02/jesus_storybook_bible_currkit_ot_NoMoreTears.compressed.pdf.

LET'S BE FRIENDS!

BLOG

We're here to help you grow in your faith, develop as a leader, and find encouragement as you go.

lifewaywomen.com

SOCIAL

Find inspiration in the in-between moments of life.

@lifewaywomen

NEWSLETTER

Be the first to hear about new studies, events, giveaways, and more by signing up.

lifeway.com/womensnews

APP

Download the Lifeway Women app for Bible study plans, online study groups, a prayer wall, and more!

Google Play   App Store

Lifeway women

MORE FROM
SCARLET

AVAILABLE WHERE BOOKS ARE SOLD

Get the most from your study.

Customize your Bible study time with a guided experience.

In this 8-session study with Scarlet Hiltibidal, learn that when we trust the Lord rather than fearing the brokenness in our world, we are able to take hold of the perfect peace that is only available in Him.

In this study you'll:

- Learn how to fight your anxiety with the Word of God so you can take hold of the abundant life Jesus has purchased for you.
- Realize you're not alone in your struggle with anxiety by prioritizing community and confession over isolation.
- Practice bringing your anxieties to God and come to know prayer as a pathway to peace.

Video Access (included in this Bible study book)

- Promo (1:38)
- Session One: Introduction—Anxious to Be Here (10:05)
- Session Two: Anxious David (10:04)
- Session Three: Anxious Jonah (8:45)
- Session Four: Anxious Moses (5:54)
- Session Five: Anxious Esther (9:21)
- Session Six: Anxious Prayer (6:34)
- Session Seven: Anxious Reader (7:36)
- Session Eight: Anxious Together (7:29)

ADDITIONAL RESOURCES

Visit **lifeway.com/anxious** to explore the entire study family—Bible study book with video access, eBook with video access, and teen girls' Bible study—along with a free session sample, video clips, and church promotional material.